# Praise for  數位 |

*Plurality* is...a truly fascinating...potential collaboration that is African in perspec... ...must read and a must-co-create for African thought leaders...who have embraced the challenge of making the 21st century the African century.

— Oby Ezekwesili, Co-Founder of Transparency International, #BringBackOurGirls, Founder of the School of Politics, Policy and Governance and #FixPolitics, and Nigerian political leader

With wit, erudition and optimism, Audrey Tang and her collaborators argue that we can harness digital technology to confront authoritarianism, and that we can do so by leaning into, rather than shying away from, the principles of an open society.

— Anne Applebaum, winner of the Pulitzer Prize and author of The Twilight of Democracy and Red Famine

Glen and Audrey lead a team offering a master class in how to harness advanced computation to augment rather than replace human social and economic systems, simultaneously showing and telling us how digital technology can make the world dramatically more cooperative and productive.

— Michael I. Jordan, Pehong Chen Distinguished Professor of Computer Science and Statistics at the University of California, Berkeley, inaugural winner of the World Laureates Association Prize in Computer Science or Mathematics, and named by Science as the most influential computer scientist in the world in 2016.

In financial technology and digital infrastructure, Kenya and other African countries are...ahead of outdated models in the North. With *Plurality* we (can)...take this...deeper...to accelerate our growth and be part of global models of a more inclusive, participatory and productive future.

— Ory Okolloh-Mwangi, Co-Founder of Ushahidi and Partner at Verod-Kepple Africa Ventures

Digital technologies that were supposed to support freedom and democracy have turned into weapons of misinformation, extremism and surveillance. This wonderful book outlines a technical and philosophical strategy, grounded in practical applications in Taiwan, for doing this all better

— Daron Acemoglu, Elizabeth and James Killian Professor of Economics at the Massachusetts Institute of Technology, Winner of the John Bates Clark Medal and co-author of *Power and Progress* and *Why Nations Fail*

What would the world be like if our dearest dreams in the social justice...movement had come to pass? (They) offer radical yet pragmatic solutions to...reinventing democracy...(to) truly serve the people...Some...have ...been implemented, serving as a beacon ...to make real change.

— Stav Shaffir, leader of the Israeli Social Justice protests that inspired "Occupy" and youngest woman Member of the Knesset

For too long, diversity and technology have been used as swords by the forces of secularization. Remarkably, in the skilled hands of these authors, they are here reforged into a shield for the faithful.

— Rev. Johnnie Moore Jr., President of the Congress of Christian Leaders, former member of the United States Commission on International Religious Freedom and informal advisor to Fmr. US President Donald Trump

Audrey Tang sets a new standard for what it means to be a pioneering leader. I hope we will all have the courage to follow in her path, as she lays out so eloquently here.

— Claudia López Hernández, former Mayor and first woman mayor of Bogotá, Colombia and highest ever LGBT elected official in the Global South

It is clear...technologies will impact the future of culture and democracy. We lack a pluralistic...vision of living with them! Fortunately, this book embodies the principles it advocates. Like AI, it is a monumental collective accomplishment, greater than the sum of its parts.

— Holly Herndon, musician, artist, Co-Host of *Interdependence* and Co-Founder of Spawning

Audrey Tang and Glen Weyl's project will be effective and meaningful in helping Taiwan (and other countries) move in the direction of a new social democracy.

— Karatani Kōjin, Author of *The Structure of World History* and winner of the Berggruen Prize for Culture and Philosophy

*Plurality* unveils the powerful blueprint of Taiwan's resilient digital transformation...provides valuable insight for concerned citizens everywhere and...can help preserve democracy amidst...a precarious moment in history for liberty and open societies around the world.

— Frank McCourt, Founder of McCourt Global and Project Liberty and co-author of *Our Biggest Fight*

I find it exhilarating to read the rules to new games and imagine the world that they build; I get that excitement here, but the game is global affairs and the way communities work together. Fantastic!

— Richard Garfield, creator of Magic: The Gathering

(They) have written a brilliant book of breathtaking possibility, offering...hope in a dark time...drawing on disciplines from mathematics to literature...readers are likely to find plenty of things to ponder and challenge...(and) are invited to join the conversation!

— Anne-Marie Slaughter, CEO of the New America Foundation, former Director of Policy Planning at the US Department of State and author of *Unfinished Business* and *The Chess Board and the Web*

Rejoice! Here is a burst of creativity that gives us a peek at the humanistic high-tech future we suspected was possible.

— Jaron Lanier, inventor of Virtual Reality, author of *Who Owns the Future?* and *The Dawn of the New Everything* and Microsoft's Office of the Chief Technology Officer Prime Unifying Scientist (OCTOPUS)

At last, we have a book that centers plurality – both in theory and in practice. This is a much-needed guide for developing new strategies to navigate the relationship between technology and democracy, and for thinking beyond the usual Western frame.

— Kate Crawford, Senior Researcher at Microsoft Research, research professor at the University of Southern California, artist, musician, and author of *Atlas of AI*

(P)opulists globally use technology to divide nations...*Plurality* invites a new journey where we can indeed use technology to reclaim that space in world of canceling to become more connected, and bring back our sense of humanity, UBUNTU as we say in Africa.

— Mmusi Maimaine, South African Presidential candidate, former Leader of the Opposition, Founder of Build One South Africa and pastor and elder of Liberty Church

Here in lucid and non-technical prose is a sweeping vision for how to integrate so much of what we've learned about technology and society in the past decades to remake the future of democracy, from someone who is actually doing it on the ground.

— Alex "Sandy" Pentland, Inaugural Academic Head of the MIT Media Lab and founding father of Computational Social Science and Data Science

If internet technology has accelerated fragmentation, it should be possible to achieve a comfortable coexistence. *Plurarity* is full of hints for this purpose.

— Yoshihisa Aono, Co-Founder and CEO of Cybozu

(A) remarkable book which provides accessible, deep and novel insights into the way in which technology has, is, will and should shape our lives. It draws on a wealth of evidence to provide a powerful case in favour of promoting plurality...It holds important lessons for all of us.

— Colin Mayer, Peter Moores Professor of Management Studies at the Oxford Saïd School of Management, and author of *Prosperity: Better Business Makes the Greater Good*

Plurality is an important book on one of today's central challenges—building collaboration and shared purpose across diversity. The authors approach this challenge not simply in ... politics...but also offer valuable insights on...technology, economics, and beyond.

— Julius Krein, Founder and Editor-in-Chief, American Affairs

Drawing inspiration from Taiwan, the world's most under-appreciated democracy, *Plurality* makes a powerful case that digital technologies can be harnessed to facilitate...a more democratic future...Reading this brilliant book left...a new sense of urgency, but it also provided real reasons for hope.

— Steven Levitsky, David Rockerfeller Professor of Government at Harvard and co-author of *How Democracies Die* and *Tyranny of the Minority*

In an era of anxiety and division, Glen Weyl and Audrey Tang provide a rare, grounded vision for how technology and democracy can harmonize, and propel us to a better future.

— Tristan Harris, Co-Founder of the Center for Humane Technology and star of *The Social Dilemma*

An exciting, creative and provocative set of ideas on how to make progress on some of the most fundamental problems in the world. You will never think the same way again after reading this book.

— Jason Furman, Former Chair of the Council of Economic Advisors and Aetna Professor of the Practice of Economic Policy, Harvard University

(T)his book...places Taiwan at the center of the world. Will it be the fulcrum of conflict or...apex of a...democratizing revolution of peace, humanity, and technology? This is our century's question. Tang, Weyl, and their collaborators have written a guide to finding the answer.

— Michael Hartley Freedman, winner of the Fields Medal, the MacArthur Fellowship and the National Medal of Science and former director of Microsoft's Station Q quantum computing research unit

It is a delight to finally see a vision for the future of human progress so clearly grounded in its past. With Plurality, we have a framework for building the engines that harness the abundant energy latent in human diversity to power the next hundred years of economic growth.

— Oded Galor, Author of *The Journey of Humanity* and Herbert Goldberger Professor of Economics at Brown University

(V)isionary in design, execution, and substance.

— Brad Carson, President of University of Tulsa and Americans for Responsible Innovation, Fmr. US Congressman and Undersecretary of the Army

At once optimistic and pragmatic, Plurality offers a roadmap to reforge democracy for the AI era...we need not limit ourselves to the libertarian or authoritarian visions...a third way...leans into openness, plurality, and the human spirit. So worth reading!

— Mark Surman, President and Executive Director of the Mozilla Foundation

Can the public sector move as fast to harness emerging technologies as the rest of society? Audrey Tang has shown on the ground that it can, and here she teaches you how to do the same.

— Shlomit Wagman, former Director General of the Israel Money Laundering and Terror Financing Prohibition Authority and Privacy Protection Authority

(S)ingularity... elicit(s) fear about how technology will overtake humans. This seminal book provides...a compelling, bold alternative. Weyl and Tang present...how technology can advance a pluralistic world...to strengthen relationships and bring people together across diversity.

— Mike Kubzansky, CEO of the Omidyar Network

"Regulation" remains elusive as a path to taming our technofeudal masters. It will not succeed in dispersing power. *Plurality* charts a different path for us to take - open and democratic - to bypass and dis-intermediate these powers.

— Cristina Caffarra, Honorary Professor at University College London and Co-Founder of the CEPR Competition Research Policy Network

數位

# PLURALITY

## THE FUTURE OF COLLABORATIVE TECHNOLOGY AND DEMOCRACY

E. Glen Weyl, Audrey Tang & Community

This book is in the public domain, licensed under a Creative Commons 1.0 Universal (CC0) "No Rights Reserved" license. Contents may be used in any fashion and for any purpose by anyone, subject to general laws on speech in the relevant jurisdiction. To view a copy of this license, visit https://creativecommons.org/publicdomain/zero/1.0/legalcode.

All images and illustrations are either public domain or used with permission from the original sources, with the license information included in the caption. Any unlabeled images are licensed CC0.

E. Glen Weyl, Audrey Tang & ⌘ Community

www.plurality.net

ISBN: 9798321247181

Printed in the USA

# About the Authors

*E. Glen Weyl* is Founder of *RadicalxChange*, *Microsoft Research*'s *Plural Technology Collaboratory* & *Plurality Institute* & co-author of *Radical Markets*.

*Audrey Tang* is the inaugural *Minister of Digital Affairs* in 🇹🇼 & the inaugural ≋ minister in the 🌐.

This book is open-source, and its contents may be freely copied, with or without attribution. In addition to the primary named authors, dozens of members of the ⌬ community around the world contributed to the book, doing most of the total work. These contributors, categorized by type of contribution and highlighted to the extent of their contribution, are listed on the next page, and represented in this machine-generated blending of their faces, tiled by their individual faces. The free online version of this book at https://www.plurality.net/ will continue to evolve, governed according to the principles described in this book by this community.

# Credits

The below represents the current state of 🖾 credits in the project, a community currency we used to track contributions as discussed further in the text. Every contributor is categorized in terms of exactly one contribution area, even if they made multiple types of contribution. Order within categories and font size overall indicate quantitative holdings of 🖾 as of early April, 2024 and we used the same weights to create the composite image above. The list excludes the two primary authors as they are sufficiently highlighted above, as well as anyone who only received credit for endorsing, as they are listed in order of credit on the opening pages of this book or on its exterior. We apologize for any errors in the ledger due to the experimental nature of the technology we used to track it and will correct these online and in future editions.

*Writing*

# Gisele Chou

# Judith Amores

# Puja Ohlhaver

## Nick Pyati

## Jeremy Lauer

## Noah Yeh

JJ Reynolds-Strange

Kinney Zalesne

Tantum Collins

Geordan Shannon

Matt Prewitt

Holly Herndon

Mat Dryhurst

Michele Zanini

Jonas Kgomo

*Editing*

Vitalik Buterin

NISHIO Hirokazu

Greg Wang

Christian Paquin

Omoaholo Omakhalen

Evan David Paul

Kaliya Young

Teddy Lee

Wes Chow

Zoë Hitzig

Isaiah Kuhle

Ko Ju-Chun

Billy Zhe-Wei Lin

Michael Zhuang

*Technical*

# Akinori Oyama
# Petar Maymounkov
# Kasia Sitkiewicz
# Derek Worthen

John Hadaway

Tyler Flajole

Julia Metcalf

*Translation*

# Jacky (taipeicity.eth)

Andreas Fauler

Daniel Alsterholm

Max Semenchuk

Michal

Vassilis Tziokas

Haju Chang

Leon Erichsen

Jennifer Victoria Scurrel

Mashbean

*Visuals*

# Tofus Wang

## Lillian Wang

Andrea Bonaceto

Kevin Owocki

*Data*

# Carl Cervone

Jordan Usdan

Jeffrey Fossett

*Management*

# Jason Entenmann

*Public relations*

# Shaurya Dubey

Malik Lakoubay

Andreas Fauler

Gideon Litchfield

*Research*

Nick Vincent

Mateo Patel

James Allen Evans

Junsol Kim

Joshua Yang

Shrey Jain

Peter E. Hart

Jamie Joyce

Dan Silver

# Finding Your Dao

As we discuss below, linear book narratives have a significant disadvantage of forcing every reader down a single learning path. While the online version avoids this through the extensive use of hyperlinks, those who hold a physical copy will find this more challenging to navigate. To partially alleviate this problem, we have structured the text in a "circular" manner, where readers can start at a variety of points, read from there and circle back to the "earlier" material at the end.

We recommend that:

- Those with a primarily topical, political, or **current affairs** interest begin at the beginning of the book, with the preface and read straight through.

- Those with a more conceptual, theoretical, or broadly **intellectual** interest consider skipping Parts 1 and 2 and beginning in Part 3.

- Those with a more **technical**, technological, or engineering focus consider beginning with Part 4.

- Those with an interest in concrete technologies and their **applications** consider beginning with Part 5.

- Those with an interest in real-world **impact** in specific social sectors consider beginning with Part 6.

- Those with a focus on public **policy**, government and social mobilization consider beginning with Part 7.

Regardless of the starting point, we expect most readers who find value wherever they begin will find it worthwhile to continue reading, looping back, and filling in the theoretical frameworks of "later" parts of the book with the material that comes earlier.

This book is a living document. If you are reading a printed version, it is almost certainly out of date already and you can read or download for free the latest version at *https://www.plurality.net/*.

More importantly, we hope you will view yourselves not just as readers but as collaborators on this project. You may at any time submit a concern or problem with the text (as an "issue") for the community to prioritize or a revision (as a "pull request") for consideration by the community at *https://github.com/pluralitybook/plurality*. *All contributions are credited* and earn the contributor recognition and governance rights as we describe below.

If we made a mistake, take it as an invitation. If you feel we are wrong, set us straight. If we are not speaking in the language of your community, create a version that does. If you don't want to deal with the community, the material has no copyright so take anything you want and leave the rest. *Ask not "why is nobody doing this?" You are the nobody.*

# Table of Contents

Part 1: Preface ............................................................. 1
  1 Seeing Plural ....................................................... 1

Part 2: Introduction ..................................................... 3
  2-0 Information Technology and Democracy: A Widening Gulf ... 3
  2-1 A View from Yushan ........................................... 47
  2-2 The Life of a Digital Democracy ........................... 64

Part 3: Plurality .......................................................... 88
  3-0 What is ⌘? ....................................................... 88
  3-1 Living in a ⌘ World ........................................... 94
  3-2 Connected Society ............................................ 112
  3-3 The Lost Dao ................................................... 132

Part 4: Freedom ........................................................ 161
  4-0 Rights, Operating Systems and ⌘ Freedom ........... 161
  4-1 Identity and Personhood ................................... 179
  4-2 Association and ⌘ Publics ................................. 208
  4-3 Commerce and Trust ......................................... 230
  4-4 Property and Contract ....................................... 251
  4-5 Access ............................................................ 277

Part 5: Democracy .................................................... 285
  5-0 Collaborative Technology and Democracy ............ 285
  5-1 Post-Symbolic Communication .......................... 305
  5-2 Immersive Shared Reality .................................. 317
  5-3 Creative Collaborations ..................................... 332
  5-4 Augmented Deliberation ................................... 345

5-5 Adaptive Administration ............................................................. 363

5-6 ⌗ Voting .......................................................................................... 377

5-7 Social Markets ............................................................................. 390

Part 6: Impact ............................................................................................ 411

6-0 From ⌗ to Reality ....................................................................... 411

6-1 Workplace .................................................................................... 427

6-2 Health ........................................................................................... 444

6-3 Media ............................................................................................ 462

6-4 Environment ............................................................................... 473

Part 7: Forward ......................................................................................... 479

7-0 Policy ............................................................................................ 479

7-1 Conclusion ................................................................................... 510

Index .......................................................................................................... 521

xxii

# Part 1: Preface

## 1 Seeing Plural

*In order to carry out a positive action we must develop here a positive vision… It is under the greatest adversity that there exists the greatest potential for doing good, both for oneself and others.*

— Dalai Lama XIV

---

The advent of the internet unfurled the world. Beginning in the 1960s, this new technology created unprecedented possibilities to tie distant communities together across space and time. Knowledge transcended borders, spreading instantaneously across languages and cultures.

At the same time, globalization ushered in an era marked by increased disparities in wealth and social standing. The rapid evolution of digital technology fueled the rise of towering tech giants, which lured individuals into polarized enclaves.

The internet is a powerful technology for tying people together in new collaborations across vast differences. Unfortunately, it has also recently proven to be a powerful tool for thwarting those collaborations and sowing new forms of division.

It is no coincidence that democracy now finds itself at a low tide. Authoritarian regimes now command nearly half of the global GDP. Only a modest one billion people find solace under the umbrella of democratic systems, while over two billion dwell under authoritarian rule.[1]

Every culture, akin to a river, tells its own tale. We see the river of democracy as a conduit of hope. As its waters wane, we must replenish it.

This book, a surging communal effort, is one attempt to restore the flow – and with it, hope.

In Mandarin, 數位 means both "digital" and "plural." To be plural is to be digital. To be digital is to be plural.

Plurality captures the symbiotic relationship between democracy and collaborative technology. Together, democracy and collaborative technology can power infinite diversity in infinite combinations.

Let's free the future — together.

---

[1] V-Dem Institute, *Democracy Report 2023* (Gothenburg, Sweden: V-Dem Institute, 2023): 7.

# Part 2: Introduction

## 2-0 Information Technology and Democracy: A Widening Gulf

> *Surveillance capitalism is...a coup from above...an overthrow of the people's sovereignty and a prominent force in the perilous drift towards democratic deconsolidation...*
>
> — Shoshana Zuboff, *The Age of Surveillance Capitalism*[1], 2019
>
> *We are being lied to...told that technology takes our jobs, reduces our wages, increases inequality, threatens our health, ruins the environment, degrades our society, corrupts our children, impairs our humanity, threatens our future, and is ever on the verge of ruining everything.*
>
> — Marc Andreessen, "The Techno-Optimist Manifesto"[2], 2023

---

Anxiety over technology and geopolitics is pervasive today. Yet there is a more fundamental conflict underway than that between great powers over technical supremacy. More deeply, the path technology and democracy as systems have taken

---

[1] Shoshanna Zuboff, *The Age of Surveillance Capitalism* (New York: Public Affairs, 2019): 513.

[2] Marc Andreessen, "The Techno-Optimist Manifesto", *Andreessen Horowitz Blog*, October 16, 2023, https://a16z.com/the-techno-optimist-manifesto/.

have put them at loggerheads and the ensuing battle has claimed victims on both sides.

The dominant trends in technology in recent decades have been artificial intelligence and blockchains. These have, respectively, empowered centralized top-down control and turbo-charged atomized polarization and financial capitalism. Both outcomes are corrosive to the values of democratic pluralism. It is hardly surprising, then, that technology is widely seen as one of the greatest threats to democracy and as a powerful tool for both external authoritarians and those who would subvert democracies from within.

At the same time, democracy was once a radical experiment to scale the governance of a city-state to many millions of citizens spread across continents. A quote on the wall of the memorial in Washington, D.C. to United States Founding Father Thomas Jefferson reads "(L)aws and institutions must go hand in hand with the progress of the human mind... We might as well require a man to wear still the coat which fitted him when a boy as civilized society to remain ever under the regimen of their barbarous ancestors." Yet today democracy has become a synonym in much of the world for the increasingly desperate effort to preserve rigid, outmoded, polarized, paralyzed, and increasingly illegitimate governments. We should not be shocked, therefore, at the disdain that so many technologists have for democratic participation, viewing it as an impediment to progress, nor should we be surprised by the fear among so many advocates of democracy that technical advance will result in the dominance of authoritarian adversaries or internal collapse.

In this book, we hope to show that this tragic conflict is avoidable and that, properly conceived, technology and democracy can be powerful and natural allies. However, it is no accident that arguments in this direction evoke eye-rolling in many quarters. A gulf of grievance and distrust between the two sides of this divide has developed over the last decade and will not easily be laid to rest. Only by fully acknowledging and embracing the legitimate concerns and critiques of both sides of this conflict shall we have a chance to see its root cause and seek to transcend it. Thus, we begin by drawing out these grievances with a generous spirit, accepting critiques that have raised broad concerns even when they are imperfectly supported by the available evidence. Trying to reconcile these extreme divergences offers an opportunity to raise the ambition of democratic technology.

## Technology's attack on democracy

The last decade of information technology has threatened democracy in two related yet opposite ways. As Daron Acemoglu and James A. Robinson famously argued, free democratic societies exist in a "narrow corridor" between social collapse and authoritarianism[3]. From both sides, information technologies seem to be narrowing the corridor, squeezing the possibility of a free society.

On the one hand, technologies (e.g., social media, cryptography, and some other financial technology) are seen to be breaking down the social fabric, heightening polarization, eroding norms, undermining law enforcement, and accelerating the speed and expanding the reach of financial markets to the point where they are unaccountable to democratic polities. We shall call these threats "anti-social". On the other hand, technologies (e.g., machine learning, foundation models, the internet of things) are increasing the capacity for centralized surveillance, the ability of small groups of engineers to set patterns in systems that shape the rules of social life for billions of citizens and customers and reduce the scope for people to meaningfully participate in shaping their

---

[3] Daron Acemoglu, and James A Robinson, *The Narrow Corridor: States, Societies, and the Fate of Liberty*. (New York: Penguin Books, 2020).

lives and communities. We will call these threats "centralizing". Both threats strike at the heart of democracy, which, as Alexis de Tocqueville famously highlighted in *Democracy in America*, depends on deep and diverse, non-market, decentralized social and civil connections to thrive[4].

The antisocial threat from recent technologies has social, economic, legal, political, and existential faces.

- Socially, there is growing evidence that while social media have offered powerful new platforms for those who have previously been socially isolated (e.g. sexual or religious minorities in conservative locales) to forge connections, on average these tools have contributed to exacerbating social isolation and feelings of exclusion[5].

- Economically, the geographic, temporal, and multiemployer flexibility facilitated by the internet and increasingly by telecommuting have expanded opportunities for many workers in developing countries or who fit poorly in traditional labor markets. Yet they have largely been unmatched by the emergence of appropriate labor market institutions (such as unions and labor regulations) that allow workers to share the

---

[4] Such relationships differ from those established in markets, which are based on bilateral, transactional exchange in a "universal" currency, as they denominate value in units based on local value and trust.

[5] Mary Gray, *Out in the Country: Youth, Media, and Queer Visibility in Rural America* (New York: NYU Press, 2009). See also O'Day, Emily B., and Richard G. Heimberg, "Social Media Use, Social Anxiety, and Loneliness: A Systematic Review," *Computers in Human Behavior Reports 3*, no. 100070 (January 2021), https://doi.org/10.1016/j.chbr.2021.100070; and see also Hunt Allcott, Luca Braghieri, Sarah Eichmeyer, and Matthew Gentzkow, "The Welfare Effects of Social Media," *American Economic Review* 110, no. 3 (March 1, 2020): 629-76. https://doi.org/10.1257/aer.20190658.

potential benefits of these arrangements. Thus, they have tended to raise workplace precarity and contribute to the "hollowing-out" of the middle class in many developed countries[6].

- Politically, polarization and the influence of extremist parties have been steadily rising in many developed democracies. While the role of the internet-based social media landscape is a topic of significant academic debate, recent surveys suggest that these tools have fallen far short of their promise of strengthening social and political bonds across differences and may well have contributed to the secular rise in polarization since 2000, especially in the US[7].

- Legally, the proliferation of financial innovation in the past few decades has led to limited measurable

---

[6] Siddharth Suri, and Mary L Gray, *Ghost Work: How to Stop Silicon Valley from Building a New Global Underclass*, (Boston: Houghton Mifflin Harcourt, 2019). David H. Autor, "Why Are There Still So Many Jobs? The History and Future of Workplace Automation", *Journal of Economic Perspectives* 29, no. 3 (2015): 3-30, https://www.aeaweb.org/articles?id=10.1257%2Fjep.29.3.3&source=post_page.

[7] Steven Levitsky, and Daniel Ziblatt. *How Democracies Die*, (New York: Broadway Books, 2018).; See also Yascha Mounk, *The People vs. Democracy: Why Our Freedom Is in Danger and How to Save It*, (Cambridge, Massachusetts: Harvard University Press, 2018); Cass Sunstein, *#Republic: Divided Democracy in the Age of Social Media*, (Princeton, New Jersey: Princeton University Press, 2017; Kathleen Jamieson, and Joseph Cappella, *Echo Chamber: Rush Limbaugh and the Conservative Media Establishment*, (Oxford, New York: Oxford University Press, 2008). Levi Boxell, Matthew Gentzkow and Jesse M. Shapiro, "Greater Internet Use is Not Associated with Faster Growth in Political Polarization among US Demographic Groups" *Proceedings of the National Academy of Sciences* 114, no. 40: 10612-10617. Levi Boxell, Matthew Gentzkow and Jesse M. Shapiro, "Cross-Country Trends in Affective Polarization" *Review of Economics and Statistics* Forthcoming.

consumer benefits (in terms of risk reduction, capital allocation or access to credit) while increasing risk in much of the financial system and proliferating financial instruments, thereby challenging, or even skirting, existing regulatory regimes intended to mitigate these harms[8]. While innovations surrounding housing finance leading up to the 2008 financial crisis were some of the most important examples, perhaps the most extreme (if more contained) case has been the recent activity around digital "crypto" assets and currencies. Given their mismatch for existing regulatory regimes, they have offered pervasive opportunities for speculation, gambling, fraud, regulatory and tax evasion, and other anti-social activities[9].

---

[8] Alp Simsek, "The Macroeconomics of Financial Speculation," *Annual Review of Economics* 13, no. 1 (May 11, 2021), https://doi.org/10.1146/annurev-economics-092120-050543.

[9] Ben McKenzie, and Jacob Silverman, *Easy Money: Cryptocurrency, Casino Capitalism, and the Golden Age of Fraud*, (New York: Abrams, 2023); "Financial Stability Board, "Regulation, Supervision and Oversight of Crypto-Asset Activities and Markets Consultative Document," 2022, https://www.fsb.org/wp-content/uploads/P111022-3.pdf; Greg Lacurci, "Cryptocurrency Poses a Significant Risk of Tax Evasion," *CNBC*, May 31, 2021, https://www.cnbc.com/2021/05/31/cryptocurrency-poses-a-significant-risk-of-tax-evasion.html; Arianna Trozze, Josh Kamps, Eray Akartuna, Florian Hetzel, Bennett Kleinberg, Toby Davies, and Shane Johnson, "Cryptocurrencies and Future Financial Crime," *Crime Science* 11, no. 1 (January 5, 2022), https://doi.org/10.1186/s40163-021-00163-8; Baer, Katherine, Ruud De Mooij, Shafik Hebous, and Michael Keen, "Crypto Poses Significant Tax Problems—and They Could Get Worse," *IMF*, July 5, 2023, https://www.imf.org/en/Blogs/Articles/2023/07/05/crypto-poses-significant-tax-problems-and-they-could-get-worse; and "Crypto-Assets: Implications for Financial Stability, Monetary Policy, and Payments and Market Infrastructures." *ECB Occasional Paper*, no. 223 (May 17, 2019), https://papers.ssrn.com/sol3/papers.cfm?abstract_id=3391055.

- Existentially, there is growing concern that the fragmentation of the social sense-making and collective action capacity is dangerous in the face of the increasing sophistication of technologies of mass destruction with impact ranging from environmental devastation (e.g., climate change, biodiversity loss, ocean acidification) to the potentially apocalyptic disruptions of more direct weapons (e.g., misaligned artificial intelligence and bioweapons)[10].

Yet even as technology is seen to erode the cohesion of democratic societies, it is also increasingly seen to threaten democracy by strengthening the control of governments and centralizing power in the hands of a small group of private actors.

- Socially, perhaps the most consistent effect of information technology has been to expand the availability and accelerate the spread of information. This has dramatically eroded the sphere of private life, making an increasing range of information publicly available. While such transparency might in principle have a range of social effects, the power to process and make sense of such information has increasingly concentrated in the hands of corporations and firms that have a combination of privileged access to the information and the capital to invest in large scale statistical models (viz. "AI") to make these data actionable. Furthermore, because these models

---

[10] Tristan Harris, "Ethics for Designers – How Technology Hijacks People's Minds – from a Magician and Google's Design Ethicist," Ethics for Designers, March 4, 2017, https://www.ethicsfordesigners.com/articles/how-technology-hijacks-peoples-minds; https://www.youtube.com/watch?v=7LqaotiGWjQ; and Daniel Schmachtenberger, "Explorations on the Future of Civilization," n.d. https://civilizationemerging.com/.

improve greatly with access to more data and capital, societies where central actors have access to very large pools of both have tended to pull ahead in the perceived "AI race", putting pressure on all societies to allow such concentration of informational power to compete[11]. Together, these forces have normalized unprecedented systems of surveillance and centralized control over information flow.

- Legally, the speed of recent advances in AI have overwhelmed core rights of many democratic societies, leaving critical choices in the hands of restricted groups of engineers from similar social backgrounds. Intellectual property law and other protections of creative activity have been largely obviated by the capacity of large AI models to "remix and replace" content; privacy regimes have failed to keep up with the explosive spread of information; discrimination law is woefully unsuited to address issues raised by the potential emergent biases of black box AI systems. The

---

[11] Shoshana Zuboff, *The Age of Surveillance Capitalism: The Fight for a Human Future at the New Frontier of Power*, (New York, NY: PublicAffairs, 2019); Cathy O'neil, *Weapons of Math Destruction: How Big Data Increases Inequality and Threatens Democracy*, (New York: Crown, 2016); Evangelos Simoudis, *The Big Data Opportunity in Our Driverless Future*. (Menlo Park, Ca: Corporate Innovators, Llc, 2017); Philippe Aghion, Benjamin Jones, and Charles Jones, "Artificial Intelligence and Economic Growth," 2017, https://web.stanford.edu/~chadj/AI.pdf; Ford, Martin, *Rise of the Robots: Technology and the Threat of a Jobless Future*, (New York: Basic Books, 2015); Kai-Fu Lee, *AI Superpowers China, Silicon Valley, and the New World Order*, (Boston: Houghton Mifflin Harcourt, 2018); David Brin, *The Transparent Society: Will Technology Force Us to Choose between Privacy and Freedom?* (New York: Basic Books, 1999); Safiya Noble, *Algorithms of Oppression: How Search Engines Reinforce Racism* (New York: New York University Press, 2018); and Virginia Eubanks, *Automating Inequality: How High-Tech Tools Profile, Police, and Punish the Poor*, (New York: St. Martin's Press, 2018).

engineers who could potentially address these issues, on the other hand, typically work for profit-seeking companies or the defense sector, come overwhelmingly from a very specific educational and demographic background (typically white or Asian, male, atheist, highly educated, etc.). This has challenged the core tenets of democratic legal regimes that aim to represent the will of the broad society they govern[12].

- Economically, there is growing evidence that AI and the related broader tendency of information technology since the mid-1980s to replace rather than complement (especially low-educated) human labor has been a central factor in the dramatic rise in the share of income accruing to capital (rather than labor) in past decades and thereby has been a core cause of increased income inequality in developed countries.[13] A rise in market power, mark-ups and (less consistently) industrial concentration around the world has accompanied this

---

[12] Meredith Broussard. *Artificial Unintelligence*: (Cambridge, Massachusetts: The MIT Press, 2018), https://doi.org/10.7551/mitpress/11022.001.0001; Cathy O'neil, *Weapons of Math Destruction: How Big Data Increases Inequality and Threatens Democracy*, (New York: Crown, 2016); Ruha Benjamin, "Race after Technology: Abolitionist Tools for the New Jim Code," *Social Forces* 98, no. 4 (December 23, 2019), https://doi.org/10.1093/sf/soz162; Victor Margolin, *The Politics of the Artificial: Essays on Design and Design Studies*, (Chicago: The University of Chicago Press, 2002).

[13] Daron Acemoglu, and Pascual Restrepo, "The Race between Man and Machine: Implications of Technology for Growth, Factor Shares, and Employment," *American Economic Review* 108, no. 6 (June 2018): 1488–1542. https://doi.org/10.1257/aer.20160696; Jonathan Haskel, and Stian Westlake, "Capitalism without Capital: The Rise of the Intangible Economy (an Excerpt)," *Journal of Economic Sociology* 22, no. 1 (2021): 61–70, https://doi.org/10.17323/1726-3247-2021-1-61-70; Ajay Agrawal, Joshua Gans, Avi Goldfarb, and Catherine Tucker, *The Economics of Artificial Intelligence*, (Illinois: University of Chicago Press, 2024).

decline in labor's share, particularly in countries and sectors that have most heavily adopted information technology[14].

- (Geo-)Politically, the above forces have strengthened authoritarian regimes and political movements against democratic countries. Creating both the tools and incentives for mass surveillance, AI, and other large-scale data processing tools, has made it easier for governments to directly maintain censorship and social control. Indirectly, by concentrating economic power and the levers of social control in a small set of (often corporate) choke points, the increase in capital income and market power and the increasing authority of small groups of engineers have made it easier for authoritarian regimes to manipulate or seize the "commanding heights" of the economy and society when they wish[15].

---

[14] Jan De Loecker, Jan Eeckhout, and Gabriel Unger. "The Rise of Market Power and the Macroeconomic Implications," *The Quarterly Journal of Economics* 135, no. 2 (January 23, 2020): 561–644, https://doi.org/10.1093/qje/qjz041; John Barrios, Yael V. Hochberg, and Hanyi Yi. "The Cost of Convenience: Ridehailing and Traffic Fatalities," SSRN Electronic Journal, 2019, https://doi.org/10.2139/ssrn.3361227; and Tali Kristal, "The Capitalist Machine: Computerization, Workers' Power, and the Decline in Labor's Share within U.S. Industries," *American Sociological Review* 78, no. 3 (May 29, 2013): 361–89. https://doi.org/10.1177/0003122413481351.

[15] Kai-Fu Lee, *AI Superpowers China, Silicon Valley, and the New World Order*, (Boston Houghton Mifflin Harcourt, 2018); Bruce Dickson, *The Dictator's Dilemma: The Chinese Communist Party's Strategy for Survival*, (Oxford, England, New York: Oxford University Press, 2016); Nick Couldry, and Ulises Mejias, "Data Colonialism: Rethinking Big Data's Relation to the Contemporary Subject," *Television & New Media* 20, no. 4 (September 2, 2019): 336–49. Steven Feldstein, *The Rise of Digital Repression: How*

Furthermore, these two threats intersect: authoritarian regimes have increasingly harnessed the "chaos" of social media and cryptocurrencies to sow internal division and conflict in democratic countries. Centralized social media platforms have leveraged AI to optimize user engagement with their services, often helping fuel the centrifugal tendencies of misinformation and "echo chambers". Even when they are not actively complementing each other and have opposite motivations, both forces have pressured democratic societies and helped undermine confidence in them, confidence that is now at its lowest ebb in much of the developed democratic world since it has been measured.[16]

---

*Technology Is Reshaping Power, Politics, and Resistance*, (New York: Oxford University Press, 2021).

[16] Richard Wike and Jannell Fetterolf, "Global Public Opinion in an Era of Democratic Anxiety" *Pew Trust Magazine* May 27, 2022. Ironically, in fragile democracies where the state has limited capacity for technology governance, chaos (the collapse of the prevailing order through disruptive technologies) could be an ally of democracy. From the Arab Spring that swept across North Africa in the early 2010s to Nigeria's #EndSARS movement in 2020, autocracies and fragile democracies have recorded the rise of an emerging class of social media-savvy, financial technology (fintech)-enabled and cryptocurrency-empowered class of young citizens deploying these technologies to challenge authoritarian state institutions. These disruptors have been aided by the algorithms of the technology companies, albeit to the extent that the objectives of such social movements align with the commercial interests of the corporations. Michael Etter and Oana Albu, "Activists in the Dark: Social Media Algorithms and Collective Action in Two Social Movement Organizations." *Organization* 28, no. 1 (September 29, 2020): 135050842096153. https://doi.org/10.1177/1350508420961532. In some cases, such movements have been boosted by the explicit endorsement and backing of the influential founder. Jack Dorsey (@Jack) "Donate via #Bitcoin to help #EndSARS NG…," X, October 14, 2020, 10.05pm, https://twitter.com/jack/status/1316485283777519620? Without a doubt, such interventions foster democratic movements and amplify the otherwise repressed voices of citizens. However, aside from the risk of poor

🗔 數位 Plurality: Part 2: Introduction
## Democracies' hostility to technology

Yet the hostilities have been far from one-sided. Democracies have, by and large, returned this hostility, viewing technology increasingly as a monolithic. Where once the public sector in democratic countries was the global driving force behind the development of information technology (e.g. the first computers, the internet, global positioning satellites), today most democratic governments are focused instead on constraining its development and are failing to respond to both opportunities and challenges it creates.

This failure has manifested in four ways. First, public opinion in democratic countries and their policymakers are increasingly hostile to large technology companies and even many technologists, a trend commonly called the "techlash". Second, democratic countries have significantly reduced their direct investment in the development of information technology. Third, democratic countries have been slow to adopt technology in public sector applications or that requires significant public sector participation. Finally, and relatedly, democratic governments have largely failed to address the areas where most technologists believe public participation, regulation, and support are critical to technology advancing in

---

understanding of context and potential divisiveness that such foreign interventions could be prone to, they underscore the debate around the impact of non-state actors such as the global corporation on state sovereignty in Africa and the global South by extension. Ohimai Amaize, *How Twitter Amplified the Divisions That Derailed Nigeria's #EndSARS Movement*, Slate Magazine, April 20, 2021, https://slate.com/technology/2021/04/endsars-nigeria-twitter-jack-dorsey-feminist-coalition.html.

a sustainable way, focusing instead on more familiar social and political problems.[17]

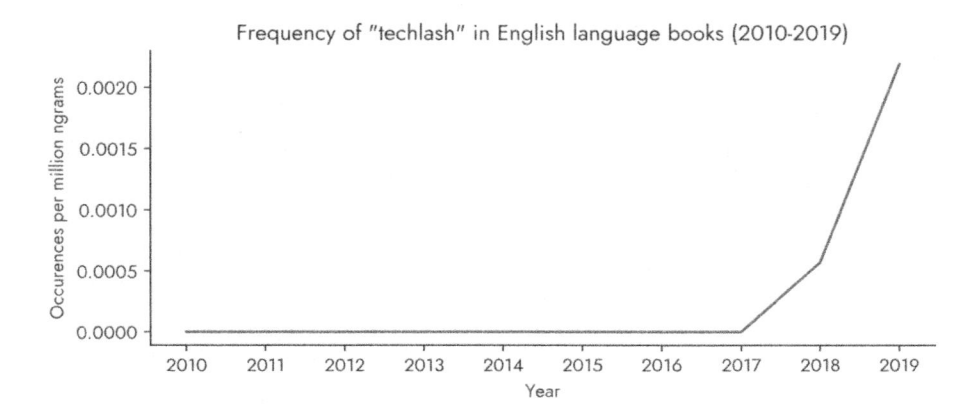

**Frequency of "techlash" in English language books (2010-2019)**

**Figure 2-0-A.** The rise of the Techlash. Source: Google Ngram Viewer.[18]

Public and policymaker attitudes towards technology took a decidedly negative turn during the 2010s. While at the end of the 2000s and early 2010s, social media and the internet were seen as forces for openness and participation, in the late 2010s they were widely blamed in commentary and to a lesser extent

---

[17] European Commission published a study on the impact of open-source software (OSS). Strict control of data in the EU has led to a lack of competition and innovation, as well as an increased risk of the market. However, we can see more investments in OSS in response to the steps of innovation in many eastern European countries. If the West fails to maintain and keep its investment in digital tech, it will experience huge losses in the future. For instance, we see the importance of digital OSS in the war between Ukraine and Russia. For more on Europe's digital position, see "Open Technologies for Europe's Digital Decade," OpenForumEurope, n.d, https://openforumeurope.org/.

[18] Google ngram Viewer, op. cit.

in public opinion surveys for many of the ills listed above [19]. This shift in attitudes has perhaps been most clearly reflected in elite attitudes, with best-selling books on technology, such as *Weapons of Math Destruction* by Cathy O'Neil and *The Age of Surveillance Capitalism* by Shoshanna Zuboff and films like *The Social Dilemma*, dominating the public conversation and political leaders across the spectrum (e.g., Jeremy Corbyn on the left and Josh Hawley on the right) taking an increasingly pessimistic and aggressive tone on the technology industry. The techlash rose to prominence to describe these concerns and is pictured in Figure A. This has been reinforced by the rise of a "cancel culture" that often harnesses social media to attack or reduce the cultural currency of prominent figures and has frequently targeted leaders in the technology industry.

Regulators in both the EU and US have responded with a range of actions, including dramatically increased antitrust scrutiny of leading technology companies, a series of regulatory interventions in Europe including the General Data Protection Regulation and the trio of the Data Governance Act, the Digital Markets Act, and the Digital Services Act. All these actions have clear policy rationales and could well be part of a positive technology agenda. However, the combination of negative tone, relative disconnection from naturally allied developments in technology and general reticence on the part of commentators and policymakers in developed democracies to articulate a positive technology vision has created an impression of an industry under siege.

---

[19] "Views of Big Tech Worsen; Public Wants More Regulation," Gallup.com, February 18, 2021, https://news.gallup.com/poll/329666/views-big-tech-worsen-public-wants-regulation.aspx; but see also "Europeans Strongly Support Science and Technology according to New Eurobarometer Survey," European Commission, September 23, 2021, https://ec.europa.eu/commission/presscorner/detail/en/IP_21_4645.

2-0 Information Technology and Democracy: A Widening Gulf

Perhaps the clearest quantitative mark for this declining proactive public interest in information technology has been falling public expenditures on research and development (R&D) as a share of gross domestic product (GDP), especially in information technology. In the great majority of developed democracies, public sector research and development expenditure as a share of GDP has been declining in recent decades even as business spending on R&D has dramatically expanded and spending by the People's Republic of China (PRC) government has dramatically increased as a share of GDP and focused on information technology.[20] Figure B shows the example of the US.

---

[20] See Fredrik Erixon, and Björn Weigel, *The Innovation Illusion: How so Little Is Created by so Many Working so Hard*, (New Haven: Yale University Press, 2017) and Robert Gordon, The Rise and Fall of American Growth: The U.S. Standard of Living since the Civil War, (Princeton; Oxford Princeton University Press, 2017). See also Carl Benedikt, and Michael Osborne, "The Future of Employment: How Susceptible Are Jobs to Computerisation," The Oxford Martin Programme on Technology and Employment, 2013. https://www.oxfordmartin.ox.ac.uk/downloads/academic/future-of-employment.pdf. Erik Brynjolfsson, and Andrew McAfee, *The Second Machine Age: Work, Progress, and Prosperity in a Time of Brilliant Technologies*, (New York: W.W. Norton & Company, 2014). Calestous Juma. Innovation and Its Enemies: Why People Resist New Technologies. (New York: Oxford University Press, 2019). Paul De Grauwe, and Anna Asbury. The Limits of the Market: The Pendulum between Government and Market. Oxford: Oxford University Press, 2019. For data sources, see "Gross Domestic Spending on R&D," 2022. https://data.oecd.org/rd/gross-domestic-spending-on-r-d.htm.; OECD. "OECD Main Science and Technology Indicators," OECD, March 2022. https://web-archive.oecd.org/2022-04-05/629283-msti-highlights-march-2022.pdf.; and "R&D Expenditure," Eurostat, n.d., https://ec.europa.eu/eurostat/statistics-explained/index.php?title=R%26D_expenditure&oldid=590306.

數位 Plurality: Part 2: Introduction

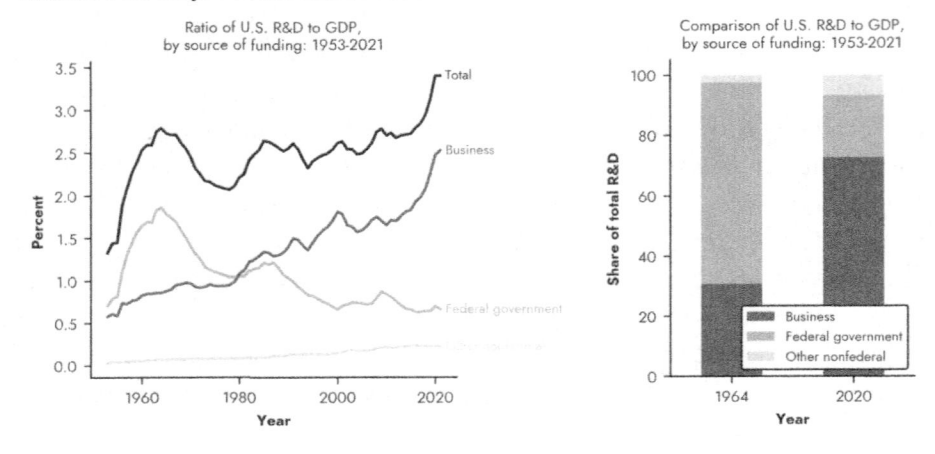

**Figure 2-0-B.** The decline over time in government funding for research and development and its eclipse by the private sector. Source: National Center for Science and Engineering Statistics.[21]

Beyond this quantitative story, the declining appearance of public financial support for information technology development has been at least as dramatic. Where once the public sector took the lead in developing what became the internet (in the US), foundations of the personal computer and analogous projects in other democratic countries (e.g., *France's Minitel*), today almost all major breakthroughs in information technology are driven by the private sector.[22]

---

[21] Gary Anderson and Francisco Moris, "Federally Funded R&D Declines as a Share of GDP and Total R&D", *National Center for Science and Engineering Statistics* NSF 23-339 (Alexandria, VA: National Science Foundation, 2023) available at https://ncses.nsf.gov/pubs/nsf23339/.

[22] See Julien Mailland and Kevin Driscoll, *Minitel: Welcome to the Internet* (Cambridge, MA: MIT Press, 2017). For example, even public interest open source code is mostly invested in by private actors, though recently the US Government has made some efforts to support that sector with the launch of code.gov.

## 2-0 Information Technology and Democracy: A Widening Gulf

While the original internet was almost entirely developed by the public and academic sectors (see our chapter *The Lost Dao* below) and based on open standards, the "Web 2.0" wave that dominated the late first two decades of the new millennium and the recent movements around "web3" and decentralized social technologies have received virtually no public financial support, as governments in democratic countries struggle to explore the potential of digital currencies, payments, and identity systems.

While many of the most fundamental advances in computing arose from democratic governments during World War II and the Cold War, today governments have played virtually no role in the breakthroughs in "foundation models" that are revolutionizing computer science. In fact, OpenAI Founders Sam Altman and Elon Musk report having initially sought government funding and only having turned to private, profit-driven sources after being repeatedly turned down; OpenAI went on to develop the Generative Pretrained Transformer (GPT) models that have increasingly captured the public's imagination about the potential of AI.[23] Again, this contrasts sharply with authoritarian regimes, like the PRC and the United Arab Emirates, that have laid out and to a large extent successfully deployed ambitious public information technology strategies, including developing their own cutting-edge competitors to GPTs.[24]

---

[23] "Transcript: Ezra Klein Interviews Sam Altman," *The New York Times*, June 11, 2021, sec. Podcasts.
https://www.nytimes.com/2021/06/11/podcasts/transcript-ezra-klein-interviews-sam-altman.html.

[24] Emily Crawford, "Made in China 2025: The Industrial Plan That China Doesn't Want Anyone Talking About," *Frontline PBS*, May 7, 2019.
https://www.pbs.org/wgbh/frontline/article/made-in-china-2025-the-industrial-plan-that-china-doesnt-want-anyone-talking-about/; Ramnath

This lack of public sector engagement with technology extends beyond research and development to deployment, adoption, and facilitation. The easiest areas to measure this are the quality and availability of digital connectivity and education. Here the data are somewhat mixed, as many high-functioning democracies (such as the Scandinavian countries) have high quality and high availability internet. But it is striking that leading authoritarian regimes dramatically outperform democracies at similar development levels, especially in the latest connectivity technology. For example, according to Speedtest.net, the PRC ranks 16th in internet speeds in the world, while only 72nd in income per head; Saudi Arabia and other Gulf monarchies similarly punch above their weight[25]. Performance on 5G, the latest generation of mobile connectivity, is more dramatic: a range of surveys find Saudi Arabia and the PRC consistently in the top 10 best-covered jurisdictions by 5G, far above their income levels.

---

Reghunadhan, "Innovation in China: Challenging the Global Science and Technology System," Asian Affairs 50, no. 4 (August 8, 2019): 656-57. https://doi.org/10.1080/03068374.2019.1663076. *United Arab Emirates National Strategy for Artificial Intelligence* (2018) available at https://ai.gov.ae/wp-content/uploads/2021/07/UAE-National-Strategy-for-Artificial-Intelligence-2031.pdf.

[25] See Robert Mcchesney, *Digital Disconnect: How Capitalism Is Turning the Internet against Democracy*, (New York; London: The New Press, 2013). See also Matthew Hindman, *The Internet Trap: How the Digital Economy Builds Monopolies and Undermines Democracy*, (Princeton, New Jersey: Princeton University Press, 2018); Adam Segal, *The Hacked World Order: How Nations Fight, Trade, Maneuver, and Manipulate in the Digital Age*, (New York: Publicaffairs, September, 2017); Richard Stengel, *Information Wars: How We Lost the Global Battle against Disinformation and What We Can Do about It*, (St. Louis: Grove Press Atlantic, 2020); and Tim Wu, *The Attention Merchants: The Epic Scramble to Get inside Our Heads*, (New York: Vintage Books, 2017).

More central to the heart of governmental responsibility in democracies, however, is the digitization of public services. Many middle-income and wealthy democracies invest less in e-government compared to authoritarian counterparts. The UN e-government development index (EGDI) is a composite measure of three important dimensions of e-government, namely: provision of online services, telecommunication connectivity, and human capital. In 2022, several authoritarian governments ranked highly, including UAE (13th), Kazakhstan (28th), and Saudi Arabia (31st), ahead of many democracies including notably Canada (32nd), Italy (37th), Brazil (49th), and Mexico (62nd).[26]

Digitization of conventional public services is perhaps the least ambitious dimension along which one might expect democracies to advance in adopting technology. Technology has redefined what services are relevant and in these novel areas, democratic governments have almost entirely failed to keep up with changing times. Where once government-provided postal services and public libraries were the backbone of democratic communication and knowledge circulation, today most communication flows through social media and search engines. Where once most public gatherings took place in parks and literal public squares, today it is almost a cliché that the public square has moved online.

Yet democratic countries have almost entirely ignored the need to provide and support digital public services. While privately-owned X (once Twitter) is the target of constant abuse by public figures, its most important competitor, the non-profits Mastodon and the open Activity Pub standard on which it runs have received a paltry few hundreds of thousands of dollars in

---

[26] *United Nations Department of Economic and Social Affairs*. E-Government Knowledge Database, 2022 available at https://publicadministration.un.org/egovkb/Data-Center

public support, running instead on Patreon donations.[27] More broadly, open source software and other commons-based public goods like Wikipedia have become critical public resources in the digital age; yet governments have consistently failed to support them and have even discriminated against them relative to other charities (for example, open source software providers generally cannot be tax-exempt charities). While authoritarian regimes plow ahead with plans for Central Bank Digital Currencies, most democratic countries are only beginning explorations.

Most ambitiously, democracies could, as so many autocracies have been doing, help facilitate radical experiments with how technologies could reshape social structures. Yet, here again, democracy seems so often to stand in the way rather than facilitate such experimentation. The PRC government has built cities and reimagined regulations to facilitate driverless cars, such as Shenzhen, and has more broadly built a detailed national technology strategy covering nearly every aspect of policy, regulation and investment.[28] Saudi Arabia is busy building a new smart city in the desert, Neom, to showcase a range of green and smart city technology, while even the most modest localized projects in democratic countries, such as

---

[27] Sara Perez, "Amid Twitter chaos, Mastodon grew donations 488% in 2022, reached 1.8M monthly active users", *Tech Crunch*, October 2, 2023 at https://techcrunch.com/2023/10/02/amid-twitter-chaos-mastodon-grew-donations-488-in-2022-reached-1-8m-monthly-active-users/)

[28] See Rogier Creemers, Hunter Dorwart, Kevin Neville, Kendra Schaefer, Johanna Costigan, and Graham Webster, "Translation: 14th Five-Year Plan for National Informatization – Dec. 2021." *DigiChina*, January 24, 2022, https://digichina.stanford.edu/work/translation-14th-five-year-plan-for-national-informatization-dec-2021/.

Google's Sidewalk Labs, have been swamped by local opposition.[29]

Even when it comes to areas where technologists agree regulation and caution are critical, democracies are falling ever further behind the needs of industry to find solutions to social challenges. There is a growing consensus among technologists that a range of emerging technologies may pose catastrophic or even existential risks that will be hard to prevent after they start to emerge. Examples include artificial intelligence systems that could rapidly self-improve their capacities, cryptocurrencies that could pose systemic financial risks, and the development of highly contagious bioweapons. They regularly bemoan the failure of democratic governments to even contemplate much less plan to confront such risks. Yet, beyond these catastrophic possibilities, a whole range of new technologies require regulatory change to be sustainable. Labor law misfits geographically and temporally flexible work empowered by technology. Copyright is far too rigid to deal with the attribution of value to data inputs to large AI models. Blockchains are empowering new forms of corporate governance that securities laws struggle to make sense of and are often put into legal jeopardy.

Yet while bold experiments with new visions of the public sector are more common in autocracies, there is an element far more fundamental to democracy itself: the mechanisms of public consent, participation, and legitimation, including voting, petitioning, soliciting citizen feedback and so forth. Voting in nearly all democracies occurs for major offices once every several years according to rules and technologies that have been largely unchanged for a century. While citizens communicate instantaneously across the planet, they are

---

[29] Josh O'Kane, *Sideways: The City Google Couldn't Buy* (Toronto: Random House Canada, 2022).

represented in largely fixed geographic configurations at great expense with low fidelity. Few modern tools of communication or data analysis are regular parts of the democratic lives of citizens.

At the same time, autocracies have increasingly harnessed the latest digital innovations to empower their regimes of surveillance (for good and ill) and social control. For example, the PRC government has widely used facial recognition to monitor population movements, has encouraged the adoption of its Digital Yuan and other surveilled digital payments (while cracking down on more private alternatives) to facilitate financial surveillance, and has even worked on developing a comprehensive "social credit score" that would track a wide range of citizen activities and condense them to a single and widely-consequential "rating".[30] For several years, the Russian government has been using facial recognition to determine who is participating in protests and detain them after the fact, allowing it to remove dissenters on a large scale with much lower risks to the regime or its police forces.[31] These techniques

---

[30] See, for, instance, John, Alun, Samuel Shen, and Tom Wilson. "China's Top Regulators Ban Crypto Trading and Mining, Sending Bitcoin Tumbling." *Reuters*, September 24, 2021, https://www.reuters.com/world/china/china-central-bank-vows-crackdown-cryptocurrency-trading-2021-09-24/. See also Bernhard Bartsch, Martin Gottske, and Christian Eisenberg, "China's Social Credit System," n.d., https://www.bertelsmann-stiftung.de/fileadmin/files/aam/Asia-Book_A_03_China_Social_Credit_System.pdf.

[31] Gleb Stolyarov, and Gabrielle Tétrault-Farber, "'Face Control': Russian Police Go Digital against Protesters," *Reuters*, February 11, 2021, https://www.reuters.com/article/us-russia-politics-navalny-tech-idUSKBN2AB1U2. See also Mark Krutov, Maria Chernova, and Robert Coalson, "Russia Unveils a New Tactic to Deter Dissent: CCTV and a 'Knock on the Door,' Days Later," *Radio Free Europe/Radio Liberty*, April 28, 2021, https://www.rferl.org/a/russia-dissent-cctv-detentions-days-later-strategy/31227889.html.

have intensified and have also been used to enforce war conscription since the full-scale invasion of Ukraine in February 2022.[32] In some sense, democracy is being left behind by technology as much by its neglect of technology, compared to many authoritarian states' eager willingness to embrace it for their own ends, as by any anti-democratic tendencies of technology itself.

**You get what you pay for**

How did we end up here? Are these conflicts the natural course of technology and of democratic societies? Is a different future possible?

A range of work suggests that technology and democracy could co-evolve in a diversity of ways and that the path most democracies are on is a result of collective choices they have made through policies, attitudes, expectations, and culture. The range of possibilities can be seen through a variety of lenses, from science fiction to real-world cases.

Science fiction shows the astonishing range of futures the human mind is capable of imagining. In many cases, these imaginations are the foundation of the technologies that researchers and entrepreneurs end up developing. Some correspond to the directions we have seen technology take recently. In his 1992 classic, *Snow Crash*, Neal Stephenson imagines a future where most people have retreated to live much of their lives in an immersive "metaverse".[33] In the process they undermine the engagement necessary to support real-world communities, governments, and the like, making space

---

[32] Anastasiia Kruope, "Russia Uses Facial Recognition to Hunt down Draft Evaders," *Human Rights Watch*, October 26, 2022, https://www.hrw.org/news/2022/10/26/russia-uses-facial-recognition-hunt-down-draft-evaders.

[33] Neal Stephenson, *Snow Crash* (New York: Bantam, 1992).

for mafias and cult leaders to rule and develop weapons of mass destruction. This future closely corresponds to elements of the "antisocial" threats to democracy from technology we discussed above.

Stephenson and other writers further extend these possibilities, which have had a profound effect in shaping technology development; for example, Meta Platforms is named after Stephenson's metaverse. Similar examples are possible for the tendency of technology to concentrate power through creating "superintelligences" as in the *fiction of* Isaac Asimov *and* Ian Banks, *the predictive futurism of* Ray Kurzweil *and* Nicholas Bostrom, *and films* like *Terminator* and *Her*.[34]

But these possibilities are both very different from each other and are far from the only visions of the technological future to be found in sci-fi. In fact, some of the most prominent science fiction shows very different possibilities. Two of the most popular sci-fi television shows of all time, *The Jetsons* and *Star Trek*, show futures where, respectively, technology has largely reinforced the culture and institutions of 1950s America and one where it has enabled a post-capitalist world of diverse intersecting alien intelligences (on which more below). But these are two among thousands of examples, from the post-gender and post-state imagination of Ursula Le Guin to the post-colonial futurism of Octavia Butler. All suggest a dizzying range of ways technology could coevolve with society[35].

---

[34] Isaac Asimov, *I, Robot* (New York: Gnome Press: 1950). Ian Banks, *Consider Phlebas* (London: Macmillan, 1987). Ray Kurzweil, *The Age of Spiritual Machines* (New York: Viking, 1999). Nicholas Bostrom, *Superintelligence* (Oxford, UK: Oxford University Press, 2014).

[35] Ursula K. LeGuin, *The Dispossessed: An Ambiguous Utopia* (New York: Harper & Row, 1974). Octavia E. Butler, *Wild Seed* (New York: Doubleday, 1980). Marge Piercy, *Woman on the Edge of Time* (New York: Knopf,

But science fiction writers are not alone. The primary theme of the field of Science and Technology Studies, including the philosophy, sociology, and history of science, has been the contingency and possibility inherent in the development of science and technology and the lack of any single necessary direction for their evolution[36]. These conclusions have been increasingly accepted in social sciences, like political science and economics, that traditionally viewed technological progress as fixed and linear. Two of the world's leading economists, Daron Acemoglu and Simon Johnson, have recently published a book that argues that the direction of technological progress is a key target for social policy and

---

1976). Karl Schroeder, "Degrees of Freedom" in Ed Finn and Kathryn Cramer eds. *Hieroglyph: Stories & Visions for a Better Future* (New York: William Morrow, 2014). Karl Schroeder, *Stealing Worlds* (New York: Tor Books, 2019) Annalee Newitz, *The Future of Another Timeline* (New York: Tor Books, 2019). Cory Doctorow, *Walkaway* (New York: Tor Books, 2017). Malka Older, *Infomocracy* (New York: Tor Books, 2016). Naomi Alderman, *The Power*, (New York:Viking, 2017) Cixin Liu, *The Three-Body Problem* (New York: Tor Books, 2014) Paolo Bacigalupi, *The Windup Girl* (New York: Start Publishing LLC, 2009). Neal Stephenson, *The Diamond Age* (New York: Spectra, 2003). William Gibson, *The Peripheral* (New York: Berkley, 2019).

[36] Jacques Ellul, *The Technological Society* (New York: Vintage Books, 1964). Paul Hoch, Donald MacKenzie, and Judy Wajcman, "The Social Shaping of Technology," *Technology and Culture* 28, no. 1 (January 1987): 132 https://doi.org/10.2307/3105489. Andrew Pickering, "The Cybernetic Brain: Sketches of Another Future," *Kybernetes* 40, no. 1/2 (March 15, 2011) https://doi.org/10.1108/k.2011.06740aae.001. Deborah Douglas, Wiebe E. Bijker, Thomas P. Hughes, and Trevor Pinch, *The Social Construction of Technological Systems: New Directions in the Sociology and History of Technology* (Cambridge, Massachusetts: MIT Press, 2012), available at: https://www.jstor.org/stable/j.ctt5vjrsq. Charles C. Mann, *1491: New Revelation of the Americas Before Columbus* (New York: Knopf, 2005).

reform while documenting the historical contingencies that led to the directions of technology we have seen in the past.[37]

Perhaps the most striking illustration comes from comparing the ways technology has advanced across countries today. Where once leading thinkers predicted the power of technology to sweep away social differences, today the technological systems of powers great and sometimes small define their competing social systems as much as their formally stated ideologies: the PRC surveillance regime looks like one technological future, while the Russian hacking networks seem another, the growing space of web3-driven communities and adjacent work in Africa and Latin America focused on interoperability a third, the mainstream Western capitalist countries on which we have focused a fourth and the heterogeneous digital democracies of India, Estonia, and Taiwan something else entirely that we will explore in depth below. Far from converging, technology seems to be proliferating possible futures.

So, if our current trajectory of technology and social relationship to it in Western liberal democracies is not inevitable, in what ways are we choosing to be on this conflictual path? And how might we get off it?

While there are many ways to describe the choices democratic societies have made about technology, perhaps the most concrete and easiest to quantify are the investments realized. These show clear choices about technological paths that Western liberal democracies (and thus most of the financial capital in the world) have made about investments in the future of technology, many are of quite recent origin. While these

---

[37] Daron Acemoglu and Simon Johnson, *Power and Progress: Our Thousand-Year Struggle over Technology and Prosperity* (New York: PublicAffairs, 2023).

have recently been driven primarily by the private sector, they reflect earlier priorities set by governments that are in many ways just beginning to filter through to private sector applications.

Beginning with recent trends in the increasingly well-measured venture capital industry, the last decade has seen a dramatic and overwhelming focus of venture capital within the high technology sector into artificial intelligence and cryptocurrency-adjacent "web3" technologies. Figure C displays data on private investment in AI collected by NetBase Quid and charted by Stanford's Center for Human-Centered Artificial Intelligence's 2022 AI Index Report, showing its explosive growth over the course of the 2010s, growth that has come to dominate private technology investment; Figure D shows the same (over a different period and quarterly) for the web3 space based on data from Pitchbook.

However, while these priorities are relatively recent and appear to emerge from the logic of "the market", they reflect a much longer running and collectively direct set of choices. These stem from the investments governments in democratic countries have made. [38]

---

[38] According to a report by the research and advisory company, Gartner, worldwide government spending on AI is expected to reach 37 billion in 2021, a 22.4% increase from the previous year. - China leads the world in AI investment: Chinese companies invested 25 billion in AI in 2017, compared to 9.7 billion in the US. In 2021, the US Senate passed a 250 billion bill that includes $52 billion for semiconductor research and development, which is expected to boost the country's AI capabilities. Additionally, in the same year, the European Union announced an 8.3 billion investment in artificial intelligence, cybersecurity, and supercomputers as part of its Digital Decade plan. In 2021, the Bank of Japan started experimenting with central bank digital currency (CBDC) and China's central bank launched a digital yuan trial program in several cities.

數位 Plurality: Part 2: Introduction

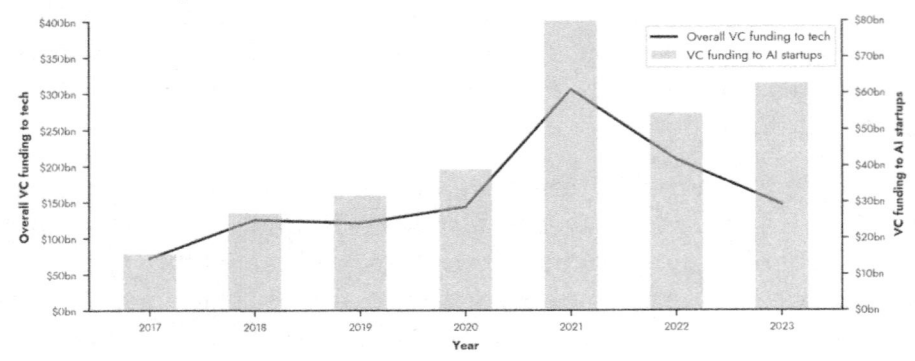

**Figure 2-0-C.** Private investment in AI over the last seven years. Source: NetBase Quid via 2023 AI Index Report[39]

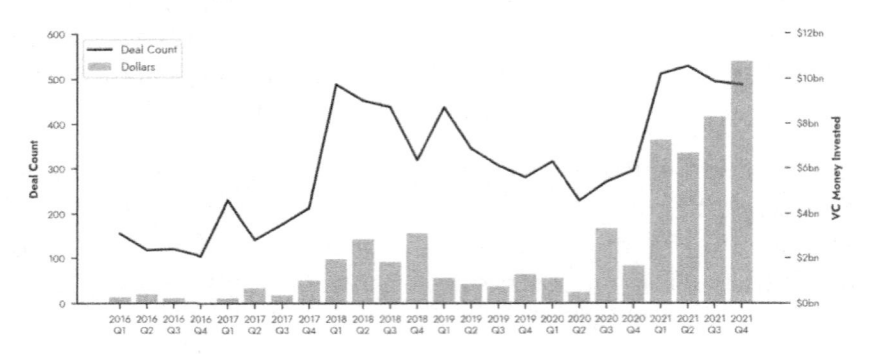

**Figure 2-0-D.** Time trend in crypto VC deals and investment. Source: National Venture Capital Association and Pitchbook[40]

---

[39] Nestor Maslej, Loredana Fattorini, Erik Brynjolfsson, John Etchemendy, Katrina Ligett, Terah Lyons, James Manyika, Helen Ngo, Juan Carlos Niebles, Vanessa Parli, Yoav Shoham, Russell Wald, Jack Clark, and Raymond Perrault, "The AI Index 2023 Annual Report," AI Index Steering Committee, Institute for Human-Centered AI, Stanford University, Stanford, CA, April 2023.

[40] Pitchbook, "Crypto Report" Q4 2023 at https://pitchbook.com/news/reports/q4-2023-crypto-report.

## 2-0 Information Technology and Democracy: A Widening Gulf

Frequency of "artificial intelligence" in English language books (1950-2019)

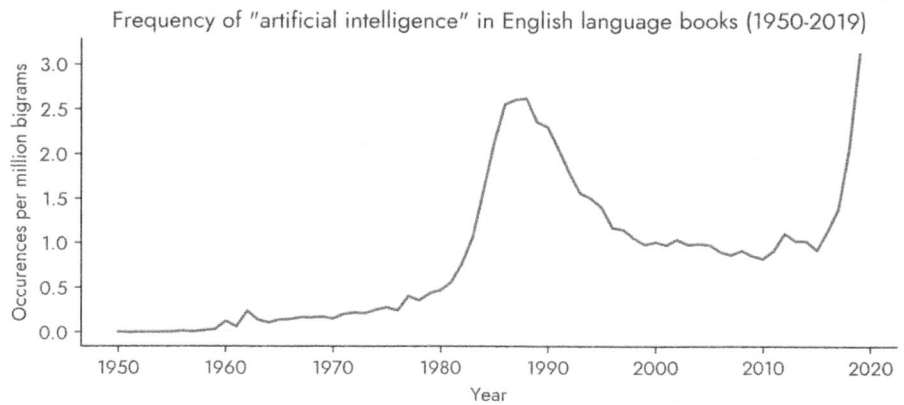

**Figure 2-0-E.** The relative frequency of "artificial intelligence in English books 1950-2019. Source: Google Ngrams[41]

Furthermore, these investments are not just choices that could have been made differently; they are quite recent and *were* made very differently immediately prior. These investments are reflected in the canonical technologies of the last few decades. Artificial intelligence was heralded as a coming revolution throughout much of the 1980s, as reflected in Figure E showing the relative frequency of this phrase in English books as tracked by Google Ngrams. Yet the defining technology of the 1980s was quite opposite: the personal computer that made computing a complement to individual human creativity. The 1990s were haunted by Stephenson's imagination of the possibilities of escapist virtual worlds and atomizing cryptography, the connective tissue of the internet swept the world, ushering in an unprecedented age of communication and cooperation. Mobile telephony in the 2000s, social networking in the 2010s, and the scaffolding of remote work in

---

[41] Derived from Google nGrams viewer at https://books.google.com/ngrams.

the 2020s...none of these have focused on either cryptographic hypercapitalism or artificial superintelligence. This reflects, with an extensive lag, the shift in investments made by public sector research funders away from supporting these technologies and towards investment in cryptography and artificial intelligence, as we discuss in The Lost Dao below, driven by a variety of (geo)political factors.

## Ideologies of the twenty-first century

If the path of technology is not predetermined and instead can be significantly shaped by collective choices regarding investment, how should we think about the flexibility we have as a society in choosing among possible directions? How much scope is there for choice and what do these look like?

One useful analogy for thinking about choice over directions a society might take is ideologies. It is "common sense" that different societies have chosen or might choose to organize themselves in terms of different (combinations of) ideologies: communism, capitalism, democracy, fascism, theocracy, etc. Each of these incorporates strengths and weaknesses, appeals to some more than to others, and coheres and prescribes to differing degrees. There may be configurations of these ideologies that simply do not work or require specific historical and social conditions.

We might look at different trajectories for technology in a similar way. The range of futures is not unlimited or infinitely malleable: some things are easier, harder, or outright impossible. But neither is it predetermined. There are clusters of plausible visions of the future and technologies that empower these; through our collective technological investments, we help choose among these possibilities.

While a bit less familiar than the linear and progressive story about technology that is most common today, this perspective is very far from original. It is a recurring theme in literature, scholarship, and even entertainment. One striking example is the series of computer games *Civilization* created by Sid Meier, in which the player charts a course for a people from prehistory to the future. A defining characteristic of the game is the diversity of possible technological paths and the way these interact with social systems a society may adopt.

The latest entry in the series, *Civilization VI*, and specifically the "Gathering Storm" expansion pack for it, illustrates our argument quite elegantly. In that game, the "Information Era" features a choice among three ideologies: "Synthetic Technocracy," "Corporate Libertarianism", and "Digital Democracy", with corresponding strengths, weaknesses, and connections to technological development. While the names for each of these are a bit awkward and we shorten them below, we will argue in what follows that they do a good job describing in broad strokes, like Communism, Fascism and Democracy in the 20th century, the great techno-ideological debate of our time.

*Artificial Intelligence and technocracy*

The first and most widely expressed vision of the future of technology today centers around Artificial Intelligence (AI) and the way social systems will have to adapt to it; it is captured by the Civilization VI "Synthetic Technocracy" category, or Technocracy for short.

Technocracy focuses on the potential of AI to create what OpenAI Founder Sam Altman calls *"Moore's Law for Everything"*: a transformation where AI makes all material goods cheap and abundant and thus allows the abolition, at least in principle, of material scarcity.[42] Yet this potential abundance may not be equally distributed; it is plausible that

---

[42] Sam Altman, "Moore's Law for Everything", March 16, 2021 https://moores.samaltman.com/.

its value will concentrate in a small group that controls and directs AI systems. A key element of the technocratic social vision is therefore material redistribution, usually through a "universal basic income" (UBI). Another central focus is on the risk of AI(s) getting out of human control and threatening human survival, and thus on the need for strong and often centralized control over who has access to these technologies, as well as ensuring they are built to faithfully execute human desires. While the precise contours differ across the exponents of this view, the idea of "Artificial General Intelligence" (AGI) is central: machines that exceed human capabilities in some generalized way, leaving little measurable utility in human individual or collective cognition.

Leading exponents of this view in Silicon Valley are Altman and his mentor Reid Hoffman and until recently Altman's OpenAI co-founder Elon Musk. The view is also popular in the PRC, where it has been advanced by Jack Ma, economist Yu Yong-Ding and even by the PRC's official New Generation Artificial Intelligence Development Plan with a strong reliance on the Marxist idea of "central planning". It also appears throughout science fiction, particularly the work of authors mentioned above like Asimov, Banks, Kurzweil and Bostrom. Bostrom's latest book, *Deep Utopia: Life and Meaning in a Solved World*, is perhaps the purest expression of this view.[43]

Leading organizations aligned with this perspective include OpenAI, DeepMind, and other advanced artificial intelligence projects. The political campaigns of Andrew Yang in the United States helped bring this perspective to the mainstream of politics and technocratic ideas show up in toned-down forms in

---

[43] Nicholas Bostrom, *Deep Utopia: Life and Meaning in a Solved World* (Washington, DC: Ideapress, 2024).

much of the thought of the "tech left", including commentators like Ezra Klein, Matthew Yglesias, and Noah Smith.

*Crypto and hyper-capitalism*

A second view is much less common in the mainstream media but has been a dominant theme in the community that has built around Bitcoin and other cryptocurrencies and in various related internet communities; it is captured by the Civilization VI "Corporate Libertarianism" category, which we will abbreviate to "Libertarianism" below.

Libertarianism focuses on the potential (or in some telling inevitability) of cryptography and networking protocols supplanting the role of human collective organization and politics, liberating individuals to participate in unfettered markets free from government and other collective "coercion" and regulation. Fiction has been the central inspiration for libertarian thinking, including the work of *Ayn Rand* and Stephenson.[44] Stephenson's books, especially *Snow Crash* discussed above and *Cryptonomicon* (1999), while seemingly and expressly intended as dystopian warnings, have been adopted as blueprints by adherents of Libertarianism.[45] Exemplary technologies in these works and have since become central to the Libertarian community are immersive virtual worlds (viz. Stephenson's metaverse), digital currencies independent of governments, private sovereignties especially based in ungoverned spaces such as floating cities or "seasteads" and strong cryptography as a means of evading collective control/law. The Bitcoin, Web3, 4Chan, and other "peripheral" but influential online communities are core to the social base of the Libertarian perspective.

---

[44] Ayn Rand, *Atlas Shrugged* (New York: Random House, 1957).

[45] Neal Stephenson, *Cryptonomicon* (New York: Avon, 1999).

Perhaps partly because it is less mainstream than Technocracy, Libertarianism has a much clearer intellectual canon and set of leaders. *The Sovereign Individual* by James Dale Davidson and Lord William Rees-Mogg, *the writings* of Curtis Yarvin under the pen name Mencius Moldbug, *The Network State* by Balaji Srinavasan and *Bronze Age Mindset* are widely read and cited in the community.[46] Venture capitalist Peter Thiel is widely seen as the central intellectual leader, along with others (such as the authors mentioned) whom he has funded or promoted the work of.

Libertarianism has a close, but also somewhat complicated, relationship with the nationalist and far-right in democratic countries. On the one hand, most participants identify with this group and support it, to the extent they engage with politics, as illustrated by Thiel's emergence as a primary financial supporter of Donald Trump and his supporters. In fact, several leading hard right politicians are closely connected to the Libertarian worldview: prominent British Conservative Member of Parliament Jacob Rees-Mogg is the son of Lord William Rees-Mogg, Thiel employs former Austrian Chancellor Sebastian Kurz and Thiel protégés Blake Masters and J. D. Vance ran for Senate in 2022, with the latter winning a seat.

On the other hand, Libertarianism is consistently hostile to nationalism (or any other form of collectivism or solidarity) and Libertarian followers routinely mock and dismiss many core religious, national and cultural values associated with the right. This apparent contradiction may be resolved by a shared antipathy to what they perceive as dominant left-wing cultural

---

[46] James Dale Davidson and Lord William Rees-Mogg, *The Sovereign Individual: Mastering the Transition to the Information Age* (New York: Touchstone, 1999). Mencius Moldbug, *Unqualified Reservations* https://www.unqualified-reservations.org/. Balaji Srinavasan, *The Network State* (Self-published, 2022) available at https://thenetworkstate.com/. Bronze Age Pervert, *Bronze Age Mindset* (Self-published, 2018).

values or by an "accelerationist" attitude as advocated by Yarvin, Davidson and Rees-Mogg that views the "nationalist backlash" to the inevitable technological trends as an accelerant and possible ally in the dissolution of the nation-state.

## Stagnation and inequality

These two ideologies have, to a significant extent though often in moderated form, dominated public imagination about the future of technology in most liberal democracies and thus shaped the direction of technology investment for most of the last half-century. While the Technocratic story sounds fresh and related to recent progress in AI, related discussions around AI were almost as fever pitched as far back as the 1980s, as illustrated by Figure E. While the recent discussions around web3 technologies have raised its profile, Libertarianism was arguably at its peak in the 1990s, with John Perry Barlow's *"Declaration of the Independence of Cyberspace"*, Stephenson's novels and the publication of *The Sovereign Individual*.

The radical promises of these visions led many to anticipate dramatic economic and productivity growth from information technology, as well as the waves of privatization, deregulation and tax cuts that went along with them in most liberal democracies beginning roughly half a century ago. Yet these promises are far from bearing fruit and economic analysis increasingly suggests these directions for technology may play a key role in explaining that failure.

數位 Plurality: Part 2: Introduction

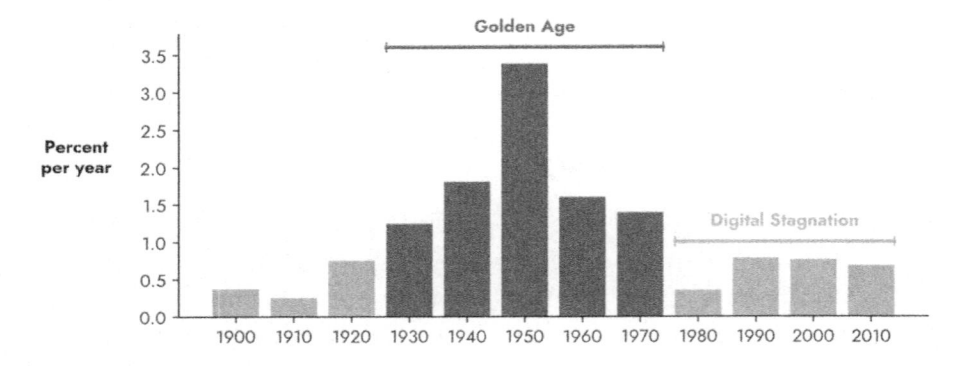

**Figure 2-0-F.** Improvement in technology represented by growth in "Total Factor Productivity". Source: Gordon, *The Rise and Fall of American Growth.*[47]

Instead of the promised explosion of economic possibility, the last half-century has seen a dramatic deceleration of economic and especially productivity growth. Figure F shows the growth in the United States of "Total Factor Productivity (TFP)", economists' most inclusive measure of the improvement in technology, averaged by decades from the beginning of the 20th century to today. Rates during the mid-century "Golden Age" roughly doubled their levels both before and after during the period we dub the "Digital Stagnation". The pattern is even more dramatic in other liberal democratic countries in Europe and in most of democratic Asia, with South Korea and Taiwan as notable exceptions.

To make matters worse, this period of stagnation has also been one of dramatically rising inequality, especially in the United States. Figure G shows average income growth in the US by income percentile during the Golden Age and Great

---

[47] Robert J. Gordon, op. cit.

Stagnation respectively. During the Golden Age, income growth was roughly constant across the distribution, but trailed off for top-income earners. During the Digital Stagnation, income growth was higher for higher earners and only exceeded the average level during the Golden Age for those in the top 1%, with even smaller groups earning the great majority of the overall much lower income gains.

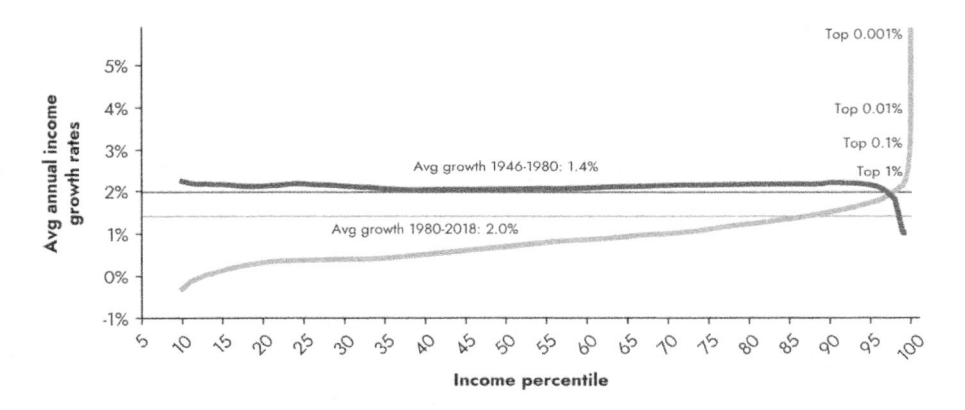

**Figure 2-0-G.** Average income growth in the US by income percentile during the Golden Age and Great Stagnation. Source: Saez and Zucman, "The Rise of Income and Wealth Inequality".[48]

What has gone so wrong in the last half-century compared to the one before? Economists have studied a range of factors, from the rise of market power and the decline of unions to the progressively greater challenge of innovating when so much has already been invented. But increasing evidence focuses on two factors closely tied to the influence of Technocracy and

---

[48] Emmanuel Saez and Gabriel Zucman, "The Rise of Wealth and Inequality in America: Evidence from Distributional Macroeconomic Accounts," *Journal of Economic Perspectives* 34, no. 4 (2020): 3-26.

Libertarianism respectively: the shift in the direction of technological progress towards automation and away from labor augmentation and the shift in the direction of policy away from proactively shaping industrial development and relations and towards an assumption that "free markets know best".

On the first point, in a series of recent papers, Acemoglu, Pascual Restrepo, and collaborators have documented the shift in the direction of technical progress from the Golden Age to the Digital Stagnation. Figure H summarizes their results, plotting cumulative changes in productivity over time from labor automation (what they call "displacement") and labor augmentation (what they call "reinstatement").[49] During the Golden Age, reinstatement roughly balanced displacement, leaving the share of income going to workers essentially constant. During the Digital Stagnation, however, displacement has slightly accelerated while reinstatement has dramatically fallen, leading to slower overall productivity growth and a significant reduction in the share of income going to workers. Furthermore, their analysis shows that the inegalitarian effects of this imbalance have been exacerbated by the concentration of displacement among low-skilled workers.

---

[49] Daron Acemoglu and Pascual Restrepo, "Automation and New Tasks: How Technology Displaces and Reinstates Labor." *Journal of Economic Perspectives* 33, no. 2 (May 2019): 3-30.
https://doi.org/10.1257/jep.33.2.3. Note that the precise Golden Age-Digital Stagnation cutoff differs across these studies, but it is always somewhere during the 1970s or 1980s.

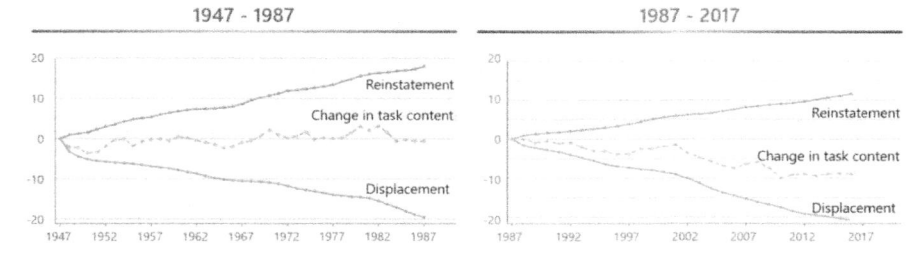

## 2-0 Information Technology and Democracy: A Widening Gulf

**Figure 2-0-H.** Cumulative changes in productivity over time from Displacement (labor automation) and Reinstatement (labor augmentation) during the Golden Age and Great Stagnation. Source: Acemoglu and Restrepo, "Automation and New Tasks: How Technology Displaces and Reinstates Labor".[50]

The role of "neoliberal" policies in contributing to the stagnation and inequality of this period is widely debated and we suspect most readers have formed their own views on the matter. One of us was also co-author of a book that contains a review of the evidence as of roughly a decade ago.[51] We will thus not go into detail here and refer readers to instead to that or other related writing.[52] However, clearly, the defining ideological and policy direction of this period was an embrace of capitalist market economics, often closely tied to claims that such an embrace was necessitated by the globalization of technology and the resulting impossibility of collective

---

[50] Ibid.

[51] Eric Posner, Glen Weyl, and Vitalik Buterin, *Radical Markets: Uprooting Capitalism and Democracy for a Just Society*, (Princeton: Princeton University Press, 2019).

[52] Thomas Philippon, *The Great Reversal: How America Gave up on Free Markets*, (Cambridge, Massachusetts: The Belknap Press Of Harvard University Press, 2019); Jonathan Tepper, *The Myth of Capitalism: Monopolies and the Death of Competition*, New York: Harper Business, 2018).

governance/action that is core to the Libertarian ideology. The, largely failed, last half-century of technology and policy has thus been characterized by the dominance of Technocracy in the sphere of technology and Libertarianism in the sphere of policy.

Of course, the last half century has hardly been devoid of technological breakthroughs that have genuinely brought about positive, if uneven and sometimes fraught, transformations. Personal computers empowered unprecedented human creativity in the 1980s; the internet allowed communication and connection across previously unimaginable distances in the 1990s; smartphones integrated these two revolutions and made them ubiquitous in the 2000s. Yet, it is striking that none of these most canonical innovations of our time fit neatly into the Technocratic or Libertarian stories. They were clearly all technologies that augmented human creativity, often called "intelligence augmentation" or IA, rather than AI.[53] Yet neither were they envisioned primarily as tools to escape existing social institutions; they facilitated rich communication and connection rather than market transactions, private property, and secrecy. As we will see, these technologies emerged from a very different tradition than either of these two. Thus, even the few major technological leaps in this period were largely independent of or in contrast to these visions.

## A fraying social contract

Yet the economic conditions surrounding the embrace of Technocracy and Libertarianism are only the easiest to quantify and thus most headline-grabbing. Deeper, more insidious, and ultimately more damaging have been the corrosion of the

---

[53] John Markoff, *Machines of Loving Grace: The Quest for Common Ground Between Humans and Robots* (New York: Ecco, 2015).

confidence, faith, and trust on which social support of both democracy and technology rest.

Faith in democratic institutions has been falling, especially in the last decade and a half in all democracies, but especially in the US and developing democracies. In the US, dissatisfaction with democracy has gone from being the opinion of a fringe (less than 25%) to being the majority opinion in the last 3 decades.[54] While it is less consistently measured, faith in technology, especially leading technology companies, has been similarly declining. In the US, the technology sector has fallen from being considered the most trusted sector in the economy in the early and mid-2010s to amongst the least trusted, based on surveys by organizations like the Public Affairs Council, Morning Consult, Pew Research and Edelman Trust Barometer.[55]

---

[54] Fred Lewsey, "Global Dissatisfaction with Democracy at a Record High," *University of Cambridge*, January 29, 2020, https://www.cam.ac.uk/stories/dissatisfactiondemocracy.

[55] According to the 2021 Edelman Trust Barometer, only 57% of global respondents trust technology as a reliable source of information. This represents a decline of 4 points from the previous year's survey. A 2020 survey by Pew Research Center found that 72% of Americans believe that social media companies have too much power and influence over the news that people see. Additionally, 51% of respondents said they were very or somewhat concerned about the role of technology in political polarization. A 2019 survey by the Center for the Governance of AI at the University of Oxford found that only 33% of Americans believe that tech companies are generally trustworthy. In a 2020 survey of 9,000 people in nine countries, conducted by Ipsos MORI, only 30% of respondents said that they trust social media companies to behave responsibly with their data. These data points suggest that there is a growing sense of skepticism and concern about the role of technology in society, including its impact on democracy. See Richard Wike, Laura Silver, Janell Fetterolf, Christine Huang, Sarah Austin, Laura Clancy, and Sneha Gubbala. "Social Media Seen as Mostly Good for Democracy across Many Nations, but U.S. Is a Major Outlier," *Pew*

數位 Plurality: Part 2: Introduction

These concerns have spilled out more broadly to a general loss of faith in a range of social institutions. The fraction of Americans expressing high confidence in several leading institutions (including organized religions, federal governments, public schools, media, and law enforcement) has

---

*Research Center*, December 6, 2022,
https://www.pewresearch.org/global/2022/12/06/social-media-seen-as-mostly-good-for-democracy-across-many-nations-but-u-s-is-a-major-outlier/. Pew Research shows ordinary citizens see social media as both a constructive and destructive component of political life, and overall most believe it has actually had a positive impact on democracy. Across the countries polled, a median of 57% say social media has been more of a good thing for their democracy, with 35% saying it has been a bad thing. There are substantial cross-national differences on this question, however, and the United States is a clear outlier: Just 34% of U.S. adults think social media has been good for democracy, while 64% say it has had a bad impact. In fact, the U.S. is an outlier on a number of measures, with larger shares of Americans seeing social media as divisive. See OAIC, "Australian Community Attitudes to Privacy Survey 2020 Prepared for the Office of the Australian Information Commissioner by Lonergan Research," 2020, https://www.oaic.gov.au/__data/assets/pdf_file/0015/2373/australian-community-attitudes-to-privacy-survey-2020.pdf. Many consumer respondents to a recent Australian survey (58%) admitted they do not understand what firms do with the data they collect, and 49% feel unable to protect their data due to a lack of knowledge or time, as well as the complexity of the processes involved (OAIC, 2020). "Twitter, Facebook, YouTube, and Instagram are critical in disseminating the rapid and far-reaching spread of information," a systematic review by WHO explains. See World Health Organization, "Infodemics and Misinformation Negatively Affect People's Health Behaviours," September 1, 2022. https://www.who.int/europe/news/item/01-09-2022-infodemics-and-misinformation-negatively-affect-people-s-health-behaviours-new-who-review-finds. The repercussions of misinformation on social media include such negative effects as "an increase in erroneous interpretation of scientific knowledge, opinion polarization, escalating fear and panic or decreased access to health care". See Janna Anderson, and Lee Rainie, "Concerns about Democracy in the Digital Age," *Pew Research Center*, February 21, 2020.
https://www.pewresearch.org/internet/2020/02/21/concerns-about-democracy-in-the-digital-age/.

fallen to roughly half its level when such surveys began, around the end of the Golden Age in most cases.[56] Trends in Europe are more moderate and the global picture is uneven, but the general trend towards declining institutional confidence in democratic countries is widely accepted.[57]

**Reclaiming our future**

Technology and democracy are trapped between two sides of a widening gulf. That divide is damaging both sides of the conflict, undermining democracy and slowing technological development. As collateral damage, it is retarding economic growth, undermining confidence in social institutions, and fueling inequality. This conflict is not inevitable; it is the product of the technological directions liberal democracies have collectively chosen to invest in, once fueled by ideologies about the future that are antithetical to democratic ideals. Because political systems depend on technologies to thrive, democracy cannot thrive if we continue down this path.

Another path is possible. Technology and democracy can be each other's greatest allies. In fact, as we will argue, large-scale "Digital Democracy" is a dream we have only begun to imagine, one that requires unprecedented technology to have any chance of being realized. By reimagining our future, shifting public investments, research agendas, and private development, we can build that future. In the rest of this book,

---

[56] Gallup, "Confidence in Institutions," n.d., https://news.gallup.com/poll/1597/confidence-institutions.aspx.

[57] United Nations Department of Economic and Social Affairs, "Trust in Public Institutions: Trends and Implications for Economic Security," n.d., https://social.desa.un.org/publications/trust-in-public-institutions-trends-and-implications-for-economic-security. See also Marta Kolczynska, Paul-Christian Bürkner, Lauren Kennedy, and Aki Vehtari, "Modeling Public Opinion over Time and Space: Trust in State Institutions in Europe, 1989-2019," *SocArXiv*, August 11, 2020. https://doi.org/10.31235/osf.io/3v5g7.

數位 Plurality: Part 2: Introduction

we hope to show you how. And we will begin by telling you the story of a place that has gone farther than any other in realizing that future, a place where democracy and digital technology are not just allies, but deeply mutually entwined.

## 2-1 A View from Yushan

*Swirling ocean, beautiful islands;*
*A transcultural republic of citizens.*[1]

---

Standing at the summit of East Asia's highest peak, Yushan (Jade Mountain), one can not only look down on Taiwan, but also feel how this small, mountainous island nation is a global crossroad. Located at the junction of the Eurasian and Pacific tectonic plates, Taiwan's geological fault line yearly pushes it up, even as it also regularly causes earthquakes, like that experienced in early April, against which rigorous building codes and resilient infrastructure protect inhabitants. In the same way, the clash of Taiwan's diverse culture, history and values has built a prosperous and innovative society, while pro-social digital innovation has managed to protect it from polarization.

Today, with a voter turnout rate over 70%[2], second-highest religious diversity in the world[3], and 90% of global supply capacity for advanced chips, Taiwan has broken through geographic constraints and demonstrated the resilience of a democratic society to collaborate with its region and the world.

---

[1] This is an alternate interpretation of 中華民國 (lit. "amidst" "cultures" "citizens" "nation"), usually translated as "Republic of China".

[2] "Billing Profile Information," Central Election Commission, n.d, https://db.cec.gov.tw/ElecTable/Election?type=President.

[3] Joseph Liu, "Global Religious Diversity," *Pew Research Center*, April 4, 2014. https://www.pewresearch.org/religion/2014/04/04/global-religious-diversity/.

Taiwan's ability to achieve among the world's lowest fatality rates without any lockdowns during the Covid crisis — while maintaining among the fastest economic growth rates in the world — show the results of the plural spirit of Taiwan's information society. Whether it's a map of masks or a social safety distance, these are all manifestations of technologies for collaborative diversity, deeply rooted in daily life.[4]

## Place of convergence

One etymology of Taiwan's name is from the indigenous word "Taivoan", meaning "place of convergence". Taiwan has arguably been a launching point for long-distance cooperation longer than anywhere on earth, being believed to be the starting point for the journeys of thousands of miles by Polynesian voyagers in the second millennium BCE.[5] The story of this island and its people, influenced by indigenous cultures, colonial powers, and political ideologies from the region and world, centers on the ongoing conflict and co-creation between different notions of what this place is and what it can be. This raucous and rich clash has poured out a unique form of democracy forged by a history of constant upheaval.

Two dramatic personal experiences of the lead authors of this book illustrate this unique cultural and political setting. On March 18, 2014, a group of students frustrated by the substance and process of a new trade deal with Beijing and inspired by the global "Occupy" movement climbed over the fence surrounding the legislature building. A similar, if more

---

[4] "Tracking Covid-19 Excess Deaths across Countries," The Economist, October 20, 2021. https://www.economist.com/graphic-detail/coronavirus-excess-deaths-tracker.

[5] Peter Bellwood, *Man's Conquest of the Pacific: the Prehistory of Southeast Asia and Oceania* (Oxford, UK: Oxford University Press, 1979).

violent, occupation of the American legislative Capitol almost seven years later lasted only a few hours and yet is one of the most divisive events in American history. In contrast, the "Sunflower" (318) occupation lasted more than a hundred times as long (more than 3 weeks) and yet the demands of the protesters were eventually largely accepted as a consensus; the movement led to a change of government and the rise of new political parties.

Perhaps most importantly, the movement led to a deeper and more lasting shift in politics, as the government at the time gained respect for the movement and ministers invited younger "reverse mentors" to help them learn from youth and civil society. One particularly proactive minister, one of the world's first ministers in charge of digital participation, Jaclyn Tsai, recruited one of us to begin our journey of public service. Eventually this led to her taking that role in 2016 and in 2022 becoming the first Minister of Digital Affairs.

Almost a decade after these events, the other primary author of this book visited to witness the general election held January 13, 2024, which launched a "year of elections" in which more people than in any previous year will vote and followed hot on the heels of the "year of AI", when generative models like GPT burst into the public consciousness. Many expect these models to turbocharge information manipulation and interference by authoritarian actors. This election seemed a test case, with a more concerted, better-funded adversary focused on a small population than anywhere in the world.[6] Walking the streets of Taipei on the eve of that election, he saw no shortage of divisions for such attacks to exploit. At the rally of the ruling Democratic Progressive Party (DPP) he found not a single

---

[6] "Disinformation in Taiwan: International versus Domestic Perpetrators," V-Dem, 2020. https://v-dem.net/weekly_graph/disinformation-in-taiwan-international-versus

official flag, only placards of the island, the party's signature green color and occasional rainbow flags ▬. At the rally of the opposition Kuomintang (KMT or Nationalist) party, he saw only the flag of the Republic of China (ROC) 🇹🇼. It made him imagine how much more extreme the divisions of his American home would be if Democrats waved a historical British flag and Republicans the stars and stripes.

Yet, despite these extreme divides and harnessing the technologies developed partly because of the Sunflower movement, the January 13 election has become a positive model to the world, with the candidate of the party opposed by the authoritarian adversary outperforming opinion polls, calm prevailing after the election and a largely consensual outcome being reached across the society. This capacity to harness technology and social organization to channel widely divergent attitudes towards shared progress was most sharply manifested in the decade of work following the Sunflower movement. Yet it has far deeper historical roots, roots that come from different starting points and converge on this fateful decade of digital democracy.

## Taiwan's historical lineage

The divergent identities emphasized by the DPP and KMT correspond to different facets and imaginations of what "this place is." These resonate with an alternate etymology for the island's name: "tayw"-"an", which means "people"-"place" in another, closed-related indigenous language (Siraya). For the KMT (identified with blue), Taiwan is defined by most of its people speaking Chinese languages such as Mandarin, Taigi (Taiwanese Hokkien) and Hakka. Some would go as far as to argue that Taiwan is more ethno-historically "Chinese" than the PRC, with more than 80% speaking Mandarin as a primary language (compared to 70% in PRC), more than 40% following traditional religions such as Daoism (compared to less than 20% in PRC) and the official government ideology being

## 2-1 A View from Yushan

Tridemism (more below) rather than imported Marxism. In contrast, for those influenced by the DPP (identified with green) view, Taiwan is a place, an island whose history is diverse and transcultural, spent only two centuries as a periphery under Qing Chinese rule and should be the center of determining its own future. To make sense of these divides, we must therefore trace briefly both the history of this island and of the ROC government.

The island's history is replete with war, rebellion, colonizers, and national independence narratives at every turn. Like many islands in the South China Sea, indigenous peoples in Taiwan encountered larger imperial powers, such as the Spanish, the Japanese, and the Dutch, through colonial expansion. By the seventeenth century, the Dutch settled in the southern part of the island while the Spanish settled in the northern region; both settlements were ports intended for trade, while much of the island remained inaccessible due to terrain and indigenous peoples violently opposing colonial control.[7]

South China Sea merchants (or pirates, depending on how you encountered them), all hailing from Japan, China, and Southeast Asia, also settled on the island or used the ports. In 1662, Zheng Chenggong, or Koxinga, in open rebellion against the newly established Qing dynasty (1644-1911), forcibly removed the Dutch from their seat of power in the southern region and continued his campaign against the Qing from Taiwan.[8] By 1683, the Zheng family-led rebellion was defeated, and Taiwan came nominally under the control of the Qing.

---

[7] Emma Teng, *Taiwan's Imagined Geography: Chinese Colonial Travel Writing and Pictures, 1683-1895*, (Cambridge, Mass.: Harvard University Asia Center, 2004), 33.

[8] Ibid.

Little more than two hundred years later, in 1895, Qing dynasty's defeat in the Sino-Japanese war set in motion two sequences of events that would define the modern history of Taiwan. First, Qing ceded Taiwan and its immediately surrounding islands to Japan, marking the beginning of a half-century of Japanese colonial rule in Taiwan. Second, this defeat fueled the rise of a nationalist movement that created the ROC.[9] We must follow each of these strands as they diverge.

In Taiwan, Japanese occupation marked the beginning of the democracy movement. Governor Tang Jingsong took advantage of the change in leadership to establish a short-lived independent Formosa Republic, which was in turn suppressed at the cost of 12,000 lives in a 36,000-square-kilometer island.

During Japanese colonial rule, the policy of "dōka" (assimilation) once again attempted to incorporate the Taiwanese into the Japanese cultural and linguistic system. The policy in the Japanese Empire acted to thoroughly integrate language, governmental structure, urban construction, and the education of Taiwan's elite and intelligentsia with Japan's, including bringing many to Japan for education.

Despite the enormous efforts and funds invested by the Japanese empire, Taiwan's resistance and identity remained. Different ethnic groups were considered more or less "civilized"; the less civilized a group of people was, the harsher and more violent the Japanese government was, thus creating fundamentally different experiences for indigenous, Taigi and Hakka people under Japanese control.[10] The rise of the global

---

[9] Suisheng Zhao, *The Dragon Roars Back: Transformational Leaders and Dynamics of Chinese Foreign Policy*, (Stanford, California: Stanford University Press, 2022), 132.

[10] Jeffrey Jacobs, *Democratizing Taiwan*, (Boston: Brill, 2012), 22.

anti-colonial movement and the Taishō democratic reforms within Japan at the beginning of the 20th century provided intellectuals and activists in Taiwan with the ideological foundation for self-determination. Local elections held in 1935 that included a small fraction of property-owning men as electors provided a first taste of democratic participation at least to Taiwanese elites, encouraging the pursuit of greater autonomy and expression.[11]

**Tridemism**

Across the Taiwan strait, a young, American-educated, Christian doctor and activist, Sun Yat-Sen, was similarly influenced in a revolutionary democratic direction by Qing's defeat at Japan's hands, but for a very different reason. Concluding that the dynasty was unreformable, Sun and his "Revive China Society" led a series of unsuccessful uprisings that forced him into exile in Japan, where he (like the Taiwanese elites sent to Japan to be educated) absorbed nascent democratic reform. Drawing on these Japanese, Christian and American influences as well as Confucian traditions, Sun articulated his *Three Principles of the People* in 1905, laying the foundation of the "Tridemism" that would become the official philosophy (and national anthem) of the ROC.

The first principle is 民族/Minzú (literally "civil clan"), which is typically translated as "nationalism". However, perhaps more notable was its emphasis on ethnic pluralism (五族共和)

---

[11] Ashley Esarey, "Overview: Democratization and Nation Building in Taiwan" in *Taiwan in Dynamic Transition: Nation Building and Democratization*, edited by Thomas Gold, (Seattle: University of Washington Press, 2020), 24

reflected in the original flag of the ROC[12], which included colors for each of the major ethnicities at the time (Han, Tibetan, Manchu, Mongolian and Muslim Hui. The second is 民權/Mínquán (literally "civil rights"), usually translated as "democracy" and articulated as a combination of rights of election, recall, initiative and referendum and division of powers among five "Yuans" (the Legislative, Executive and Judicial of the European tradition plus the Control and Examination divisions of the Confucian tradition). The third is 民生/Mínshēng (literally "civil livelihood"), usually translated as "socialism", draws from a variety of economic philosophies, including the ideas of Henry George, an American political economist known for his advocacy of land rights equality, anti-monopoly stances, and support for cooperative enterprises. We will discuss these ideas much more extensively in the next part of the book.

Harnessing these ideas, Sun built international support from foreign allies and expatriates around the world that eventually allowed him and his allies to overthrow the Qing in 1911 and found the ROC in 1912. Despite this initial success, internal conflict quickly forced him again into exile and then back to take part in a civil war. In 1919, he managed to marshal his forces and found the modern KMT.

That year he also met another crucial influence on the ideas of the ROC, a disciple of Henry George who was visiting China partly to see how George's ideas might play out on a social scale. John Dewey was perhaps the most respected American philosopher and among the most esteemed educators and philosophers of democracy globally. Dewey's "pragmatic" theory of democracy (translated by his Chinese student Hu Shih

---

[12] "Flag of China (1912-1928)," n.d. Wikimedia Commons, https://commons.wikimedia.org/wiki/File:Flag_of_China_(1912%E2%80%931928).svg.

as "experimentalism"), which we will discuss in greater detail in the next part of this book, resonated with the uncertain and exploratory atmosphere of early ROC.

On the one hand, this fluid, experimental and emergent approach shared much with Taoist traditions popular among democratic opponents of Qing and warlord monarchy.[13] On the other hand, unlike many more imperialistic foreign observers, Dewey advocated the ROC following its own path of "collaborative problem solving" as the axis of modern experimental model schools. This led Dewey to become something of a bridge between the ROC and the West, especially the US, giving over 200 lectures in China while writing monthly columns on his experiences for emerging outlets such as *The New Republic*. In the process, he helped forge a deep and enduring connection between the ROC and the US.

The roughly concurrent success of the Russian revolution brought financial support and military training to the previously marginal Chinese Communist Party (CCP). While inspired by a different, Marxist vision of socialism, Sun allied with the communists to unify the country. This effort, nearly successful at the time of his death in 1925, has made Sun the "Father of the Nation" for the Nationalists and the "Forerunner of the Revolution" for the Communists.

That moment of unity was, however, short-lived, with the communists (under Mao Zedong) and nationalists (under Chiang Kai-shek) alternatingly engaging in civil war and alliances against warlords and Japanese occupiers during the next twenty years, until the final defeat of the Japanese in 1945.

---

[13] Richard Shusterman, "Pragmatism and East-Asian Thought," *Metaphilosophy* 35, no. 1-2 (2004): 13, https://www.academia.edu/3125320/*Pragmatism_and_East_Asian_Though t*.

數位 Plurality: Part 2: Introduction

Focused overwhelmingly on both the struggle for national liberation and against each other, neither the Communists nor the Nationalists thought much of Taiwan.[14]

## Postbellum Taiwan

In 1949, having been defeated by Communists, Chiang and two million ROC soldiers and civilians relocated to Taiwan, declaring it the home of "free China", while simultaneously imposing martial law on the eight million native, primarily Taigi- and Hakka-speaking population that came to be known as the "White Terror". Acting as dictator, Chiang positioned the ROC to the world as the true representatives of China. Internally, people in Taiwan experienced a violent outsider government, one that had swiftly taken control of the island and began to suppress any sign of Taiwanese identity systematically and ruthlessly.[15]

At the same time, the government whose official ideology was Tridemism began sowing many seeds of social reform that would eventually sprout into democratic movements in Taiwan. Given his lack of ties to the island and its local elites, Chiang was able to impose the Rural Land Reform, including a rent reduction to 37.5% in 1949, the release of public land in 1951 and the breaking up of large estates in the 1953 policy of "land to the tiller". This one-time reform was institutionalized more permanently with a creative form of Georgist land tax based on "self-assessment" that we discuss further below in our Property

---

[14] Yet, to the extent they did address it, Mao supported Taiwan as an independent communist state much as he hoped for Korea and Vietnam, while Chiang (almost as an afterthought) requested the return of Taiwan after the war along with other territories formerly occupied by Japan, including Manchuria.

[15] Chien-Jung Hsu, *The Construction of National Identity in Taiwan's Media, 1896-2012*, (Leiden: Brill, 2014), 71.

## 2-1 A View from Yushan

and Contract and Social Markets chapters.[16] Together, as many scholars have argued, these reforms laid an egalitarian economic foundation that proved critical to Taiwan's later social and economic development.[17]

Another outgrowth of Tridemism was a focus on cooperative enterprise, enshrined in Articles 145 of the ROC Constitution, which states that "private wealth and privately-operated enterprises, the State shall restrict them by law if they are deemed detrimental to a balanced development... Cooperative enterprises... and foreign trade shall receive encouragement." While influenced by Georgist ideas, this support for industrial cooperatives and participative production also drew heavily on traditions of agricultural and industrial cooperation developed during the Japanese colonial rule, further influenced by American thinkers like W. Edwards Deming who emphasized the empowerment of line workers in improving production under the US occupation of Japan that he worked for.[18]

---

[16] Yun-chien Chang, "Self-Assessment of Takings Compensation: An Empirical Study" *The Journal of Law, Economics, and Organization*, 28, No. 2 (2012): 265–285.

[17] Joe Studwell, "How Asia Works: Success and Failure in the World's Most Dynamic Region," (London: Profile, 2013).

[18] After World War II, Japan's industrial infrastructure was devastated, and product quality was poor. In this context, Deming was invited by the Union of Japanese Scientists and Engineers(JUSE) in 1950. He introduced Statistical Process Control (SPC) and the PDCA (Plan-Do-Check-Act) cycle, emphasizing continuous improvement (Kaizen) and the importance of employee involvement. His principles were particularly embraced by the Japanese automotive industry, notably Toyota and became integral to the Toyota Production System (TPS). In 1990, James P. Womack and others published *The Machine That Changed the World*, analyzing the Toyota Production System and introducing it as the Lean manufacturing to a global audience. James P. Womack, Daniel T. Jones and Daniel Roos, *The*

Together these influences fostered the development of a robust civil and cooperative sector in Taiwan (which we collectively call the Third Sector), critical to its industrial and political future. Furthermore, the constitutional and historical focus on trade, as well as public investment in export-supporting infrastructure, propelled Taiwan's rise. By the 1970s, Taiwan became a major supplier of components for advanced Western technologies.

Taiwan's education system was similarly influenced by the intellectual ferment of the early ROC period, with Dewey's student Hu fleeing to Taiwan alongside the KMT that he sometimes feuded with. As President of the national research institute Academia Sinica and a leading intellectual, Hu became a central influence on the development of Taiwan's educational system. His fusion of Confucian traditions with Deweyian pragmatism, egalitarianism and democracy helped shape Taiwanese education into the envy of the world, topping world league tables on a range of benchmarks.[19]

## Coming of democracy

The 1960s, parallel to the American Civil Rights movement, saw an outburst of demands against the KMT and Chiang Kai-Shek for Taiwan's independence and a truly democratic government. Taiwan-born National Taiwan University Professor Peng Ming-min (1921-2022) and two of his students, Hsieh Tsung-min and Wei Ting-chao, circulated the Taiwan Self-Salvation Manifesto, which called for a freed and independent

---

*Machine that Changed the World* (New York: Free Press, 2007). In 2011, Eric Ries, who coined the term "Lean Startup," drew inspiration from the Lean manufacturing principles in entrepreneurship. Eric Ries, *The Lean Startup* (New York: Crown Currency, 2011).

[19] "John Dewey and Free China," Taiwan Today, January 1, 2003, https://taiwantoday.tw/news.php?unit=12.

Taiwan, decrying the ROC as an illegitimate government.[20] Though this moment ended with Peng's exile, the manifesto sparked a national conversation that further spurred democratic advocates to demand access to national elections.

The United Nations was central to the ROC's early identity under the White Terror as it was not only one of the founding members of the UN, but also the only Asian permanent member of the Security Council. This prominent international role was the leading irritant to the People's Republic of China (PRC) regime, preventing it from participating in international affairs and leading the CCP to change its position from initially supporting Taiwanese independence to an ideological focus on conquering Taiwan. However, as the US sought to contain its failures in Vietnam, President Richard Nixon secretly pursued accommodation with the PRC, including supporting an Albanian-sponsored Resolution 2758 by the General Assembly on October 25, 1971 that transferred recognition of "China" from the ROC to the PRC, finally culminating in Nixon's visit to PRC in 1972. As a result, the ROC "withdrew" from the UN, transforming its identity and international standing.

On the one hand, this withdrawal severely limited the scope of Taiwan's international diplomacy and trade. It also led the US and much of the non-Communist world to shift from a position of unconditional alliance with the ROC to one of careful balancing of interests and ambiguity, seeking to prevent PRC's violence over Taiwan while also supporting a policy of acknowledging its "One China" position.

Internally, this change in identity undermined much of the rationale for the White Terror, as the prospect of global support for a war to suppress the "Communist rebellion"

---

[20] Ryan Dunch, and Ashley Esarey, *Taiwan in Dynamic Transition: Nation-Building and Democratization*, (Seattle: University Of Washington Press, 2020), 28.

withered and undermined the aspirational identity of "free China". The contradictions between the increasingly egalitarian, Third Sector-driven and highly progressively educated population, on the one hand, and an authoritarian repressive state on the other thus became increasingly overwhelming, especially with the development of labor unions and political civic associations and the death of Chiang all before the end of the 1970s. The lives of the parents of one of the authors of this book are a perfect illustration of these trends: as pioneers of community college and consumer cooperative movements, they benefited from the cooperative support in the ROC constitution. Yet, as journalists, they covered and helped support those repressed by the state, such as in the Kaohsiung Incident of 1979 when leaders of the political opposition were imprisoned, building the foundation for democratization.

Taiwan's weakened international position also allowed dissidents exiled during the White Terror to put increasing pressure on Chiang's son and successor Chiang Ching-Kuo. The liberalization of Taiwan under the younger Chiang in the 1980s created an environment where democratic action, protests, essays, songs, and art reflected the growing belief for general elections. Those who called for democracy were still in exile or jailed, but their relatives and friends began to run for local and national political offices.[21]

## Vibrant democratic generation

In 1984, Chiang Ching-Kuo selected Lee Teng-hui (1923-2020) as the first Taiwan-born vice president. This choice signaled a

---

[21] Ryan Dunch, and Ashley Esarey, *Taiwan in Dynamic Transition: Nation-Building and Democratization*, (Seattle: University Of Washington Press, 2020), 31.

## 2-1 A View from Yushan

change in the political landscape of Taiwan.[22] When Lee became President in 1988, he quickly instituted a range of democratic reforms, calling for the direct election of the President and vesting the sovereignty of the country in the "citizens of the Free Area" of the ROC (those living on the Taiwan islands). This led him to become the first directly elected President in 1996, just a few months after the Bill Gates's *Internet Tidal Wave* memo heralded the mainstream arrival of the internet age.[23]

Already among the most technology-intensive export economies in the world, this tidal wave swept the Taiwanese economy and society with the same force as democratization. Thus, the internet and democracy were something of Siamese twins in Taiwan. Four years later, the first DPP President, Chen Shui-bian, narrowly won election as the Blue camp splintered. With the return of the KMT to the Presidency eight years later in 2008, a system of alternation between the Blue vision of "free China" and the Green vision of "island nation" was established as the pattern of politics.

Yet despite this deep and persistent division that fueled the Sunflower movement, the overlapping consensus between these perspectives is striking:

1. Pluralism: Both the Blue and Green stories share a strong emphasis on pluralism. For Blue, it's about fusing both contemporary and traditional culture (exemplified by the National Palace Museum) and the Tridemist tradition of ethnic pluralism, while highlighting ROC's role as a cultural inheritor and leader; while the Greens focus on

---

[22] Jeffrey Jacobs, *Democratizing Taiwan*, (Boston: Brill, 2012), 62.

[23] Bill Gates, "The Internet Tidal Wave" May 26, 1995 available athttps://www.fastcompany.com/4039009/22-years-ago-today-bill-gates-wrote-his-legendary-internet-tidal-wave-memo.

the diversity of those who have settled in Taiwan, including the indigenous peoples, Japanese, Taigi, Hakka, Westerners, and new immigrants.
2. Diplomatic nuance: To navigate the challenging relationship with the PRC, both have had to embrace a range of complex and nuanced public positions around the security posture of the US and other allies, the meaning of ROC and Taiwan, as well as the concept of "independence".
3. Democratic freedom: The ideas of "democracy" and "freedom" are core to both ideologies. To Blues, these ideas are core to Tridemism and thus, in their eyes, qualities that a ROC leadership must focus on. For Greens, these ideas are the core of Taiwan's rallying cries overcoming both the White Terror and PRC authoritarianism.
4. Anti-authoritarianism: Both are deeply concerned about growing authoritarianism in the PRC, especially in the last decade with the failure of the "One Country, Two Systems" formula in Hong Kong.
5. Export-orientation: Both parties celebrate success as a commercial exporter and see the ability to export ideas and culture as central to the future. For Blues this focuses more on influencing the PRC to be more like Taiwan, while for Greens it focuses on gaining respect in the "free world" that Taiwan needs to defend itself.

In addition to this ideological overlap, the two sides have both benefited from and been immersed in the central role the island has come to play in the global electronics industry. As the center of the semiconductor and smartphone supply chain, while also having the fastest internet in the world, no country is more thoroughly immersed in the digital world than Taiwan.[24]

This combination of an overlapping consensus on plural, complex, free, world-facing democracy, where digital tools are easily available to help navigate the resulting ambiguity, has allowed Taiwan to become, in the last decade, the world's leading example of digital democracy.

---

[24] Taiwan News, "Taiwan Has No. 1 Fastest Internet in World," October 23, 2023. https://www.taiwannews.com.tw/en/news/5025449.

## 2-2 The Life of a Digital Democracy

*When we see "internet of things,"*
*let's make it an **internet of beings**.*
*When we see "virtual reality,"*
*let's make it a **shared reality**.*
*When we see "machine learning,"*
*let's make it **collaborative learning**.*
*When we see "user experience,"*
*let's make it **about human experience**.*
*When we hear "the singularity is near" —*
*let us remember: The **Plurality** is here.*

— Audrey Tang, Job Description, 2016

---

Without living in Taiwan and experiencing it regularly, it is hard to grasp what such an achievement means, and for those living there continuously many of these features are taken for granted. Thus, we aim here to provide concrete illustrations and quantitative analyses of what distinguishes Taiwan's digital civic infrastructure from those of most of the rest of the world. Because there are far too many examples to discuss in detail, we have selected six diverse illustrations that roughly cover a primary focal project for each two-year period since 2012; after we briefly list a wide range of other programs.

### Illustrations

*g0v*

More than any other institution, g0v (pronounced gov-zero) symbolizes the civil-society foundation of digital democracy in Taiwan. Founded in 2012 by civic hackers including Kao Chia-liang, g0v arose from discontent with the quality of

## 2-2 The Life of a Digital Democracy

government digital services and data transparency.[1] Civic hackers began to scrape government websites (usually with the suffix gov.tw) and build alternative formats for data display and interaction for the same website, hosting them at g0v.tw. These "forked" versions of government websites often ended up being more popular, leading some government ministers, like Simon Chang to begin "merging" these designs back into government services.

g0v built on this success to establish a vibrant community of civic hackers interacting with a range of non-technical civil society groups at regular hackathon, called "jothons" (based on a Mandarin play on words, meaning roughly "join-athon"). While hackathons are common in many parts of the world, some of the unique features of g0v practices include the diversity of participants (usually a majority non-technical and with nearly full gender parity), the orientation towards civic problems rather than commercial outcomes and the close collaboration with a range of civic organizations. These features are perhaps best summarized by the slogan "Ask not why nobody is doing this. You are the 'nobody'!", which has led the group to be labeled the "nobody movement". They are also reflected in a Venn diagram commonly used to explain the movement's intentions shown in Figure A. As we will note below, most of the initiatives we highlight grew out of g0v and closely aligned projects.

---

[1] *g0v Manifesto* defines it as "a non-partisan, not-for-profit, grassroots movement". MoeDict, an early g0v project, was led by one of the authors of this book.

數位 Plurality: Part 2: Introduction

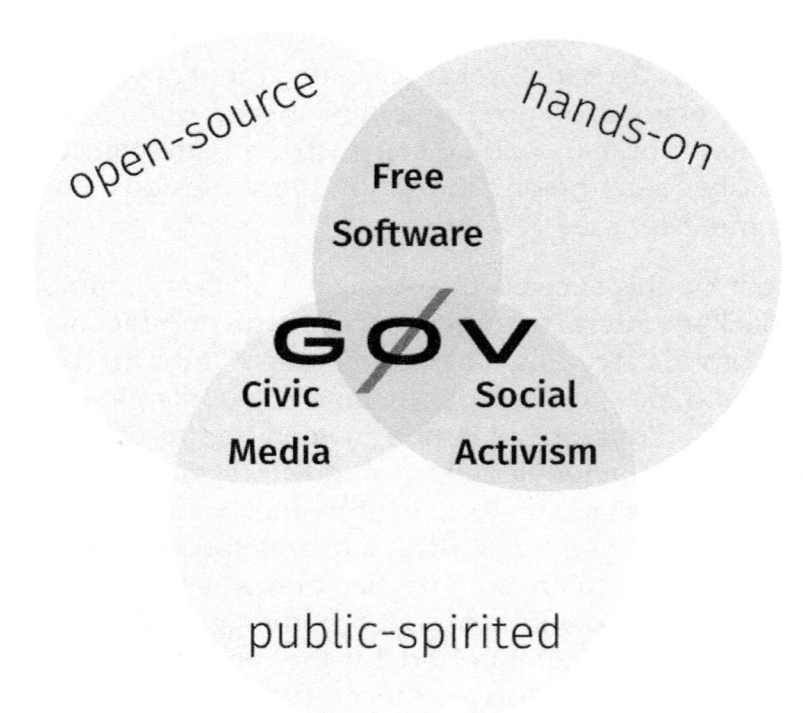

**Figure 2-2-A.** Principles of g0v displayed in a Venn diagram.

*Sunflower*

While g0v gained significant public attention and support even in its earliest years, it burst most prominently onto the public scene during the Sunflower Movement we described above. Hundreds of contributors in the g0v community were present during the occupation of the Legislative Yuan (LY), aiding in broadcasting, documenting, and communicating civic actions. Livestream-based communication sparked heated discussion among the public. Street vendors, lawyers, teachers, and designers rolled up their sleeves to participate in various online and offline actions. Digital tools brought together resources for crowdfunding, rallies, and international voices of support.

On March 30, 2014, half a million people took to the streets in the largest demonstration in Taiwan since the 1980s. Their demands, thus formulated, for a review process prior to the passage of the Cross-Straits Services Trade Agreement was accepted by LY Speaker Wang Jin-pyng on April 6, about three weeks after the start of the occupation, leading to its dispersal soon thereafter. The contributions of g0v to both sides and the resolution of their tensions led the sitting government to see the merit in g0v's methods and in particular cabinet member Jaclyn Tsai recruited one of us as a youth "reverse mentor" and began to attend and support g0v meetings, putting an increasing range of government materials into the public domain through g0v platforms.

Many Sunflower participants devoted themselves to the open government movement; the following local (2014) and general (2016) elections saw a dramatic swing in outcomes of roughly 10 percentage points towards the Green camp, as well as the establishment of a new political party by the Sunflower leaders, the New Power Party, including leading Taiwanese rock star Freddy Lim. Together, these events significantly added to the momentum behind g0v and led to one of our appointment as Minister without Portfolio responsible for open government, social innovation and youth participation.

*vTaiwan and Join*

During this process of institutionalization of g0v, there was growing demand to apply the methods that had allowed for these dispute resolutions to a broader range of policy issues. This led to the establishment of vTaiwan, a platform and project developed by g0v for facilitating deliberation on public policy controversies. The process involved many steps (proposal, opinion expression, reflection, and legislation) each harnessing a range of open source software tools, but has become best known for its use of the at-the-time(2015)-novel machine learning based open-source "wikisurvey"/social media tool Polis, which we discuss further in our chapter on Augmented Deliberation below. In short, Polis functions similarly to conventional microblogging services like X, except that it employs dimension reduction techniques to cluster opinions as shown in Figure B. Instead of displaying content that maximizes engagement, Polis shows the clusters of opinion that exist and highlights statements that bridge them. This approach facilitates both consensus formation and a better understanding of the lines of division.

vTaiwan was deliberately intended as an experimental, high-touch, intensive platform for committed participants. It had about 200,000 users or about 1% of Taiwan's population at its peak and held detailed deliberations on 28 issues, 80% of which led to legislative action. These focused mostly on questions around technology regulation, such as the regulation of ride sharing, responses to non-consensual intimate images, regulatory experimentation with financial technology and regulation of AI.

2-2 The Life of a Digital Democracy

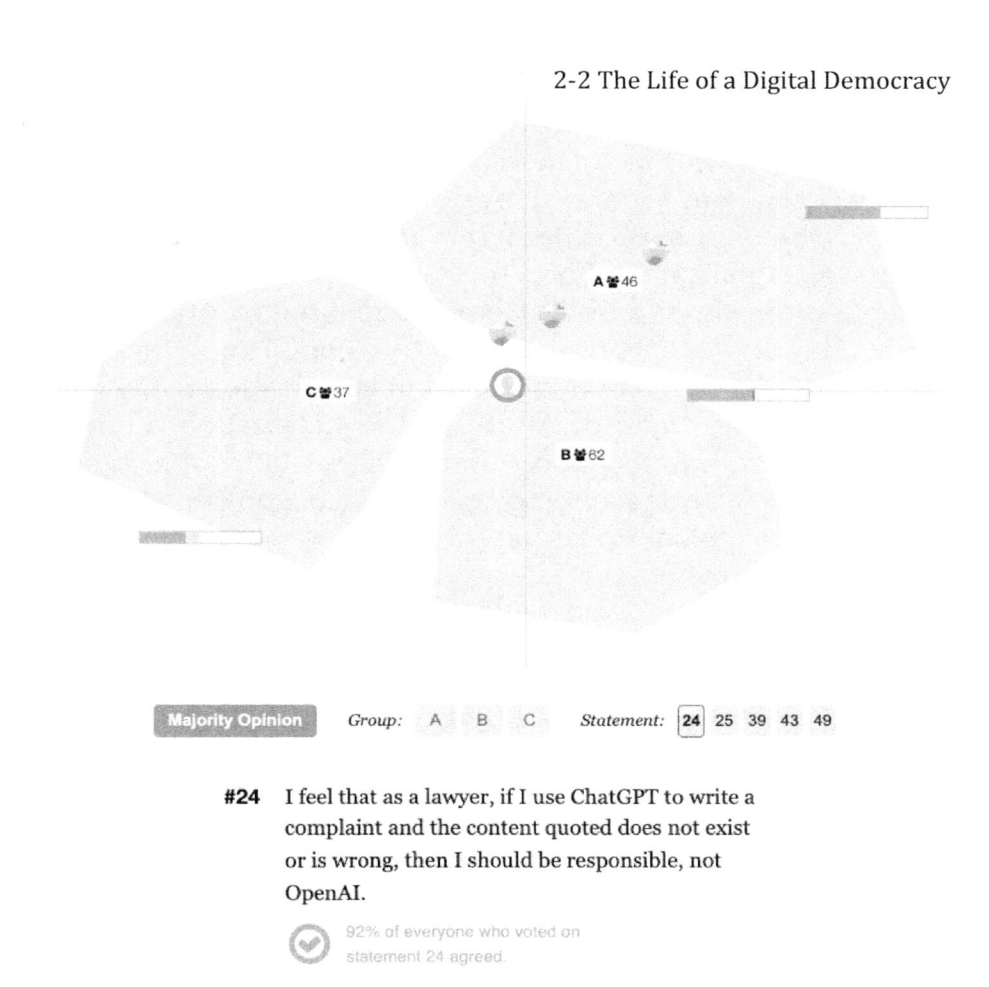

**#24** I feel that as a lawyer, if I use ChatGPT to write a complaint and the content quoted does not exist or is wrong, then I should be responsible, not OpenAI.

92% of everyone who voted on statement 24 agreed.

**Figure 2-2-B.** Clusters of consensual opinions generated by Polis on vTaiwan. Source: vTaiwan.tw, CC0 license.

As a decentralized, citizen-led community, vTaiwan is also a living organism that naturally evolves and adapts as citizen volunteers participate in various ways. The community's engagement experienced a downturn following the onset of the COVID-19 pandemic, which interrupted face-to-face meetings and led to decreased participation. The platform faced challenges due to the intensive volunteering effort required, the absence of mandates for governmental responses, and its somewhat narrow focus. In response to these challenges, vTaiwan's community has sought to find a new role between the public and the government and extend its outreach beyond the realm of Taiwanese regulation in recent years. A significant effort to revitalize vTaiwan was its collaboration with OpenAI's Democratic Input to AI project in 2023. Through partnerships with Chatham House and the organization of several physical and online deliberative events centered on the topic of AI ethics and localization, vTaiwan successfully integrated local perspectives into the global discourse on AI and technology governance. Looking ahead to 2024, vTaiwan plans to engage in deliberations concerning AI-related regulations in Taiwan and beyond. In addition to Polis, vTaiwan is constantly experimenting with new deliberation and voting tools, integrating LLMs for summarization. The vTaiwan community remains committed to democratic experimentation and finding consensus among the public for policymaking.

The Public Digital Innovation Space (PDIS) that one of us established in 2016 to work with vTaiwan and other projects we discuss below in the ministerial role therefore supported a second, related platform Join. While Join also sometimes used Polis, it has a lighter-weight user interface and focuses primarily on soliciting input, suggestions and initiatives from a broader public, and has an enforcement mechanism where government officials must respond if a proposal receives sufficient support. Unlike vTaiwan, furthermore, Join addresses a range of policy issues, including controversial non-technological issues such as high school's start time, and has strong continuing usage today of roughly half of the population over its lifetime and an average of 11,000 unique daily visitors.

## 2-2 The Life of a Digital Democracy
### Hackathons, coalitions, and quadratic signals

While such levels of digital civic engagement may seem surprising to many Westerners, they can be seen simply as the harnessing of a small portion of the energy typically wasted on conflict on (anti-)social media towards solving public problems. Even more concentrated applications of this principle have come by placing the weight of government behind the g0v practice of hackathons through the Presidential Hackathon (PH) and a variety of supporting institutions.

The PH convened mixed teams of civil servants, academics, activists, and technologists to propose tools, social practices and collective data custody arrangements that allowed them to "collectively bargain" with their data for cooperation with government and private actors supported by the PDIS-supported program of "data coalitions" to address civic problems. Examples have included the monitoring of air quality and early warning systems for wildfires. Participants and broader citizens were asked to help select the winners using a voting system called Quadratic Voting that allows people to express the extent of their support across a range of projects and that we discuss in our 🗳 Voting chapter below. This allowed a wide range of participants to be at least partial winners, by making it likely everyone would have supported some winner and that if someone felt very strongly in favor of one project they could give it a significant boost. Winning project received a trophy – a micro projector showing the President of Taiwan giving the award to the winners, leverage they could use to induce relevant government agencies or localities to cooperate in their mission, given the legitimacy g0v has gained as noted above.

More recently, this practice has been extended beyond developing technical solutions to envisioning of alternative futures and production of media content to support this through "ideathons". It has also gone beyond symbolic support to awarding real funding to valued projects (such as around agricultural and food safety inspections) using an extension of Quadratic Voting to Funding as we discuss in our *Social Markets* chapter.

*Pandemic*

These diverse approaches to empowering government to more agilely leverage civil participation most dramatically came to a head during the Covid-19 pandemic. Taiwan is widely believed (based on statistics we will discuss in the next section of this chapter) to have had one of the world's most effective responses to the crisis stage of the pandemic. Notably, it achieved among the lowest global death rates from the disease during that stage without using lockdowns and while maintaining among the fastest rates of economic growth in the world. While being an island, having as Taiwan did an epidemiologist ready for an instant response as Vice-President and restricting travel clearly played a key role, a range of technological interventions played an important role as well.

The best documented example and the one most consistent with the previous examples was the "Mask App". Given previous experience with SARS, masks in Taiwan were beginning to run into shortages by late January, when little of the world had even heard of Covid-19. Frustrated, civic hackers led by Howard Wu developed an app that harnessed data that the government, following open and transparent data practices harnessed and reinforced by the g0v movement, to map mask availability. This allowed Taiwan to achieve widespread mask adoption by mid-February, even as mask supplies remained extremely tight given the lack of a global production response at this early stage.

Another critical aspect of the Taiwanese response was the rigorous use of testing, tracing, and supported isolation to avoid community spread of the disease. While most tracing occurred by more traditional means, Taiwan was among the only places able to reach the prevalence of adoption of phone-based social distancing and tracing systems necessary to make these an effective part of their response. This was, in turn, largely because of the close cooperation facilitated by PDIS between government health officials and members of the g0v community deeply concerned about privacy, especially given the lack in Taiwan of an independent privacy protection regime, a point we return to below. This led to the design of systems with strong anonymization and decentralization features that received broad acceptance.

*Information integrity*

Yet perhaps the single most important digital contributor to Taiwan's pandemic response was its ability to rapidly and effectively respond to misinformation and deliberate attempts to spread disinformation. This "superpower" has extended, however, well beyond the pandemic and been critical to the successful elections Taiwan has held during a time when a lack of information integrity has challenged many other jurisdictions.

Central to those efforts, in turn, has been the g0v spin-off project "Cofacts," in which participating citizens rapidly respond to both trending social media content and to messages from private channels forwarded to a public comment box for requested response. Recent research shows that these systems can typically respond faster, equally accurately and more engagingly to rumors than can professional fact checkers, who are much more bandwidth constrained.[2]

---

[2] Andy Zhao and Mor Naaman, "Insights from a Comparative Study on the Variety, Velocity, Veracity, and Viability of Crowdsourced and Professional

數位 Plurality: Part 2: Introduction

The technical sophistication of Taiwan's civil sector and its support from the public sector have aided in other ways as well. This has allowed organizations like MyGoPen and private sector companies like Gogolook to develop and, with public support, rapidly spread chatbots for private messaging services like Line that make it fast and easy for citizens to anonymously receive rapid responses to possibly misleading information. Government leaders' close cooperation with such civil groups has allowed them to model and thus encourage policies of "humor over rumor" and "fast, fun and fair" responses. For example, when a rumor began to spread during the pandemic that there would be a shortage of toilet paper created by the mass production of masks, Taiwan's Premier Su Tseng-chang famously circulated a picture of himself wagging his rear to indicate it had nothing to fear.

Together these policies have helped Taiwan fight off the "infodemic" without takedowns, just as it fought of the pandemic without lockdowns. This culminated in the January 13, 2024 election we mentioned above, in which a PRC campaign of unprecedented size and AI-fueled sophistication failed to polarize or noticeably sway the election.

*Other programs*

While these are some of the most prominent examples of Taiwanese digital democratic innovation, there are many other examples we lack the space to discuss in detail but will briefly list here.

1. Alignment assemblies: Taiwan has pioneered convening, increasingly common around the world, of

---

Fact-Checking Services", *Journal of Online Trust and Safety* 2, no. 1. https://doi.org/10.54501/jots.v2i1.118.

## 2-2 The Life of a Digital Democracy

citizen participation in the regulation and steering of AI foundation models.

2. Information security: Taiwan has become a world leader in the use of distributed storage to guard against malicious content takedowns and of "zero trust" principles in ensuring the security of citizen accounts.
3. Gold cards: Taiwan has among the most diversely accessible paths to permanent residence through its "gold card" program, including in a "digital field" to those who have contributed to open source and public interest software.
4. Transparency: Building on and extending broader government policies of data transparency, one of us has modeled this idea by making recordings and/or transcripts all of her official meetings public without copyrights.
5. Digital competence education: Since 2019, Taiwan has pioneered a 12-Year Basic Education Curriculum that enshrines "tech, info & media literacy" as a core competency, empowering students to become active co-creators and discerning arbiters of media, rather than passive consumers.
6. Land and spectrum: Building on the ideas of Henry George, Taiwan has among the most innovative policies in the world to ensure full utilization of natural resources, land and electromagnetic spectrum through taxes that include rights of compulsory sale (as we discuss further in our *Property and Contract* and *Social Markets* chapters).
7. Participation Officer Network: PDIS helped create a network of civil servants across departments committed to citizen participation, collaboration across government departments and digital feedback, who could act as supporters and conduits of practices such as these.

8. Broadband access: Taiwan has one of the most universal internet access rates and has been recognized two years in a row as the fastest average internet in the world.
9. Open parliament: Taiwan has become a leader in the global "open parliament" movement, experimenting with a range of ways to make parliamentary procedures transparent to the public and experimenting with innovative voting methods.
10. Digital diplomacy: Based on these experiences, Taiwan has become a leading advisor and mentor to democracies around the world confronting similar challenges and with similar ambitions to harness digital tools to improve participation and resilience.

Furthermore, this work sufficiently won the confidence of both the public and the government that in August 2022 Taiwan created a Ministry of Digital Affairs, elevating one of us from Minister without Portfolio to lead this new ministry.

## Decade of accomplishment

While this is an interesting set of programs, one might naturally inquire about evidence of their efficacy. Tracing causal impacts precisely for so many projects is obviously an arduous task beyond our scope here. But at very least it is reasonable to ask how Taiwan has performed overall on the range of challenges that has so troubled most liberal democracies in the last decades. We consider each category of these in turn. Unfortunately, the quality of analysis and comparison possible is not all it could be given the complex geopolitics around Taiwan's international status meaning that many standard international comparators choose not to include it in their data.

## Economic

While the economic lens of Taiwan's performance is far from the most important, it is one of the easier to quantify and provides a useful baseline for understanding the starting point for the rest. In one sense, Taiwan is an upper-middle income country, like much of Europe, with a Gross Domestic Product (GDP) per capita of $34,000 per person in 2024 according to the International Monetary Fund (IMF).[3] However, prices are much lower in Taiwan on average than in almost any other rich country; making this adjustment (which economists call "purchasing power parity") makes Taiwan the second richest country on average other than the US with more than 10 million people in the world. Furthermore, as we discuss below, most sources suggest that Taiwan is much more equal than the US, which means it is likely the country of that size with the highest median living standards in the world. Thus, Taiwan is best thought of as among the absolute most developed economies in the world, rather than as a middle-income country.

The sectoral focus of Taiwan's economy stands out as well. While perfectly comparable data are hard to come by, Taiwan is almost certainly the most digital export-intensive economy in the world, with exports of electronics and information and communication products accounting for roughly 31% of the economy, compared to less than half that fraction in other leading technology exporters such as Israel and South Korea.[4] This fact is best known to the world for what it reflects: that most of the world's semiconductors, especially the most advanced

---

[3] "GDP per Capita, Current Prices," International Monetary Fund, n.d., https://www.imf.org/external/datamapper/NGDPDPC@WEO/ADVEC/WEOWORLD/TWN/CHN.

[4] "Exports," Trading Economics, n.d., https://tradingeconomics.com/country-list/exports.

ones, are manufactured in Taiwan and Taiwan is also a major both manufacturer and domicile for manufacturers of smartphones such as Foxconn.

Taiwan is also unusual among rich countries in its relatively low tax take; according to the Asia Development Bank, Taiwan collected only 11% of GDP in taxes compared to 34% on average in the Organization of Economic Cooperation and Development (OECD) club of rich countries.[5] Relatedly, Taiwan ranked 4th in the world in the Heritage Foundation's Economic Freedom Index.[6]

Given this background, several features of Taiwan's economic performance in the last decade stand out.

1. Growth: Taiwan has averaged real GDP growth of 3% over the last decade, compared to less than 2% for the OECD, a bit over 2% for the US and 2.7% for the world overall.[7]
2. Unemployment: Taiwan has averaged an unemployment rate of just under 4% steadily in the last decade, compared to an OECD average of 6%, a US average of 5% and a world average of around 6%.

---

[5] "Key Indicators Database," Asian Development Bank, n.d., https://kidb.adb.org/economies/taipeichina; "Revenue Statistics 2015 - the United States," OECD, 2015, https://www.oecd.org/tax/revenue-statistics-united-states.pdf.

[6] "Index of Economic Freedom." The Heritage Foundation, 2023. https://www.heritage.org/index/.

[7] "GDP Growth (Annual %)," World Bank, 2023. https://data.worldbank.org/indicator/ny.gdp.mktp.kd.zg; "GDP per Capita, Current Prices," International Monetary Fund, n.d., https://www.imf.org/external/datamapper/NGDPDPC@WEO/ADVEC/WEOWORLD/TWN/CHN.

3. Inflation: While inflation has spiked and wildly fluctuated around the world including almost all rich countries, Taiwan's inflation rate has remained relatively steady the last decade in the 0-2% range, averaging 1.3% according to the IMF.
4. Inequality: The last decade has seen significant debate about methods in calculating inequality statistics. Using more traditional methods, Taiwan's Survey of Family Income and Expenditure has found that Taiwan's Gini Index of inequality (ranging from 0 for perfectly equal to 1 for perfectly unequal) has been steady at around .28 for the last decade, placing it around the level of Austria on the lower end of global inequality and far lower than the roughly .4 of the US. Other analyses, using innovative but controversial administrative approaches pioneered by economists including Emmanuel Saez, Thomas Piketty, and Gabriel Zucman show Taiwan's top 1% income share at 19%, not far behind the US at 21% and well above a country like France at 13%. However, even in these data, Taiwan's top 1% share has fallen by about a tenth in the last decade, while in both France and the US it has risen by a similar proportion. Furthermore, a number of studies have recently argued these methods tend to find higher inequality in countries and time periods with lower and less progressive taxes as they rely on tax administration data and struggle to fully account for induced avoidance.[8] Given Taiwan's dramatically lower tax take than either the US or France, it seems likely that if these

---

[8] Gerald Auten, and David Splinter, "Income Inequality in the United States: Using Tax Data to Measure Long-Term Trends," *Journal of Political Economy*, November 14, 2023. https://doi.org/10.1086/728741.

issues apply anywhere, they would lead to a substantial overstatement of Taiwanese inequality.[9]

Putting these facts together, what is notable is that Taiwan's economic performance has been strong and fairly egalitarian or at least not becoming more unequal *despite its wealth and extreme tech-intensity*. As we documented above, economists have widely blamed the role of technology for many recent economic woes, including slow growth, unemployment, and rising inequality. In the world's most tech-intensive economy, this seems not to be the case.

## Social

Internationally comparable social indicators are far more difficult than even economic ones for Taiwan, given that it is excluded from the World Health Organization (WHO). However, we were able to find roughly comparable data on two commonly cited social indicators: loneliness and self-reported technology addiction. Loneliness among older adults (above 65) in Taiwan stands at roughly 10%, which puts it around similar rates in the least affected countries in the world (mostly in Northern Europe), better than in North America (roughly 20%) and much better than in the PRC (more than 30%).[10] Another comparison is self-reported cellphone addiction rates, which are fairly high in Taiwan (at roughly 28%) but much lower

---

[9] The most interesting statistic we woudl like to report on is labor's share of income and its trends in Taiwan. However, to our knowledge no persuasive and internationally comparable study of this exists. We hope to see more research on this soon.

[10] S. Schroyen, N. Janssen, L. A. Duffner, M. Veenstra, E. Pyrovolaki, E. Salmon, and S. Adam, "Prevalence of Loneliness in Older Adults: A Scoping Review." *Health & Social Care in the Community 2023* (September 14, 2023): e7726692. https://doi.org/10.1155/2023/7726692.

## 2-2 The Life of a Digital Democracy

than in the US (at 58%).[11] Differences in rates of addiction to controlled substances are even more dramatically different, with about 10 times as many Americans reporting using illegal drugs at least monthly than Taiwanese *who have ever tried an illegal drug*.[12]

Taiwan is also marked by a unique experience with religion among rich countries, almost all of which (especially the United States) are both dominated by a single broad religious group (e.g. Christianity) and have seen dramatic declines in a range of measures of religiosity including affiliation and participation in the past decades.[13] Religion in Taiwan, by contrast, is far more diverse with a roughly equal mix of followers of four distinct religious traditions: folk religion, Taoism, Buddhism, Western/minority religions, with about an equal proportion as each of these being non-believers.[14] At the same time, while

---

[11] "More than Half of Teens Admit Phone Addiction ." Taipei Times, February 4, 2020.
https://www.taipeitimes.com/News/biz/archives/2020/02/04/2003730302; "Study Finds Nearly 57% of Americans Admit to Being Addicted to Their Phones - CBS Pittsburgh." CBS News, August 30, 2023.
https://www.cbsnews.com/pittsburgh/news/study-finds-nearly-57-of-americans-admit-to-being-addicted-to-their-phones/.

[12] "NCDAS: Substance Abuse and Addiction Statistics [2020]," National Center for Drug Abuse Statistics, 2020, https://drugabusestatistics.org/; Ling-Yi Feng, and Jih-Heng Li, "New Psychoactive Substances in Taiwan," *Current Opinion in Psychiatry* 33, no. 4 (March 2020): 1, https://doi.org/10.1097/yco.0000000000000604.

[13] Ronald Inglehart, "Giving up on God: The Global Decline of Religion," *Foreign Affairs* 99 (2020): 110.
https://heinonline.org/HOL/LandingPage?handle=hein.journals/fora99&div=123&id=&page=.

[14] "2022 Report on International Religious Freedom: Taiwan," American Institute in Taiwan, June 8, 2023, https://www.ait.org.tw/2022-report-on-international-religious-freedom-taiwan/#:~:text=According%20to%20a%20survey%20by.

there has been some shift among these groups, there has hardly been any significant increase in non-belief or non-practicing in Taiwan in the past decades.[15]

*Political*

Taiwan is widely recognized both for the quality of its democracy and its resilience against technology-driven information manipulation. Several indices, published by organizations such as Freedom House[16], the Economist Intelligence Unit[17], the Bertelsmann Foundation and V-Dem, consistently rank Taiwan as among the freest and most effective democracies on earth.[18] While Taiwan's precise ranking differs across these indices (ranging from first to merely in the top 15%), it nearly always stands out as the strongest democracy in Asia and the strongest democracy younger than 30 years old; even if one includes the wave of post-Soviet democracies immediately before this, almost all are less than half Taiwan's size, typically an order of magnitude smaller. Thus, Taiwan is at least regarded as Asia's strongest democracy and the strongest young democracy of reasonable size and by many as the world's absolute strongest. Furthermore, while democracy has generally declined in every region of the world in the last

---

[15] "Religion in Taiwan," Wikipedia, Wikimedia Foundation, January 12, 2020. https://en.wikipedia.org/wiki/Religion_in_Taiwan.

[16] "Freedom in the World," Freedom House, 2023, https://freedomhouse.org/report/freedom-world.

[17] "Democracy Index 2023," Economist Intelligence Unit, n.d., https://www.eiu.com/n/campaigns/democracy-index-2023.

[18] "Democracy Indices," Wikipedia, Wikimedia Foundation, March 5, 2024. https://en.wikipedia.org/wiki/Democracy_indices#:~:text=Democracy%20indices%20are%20quantitative%20and..

decade according to these indices, Taiwan's democratic scores have substantially increased.

In addition to this overall strength, Taiwan is noted for its resistance to polarization and threats to information integrity. A variety of studies using a range of methodologies have found that Taiwan is one of the least politically, socially, and religiously polarized developed countries in the world, though some have found a slight upward trend in political polarization since the Sunflower movement.[19] This is especially true in *affective polarization*, the holding of negative or hostile personal attitudes towards political opponents, with Taiwan consistently among the 5 least affectively polarized countries.

This is despite analyses consistently finding Taiwan to be the jurisdiction targeted for the largest volume of disinformation on earth.[20] One reason for this paradoxical result may be the finding by political scientists Bauer and Wilson that unlike in many other contexts, foreign manipulation fails to exacerbate partisan divides in Taiwan. Instead, it tends to galvanize a unified stance among Taiwanese against external interference.[21]

---

[19] Laura Silver, Janell Fetterolf, and Aidan Connaughton, "Diversity and Division in Advanced Economies," Pew Research Center, October 13, 2021, https://www.pewresearch.org/global/2021/10/13/diversity-and-division-in-advanced-economies/.;

[20] Adrian Rauchfleisch, Tzu-Hsuan Tseng, Jo-Ju Kao, and Yi-Ting Liu, "Taiwan's Public Discourse about Disinformation: The Role of Journalism, Academia, and Politics," *Journalism Practice* 17, no. 10 (August 18, 2022): 1–21, https://doi.org/10.1080/17512786.2022.2110928.

[21] Fin Bauer, and Kimberly Wilson, "Reactions to China-Linked Fake News: Experimental Evidence from Taiwan," The China Quarterly 249 (March 2022): 1–26. https://doi.org/10.1017/S030574102100134X.

## Legal

Taiwan consistently ranks among the top five safest countries in the world and stands, by a significant margin, as the safest democracy for populations that exceed 100,000 people.[22] When one of us first traveled to Taiwan, he was shocked to receive compensation for his flight as a large envelope of cash, which most Taiwanese feel comfortable carrying given the extreme safety. Furthermore, crime in Taiwan continues to trend steadily downward even as countries like the US have seen dramatic surges in especially violent crime.[23] It is worth noting, however, that it has achieved this historically with a strong police presence (somewhat higher than the US) and an incarceration rate that while far short of the US is high by global standards.

Taiwan's legal-political system has also distinguished itself for its ability to adapt to inclusively resolve long-standing social conflicts. In 2017, the Constitutional Court ruled that the government must pass a law to legalize same-sex marriage within two years. After the failure of a referendum on a straightforward same-sex marriage proposal in 2018, the government found a creative way to respond to the interests of all sides. Many who opposed same-sex marriage were concerned that because of traditions of extended families being bound together by marriage, family members opposing the practice could be forced to participate. At the same time, most young people who planned to take advantage of the new provision had more individualistic, partner-based visions of marriage and had no desire to bind their families either, leading

---

[22] "Crime Index by Country," Numbeo, 2023, https://www.numbeo.com/crime/rankings_by_country.jsp.

[23] "Taiwan: Crime Rate," Statista, n.d, https://www.statista.com/statistics/319861/taiwan-crime-rate/#:~:text=In%202022%2C%20around%201%2C139%20crimes.

the government to pass a legalization bill that exempted kin from the same-sex marriage process.

*Existential*

Crises come rarely and with low probability. It is thus hard to know how well Taiwan might perform in avoiding or mitigating one. However, perhaps the closest one can reach for is an emergency that did occur: the Covid-19 pandemic. As noted above, Taiwan was widely seen as among the best if not the very best performing country in the world during this episode and here we discuss the quantitative reasons for this esteem.

The exceptional performance that won Taiwan this international acclaim occurred during the focal early stages of the pandemic, during which much of the world was in rolling lockdowns prior to the availability of the vaccine. We can call this the "crisis" stage of the pandemic and declare it to have ended in April 2021, when vaccines were widely available in the US. From the start of the pandemic to April 2021, Taiwan suffered only 12 deaths to the pandemic, giving it by far the lowest death rate to that point of any jurisdiction with estimates considered internationally accurate. Furthermore, Taiwan achieved this without any lockdowns and achieved the fastest economic growth of any rich country bar Ireland in 2020. More broadly, Taiwan's health system has for the better part of a decade been ranked as the world's most efficiently performing by Numbeo, though life expectancy in Taiwan is merely among the highest in the world.[24]

It is important to note, however, that Taiwan performed much less impressively during the "post-crisis" phase following mid-2021, during which vaccine availability and uptake were the most critical components of response and challenges with domestic vaccine production and distribution led to significant

---

[24] https://www.numbeo.com/health-care/rankings_by_country.jsp

loss of life in the coming years. Taiwan still had among the lowest death rates and best economic performance reliably measured by a rich jurisdiction of significant size, but its exceptional leadership early in the pandemic did not fully persist after the crisis phase. This may indicate that the cohesion and civic engagement fostered by crises (like Sunflower and the Pandemic) allow Taiwan to respond more effectively than anywhere in the world, but that additional care and focus is needed to ensure these efforts are institutionalized and sustainable, an important direction for the future we discuss further below.

Another slow-burning crisis that may illustrate this challenge is climate change. While Taiwan has joined many other countries in enshrining its 2050 net zero ambitions into law and has won praise for its plans to reach this goal, its progress thus far has been modest.[25] More broadly, Taiwan has a strong but not outstanding record on environmental protection.[26]

Taiwan nonetheless exhibits unusually high levels of participation and trust in institutions, particularly in its democracy. Voter turnout is among the highest in the world outside countries where voting is compulsory.[27] 91% consider democracy to be at least "fairly good", a sharp contrast to the

---

[25] "Net Zero Tracker," Energy & Climate Intelligence Unit, 2023. https://eciu.net/netzerotracker.

[26] "2022 EPI Results," Environmental Performance Index, 2022, https://epi.yale.edu/epi-results/2022/component/epi.

[27] Drew DeSilver, "Turnout in U.S. Has Soared in Recent Elections but by Some Measures Still Trails that of Many Other Countries." Pew Research Center, November 1, 2022. https://www.pewresearch.org/short-reads/2022/11/01/turnout-in-u-s-has-soared-in-recent-elections-but-by-some-measures-still-trails-that-of-many-other-countries/.

dramatic declines in recent years in support for democracy even in many long-established democracies.[28]

In short, while like all countries it has key limitations, Taiwan deserves a leading place among global exemplars that it is too rarely afforded. Admiration for Scandinavian countries is a constant refrain on the left in the West, as is praise for Singapore on the right. While all these jurisdictions have important lessons and in fact many important points of overlap with Taiwan, few places offer the breadth of promise in addressing today's leading challenges, and appeal across the typical divides as Taiwan does. As an economically free, vibrantly participatory liberal democracy Taiwan both has something to offer all points on the political spectrum of the West and holds arguably the most compelling example available to those looking to leapfrog the practices of increasingly ailing Western democracies. This is especially true given its starting point: without abundant natural resources or strategic position, in a fragile geopolitical setting, with a deeply divided rather than homogeneous and robust sized population and only democratizing a few decades ago, rising from abject poverty in less than a century.

It will doubtless take decades of study to understand the precise causal connections between Taiwan's unique and dramatic digital democratic practices and the range of success it has found in confronting today's most vexing challenges. Yet given this appeal, in the interim, it seems critical to articulate as so many have done for Scandinavia and Singapore, the generalizable philosophy behind the strategies of the world's most admired digital democracy. It is to that task that the rest of this book is devoted.

---

[28] "Taiwan Country Report Report," BTI Transformation Index, n.d., https://bti-project.org/en/reports/country-report/TWN.

# Part 3: Plurality

## 3-0 What is ⿻?

*Action, the only activity that goes on directly between men without the intermediary of things or matter, corresponds to the human condition of plurality, to the fact that men, not Man, live on the earth and inhabit the world.*

— Hannah Arendt, *The Human Condition*, 1958[1]

*(A)n ideal of 'social connectedness'...denotes a society where bridging ties, across lines of difference are formed at a high rate.*

— Danielle Allen, "Towards a Connected Society", 2017[2]

*Democracy is a technology. Like any technology, it gets better when more people strive to improve it.*

— Audrey Tang, Interview with Azeem Azhar, 2020[3]

---

The increasing tensions between democracy and technology and the way that, starting from such extreme divisions, Taiwan seems to have overcome them naturally raises a question: is

---

[1] Hannah Arendt, *The Human Condition*, (Chicago: University of Chicago Press, 1958).

[2] Danielle Allen, "Chapter 2: Toward a Connected Society," in In Our Compelling Interests, (Princeton: Princeton University Press, 2017), https://doi.org/10.1515/9781400881260-006.

[3] "View Section: 2020-10-07 Interview with Azeem Azhar," SayIt, https://sayit.pdis.nat.gov.tw/2020-10-07-interview-with-azeem-azhar#s433950, 2020.

there a more broadly applicable lesson on how technology and democracy can interact to be gleaned? We usually think of technology as something that inexorably progresses, while democracy and politics as the static choice between different competing forms of social organization. Taiwan's experience shows us that more options may be available for our technological future, making it more like politics, and that one of these may involve radically enhancing how we live together and collaborate, progressing democracy much like we do technology. It also shows us that while social differences may generate conflict, using appropriate technology, they may also be a fundamental source of progress.

Nor is the possibility of such a direction for technology especially novel. Perhaps the most canonical work of science fiction and thus vision of a positive future is *Star Trek*, in the original series of which the heroic Vulcans maintain a philosophy of "Infinite Diversity in Infinite Combinations...a...belief that beauty, growth, progress – all result from the union of the unlike."[4] Consistent with this idea, we define "⌘ 數位 Plurality", the subject of the rest of this book, briefly as "technology for collaboration across social difference". This contrasts with a common element between Libertarianism and Technocracy: that both consider the world to be made up of atoms (viz. individuals) and a social whole, a view we call "monist atomism". While they take different positions on how much authority should go to each, they miss the core idea of ⌘ 數位 Plurality, that intersecting diverse social groups and the diverse and collaborative people whose identities are constituted by these intersections are the core fabric of the social world.

---

[4] Gene Roddenberry, *Inside Star Trek*, 1: 15.

▦ 數位 Plurality: Part 3: Plurality

# INFINITE DIVERSITY IN INFINITE COMBINATIONS

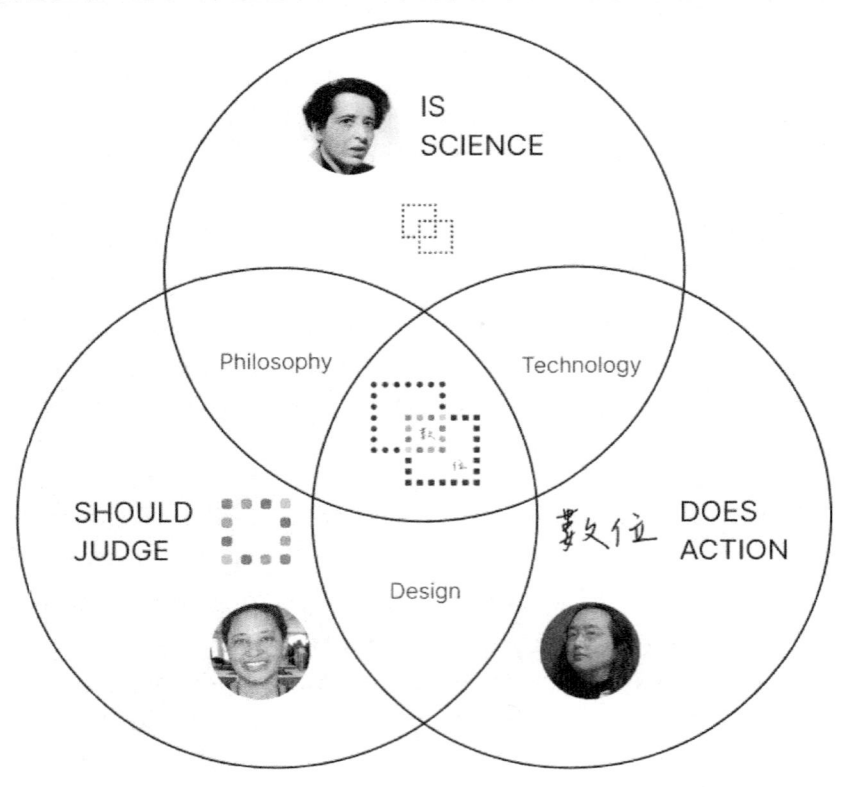

**Figure 3-0-A.** Three-part definition of ▦ 數位 Plurality.

To be more precise, we can break ▦ 數位 Plurality into three components (descriptive, normative, and prescriptive) each associated with one of three thinkers (Hannah Arendt, Danielle Allen, and Audrey Tang) each of whom has used the term in these three distinct and yet tightly connected ways, as captured in Figure A above:

1. Descriptive: **The social world is neither an unorganized collection of isolated individuals nor a monolithic whole. Instead, it is a fabric of diverse and intersecting affiliations that define both our personal identities and our collective organization.** We identify this concept with Hannah Arendt and especially her book, *The Human Condition*, where she labels Plurality as the most fundamental element of the human condition.[5] We identify this descriptive element of Plurality especially with the Universal Coded Character (Unicode) 🮰 which captures its emphasis on the intersectional, overlapping nature of identity for both groups and individuals. Furthermore, in the next chapter, *Living in a 🮰 World*, we highlight that this description applies not merely to human social life, but, according to modern (complexity) science, to essentially all complex phenomena in the natural world.

2. Normative: **Diversity is the fuel of social progress and while it may explode like any fuel (into conflict), societies succeed largely to the extent they manage to instead harness its potential energy for growth.** We identify this concept with philosopher Danielle Allen's ideal of "A Connected Society" and associate it with the rainbow elements that form at the intersection of the squares in the elaborated 🮰 image on the book cover and in the figure above. While Allen has given perhaps the clearest exposition of these ideas, as we explore in *The Lost Dao* they are deeply rooted in a philosophical tradition including many of the American thinkers who deeply influenced Taiwan, such as Henry George and John Dewey.

---

[5] Fittingly, Danielle Allen wrote the foreword for the second edition of this book.

⌬ 數位 Plurality: Part 3: Plurality

3. Prescriptive: **Digital technology should aspire to build engines that harness and avoid conflagration of diversity, much as industrial technology built the engines that harnessed physical fuel and contained its explosions.** We identify this concept by the use by one of us, beginning in 2016, of the term Plurality to refer to a technological agenda. We associate it even more closely with the use in her title (as Digital Minister) of the traditional Mandarin characters 數位 (pronounced in English as "shuwei") which, in Taiwan, mean simultaneously "plural" when applied to people and "digital" and thus capture the fusion of the philosophy arising in Arendt and Allen with the transformative potential of digital technology. In the last chapter of this part, Technology for Collaborative Diversity, we argue that, while less explicit, this philosophy drove much of the development of what has come to be called the "internet", though because it was not sufficiently articulated it has been somewhat lost since. A primary goal of the rest of the book is to clearly state this vision and thus help it become the alternative it should be to the Libertarian, Technocratic and stagnant democratic stories that dominate much discussion today.

Given this rich definition and the way it blends elements from traditional Mandarin and various English traditions, throughout the rest of the book we use the Unicode ⌬ to represent this idea set in both noun form (viz. to stand in for "Plurality") and in the adjective form (viz. to stand in for 數位).

In English this may be read in a variety of ways depending on context:

3-0 What is ⌘?

- As "Plurality" typically when used as a concept;[6]
- As "digital", "plural", "shuwei", "digital/plural" or even as a range of other things such as "intersectional", "collaborative" or "networked" when used as an adjective.

None of these existing words perfectly captures this idea set, and thus, in some cases, one might simply say "overlap" or "overlapping" to describe it literally. The rest of the book describes more deeply the content, vision, and ambition of ⌘.

---

[6] Note that ⌘ could also be used to represent the closely overlapping meanings of our interpretations of the two standard variations on the name of her jurisdiction, obviating the need for conflict over ROC v. Taiwan. However, we will leave this observation for someone else to build on given the risk of creating too much ambiguity in the meaning of ⌘.

數位 Plurality: Part 3: Plurality

## 3-1 Living in a ⬚ World

*Until lately the best thing that I was able to think in favor of civilization...was that it made possible the artist, the poet, the philosopher, and the man of science. But I think that is not the greatest thing. Now I believe that the greatest thing is a matter that comes directly home to us all. When it is said that we are too much occupied with the means of living to live, I answer that the chief worth of civilization is just that it makes the means of living more complex; that it calls for great and combined intellectual efforts, instead of simple, uncoordinated ones, in order that the crowd may be fed and clothed and houses and moved from place to place. Because more complex and intense intellectual efforts mean a fuller and richer life. They mean more life. Life is an end in itself, and the only question as to whether it is worth living is whether you have enough of it.*

— Oliver Wendell Holmes, 1900[1]

*(A)re...atoms independent elements of reality? No...as quantum theory shows: they are defined by their...interactions with the rest of the world...(Q)uantum physics may just be the realization that this ubiquitous relational structure of reality continues all the way down...Reality is not a collection of things, it's a network of processes.*

---

[1] Harper's Magazine. "Holmes – Life as Art," May 2, 2009. https://harpers.org/2009/05/holmes-life-as-art/.

3-1 Living in a ⬚ World

— Carlo Rovelli, 2022[2]

Technology follows science. If we want to understand ⬚ as a vision of *what our world could become*, we need to start off by understanding ⬚ as a perspective on *how the world already is*. The Technocratic and Libertarian perspectives are rooted in a science, namely the monist atomism we described in the previous chapter: the belief that a universal set of laws operating on a fundamental set of atoms is the best way to understand the world.

Technocracy has a long history of being justified by science and rationality. The idea of "scientific management" (a.k.a. Taylorism) that became popular in the early 1900s was justified by making analogies between social systems and simple mathematical models, and logic and reason as ways of thinking about them. High modernism in architecture is similarly inspired by the beauty of geometry.[3] Libertarianism also borrows heavily from physics and other sciences: just like particles "take the path of least action", and evolution maximizes fitness, economic agents "maximize utility". Every phenomenon in the world, from human societies to the motion of the stars, can, in the monist atomist view, ultimately be reduced to these laws.

---

[2] Carlo Rovelli, "The Big Idea: Why Relationships Are the Key to Existence." The Guardian, September 5, 2022, sec. Books. https://www.theguardian.com/books/2022/sep/05/the-big-idea-why-relationships-are-the-key-to-existence.

[3] James C. Scott, *Seeing Like a State: How Certain Schemes to Improve the Human Condition Have Failed* (New Haven, CT: Yale University Press, 1999).

These approaches have achieved great successes. Newtonian mechanics explained a range of phenomena and helped inspire the technologies of the industrial revolution. Darwinism is the foundation of modern biology. Economics has been the most influential of the social sciences on public policy. And the Church-Turing vision of "general computation" helped inspire the idea of general-purpose computers that are so broadly used today.

Yet the last century taught us how much progress is possible if we transcend the limitations of monist atomism. Gödel's Theorem undermined the unity and completeness of mathematics and a range of non-Euclidean geometries are now critical to science.[4] Symbiosis, ecology, and extended evolutionary synthesis undermined "survival of the fittest" as the central biological paradigm and ushered in the age of environmental science. Neuroscience has been reimagined around networks and emergent capabilities and given birth to modern neural networks. What all these share is a focus on complexity, emergence, multi-level organization, and multidirectional causality rather than the application of a universal set of laws to a single type of atomic entity.

數位 approaches social systems similarly. A corporation plays in the game of global competition, yet is simultaneously itself a game played by employees, shareholders, management, and customers. There is no reason to expect the resulting outcomes often to cohere as preferences. What's more, many games intersect: employees of a corporation are often influenced through their *other* relationships with the outside world (e.g. political, social, religious, ethnic), and not only through the corporation itself. Countries too are both games and players,

---

[4] Cris Moore and John Kaag, "The Uncertainty Principle", *The American Scholar* March 2, 2020 https://theamericanscholar.org/the-uncertainty-principle/.

3-1 Living in a ⌧ World

intersected by corporations, religions and much more, and there too we cannot cleanly separate actions between countries and actions within a country: the writing of this very book is a complex mix of both in multiple ways.

⌧ is thus heavy with analogies to the last century of natural sciences. Drawing out a ⌧ of these influences and analogies, without taking any too literally or universally, allows us to glimpse an inviting path ahead of inspiration and recombination. While Libertarianism and Technocracy can be seen as ideological caricatures, they can also be understood in scientific terms as ever-present threats to complexity.

Essentially every complex system, from the flow of fluids to the development of ecosystems to the functioning of the brain, can exhibit both "chaotic" states (where activity is essentially random) and "orderly" states (where patterns are static and rigid). There is almost always some parameter (such as heat or the mutation rate) that conditions which state arises, with chaos happening for high values and order for low values. When the parameter is very close to the "critical value" of transition between these states, when it sits on what complexity theorists call the "edge of chaos", complex behavior can emerge, forming unpredictable, developing, life-like structures that are neither chaotic nor orderly but instead complex.[5] This corresponds closely to the idea we highlighted above of a "narrow corridor" between centralizing and anti-social, Technocratic and Libertarian threats that we have highlighted above.

As such, ⌧ can take from science the crucial importance of steering towards and widening this narrow corridor, a process

---

[5] M. Mitchell Waldrop, *Complexity: The Emerging Science at the Edge of Order and Chaos* (New York: Open Road Media, 2019).

complexity scientists call "self-organizing criticality". In doing so, we can draw on the wisdom of many sciences, ensuring we are not unduly captured by any one set of analogies.

## Mathematics

Nineteenth century mathematics saw the rise of formalism: being precise and rigorous about the definitions and properties of mathematical structures that we are using, to avoid inconsistencies and mistakes. At the beginning of the 20th century, there was a hope that mathematics could be "solved", perhaps even giving a precise algorithm for determining the truth or falsity of any mathematical claim.[6] 20th century mathematics, on the other hand, was characterized by an explosion of complexity and uncertainty.

- **Gödel's Theorem**: Several mathematical results from the early 20th century, most notably Gödel's theorem, showed that there are fundamental and irreducible ways in which key parts of mathematics cannot be fully solved. Similarly, Alonzo Church proved that some mathematical problems were "undecidable" by computational processes.[7] This dashed the dream of reducing all of mathematics to computations on basic axioms.
- **Computational complexity**: Even when reductionism is feasible in principle/theory, the computation required to predict higher-level phenomena based on their components (its computational complexity) is so large that performing it is unlikely to be practically relevant. In some cases, it is believed that the required

---

[6] Alfred North Whitehead and Bertrand Russell, *Principia Mathematica* (Cambridge, UK: Cambridge University Press, 1910).

[7] Alonzo Church, "A note on the Entscheidungsproblem", *The Journal of Symbolic Logic* 1, no. 1: 40-41.

computation would consume far more resources than could possibly be recovered through the understanding gained by such a reduction. In many real-world use cases, the situation can often be described as a well-studied computational problem where the "optimal" algorithm takes an amount of time growing exponentially in the problem size and thus rules of thumb are almost always used in practice.

- **Sensitivity, chaos, and irreducible uncertainty**: Many even relatively simple systems have been shown to exhibit "chaotic" behavior. A system is chaotic if a tiny change in the initial conditions translates into radical shifts in its eventual behavior after an extended time has elapsed. The most famous example is weather systems, where it is often said that a butterfly flapping its wings can make the difference in causing a typhoon half-way across the world weeks later.[8] In the presence of such chaotic effects, attempts at prediction via reduction require unachievable degrees of precision. To make matters worse, there are often hard limits to how much precision is feasible known as "the Uncertainty Principle", as precise instruments often interfere with the systems they measure in ways that can lead to important changes due to the sensitivity mentioned previously.
- **Fractals**: Many mathematical structures have been shown to have similar patterns at very different scales. A good example of this is the Mandelbrot set, generated by repeatedly squaring then adding the same offset to a complex number. These illustrate why breaking structures down to atomic components may obscure rather than illuminate their inherently multi-scale structure.

---

[8] James Gleick, *Chaos: Making a New Science* (New York: Penguin, 2018).

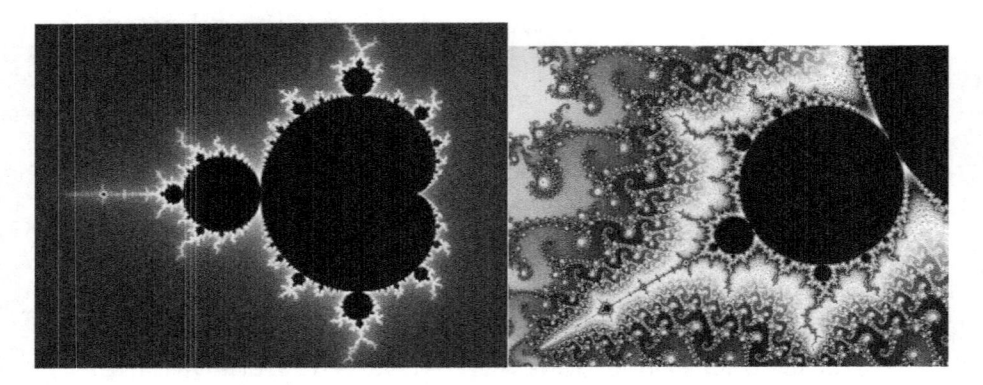

**Figure 3-1-A.** The Mandelbrot Set (characterizing the chaotic behavior of simple quadratic functions depending on parameter values in the function) shown at two scales. Source: Wikipedia CC 3.0 BY-SA.

- **Relationality**: In mathematics, different branches are often connected, and insights from one area can be applied to another. For instance, algebraic structures are ubiquitous in many branches of mathematics, and they provide a language for expressing and exploring relationships between mathematical objects. The study of algebraic geometry connects these structures to geometry. Moreover, the study of topology is based on understanding the relationships between shapes and their properties. The mix of diversity and interconnectedness is perhaps the defining feature of modern mathematics.

## Physics

In 1897, Lord Kelvin infamously proclaimed that "There is nothing new to discover in physics now." The next century proved, on the contrary, to be the most fertile and revolutionary in the history of the field.

3-1 Living in a ▨ World

- **Einstein's theories of relativity** overturned the simplicity of Euclidean geometry and Newtonian dynamics of colliding billiard balls as a guide to understanding the physical world at large scales and fast speeds. When objects travel at large fractions of the speed of light, very different rules start describing their behavior: namely, many features are relative and relational rather than absolute.
- **Quantum mechanics and string theory** similarly showed that classical physics is insufficient at very small scales. Bell's Theorem demonstrated clearly that quantum physics cannot even be fully described as a consequence of probability theory and hidden information: rather, a particle can be in a combination (or "superposition") of two states at the same time, where those two states *cancel each other out*.
- **"Heisenberg's Uncertainty Principle"**, mentioned above, puts a firm upper limit on the precision with which the velocity and position of a particle can even be measured.
- **The three body problem**, now famous after its central role in Liu Cixin's science-fiction series, shows that an interaction of even three bodies, even under simple Newtonian physics, is chaotic enough that its future behavior cannot be predicted with simple mathematical problems.[9] However, we still regularly solve *trillion-body problems* well enough for everyday use by using seventeenth-century abstractions such as "temperature" and "pressure".

Perhaps the most striking and consistent feature of the revolutions in twentieth century physics was the way they upset

---

[9] Liu Cixin, *The Three Body Problem* (Chongqing: China, Chongqing Press, 2008).

assumptions about a fixed and objective external world. Relativity showed how time, space, acceleration, and even gravity were functions of the relationship among objects, rather than absolute features of an underlying reality. Quantum physics went even further, showing that even these relative relationships are not fixed until observed and thus are fundamentally interactions rather than objects.[10] Thus, modern science often consists of mixing and matching different disciplines to understand different aspects of the physical world at different scales.

The applications of this rich and 數位 understanding of physical reality are at the very core of the glories and tragedies of the twentieth century. Great powers harnessed the atom to shape world affairs. Global corporations powered unprecedented communications and intelligence by harnessing their understanding of quantum physics to pack ever-tinier electronics into the palms of their customers' hands. The burning of wood and coal by millions of families has become the cause of ecological devastation, political conflict, and world-spanning social movements based on information derived from microscopic sensors scattered around the world.

## Biology

If the defining idea of 19th century macrobiology (concerning advanced organisms and their interactions) was the "natural selection", the defining idea of the 20th century analog was "ecosystems". Where natural selection emphasized the "Darwinian" competition for survival in the face of scarce resources, the ecosystem view (closely related to the idea of "extended evolutionary synthesis") emphasizes:

---

[10] Carlo Rovelli, "Relational Quantum Mechanics", *International Journal of Theoretical Physics* 35, 1996: 1637-1678.

- **Limits to predictability of models**: We have continued to discover limits in our ability to make effective models of animal behavior that are based on reductive concepts, such as behaviorism, neuroscience, and so forth, illustrating computational complexity.
- **Similarities between organisms and ecosystems**: We have discovered that many diverse organisms ("ecosystems") can exhibit features like multicellular life (homeostasis, fragility to destruction or over propagation of internal components, etc.) illustrating emergence and multiscale organization. In fact, many higher-level organisms are hard to distinguish from such ecosystems (e.g., multicellular life as cooperation among single-celled organisms or "eusocial" organisms like ants from individual insects). A particular property of the evolution of these organisms is the potential for mutation and selection to occur at all these levels, illustrating multi-scale organization.[11]
- **The diversity of cross-species interactions**, including traditional competition or predator and prey relationships, but also a range of "mutualism", where organisms depend on services provided by other organisms and help sustain them in turn, exemplifying entanglement, and relationality.[12]

---

[11] David Sloan Wilson and Edward O. Wilson, "Rethinking the Theoretical Foundation of Sociobiology" *Quarterly Review of Biology* 82, no. 4, 2007: 327-348.

[12] These discoveries have continually and deeply intertwined with ⬚ social thought, from "mutualism" being used almost interchangeably by early anarchist thinkers like Pierre-Joseph Proudhon to one of the authors of this book publishing his second paper on biological mutualism, then developing these ideas further into the theories we will return to in our chapter on *Social Markets*. Pierre-Joseph Proudhon, *System of Economic Contradictions* (1846). E. Glen Weyl, Megan E. Frederickson, Douglas W.

- **Epigenetics**: We have discovered that genetics codes only a portion of these behaviors, and "epigenetics" or other environmental features play important roles in evolution and adaptation, showing the multi-level and multidimensional causation inherent even to molecular biology.

This shift was not simply a matter of scientific theory. It led to some of the most important changes in human behavior and interaction with nature of the twentieth century. In particular, the environmental movement and the efforts it created to protect ecosystems, biodiversity, the ozone layer, and the climate all emerged from and have relied heavily on this science of "ecology", to the point where this movement is often given that label.

## Neuroscience

Modern neuroscience started in the late 19th century, when Camillo Golgi, Santiago Ramón y Cajal, and collaborators isolated neurons and their electrical activations as the fundamental functional unit of the brain. This analysis was refined into clear physical models by the work of Alan Hodgkin and Andrew Huxley, who built and tested on animals their electrical theories of nervous communication. More recently, however, we have seen a series of discoveries that put chaos and complexity theory at the core of how the brain functions:

- **Distribution of brain functions**: Mathematical modeling, brain imaging, and single-neuron activation experiments suggested that many if not most brain functions are distributed across regions of the brain,

---

Yu and Naomi E. Pierce, "Economic Contract Theory Tests Models of Mutualism" *Proceedings of the National Academy of Sciences* 107, no. 36, 2010: 15712-15716.

emerging from patterns of interactions rather than primarily physical localization.
- **The Hebbian model of connections:** where they are strengthened by repeated co-firing, is perhaps one of the most elegant illustrations of the idea of "relationality" in science, closely paralleling the way we typically imagine human relationships developing.
- **Study of artificial neural networks**: As early as the late 1950s, researchers beginning with Frank Rosenblatt built the first "artificial neural network" models of the brain. Neural networks have become the foundation of the recent advances in "artificial intelligence". Networks of trillions of nodes, each operating on simple principles inspired by neurons of activation triggered by crossing a threshold determined by a linear combination of inputs, are the backbone of the "foundation models" such as BERT and the GPT models.

**From science to society**

⌘ is, scientifically, the application of an analogous perspective to the understanding of human societies and, technologically, the attempt to build formal information and governance systems that account for and resemble these structures as physical technologies built on ⌘ science do. Perhaps the crispest articulation of this vision appears in the work of the leading figure of network sociology, Mark Granovetter.[13] There is no basic individual atom; personal identity fundamentally arises from social relationships and connections. Nor is there any fixed collective or even set of collectives: social groups do and must constantly shift and

---

[13] Mark Granovetter, "Economic Action and Social Structure: The Problem of Embeddedness", *American Journal of Sociology* 91, no. 3 (1985): 481-510.

reconfigure. This bidirectional equilibrium between the diversity of people and the social groups they create is the essence of 數位 social science.

Moreover, these social groups exist at a variety of intersecting and non-hierarchical scales. Families, clubs, towns, provinces, religious groups of all sizes, businesses at every scale, demographic identities (gender, sexual identity, race, ethnicity, etc.), education and academic training, and many more co-existing and intersecting. For example, from the perspective of global Catholicism, the US is an important but "minority" country, with only about 6% of all Catholics living in the US; but the same could be said about Catholicism from the perspective of the US, with about 23% of Americans being Catholic.[14]

While we do not have the space to review it in detail, rich literature provides quantitative and social scientific evidence for the explanatory power of the 數位 perspective [15]. Studies of industrial dynamics, of social and behavioral psychology, of economic development, of organizational cohesion, and much else, have shown the central role of social relationships that

---

[14] Pew Research Center, "The Global Catholic Population", February 13, 2013 https://www.pewresearch.org/religion/2013/02/13/the-global-catholic-population/.

[15] In assemblage theory, as articulated by Manuel DeLanda, entities are understood as complex structures formed from the symbiotic relationship between heterogeneous components, rather than being reducible to their individual parts. Its central thesis is that people do not act exclusively by themselves, and instead human action requires complex socio-material interdependencies. DeLanda's perspective shifts the focus from inherent qualities of entities to the dynamic processes and interactions that give rise to emergent properties within networks of relations. His book "A New Philosophy of Society: Assemblage Theory and Social Complexity" (2006) is a good starting point.

create and harness diversity[16]. Instead, we will pull out just one example that perhaps will be both the most surprising and most related to the scientific themes above: the evolution of scientific knowledge itself.

A growing interdisciplinary academic field of "Metascience" studies the emergence of scientific knowledge as a complex system from networks among scientists and ideas.[17] It charts the emergence and proliferation of scientific fields, sources of scientific novelty and progress, the strategies of exploration scientists choose, and the impact of social structure on intellectual advancement. Among other things, they find that scientific exploration is biased towards topics that have been frequently discussed within a field and constrained by social and institutional connections among scientists, which diminishes the efficiency of the scientific knowledge discovery

---

[16] Scott Page, *The Difference: How the Power of Diversity Creates Better Groups, Firms, Schools, and Societies*, (Princeton: Princeton University Press, 2007); César Hidalgo, *Why Information Grows: The Evolution of Order, from Atoms to Economies*, (New York: Basic Books, 2015); Daron Acemoglu, and Joshua Linn, "Market Size in Innovation: Theory and Evidence from the Pharmaceutical Industry," *Library Union Catalog of Bavaria*, (Berlin and Brandenburg: B3Kat Repository, October 1, 2003), https://doi.org/10.3386/w10038; Mark Granovetter, "The Strength of Weak Ties," *American Journal of Sociology* 78, no. 6 (May 1973): 1360–80; Brian Uzzi, "Social Structure and Competition in Interfirm Networks: The Paradox of Embeddedness," Administrative Science Quarterly 42, no. 1 (March 1997): 35–67. https://doi.org/10.2307/2393808; Jonathan Michie, and Ronald S. Burt, "Structural Holes: The Social Structure of Competition," *The Economic Journal* 104, no. 424 (May 1994): 685. https://doi.org/10.2307/2234645; McPherson, Miller, Lynn Smith-Lovin, and James M Cook. "Birds of a Feather: Homophily in Social Networks." Annual Review of Sociology 27, no. 1 (August 2001): 415-44.

[17] Santo Fortunato, Carl T. Bergstrom, Katy Borner, James A. Evans, Dirk Helbing, Stasa Milojevič, Filippo Radicchi, Robeta Sinatra, Brian Uzzi, Alessandro Vespignani, Ludo Waltman, Dashun Wang and Alberto-László Barbási, "Science of Science" *Nature* 359, no. 6379 (2018): eaao0185.

process.[18] Furthermore, they discover that a decentralized scientific community, made up of mostly independent, non-overlapping teams that use a variety of methods and draw upon a broad spectrum of earlier publications, tends to yield more reliable scientific knowledge. In contrast, centralized communities marked by repeated collaborations and restricted to a limited range of approaches from previous studies are likely to generate less reliable outcomes [19,20] It also finds strong connections between research team size and hierarchy with the types of findings (risky and revolutionary v. normal science) developed and documents the increasingly dominant role of teams (as opposed to individual research) in modern science.[21] Although the largest innovations tend to arise from a strong grounding in existing disciplines deployed in unusual and

---

[18] Andrey Rzhetsky, Jacob Foster, Ian Foster, and James Evans, "Choosing Experiments to Accelerate Collective Discovery," *Proceedings of the National Academy of Sciences* 112, no. 47 (November 9, 2015): 14569-74. https://doi.org/10.1073/pnas.1509757112.

[19] Valentin Danchev, Andrey Rzhetsky, and James A Evans, "Centralized Scientific Communities Are Less Likely to Generate Replicable Results." *ELife* 8 (July 2, 2019), https://doi.org/10.7554/elife.43094.

[20] Alexander Belikov, Andrey Rzhetsky, and James Evans, "Prediction of robust scientific facts from literature," *Nature Machine Intelligence* 4.5 (2022): 445-454.

[21] Lingfei Wu, Dashun Wang, and James Evans, "Large teams develop and small teams disrupt science and technology," *Nature* 566.7744 (2019): 378-382.

3-1 Living in a 🔲 World

surprising combinations [22] [23] [24], it illustrates that most incentive structures used in science (based e.g. on publication quality and citation count) create perverse incentives that limit scientific creativity. These findings have led to the development of new metrics in scientific communities that can reward innovations and offset these biases, creating a more 🔲 incentive set.[25]

Science policy research that directly accounts for and enhances 🔲 in science demonstrates advantages for both the rigor of existing knowledge and the discovery of novel insights. When more distinct communities and their approaches work to validate existing claims, those *independent* perspectives ensure their findings are more robust to rebuttal and revision. Moreover, when building analytic models based on 🔲 principles by simulating the diversity we see in the most

---

[22] Yiling Lin, James Evans, and Lingfei Wu, "New directions in science emerge from disconnection and discord," *Journal of Informetrics* 16.1 (2022): 101234.

[23] Feng Shi, and James Evans, "Surprising combinations of research contents and contexts are related to impact and emerge with scientific outsiders from distant disciplines," Nature Communications 14.1 (2023): 1641.

[24] Jacob Foster, Andrey Rzhetsky, and James A. Evans, "Tradition and Innovation in Scientists' Research Strategies," *American Sociological Review* 80.5 (2015): 875-908.

[25] Aaron Clauset, Daniel Larremore, and Roberta Sinatra, "Data-driven predictions in the science of science," *Science* 355.6324 (2017): 477-480.

scientific ventures, discoveries exceed those produced by normal human science.²⁶

Thus, even in understanding the very practice of science, a 🔲 perspective, grounded in many intersecting levels of social organization, is critical. Science of science findings regarding the driving forces behind the emergence of disruptive, innovative knowledge have been replicated in other communities of creative collaboration, such as patents and software projects in GitHub, revealing that a 🔲 outlook could transcend the advance of science and technology of any flavor.

## A future 🔲?

Yet the assumptions on which the Technocratic and Libertarian visions of the future discussed above diverge sharply from such 🔲 foundations.

In the Technocratic vision we discussed in the previous chapter, the "messiness" of existing administrative systems is to be replaced by a massive-scale, unified, rational, scientific, artificially intelligent planning system. Transcending locality and social diversity, this unified agent is imagined giving "unbiased" answers to any economic and social problem, transcending social cleavages and differences. As such, it seeks to at best paper over and at worst erase, rather than fostering and harnessing, the social diversity and heterogeneity that 🔲 social science sees as defining the very objects of interest, engagement, and value.

---

²⁶ Jamshid Sourati, and James Evans, "Accelerating science with human-aware artificial intelligence," *Nature Human Behaviour* 7.10 (2023): 1682-1696.

## 3-1 Living in a ⿻ World

In the Libertarian vision, the sovereignty of the atomistic individual (or in some versions, a homogeneous and tightly aligned group of individuals) is the central aspiration. Social relations are best understood in terms of "customers", "exit" and other capitalist dynamics. Democracy and other means of coping with diversity are viewed as failure modes for systems that do not achieve sufficient alignment and freedom.

But these cannot be the only paths forward. ⿻ science has shown us the power of harnessing a ⿻ understanding of the world to build physical technology. We have to ask what a society and information technology built on an analogous understanding of human societies would look like. Luckily, the twentieth century saw the systematic development of such a vision, from philosophical and social scientific foundations to the beginnings of technological expression.

## 3-2 Connected Society

> *Industry and inventions in technology, for example, create means which alter the modes of associated behavior, and which radically change the quantity, character, and place of impact of their indirect consequences. These changes are extrinsic to political forms which, once established, persist of their own momentum. The new public, which is generated, remains long-inchoated, unorganized, because it cannot use inherited political agencies. The latter, if elaborate and well institutionalized, obstruct the organization of the new public. They prevent that development of new forms of the state which might grow up rapidly were social life more fluid, less precipitated into set political and legal molds. To form itself, the public must break existing political forms. This is hard to do because these forms are themselves the regular means of instituting change. The public which generated political forms is passing away, but the power and lust of possession remains in the hands of the officers and agencies which the dying public instituted. This is why the change of the form of states is so often affected only by revolution.*
>
> — John Dewey, *The Public and its Problems*, 1927[1]

The twentieth century saw as fundamental shifts in social as natural sciences. Henry George, author of the best-selling and most influential book on economics in American and perhaps world history, made his career as a searing critic of private property. Georg Simmel, one of the founders of sociology,

---

[1] John Dewey, *The Public and its Problems* (New York: Holt Publishers, 1927): p. 81.

originated the idea of the "web" as a critique of the individualist concept of identity. John Dewey, widely considered the greatest philosopher of American democracy, argued that the standard nation-state institutions that instantiated the idea hardly scratched the surface of what democracy required. Norbert Wiener coined the term "cybernetics" for a field studying such rich interactive systems. By perceiving the limits of the box of modernity they highlighted even as they helped construct it, these pioneers helped us imagine a social world outside it, pointing the way towards a vision of a Connected Society that harnesses the potential of collaboration across diversity.

## Limits of Modernity

Private property. Individual identity and rights. Nation-state democracy. These are the foundations of most modern liberal democracies. Yet they rest on fundamentally monist atomist foundations. Individuals are the atoms; the nation-state is the whole that connects them. Every citizen is seen as equal and exchangeable in the eyes of the whole, rather than part of a network of relationships that forms the fabric of society and in which any state is just one social grouping. State institutions see direct, unmediated relationships to free and equal individuals, though in some cases federal and other subsidiary (e.g. city, religious or family) institutions intercede.

Three foundational institutions of modern social organization represent this structure most sharply: property, identity, and voting. We will illustrate how this works in each context and then turn to the ways that 🔲 social science has challenged and offers ways past the limits of atomist monism.

*Property*

Simple and familiar forms of private property, with most restrictions on that right being imposed by governments, are the most common form of ownership in liberal democracies around the world. Most homes are owned by a single individual or family or by a single landlord who rents to another individual or family. Most non-governmental collective ownership takes the form of a standard joint stock company governed by the principle of one-share-one-vote and the maximization of shareholder value. While there are significant restrictions on the rights of private property owners based on community interests, these overwhelmingly take the form of regulations by a small number of governmental levels, such as national, provincial/state, and local/city. These practices are in sharp contrast to the property regimes that have prevailed in most human societies throughout most of history, in which individual ownership was rarely absolutely institutionalized and a diversity of "traditional" expectations governed how possessions can rightly be used and exchanged. Such traditional structures were largely erased by modernity and colonialism as they attempted to pattern property into a marketable "commodity", allowing exchange and reuse for a much broad set of purposes than was possible within full social context.[2]

## Identity

Prior to modernity, individuals were born into families rooted within kin-based institutions that provided everything, livelihood, sustenance, meaning, and that were for the most part inescapable. No "official documents" were needed or useful as people rarely traveled beyond the boundaries of those they knew well. Such institutions were eroded by the Roman Empire and the spread of Christianity in its wake.[3] As

---

[2] Karl Polanyi, *The Great Transformation* (New York: Farrar & Rinehart, 1944).

[3] Joseph Henrich, *The WEIRDest People in the World How the West Became Psychologically Peculiar and Particularly Prosperous*, (New York Macmillan, 2010).

European cities grew in the first centuries of the second millennium of the common era, impersonal pro-sociality of citizens began to take shape through the emergence of a diversity of extra-kin social institutions such as monasteries, universities, and guilds. Paper-based markers of affiliations with such institutions began to supplant informal kin knowledge. Church records of baptisms helped lay the foundation for what became the widespread practice of issuing birth certificates. This, in turn, became the foundational document on which essentially all other identification practices are grounded in modern states.[4]

This helped circumvent the reliance on personal relationships, building the foundation of identity in a relationship to a state, which in turn served as a trust anchor for many other types of institutions ranging from children's sports teams to medical care providers. These abstract representations enabled people to navigate the world not based on "who they know" or "where they fit" in a tight social world but as who they are in an abstracted universal sense relative to the state. This "WEIRD" (Western Educated Industrialized Rich Democratic) universalism thus broke with the social embedding of identity while thereby "freeing" people to travel and interact much more broadly using modern forms of identification issued by governments like passports and national identity cards. While other critical credentials, such as educational attainment are more diverse, they almost uniformly conform to a limited structure, implying one of a small number of "degrees" derived from courses with a particular "Carnegie unit" structure (in theory, 120 hours spent with an instructor), in contrast to the

---

[4] It is worth noting, however, that universal birth registration is a very recent phenomenon and only was achieved in the US in 1940. Universal registration for Social Security Numbers did not even begin until 1987 when Enumeration at Birth was instituted at the federal level in collaboration with county level governments where births are registered.

broad range of potential recognition that could be given to learning attainment as illustrated in Figure A. In short, just as modernity abstracted ownership private property, removing it from its many social entanglements, it also abstracted personal identity from the social anchoring that limited travel and the formation of new relationships.

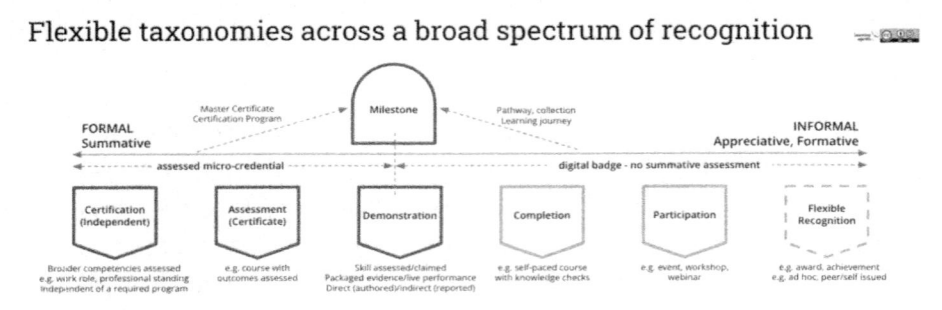

**Figure 3-2-A.** Flexible taxonomies across a broad spectrum of recognition. Source: Learning Agents Inc. (https://www.learningagents.ca).

*Voting*

In most liberal democracies, the principle of "one-person-one-vote" is viewed as a sacred core of the democratic process. Of course, various schemes of representation (multi-member proportional representation or single-member districts), checks-and-balances (mutli- v. unicameral legislatures, parliamentary v. presidential) and degrees of federalism vary and recombine in a diverse way. However both in popular imagination and in formal rules, the idea that numerical majorities (or in some cases supermajorities) should prevail regardless of the social composition of groups is at the core of how democracy is typically understood.[5] Again this contrasts with decision-making structures throughout most of the world and most of history, including ones that involved widespread and diverse representation by a range of social relationships, including family, religious, relationships of fealty, profession, etc.[6] We again see the same pattern repeated: liberal states have "extracted" "individuals" from their social embedding to make them exchangeable, detached citizens of an abstracted national polity.

This regime began to develop during the Renaissance and Enlightenment, when traditional, commons-based property systems, community-based identity and multi-sectoral representation were swept away for the "rationality" and "modernity" of what became the modern state.[7] This system solidified and literally conquered the world during the industrial and colonial nineteenth century and was canonized in the work of Max Weber, reaching its ultimate expression in the "high modernism" of the mid-twentieth century, when

---

[5] There are, of course, limited exceptions that in many ways prove the rule. The two most notable examples are "degressive proportionality" and "consociationalism". Many federal systems (e.g. the US) apply the principle of degressive proportionality to which we will return later: namely, that smaller sub-units (e.g. provinces in national voting) are over-represented relative to their population. Some countries also have consociational structures in which designated social groups (e.g. religions or political parties) agree to share power in some specified fashion, ensuring that even if one group's vote share declines they retain something of their historical power. Yet these counterexamples are few, far between and usually subjects of on-going controversy, with significant political pressure to "reform" them in the direction of a standard one-person-one-vote direction.

[6] David Graeber and David Wengrow, *The Dawn of Everything* (London: Allen Lane, 2021).

[7] Andreas Anter, *Max Weber's Theory of the Modern State*, (Palgrave Macmillan, 2014).

properties were further rationalized into regular shapes and sizes, identity documents reinforced with biometrics and one-person-one-vote systems spread to a broad range of organizations.

Governments and organizations around the world adopted these systems for some good reasons. They were simple and thus scalable; they allowed people from very different backgrounds to quickly understand each other and thus interact productively. Where once commons-based property systems inhibited innovation when outsiders and industrialists found it impossible to navigate a thicket of local customs, private property cleared a path to development and trade by reducing those who could inhibit change. Administrators of the social welfare schemes that transformed government in the twentieth century would have struggled to provide broad access to pensions and unemployment benefits without a single, flat, clear database of entitlements. And reaching subtle compromises like those that went into the US Constitution, much less ones rich enough to keep up with the complexity of the modern world, would have likely undermined the possibility of democratic government spreading.

In fact, these institutions were core to what allowed modern, wealthy, liberal democracies to rise, flourish and rule, making what Joseph Heinrich calls the "WEIRDest people in the world". Just as the insights of Newtonian mechanics and Euclidean geometry gave those civilizations the physical power to sweep the earth, liberal social institutions gave them the social flexibility to do so. Yet just as the Euclidean-Newtonian worldview turned out to be severely limited and naïve, social science was born by highlighting the limits of these atomist monist social systems.

## Henry George and the networked value

We remember Karl Marx and Adam Smith more sharply, but the social thinker that may have had the greatest influence during and immediately following his lifetime was Henry George.[8] Author of the for-years best-selling book in English other than the Bible, *Progress and Poverty*, George inspired or arguably founded many of the most successful political movements and even cultural artifacts of the early twentieth century including:[9]

- the American center-left, as a nearly successful United Labor candidate for Mayor of New York City.
- the Progressive and social gospel movements, which both traced their names to his work.
- Tridemism, which, as we saw above in our chapter *A View from Yushan*, had its economic leg firmly founded in Georgism.
- and the game Monopoly, which originated as an educational device "The Landlord's Game", to illustrate how an alternate set of rules could avoid monopoly and enable common prosperity.[10]

George wrote on many topics helping to originate, for example, the idea of a secret ballot. But he became most famous for advocating a "single tax" on land, whose value he argued could never properly belong to an individual owner. His

---

[8] Christopher William England, *Land and Liberty: Henry George and the Crafting of Modern Liberalism* (Baltimore, MD: Johns Hopkins University Press, 2023).

[9] Henry George, *Progress and Poverty: An Inquiry into the Cause of Industrial Depressions and of Increase of Want with Increase of Wealth: The Remedy* (New York: D. Appleton and Company, 1879)

[10] Mary Pilon, *The Monopolists: Obsession, Fury and the Scandal Behind the World's Favorite Board Game* (New York: Bloomsbury, 2015).

most famous illustration asked readers to imagine an open savannah full of beautiful but homogeneous land on which a settler arrives, claiming some arbitrarily chosen large plot for her family. When future settlers arrive, they choose to settle close to the first, to enjoy the company, divide labor and enjoy shared facilities like schools and wells. As more settlers arrive, they continue to choose to cluster and the value of land rises. In a few generations, the descendants of the first settler find themselves landlords of much of the center of a bustling metropolis, rich beyond imagination, through little effort of their own, simply because a great city was built around them.

The value of their land, George insisted, could not justly belong to that family: it was a collective product that should be taxed away. Such a tax was not only just, but it was also crucial for economic development, as highlighted especially by later economists including one of the authors of this book. Taxes of this sort, especially when carefully designed as they were in Taiwan, ensure property owners must use their land productively or allow others to do so. The revenue they raise can support shared infrastructure (like those schools and wells) that gives value to the land, an idea called the "Henry George Theorem". We return to all these points in our chapter on *Social Markets*.

Yet, as attractive as this argument has proven to politicians and intellectuals from Leo Tolstoy to Albert Einstein, in practice it has raised many more questions than it has answered. Simply saying that land does not belong to an individual owner says nothing about who or what it does belong to. The city? The nation state? The world?

Given this is a book about technology, an elegant illustration is the San Francisco Bay Area, where both authors and George himself lived parts of their lives and which has some of the most expensive land in the world. To whom does the enormous value of this land belong?

## 3-2 Connected Society

- Certainly not to the homeowners who simply had the good fortune of seeing the computer industry grow up around them. Then perhaps to the cities in the region? Many reformers have argued these cities, which are in any case fragmented and tend to block development, can hardly take credit for the miraculous increase in land values.
- Perhaps Stanford University and the University of California at Berkeley, to which various scholars have attributed much of the dynamism of Silicon Valley?[11] Certainly these played some role, but it would be strange to attribute the full value of Bay Area land to two universities, especially when these universities succeeded with the financial support of the US government and the collaboration of other universities across the country.
- Perhaps the State of California? Arguably the national defense industry, research complex that created the internet (as we discuss below) and political institutions played a far greater role than anything at the state level.
- Then to the US? But of course, the software industry and internet are global phenomena.
- Then to the world in general? Beyond the essential non-existence of a world government that could meaningfully receive and distribute the value of such land, abstracting all land value to such heights is a bit of an abdication: clearly many of the entities above are more relevant than simply "the entire world" to the value of the software industry; if we followed that path, global government would end up managing everything simply by default.

---

[11] AnnaLee Saxenian, *The New Argonauts: Regional Advantage in a Global Economy* (Cambridge, MA: Harvard University Press, 2007).

To make matters yet more complex, the revenue earned on the property is but one piece of what it means to own. Legal scholars typically describe property as a bundle of rights: of "usus" (to access the land), "abusus" (to build on or dispose of it) and "fructus" (to profit from it). Who should be able to access the land of the Bay Area under what circumstances? Who should be allowed to build what on it, or to sell exclusive rights to do so to others? Most of these questions were hardly even considered in George's writing, much less settled. In this sense, his work is more a helpful invitation to step beyond the easy answers private property offers, which is perhaps why his enormously influential ideas have only been partly implemented in a small number of (admittedly highly successful) places like Estonia and Taiwan.

The world George invites us to reflect on and imagine how to design for is thus one of 數位 value, one where a variety of entities, localized at different scales (universities, municipalities, nation states, etc.) all contribute to differing degrees to create value, just as networks of waves and neurons contribute to differing degrees to the probabilities of particles being found in various positions or thoughts occurring in a mind. And for both justice and productivity, property and value should belong, in differing degrees, to these intersecting social circles. In this sense, George was a founder of 數位 social science.

**Figure 3-2-B.** Georg Simmel. Source: Wikipedia, public domain.

## Georg Simmel and the intersectional (in)dividual

But if network thinking was implicit in George's work, it took another thinker, across the Atlantic, to make it explicit and, accidentally, give it a name. Georg Simmel, pictured in Figure B, was a German philosopher and sociologist of the turn of the twentieth century who pioneered the idea of social networks. The mistranslation of his work as focused on a "web" eventually went "worldwide". In his 1955 translation of Simmel's classic 1908 *Soziologie*, Reinhard Bendix chose to describe Simmel's idea as describing a "web of group-affiliations" over what he described as the "almost meaningless" direct translation "intersection of social circles".[12] While the precise lines of influence are hard to trace, it is possible that, had Bendix made an opposite choice, we might talk of the internet in terms of "intersecting global circles" rather than the "world wide web".[13]

Simmel's "intersectional" theory of identity offered an alternative to both the traditional individualist/atomist (characteristic at the time in sociology with the work of Max Weber and deeply influential on Libertarianism) and collectivist/structuralist (characteristic at the time of the sociology of Émile Durkheim and deeply influential on Technocracy) accounts. From a Simmelian point of view, both appear as extreme reductions/projections of a richer underlying theory.

In his view, humans are deeply social creatures and thus their identities are deeply formed through their social relations. Humans gain crucial aspects of their sense of self, their goals, and their meaning through participation in social, linguistic, and solidaristic groups. In simple societies (e.g., isolated, rural, or tribal), people spend most of their life interacting with the kin groups we described above. This circle comes to (primarily) define their identity collectively, which is why most scholars of simple societies (for example, anthropologist Marshall Sahlins) tend to favor methodological collectivism.[14] However, as we noted above, as societies urbanize social

---

[12] Georg Simmel, *Soziologie: Untersuchungen Über Die Formen Der Vergesellschaftung*, Prague: e-artnow, 2017.

[13] Miloš Broćić, and Daniel Silver, "The Influence of Simmel on American Sociology since 1975," *Annual Review of Sociology* 47, no. 1 (July 31, 2021): 87–108, https://doi.org/10.1146/annurev-soc-090320-033647.

[14] Marshall Sahlins, *Stone Age Economics* (Chicago: Aldine-Atherton, 1972).

## 3-2 Connected Society

relationships diversify. People work with one circle, worship with another, support political causes with a third, recreate with a fourth, cheer for a sports team with a fifth, identify as discriminated against along with a sixth, and so on. These diverse affiliations together form a person's identity. The more numerous and diverse these affiliations become, the less likely it is that anyone else shares precisely the same intersection of affiliations.

As this occurs, people come to have, on average, less of their full sense of self in common with those around them at any time; they begin to feel "unique" (to put a positive spin on it) and "isolated/misunderstood" (to put a negative spin on it). This creates a sense of what he called "qualitative individuality" that helps explain why social scientists focused on complex urban settings (such as economists) tend to favor methodological individualism. However, ironically as Simmel points out, such "individuation" occurs precisely because and to the extent that the "individual" becomes divided among many loyalties and thus dividual. Thus, while methodological individualism (and what he called the "egalitarian individualism" of nation states we highlighted above that it justified) takes the "(in)dividual" as the irreducible element of social analysis, Simmel instead suggests that individuals become possible as an emergent property of the complexity and dynamism of modern, urban societies.

Thus, the individuals that the national identity systems seek to strip away from the shackles of communities actually emerge from their growth, proliferation and intersection. As a truly just and efficient property regime would recognize and account for such networked interdependence, identity systems that truly empower and support modern life would need to mirror its structure.

## John Dewey's emergent publics

If (in)dividual identity is so fluid and dynamic, surely so too must be the social circles that intersect to constitute it. As Simmel highlights, new social groups are constantly forming, while older one's decline. Three examples he highlights are the for his time still recent formation of cross-sectoral "working men's associations" that represented the general interest of labor and the just-then-emerging feminist associations and cross-sectoral employers' interest groups. The critical pathway to creating such new circles was the establishment of places (e.g. workman's halls) or publications (e.g. working men's newspapers) where this new group could come to know one another and understand, and thus have things in common they do not have with others in the broader society. Such bonds were strengthened by secrecy, as shared secrets allowed for a distinctive identity and culture, as well as the coordination in a common interest in ways unrecognizable by outsiders.[15] Developing these shared, but hidden, knowledge allows the emerging social circle to act as a collective agent.

In his 1927 work that defined his political philosophy, *The Public and its Problems*, John Dewey (who we meet in A View from Yushan) considered the political implications and dynamics of these "emergent publics" as he called them.[16] Dewey's views emerged from a series of debates he held, as leader of the "democratic" wing of the progressive movement after his return from China with left-wing technocrat Walter Lippmann, whose 1922 book *Public Opinion* Dewey considered "the most effective indictment of democracy as

---

[15] Georg Simmel, "The Sociology of Secrecy and of Secret Societies," *American Journal of Sociology* 11, no. 4 (January 1906): 441–98, https://doi.org/10.1086/211418.

[16] John Dewey, op. cit.

currently conceived".[17] In the debate, Dewey sought to redeem democracy while embracing fully Lippmann's critique of existing institutions as ill-suited to an increasingly complex and dynamic world.

While he acknowledged a range of forces for social dynamism, Dewey focused specifically on the role of technology in creating new forms of interdependence that created the necessity for new publics. Railroads connected people commercially and socially whom they would never have met. Radio created shared political understanding and action across thousands of miles. Pollution from industry was affecting rivers and urban air. All these technologies resulted from research, the benefits of which spread with little regard for local and national boundaries. The social challenges (e.g. governance railway tariffs, safety standards, and disease propagation; fairness in access to scarce radio) arising from these forms of interdependence are poorly managed by both capitalist markets and preexisting "democratic" governance structures.

Markets fail because these technologies create market power, pervasive externalities (such as "network externalities"), and more generally exhibit "supermodularity" (sometimes called "increasing returns"), where the whole of the (e.g. railroad network) is greater than the sum of its parts; see our chapter on *Social Markets*. Capitalist enterprises cannot account for all the relevant "spillovers" and to the extent they do, they accumulate market power, raise prices, and exclude participants, undermining the value created by increasing returns. Leaving these interdependencies "to the market" thus exacerbates their risks and harms while failing to leverage their potential.

---

[17] Robert Westbrook, *John Dewey and American Democracy* (Ithaca, NY: Cornell University Press).

Dewey revered democracy as the most fundamental principle of his career; barely a paragraph can pass without him harkening back to it. He firmly believed that democratic action could address the failings of markets. Yet he saw the limits of existing "democratic" institutions just as severely as those of capitalism. The problem is that existing democratic institutions are not, in Dewey's view, truly democratic in the face of the emergent challenges created by technology.

What it means to say an institution is "democratic" is not just that it involves participation and voting. Apartheid South Africa held elections, just ones that excluded most of the population. Nor would, in Dewey's mind, a global "democracy" directly managing the affairs of a village count as democratic. Core to true democracy is the idea that the "relevant public", the set of people whose lives are shaped by the phenomenon in question, manage that challenge. Because technology is constantly throwing up new forms of interdependence, which will almost never correspond precisely to existing political boundaries, true democracy requires new publics to constantly emerge and reshape existing jurisdictions.

Furthermore, because new forms of interdependence are not easily perceived by most individuals in their everyday lives, Dewey saw a critical role for what he termed "social science experts" but we might with no more abuse of terminology call "entrepreneurs", "leaders", "founders", "pioneer" or, as we prefer, "mirror". Just as George Washington's leadership helped the US both perceive itself as a nation and a nation that had to democratically choose its fate after his term in office, the role of such mirrors is to perceive a new form of interdependence (e.g. solidarity among workers, the carbon-to-global-warming chain), explain it to those involved by both word and deed, and thereby empower a new public to come into existence. Historical examples are union leaders, founders of rural electricity cooperatives, and the leaders who founded

## 3-2 Connected Society

the United Nations. Once this emergent public is understood, recognized, and empowered to govern the new interdependence, the role of the mirror fades away, just as Washington returned to Mount Vernon.

Thus, as the mirror image of Simmel's philosophy of (in)dividual identity, Dewey's conception of democracy and emergent publics is at once profoundly democratic and yet challenges and even overturns our usual conception of democracy. Democracy, in this conception, is not the static system of representation of a nation-state with fixed borders. It is a process even more dynamic than a market, led by a diverse range of entrepreneurial mirrors, who draw upon the ways they are themselves intersections of unresolved social tensions to renew and re-imagine social institutions. Standard institutions of nation state-based voting are to such a process as pale a shadow as Newtonian mechanics is of the underlying quantum and relativistic reality. True democracy must be 🔲 and constantly evolving.

### Norbert Wiener's cybernetic society

All these critiques and directions of thought are suggestive, but none seems to offer clear paths to action and further scientific development. Could the understanding of the 🔲nature of social organization be turned into a scientific engine of new forms of social organization? This hypothesis was the seed from which Norbert Wiener sprouted the modern field of "cybernetics", from which comes all the uses of "cyber" to describe digital technology and, many would argue, the later name of "computer science" given to similar work. Wiener defined cybernetics as "the science of control and communication in (complex systems like) the animal and machine", but perhaps the most broadly accepted meaning is something like the "science of communication within and governance of, by and for networks".[18] The word was drawn from a Greek analogy of a ship directed by the inputs of its many oarsmen.

Wiener's scientific work focused almost exclusively on physical, biological and information systems, investigating the ways that organs and machines can obtain and preserve homeostasis, quantifying information transmission channels and the role they play in achieving such equilibrium and so on. Personally and politically, he was a pacifist, severe critic of capitalism as failing basic principles of cybernetic stabilization and creation of homeostasis and advocate of radically more responsible use and deployment of technology.[19] He despaired that without profound social reform his scientific work would come to worse than nothing, writing in the introduction to *Cybernetics*, "there are those who hope that the good of a better understanding of man and society which is offered by this new field of work may anticipate and outweigh the incidental contribution we are making to the concentration of power (which is always concentrated, by its very conditions of existence, in the hand of the most unscrupulous. I write in 1947, and I am compelled to say that it is a very slight hope." It is thus unsurprising that Wiener befriended many social scientists and reformers who vested "considerable…hopes…for the social efficacy of whatever new ways of thinking this book may contain."

Yet while he shared the convictions, he believed these hopes to be mostly "false". While he judged such a program as "necessary", he was unable to "believe it possible". He argued that quantum physics had shown the impossibility of precision

---

[18] Norbert Wiener, *Cybernetics, Or Control and Communication in the Animal and the Machine* (Paris: Hermann & Cie, 1948).

[19] Norbert Wiener, *Human Use of Human Beings* (Boston: Houghton Mifflin, 1950).

at the level of particles and therefore that the success of science arose from the fact that we live far above the level of particles, but that our very existence within societies meant that the same principles made social science essentially inherently infeasible. Thus, as much as he hoped to offer scientific foundations on which the work of George, Simmel and Dewey could rest, he was skeptical of "exaggerated expectations of their possibilities."

Across all these authors, we see many common threads. We see appreciation of the ▢ and layered nature of society, which often shows even greater complexity than other phenomena in the natural sciences: while an electron typically orbits a single atom or molecule, a cell is part of one organism, and a planet orbits one star, in human society each person, and even each organization, is part of multiple intersecting larger entities, often with no single of them being fully inside any other. But how might these advancements in the social sciences translate into similarly more advanced social technologies? This is what we will explore in the next chapter.

## 3-3 The Lost Dao

*(D)ecisions about the development and exploitation of computer technology must be made not only "in the public interest" but in the interest of giving the public itself the means to enter into the decision-making processes that will shape their future.*

– J. C. R. Licklider, "Computers and Government", 1980[1]

---

Can a 數位 understanding of society lay the foundation for social transformations as dramatic as those that fields like quantum mechanics and ecology have brought to natural sciences, physical technology, and our relationship to nature? Liberal democracies often celebrate themselves as pluralistic societies, which would seem to indicate they have already drawn the available lessons from 數位 social science. Yet despite this formal commitment to pluralism and democracy, almost every country has been forced by the limits of available information systems to homogenize and simplify social institutions in a monist atomist mold that runs into direct conflict with such values. The great hope of 數位 social science and 數位 built on top of it is to use the potential of information technology to begin to overcome these limitations.

---

[1] J.C.R. Licklider, "Computers and Government" in Michael L. Dertouzos and Joel Moses eds., *The Computer Age: A Twenty-Year View* (Cambridge, MA: MIT Press, 1980)

## 🚀 launches

This was the mission pursued by the younger generation that followed in Wiener's lead but had a more human/social scientific background. This generation included a range of pioneers of applied cybernetics such as the anthropologist Margaret Mead[2] (who heavily influenced the aesthetics of the internet), W. Edwards Deming[3] (whose influence on Japanese and to a lesser extent Taiwanese inclusive industrial quality practices we saw above) and Stafford Beer[4] (who pioneered business cybernetics and has become something of a guru for social applications of Wiener's ideas including in Chile's brief cybernetic socialist regime of the early 1970s). They built on his vision in a more pragmatic mode, shaping technologies that defined the information era. Yet the most ambitious and systemic impact of this work was heralded by a blip moving across the sky in October 1957, a story masterfully narrated by M. Mitchell Waldrop in his *The Dream Machine*, from which much of what follows derives.[5]

---

[2] Fred Turner, *The Democratic Surround: Multimedia and American Liberalism from World War II to the Psychedelic Sixties* (Chicago: University of Chicago Press, 2013).

[3] While we do not have space to pursue Deming's or Mead's stories in anything like the depth we do the development of the internet, in many ways the work of these two pioneers parallels many of the themes we develop and in the industrial and cultural spheres laid the groundwork for 🚀 just as Licklider and his disciples did in computation. UTHSC. "Deming's 14 Points," May 26, 2022. https://www.uthsc.edu/its/business-productivity-solutions/lean-uthsc/deming.php.

[4] Dan Davies, *The Unaccountability Machine: Why Big Systems Make Terrible Decisions - and How The World Lost its Mind* (London: Profile Books, 2024).

[5] M. Mitchell Waldrop, *The Dream Machine* (New York: Penguin, 2002).

數位 Plurality: Part 3: Plurality

## Sputnik and the Advanced Research Projects Agency

The launch by the Soviet Union of the first orbital satellite was followed a month later by the Gaither Committee report, claiming that the US had fallen behind the Soviets in missile production. The ensuing moral panic forced the Eisenhower administration into emergency action to reassure the public of American strategic superiority. Yet despite, or perhaps because of, his own martial background, Eisenhower deeply distrusted what he labeled America's "military industrial complex", while having boundless admiration for scientists.[6] He thus aimed to channel the passions of the Cold War into a national strategy to improve scientific research and education.[7]

While that strategy had many prongs, a central one was the establishment, within the Department of Defense, of a quasi-independent, scientifically administered Advanced Research Projects Agency (ARPA) that would harness expertise from universities to accelerate ambitious and potentially transformative scientific projects with potential defense applications.

While ARPA began with many aims, some of which were soon assigned to other newly formed agencies, such as the National Aeronautics and Space Administration (NASA), it quickly found a niche as the most ambitious government supporter of ambitious and "far out" projects under its second director, Jack Ruina. One area was to prove particularly representative of this

---

[6] Katie Hafner and Matthew Lyon, *Where the Wizards Stay up Late: The Origins of the Internet* (New York: Simon & Schuster, 1998).

[7] Dickson, Paul. "Sputnik's Impact on America." NOVA | PBS, November 6, 2007. https://www.pbs.org/wgbh/nova/article/sputnik-impact-on-america/.

## 3-3 The Lost Dao

risk-taking style: the Information Processing Techniques Office led by Joseph Carl Robnett (JCR) Licklider.

Licklider hailed from a different field still from the political economy of George, sociology of Simmel, political philosophy of Dewey and mathematics of Wiener: "Lick", as he was commonly known, received his PhD in 1942 in the field of psychoacoustics. After spending his early career developing applications to human performance in high-stakes interactions with technology (especially aviation), his attention increasingly turned to the possibility of human interaction with the fastest growing form of machinery: the "computing machine". He joined the Massachusetts Institute of Technology (MIT) to help found Lincoln Laboratory and the psychology program. He moved to the private sector as Vice President of Bolt, Beranek and Newman (BBN), one of the first MIT-spin off research start-ups.

Having persuaded BBN's leadership to shift their attention towards computing devices, Lick began to develop an alternative technological vision to the then-emerging field of Artificial Intelligence that drew on his psychological background to propose "Man-Computer Symbiosis", as his path-breaking 1960 paper was titled. Lick hypothesized that while "in due course…'machines' will outdo the human brain in most of the functions we now consider exclusively within its province…(t)here will…be a fairly long interim during which the main advances will be made by men and computers working together…those years should be intellectually the most creative and exciting in the history of mankind."[8]

These visions turned out to arrive at precisely the right moment for ARPA, as it was in search of bold missions with which it could secure its place in the rapidly coalescing national science

---

[8] J. C. R. Licklider. "Man-Computer Symbiosis," March 1960. https://groups.csail.mit.edu/medg/people/psz/Licklider.html.

administration landscape. Ruina appointed Lick to lead the newly formed Information Processing Techniques Office (IPTO). Lick harnessed the opportunity to build and shape much of the structure of what became the field of Computer Science.

*The Intergalactic Computer Network*

While Lick spent only two years at ARPA, they laid the groundwork for much of what followed in the next forty years of the field. He seeded a network of "time sharing" projects around the US that would enable several individual users to directly interact with previously monolithic large-scale computing machines, taking a first step towards the age of personal computing. The five universities thus supported (Stanford, MIT, UC Berkeley, UCLA and Carnegie Mellon) went on to become the core of the academic emerging field of computer science.

Beyond establishing the computational and scientific backbone of modern computing, Lick was particularly focused on the "human factors" in which he specialized. He aimed to make the network represent these ambitions in two ways that paralleled the social and personal aspects of humanity. On the one hand, he gave particular attention and support to projects he believed could bring computing closer to the lives of more people, integrating with the functioning of human minds. The leading example of this was the Augmentation Research Center established by Douglas Engelbart at Stanford.[9] On the other hand, he dubbed the network of collaboration between these hubs, with his usual tongue-in-cheek, the "Intergalactic

---

[9] "Douglas Engelbart Issues 'Augmenting Human Intellect: A Conceptual Framework' : History of Information," October 1962. https://www.historyofinformation.com/detail.php?id=801.

Computer Network", and hoped it would provide a model of computer-mediated collaboration and co-governance.[10]

This project bore fruit in a variety of ways, both immediately and longer term. Engelbart quickly invented many foundational elements of personal computing, including the mouse, a bitmapped screen that was a core precursor to the graphical user interface and hypertext; his demonstration of this work, six short years after Lick's initial funding, as the "oNLine system" (NLS) is remembered as "the mother of all demos" and a defining moment in the development of personal computers.[11] This in turn helped persuade Xerox Corporation to establish their Palo Alto Research Center (PARC), which went on to pioneer much of personal computing. US News and World Report lists four of the five departments Lick funded as the top four computer science departments in the country.[12] Most importantly, after Lick's departure to the private sector, the Intergalactic Computer Network developed into something less fanciful and more profound under the leadership of his collaborator, Robert W. Taylor.

*A network of networks*

Taylor and Lick were naturally colleagues. While Taylor never completed his PhD, his research field was also psychoacoustics and he served as Lick's counterpart at NASA, which had just

---

[10] J.C.R. Licklider, "Memorandum For: Members and Affiliates of the Intergalactic Computer Network", 1963 available at https://worrydream.com/refs/Licklider_1963_-_Members_and_Affiliates_of_the_Intergalactic_Computer_Network.pdf.

[11] Engelbart, Christina. "Firsts: The Demo - Doug Engelbart Institute." Doug Engelbart Institute, n.d. https://dougengelbart.org/content/view/209/.

[12] https://www.usnews.com/best-colleges/rankings/computer-science-overall

split from ARPA, during Lick's leadership at IPTO. Shortly following Lick's departure (in 1965), Taylor moved to IPTO to help develop Lick's networking vision under the leadership of Ivan Sutherland, who then returned to academia, leaving Taylor in charge of IPTO and the network that he more modestly labeled the ARPANET. He used his authority to commission Lick's former home of BBN to build the first working prototype of the ARPANET backbone. With momentum growing through Engelbart's demonstration of personal computing and ARPANET's first successful trials, Lick and Taylor articulated their vision for the future possibilities of personal and social computing in their 1968 article "The Computer as a Communication Device", describing much of what would become the culture of personal computing, internet and even smartphones several decades later.[13]

By 1969, Taylor felt the mission of the ARPANET was on track to success and moved on to Xerox PARC, where he led the Computer Science Laboratory in developing much of this vision into working prototypes. These in turn became the core of the modern personal computer that Steve Jobs famously "stole" from Xerox to build the Macintosh, while ARPANET evolved into the modern internet.[14] In short, the technological revolutions of the 1980s and 1990s trace clearly back to this quite small group of innovators in the 1960s. While we will turn to these more broadly known later developments shortly, it is worth lingering on the core of the research program that made them possible.

At the core of the development of what became the internet was replacing centralized, linear, and atomized structures with

---

[13] J.C.R. Licklider and Robert Taylor, "The Computer as a Communication Device" *Science and Technology* 76, no. 2 (1967): 1-3.

[14] Michael A. Hiltzik, *Dealers of Lightning: Xerox PARC and the Dawn of the Computer Age* (New York: Harper Business, 2000).

relationships and governance. This happened at three levels that eventually converged in the early 1990s as the World Wide Web:

1. packet switching to replace centralized switchboards,
2. hypertext to replace linear text,
3. and open standard setting processes to replace both government and corporate top-down decision-making.

All three ideas had their seeds at the edges of the early community Lick formed and grew into core features of the ARPANET community.

While the concept of networks, redundancy and sharing permeate Lick's original vision, it was Paul Baran's 1964 report "On Distributed Communications" that clearly articulated how and why communications networks should strive for a ▢ rather than centralized structure.[15]

Baran argued that while centralized switchboards achieved high reliability at low cost under normal conditions, they were fragile to disruptions. Conversely, networks with many centers could be built with cheap and unreliable components and still withstand even quite devastating attacks by "routing around damage", taking a dynamic path through the network based on availability rather than prespecified planning. While Baran received support and encouragement from scientists at Bell Labs, his ideas were roundly dismissed by AT&T, the national telephone monopoly in whose culture high-quality centralized dedicated machinery was deeply entrenched.

Despite the apparent threat it posed to that private interest, packet switching caught the positive attention of another

---

[15] Paul Baran, "On Distributed Communications Networks," *IEEE Transactions on Communications Systems* 12, no. 1 (1964): 1-9.

數位 Plurality: Part 3: Plurality

organization that owed its genesis to the threat of devastating attacks: ARPA. At a 1967 conference, ARPANET's first program manager, Lawrence Roberts, learned of packet switching through a presentation by Donald Davies, who concurrently and independently developed the same idea as Baran, and drew on Baran's arguments that he soon learned of to sell the concept to the team. Figure A shows the decentralized logical structure of early ARPANET that resulted.

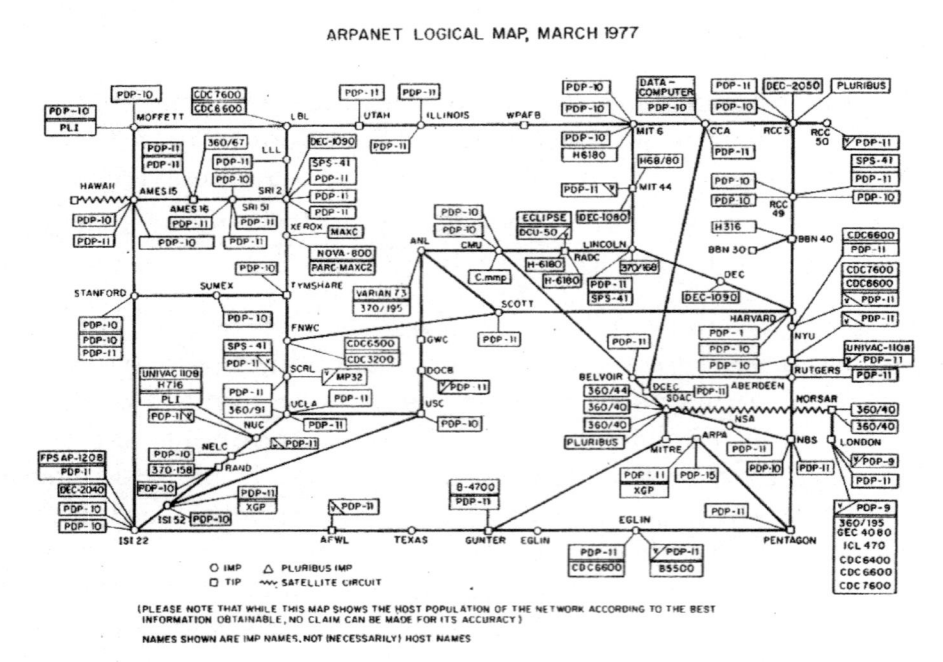

**Figure 3-3-A.** Early logical structure of ARPANET. Source: *Wikipedia*, public domain.

If one path to networked thinking was thus motivated by technical resilience, another was motivated by creative expression. Ted Nelson trained as a sociologist, was inspired in his work by a visit to campus he hosted in 1959 by cybernetic pioneer Margaret Mead's vision of democratic and pluralistic

### 3-3 The Lost Dao

media and developed into an artist. Following these early experiences, he devoted his life beginning in his early 20s to the development of "Project Xanadu", which aimed to create a revolutionary human-centered interface for computer networks. While Xanadu had so many components that Nelson considered indispensable that it was not released fully until the 2010s, its core idea, co-developed with Engelbart, was "hypertext" as Nelson labeled it.

Nelson imagined hypertext as a way to liberate communication from the tyranny of a linear interpretation imposed by an original author, empowering a "pluralism" (as he labeled it) of paths through material through a network of (bidirectional) links connecting material in a variety of sequences.[16] This "choose your own adventure"[17] quality is most familiar today to internet users in their browsing experiences but showed up earlier in commercial products in the 1980s (such as computer games based on hypercard). Nelson imagined that such ease of navigation and recombination would enable the formation of new cultures and narratives at unprecedented speed and scope. The power of this approach became apparent to the broader world when Tim Berners-Lee made it central to his "World Wide Web" approach to navigation in the early 1990s, ushering in the era of broad adoption of the internet.

While Engelbart and Nelson were lifelong friends and shared many similar visions, they took very different paths to realizing

---

[16] Theodor Holm Nelson, *Literary Machines* (Self-published, 1981), available at https://cs.brown.edu/people/nmeyrowi/LiteraryMachinesChapter2.pdf

[17] "Choose Your Own Adventure," interactive gamebooks based on Edward Packard's concept from 1976, peaked in popularity under Bantam Books in the '80s and '90s, with 250+ million copies sold. It declined in the '90s due to competition from computer games.

them, each of which (as we will see) held an important seed of truth. Engelbart, while also a visionary, was a consummate pragmatist and a smooth political operator, and went on to be recognized as the pioneer of personal computing. Nelson was an artistic purist whose relentless pursuit over decades of Xanadu embodying all his seventeen enumerated principles buried his career.

As an active participant in Lick's network, Engelbart conversely tempered his ambition with the need to persuade other network nodes to support, adopt or at least inter-operate with his approach. As different user interfaces and networking protocols proliferated, they retreated from the pursuit of perfection. Engelbart, and even more his colleagues across the project, instead began to develop a culture of collegiality, facilitated by the communication network they were building, across the often-competing universities they worked at. The physical separation made tight coordination of networks impossible but work to ensure minimal inter-operation and spreading of clear best practices became a core characteristic of the ARPANET community.

This culture manifested in the development of the "Request for Comments" (RFC) process by Steve Crocker, arguably one of the first "wiki"-like processes of informal and mostly additive collaboration across many geographically and sectorally (governmental, corporate, university) dispersed collaborators. This in turn contributed to the common Network Control Protocol and, eventually, Transmission Control and Internet Protocols (TCP/IP) under the famously mission-driven but inclusive and responsive leadership of Vint Cerf and Bob Kahn between 1974 when TCP was first circulated as RFC 675 and 1983 when they became the official ARPANET protocols. At the core of the approach was the vision of a "network of networks" that gave the "internet" its name: that many diverse and local networks (at universities, corporations and government agencies) could inter-operate sufficiently to permit the near-seamless communication across long distances, in contrast to centralized networks (such as France's concurrent Minitel) that were standardized from the top down by a government.[18] Together these three dimensions of networking (of technical communication protocols, communicative content, and governance of standards) converged to create the internet we know today.

**Triumph and tragedy**

Much of what resulted from this project is so broadly known it hardly bears repeating here. During the 1970's, Taylor's Xerox PARC produced a series of expensive, and thus commercially unsuccessful, but revolutionary "personal workstations" that incorporated much of what became the personal computer of the 1990s. At the same time, as computer components were made available to broader populations, businesses like Apple and Microsoft began to make cheaper and less user-friendly machines available broadly. Struggling to commercialize its inventions, Xerox allowed Apple Co-Founder Steve Jobs access to its technology in exchange for a stake, resulting in the Macintosh's ushering in of modern personal computing and Microsoft's subsequent mass scaling through their Windows operating system. By 2000, most Americans had a personal computer in their homes. Internet use has steadily spread, as pictured in Figure B.

---

[18] Mailland and Driscoll, op. cit.

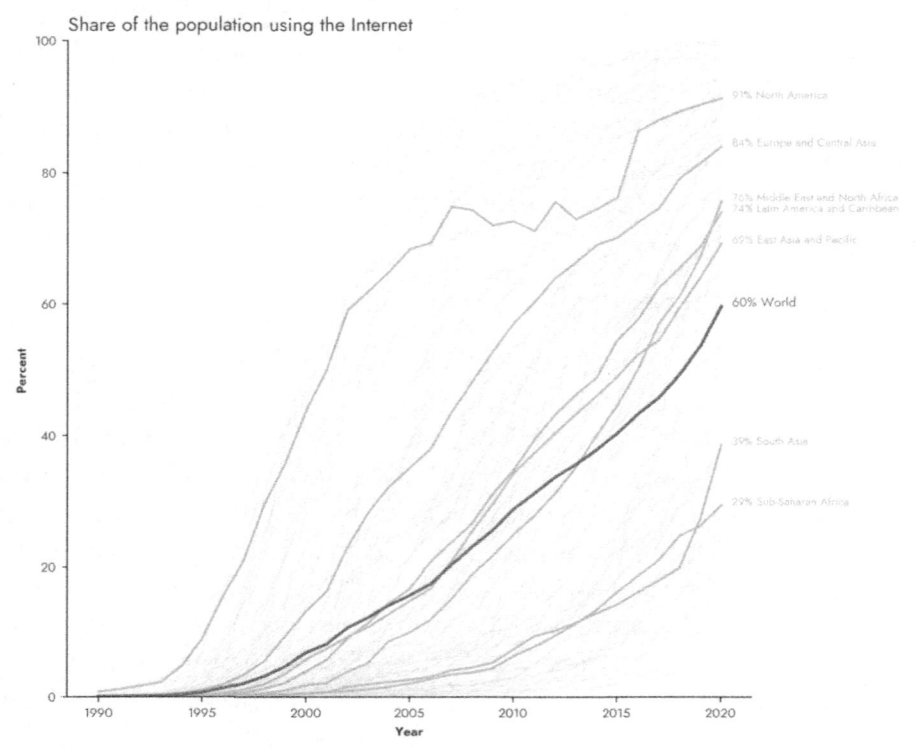

**Figure 3-3-B.** Population share with internet access over time in the world and in various regions. Source: Our World in Data.[19]

## The internet and its discontents

And much as it had developed in parallel from the start, the internet grew to connect those personal computers. During the late 1960s and early 1970s, a variety of networks grew up in parallel to the largest ARPANET, including at universities, governments outside the United States, international standards

---

[19] World Bank, "World Development Indicators" December 20, 2023 at https://datacatalog.worldbank.org/search/dataset/0037712/World-Development-Indicators.

## 3-3 The Lost Dao

bodies and inside corporations like BBN and Xerox. Under the leadership of Kahn and Cerf and with support from ARPA (now renamed DARPA to emphasize its "defense" focus), these networks began to harness the TCP/IP protocol to inter-operate. As this network scaled, DARPA looked for another agency to maintain it, given the limits of its advanced technology mission. While many US government agencies took their hand, the National Science Foundation had the widest group of scientific participants and their NSFNET quickly grew to be the largest network, leading ARPANET to be decommissioned in 1990. At the same time, NSFNET began to interconnect with networks in other wealthy countries.

One of those was the United Kingdom, where researcher Tim Berners-Lee in 1989 proposed a "web browser", "web server" and a Hypertext Mark-Up Language (HTML) that fully connected hypertext to packet-switching and made internet content far more available to a broad set of end users. From the launch of Berners-Lee's World Wide Web (WWW) in 1991, internet usage grew from roughly 4 million people (mostly in North America) to over 400 million (mostly around the world) by the end of the millennium. With internet start-ups booming in Silicon Valley and life for many beginning its migration online though the computers many now had in their home, the era of networked personal computing (of "The Computer as a Communication Device") had arrived.[20]

In the boom-and-bust euphoria of the turn of the millennium, few people in the tech world paid attention to the specter haunting the industry, the long-forgotten Ted Nelson. Stuck on his decades-long quest for the ideal networking and communication system, Nelson ceaselessly warned of the insecurity, exploitative structure and inhumane features of the

---

[20] Licklider and Taylor, op. cit.

emerging WWW design. Without secure identity systems (Xanadu Principles 1 and 3), a mixture of anarchy and land-grabs by nation-states and corporate actors would be inevitable. Without embedded protocols for commerce (Xanadu Principles 9 and 15), online work would become devalued or the financial system controlled by monopolies. Without better structures for secure information sharing and control (Xanadu Principles 8 and 16), both surveillance and information siloing would be pervasive. Whatever its apparent success, the WWW-Internet was doomed to end badly.

While Nelson was something of an oddball, his concerns were surprisingly broadly shared among even the mainstream internet pioneers who would seem to have every reason to celebrate their success. As early as 1980, while TCP/IP was coalescing, Lick foresaw in his classic essay "Computers and Government" "two scenarios" (one good, the other bad) for the future of computing: it could be dominated and its potential stifled by monopolistic corporate control or there could be a full societal mobilization that made computing serve and support democracy.[21] In the former scenario, Lick projected all kinds of social ills, one that might make the advent of the information age a net detractor to democratic social flourishing. These included:

1. Pervasive surveillance and public distrust of government.
2. Paralysis of government's ability to regulate or enforce laws, as they fall behind the dominant technologies citizens use.
3. Debasement of creative professions.
4. Monopolization and corporate exploitation.
5. Pervasive digital misinformation.

---

[21] Licklider, "Comptuers and Government", op. cit.

6. Siloing of information that undermines much of the potential of networking.
7. Government data and statistics becoming increasingly inaccurate and irrelevant.
8. Control by private entities of the fundamental platforms for speech and public discourse.

The wider internet adoption spread, the less relevant such complaints appeared. Government did not end up playing as central of a role as he imagined, but by 2000 most of the few commentators who were even aware of his warnings assumed we were surely on the path of Lick's scenario 2. Yet in a few places, concern was growing by late in the first decade of the new millennium. Virtual reality pioneer Jaron Lanier sounded the alarm in two books *You are Not a Gadget* and *Who Owns The Future?*, highlighting Nelson's and his own version of Lick's concerns about the future of the internet.[22] While these initially appeared simply an amplification of Nelson's fringe ideas, a series of world events that we discuss in the Information Technology and Democracy: a Widening Gulf above eventually brought much of the world around to seeing the limitations of the internet economy and society that had developed, helping ignite the Techlash. These patterns bore a striking resemblance to Lick and Nelson's warnings. The victory of the internet may have been far more Pyrrhic than it at first seemed.

## Losing our dao

How did we fall into a trap clearly described by the founders of hypertext and the internet? After having led the development of the internet, why did government and

---

[22] Jaron Lanier, *You Are Not a Gadget: A Manifesto* (New York: Vintage, 2011) and *Who Owns the Future?* (New York: Simon & Schuster, 2014).

universities not rise to the challenge of the information age following the 1970s?

It was the warning signs that motivated Lick to put pen to paper in 1980 as the focus of ARPA (now DARPA) shifted away from support for networking protocols towards more directly weapons-oriented research. Lick saw this resulting from two forces on opposite ends of the political spectrum. On the one hand, with the rise of "small government conservatism" that would later be labeled "neoliberalism", government was retreating from proactively funding and shaping industry and technology. On the other hand, the Vietnam War turned much of the left against the role of the defense establishment in shaping research, leading to the Mansfield Amendments of 1970, 1971 and 1973 that prohibited ARPA from funding any research not directly related to the "defense function".[23] Together these were redirecting DARPA's focus to technologies like cryptography and artificial intelligence that were seen as directly supporting military objectives.

Yet even if the attention of the US government had not shifted, the internet was quickly growing out of its purview and control. As it became an increasingly global network, there was (as Dewey predicted) no clear public authority to make the investments needed to deal with the socio-technical challenges needed to make a network society a broader success. To quote Lick

> *From the point of view of computer technology itself, export...fosters computer research and development [but that] (f)rom the point of view of mankind...the important thing would...be a wise rather than a*

---

[23] Phil Williams, "Whatever Happened to the Mansfield Amendment?" *Survival: Global Politics and Strategy* 18, no. 4 (1976): 146-153 and "The Mansfield Amendment of 1971" in *The Senate and US Troops in Europe* (London, Palgrave Macmillan: 1985): pp. 169-204.

*rapid...development...Such crucial issues as security, privacy, preparedness, participation, and brittleness must be properly resolved before one can conclude that computerization and programmation are good for the individual and society...Although I do not have total confidence in the ability of the United States to resolve those issues wisely, I think it is more likely than any other country to do so. That makes me doubt whether export of computer technology will do as much for mankind as a vigorous effort by the United States to figure out what kind of future it really wants and then to develop the technology needed to realize it.*

The declining role of public and social sector investment left abandoned core functions/layers that leaders like Lick and Nelson saw for the internet (e.g. identity, privacy/security, asset sharing, commerce) to which we return below. While there were tremendous advances to come in both applications running on top of the internet and in the WWW, much of the fundamental investment in protocols was wrapping up by the time of Lick's writing. The role of the public and social sectors in defining and innovating the network of networks was soon eclipsed.

Into the resulting vacuum stepped the increasingly eager private sector, flush with the success of the personal computer and inflated by the stirring celebrations of Reagan and Thatcher. While the International Business Machines (IBM) that Lick feared would dominate and hamper the internet's development proved unable to key pace with technological change, it found many willing and able successors. A small group of telecommunications companies took over the internet backbone that the NSF freely relinquished. Web portals, like America Online and Prodigy came to dominate most Americans' interactions with the web, as Netscape and Microsoft vied to dominate web browsing. The neglected identity functions were filled by the rise of Google and Facebook. Absent digital payments were filled in by PayPal and Stripe. Absent the protocols for sharing data, computational power and storage that motivated work on the Intergalactic Computer Network in the first place, private infrastructures (often called "cloud providers") that empowered such sharing (such as Amazon Web Services and Microsoft Azure) became the platforms for building applications.[24]

While the internet backbone continued to improve in limited ways, adding security layers and some encryption, the basic features Lick and Nelson saw as essential were never integrated. Public financial support for the networking protocols largely dried up, with remaining open-source development largely consisting of volunteer work or work supported by private corporations. As the world woke to the Age of the Internet, the dreams of its founders faded.

## Flashbacks

Yet faded dreams have a stubborn persistence, nagging throughout the day. While Lick passed away in 1990, many of the early internet pioneers lived to see their triumph and tragedy.

Ted Nelson (shown in Figure C) and many other pioneers in Project Xanadu continue to carry their complaints about and reforms to the internet forward to this day. Engelbart, until his death in 2013, continued to speak, organize, and write about his vision of "boosting Collective IQ". These activities included supporting, along with Terrence Winograd (PhD advisor to the Google founders), a community around Online Deliberation based at Stanford University that nurtured key leaders of the

---

[24] Ben Tarnoff, *Internet for the People: The Fight for Our Digital Future* (New York: Verso, 2022).

next generation of 🗆 as we will see below. While none of these efforts met with the direct successes of their earlier years, they played critical roles as inspiration and in some case even incubation for a new generation of 🗆 innovators, who have helped revive and articulate the dream of 🗆.

**Figure 3-3-C.** Ted Nelson at Keio University, Japan, 1999. Source: Wikipedia, used under CC 4.0 BY-SA.

*Nodes of light*

While, as we highlighted in the introduction, the dominant thrust of technology has developed in directions that put it on a collision course with democracy, this new generation of leaders has formed a contrasting pattern, scattered but clearly discernible nodes of light that together give hope that with renewed common action, ⬚ could one day animate technology writ large. Perhaps the most vivid example for the average internet user is Wikipedia.

This open, non-profit collaborative project has become the leading global resource for reference and broadly shared facts.[25] In contrast to the informational fragmentation and conflict that pervades much of the digital sphere that we highlighted in the introduction, Wikipedia has become a widely accepted source of shared understanding. It has done this through harnessing large-scale, open, collaborative self-governance.[26] Many aspects of this success are idiosyncratic and attempts to directly extend the model have had mixed success; trying to make such approaches more systematic and pervasive is much of our focus below. But the scale of the success is quite remarkable.[27] Recent analysis suggests that

---

[25] In fact, researchers have studied reading patterns in terms of time spent by users across the globe. Nathan TeBlunthuis, Tilman Bayer, and Olga Vasileva, "Dwelling on Wikipedia," *Proceedings of the 15th International Symposium on Open Collaboration*, August 20, 2019, https://doi.org/10.1145/3306446.3340829, (pp. 1-14).

[26] Sohyeon Hwang, and Aaron Shaw. "Rules and Rule-Making in the Five Largest Wikipedias." *Proceedings of the International AAAI Conference on Web and Social Media* 16 (May 31, 2022): 347–57, https://doi.org/10.1609/icwsm.v16i1.19297 studied rule-making on Wikipedia using 20 years of trace data.

[27] In an experiment, McMahon and colleagues found that a search engine with Wikipedia links increased relative click-through-rate (a key search metric) by 80% compared to a search engine without Wikipedia links. Connor McMahon, Isaac Johnson, and Brent Hecht, "The Substantial Interdependence of Wikipedia and Google: A Case Study on the Relationship between Peer Production Communities and Information Technologies," *Proceedings of the International AAAI Conference on Web and Social Media* 11, no. 1 (May 3, 2017): 142–51, https://doi.org/10.1609/icwsm.v11i1.14883. Motivated by this work, an

## 3-3 The Lost Dao

most web searches lead to results that prominently include Wikipedia entries. For all the celebration of the commercial internet, this one public, deliberative, participatory, and roughly consensual resource is perhaps its most common endpoint.

The concept of "Wiki," from which Wikipedia derives its name, comes from a Hawaiian word meaning "quick," and was coined by Ward Cunningham in 1995 when he created the first wiki software, WikiWikiWeb. Cunningham aimed to extend the web principles highlighted above of hypertextual navigation and inclusive 🕸 governance by allowing the rapid creation of linked databases.[28] Wikis invite all users, not just experts, to edit or create new pages using a standard web browser and to link them to one another, creating a dynamic and evolving web landscape in the spirit of 🕸.

While Wikis themselves have found significant applications, they have had an even broader impact in helping stimulate the "groupware" revolution that many internet users associate with products like Google docs but has its roots in the open source WebSocket protocol.[29] HackMD, a collaborative real-time

---

audit study found that Wikipedia appears in roughly 70 to 80% of all search results pages for "common" and "trending" queries. Nicholas Vincent, and Brent Hecht, "A Deeper Investigation of the Importance of Wikipedia Links to Search Engine Results," *Proceedings of the ACM on Human-Computer Interaction* 5, no. CSCW1 (April 13, 2021): 1-15, https://doi.org/10.1145/3449078.

[28] Bo Leuf and Ward Cunningham, *The Wiki Way: Quick Collaboration on the Web* (Boston: Addison-Wesley, 2001).

[29] The term "groupware" was coined by Peter and Trudy Johnson-Lenz in 1978, with early commercial products appearing in the 1990s, such as Lotus Notes, enabling remote group collaboration. Google Docs, originated from Writely launched in 2005, has widely popularized the concept of collaborative real-time editing.

Markdown editor, is used within the g0v community to collaboratively edit and openly share documents such as meeting minutes.[30] While collaboratively constructed documents illustrate this ethos, it more broadly pervades the very foundation of the online world itself. Open-source software (OSS) embodies this ethos of participatory, networked, transnational self-governance. Significantly represented by the Linux operating system, OSS underlies most public cloud infrastructures and connects with many through platforms like GitHub, boasting over 100 million contributors, growing rapidly in recent years especially in the developed world as pictured in Figure D. The Android OS, which powers over 70% of all smartphones, is an OSS project, despite being primarily maintained by Google. The success and impact of such "peer production" has forced the broad reconsideration of many assumptions underlying standard economic analysis.[31]

OSS emerged in reaction to the secretive and commercial direction of the software industry that emerged in the 1970s. The free and open development approach of the early days of ARPANET was sustained even after the withdrawal of public funding, thanks to a global volunteer workforce.

---

[30] *Scrapbox*, a combination of real-time editor with a wiki system, is utilized by the Japanese forum of this book. Visitors of the forum can read the drafts and add questions, explanations, or links to related topics in real time. This interactive environment supports activities like book reading events, where participants can write questions, engage in oral discussions, or take minutes of these discussions. The feature to rename keywords while maintaining the network structure helps the unification of variations in terminology and provides a process to find the good translation. As more people read through, a network of knowledge is nurtured to aid the understanding of subsequent readers.

[31] Yochai Benkler, "Coase's Penguin, Or, Linux and the Nature of the Firm," n.d. http://www.benkler.org/CoasesPenguin.PDF.

Software contributors as a share of working-age adults

2023 Q3
125,462,005
2.4% of working-age adults

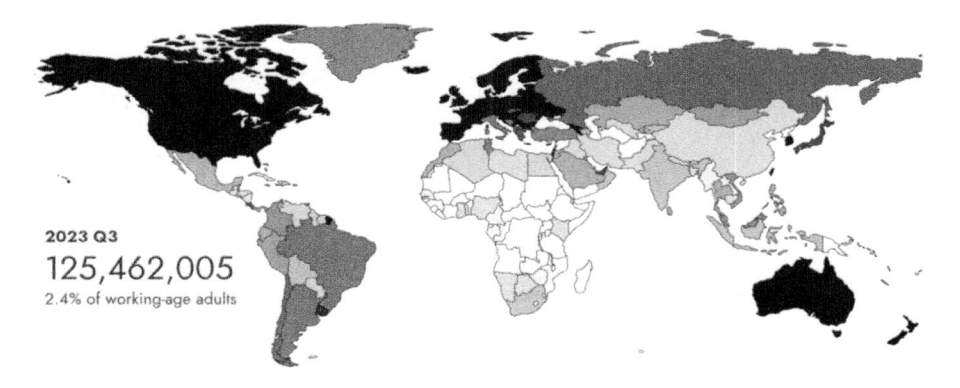

**Figure 3-3-D.** GitHub contributors as share of working-age population by country. Source: GitHub Innovation Graph[32], World Bank[33] and Taiwan Ministry of Interior[34]

Richard Stallman, opposing the closed nature of the Unix OS developed by AT&T, led the "free software movement", promoting the "GNU General Public License" that allowed users to run, study, share, and modify the source code. This was eventually rebranded as OSS, with a goal to replace Unix with an open-source alternative, Linux, led by Linus Torvalds.

OSS has expanded across various internet and computing sectors, even earning support from formerly hostile companies like Microsoft, now owner of leading OSS service company GitHub and employer of one of the authors of this book. This

---

[32] GitHub Innovation graph at https://github.com/github/innovationgraph/

[33] World Bank, "Population ages 15-64, total" at https://data.worldbank.org/indicator/SP.POP.1564.TO.

[34] Department of Household Registration, Ministry of the Interior, "Household Registration Statistics in January 2024" at https://www.ris.gov.tw/app/en/2121?sn=24038775.

represents the practice of 🗒 on a large scale; emergent, collective co-creation of shared global resources. Communities form around shared interests, freely build on each other's work, vet contributions through unpaid maintainers, and "fork" projects into parallel versions in case of irreconcilable differences. The protocol "git" supports collaborative tracking of changes, with platforms like GitHub and GitLab facilitating millions of developers' participation. This book is a product of such collaboration and has been supported by Microsoft and GitHub.

However, OSS faces challenges such as chronic financial support shortage due to the withdrawal of public funding, as explored by Nadia Eghbal (now Asparouhova) in her book *Working in Public*. Maintainers are often unrewarded, and the community's growth increases the burden on them. Nonetheless, these challenges are addressable, and OSS, despite its business model limitations, exemplifies the continuance of the open collaboration ethos (the lost dao) that 🗒 aims to support. Hence, OSS projects will be frequent examples in this book.

Another contrasting reaction to the shift away from public investment in communication networking was exemplified by the work of Lanier from above. A student and critic of AI pioneer Marvin Minsky, he sought to develop a technological program of the same ambition as AI but centered around human experience and communication. Seeing existing forms of communication as being constrained by symbols that can be processed by the ears and eyes like words and pictures, he aspired to empower deeper sharing of and empathy for experiences only expressible by sense like touch and proprioception (the internal sense). Through his research and entrepreneurship during the 1980s, this developed into the field of "virtual reality", one that has been a continual source of

## 3-3 The Lost Dao

innovation in user interaction since, from the wired glove[35] to Apple's release of the Vision Pro.[36]

Yet, as we highlighted above, Lanier carried forward not only the cultural vision of the computer as a communication device; he also championed Nelson's critique of the gaps and failings of what became the internet. He particularly emphasized the lack of base layer protocols supporting payments, secure data sharing and provenance and financial support for OSS. This advocacy combined with the emergence of (pseudonymous) Satoshi Nakamoto's invention of the Bitcoin protocol in 2008 to inspire a wave of work on these topics in and around "web3" communities that harnesses cryptography and blockchains to create shared understanding of provenance and value.[37] While many projects in the space have been influenced by Libertarianism and hyper-financialization, the enduring connection to original aspirations of the internet, especially under the leadership of Vitalik Buterin (who founded Ethereum, the largest smart contract platform), has inspired a number of projects, like GitCoin and decentralized identity, that are central inspirations for ⌗ today as we explore below.

---

[35] A wired glove is an input device like a glove. It allows users to interact with digital environments through gestures and movements, translating physical hand actions into digital responses. Jaron Lanier, *Dawn of the New Everything: Encounters with Reality and Virtual Reality* (New York: Henry Holt and Co., 2017).

[36] The Vision Pro is a head mount display, released by Apple in 2024. This device integrates high-resolution displays with sensors capable of tracking the user's movements, hand actions and the environment to offer an immersive mixed reality experience.

[37] Satoshi Nakamoto, "Bitcoin: A Peer-to-Peer Electronic Cash System" at https://assets.pubpub.org/d8wct41f/31611263538139.pdf.

Other pioneers on these issues focused more on layers of communication and association, rather than provenance and value. Calling their work the "Decentralized Web" or the "Fediverse", they built protocols like Christine Lemmer Webber's Activity Pub that became the basis for non-commercial, community based alternatives to mainstream social media, ranging from Mastodon to Twitter's now-independent and non-profit BlueSky initiative. This space has also produced many of the most creative ideas for re-imagining identity and privacy with a foundation in social and community relationships.

Finally, and perhaps most closely connected to our own paths to 數位 have been the movements to revive the public and multisectoral spirit and ideals of the early internet by strengthening the digital participation of governments and democratic civil society. These "GovTech" and "Civic Tech" movements have harnessed OSS-style development practices to improve the delivery of government services and bring the public into the process in a more diverse range of ways. Leaders in the US include Jennifer Pahlka, founder of GovTech pioneer Code4America, and Beth Simone Noveck, Founder of The GovLab.[38]

Noveck, in particular, is a powerful bridge between the early development of 數位 and its future, having been a driving force behind the Online Deliberation workshops mentioned above, having developed Unchat, one of the earliest attempts at software to serve these goals and which helped inspire the

---

[38] Jennifer Pahlka, *Recoding America: Why Government is Failing in the Digital Age and How We Can Do Better* (New York: Macmillan, 2023). Beth Simone Noveck, *Wiki Government: How Technology Can Make Government Better, Democracy Stronger, and Citizens More Powerful* (New York: Brookings Institution Press, 2010).

work of vTaiwan and more.[39] She went on to pioneer, in her work with the US Patent and Trademark Office and later as Deputy Chief Technology Officer of the US many of the transparent and inclusive practices that formed the core of the g0v movement we highlighted above.[40] Noveck was a critical mentor not just to g0v but to a range of other ambitious civic technology projects around the world from the Kenya collective crisis reporting platform Ushahidi founded by Juliana Rotich and collaborators to a variety of European participative policy-making platforms like Decidim founded by Francesca Bria and collaborators and CONSUL that arose from the "Indignado" movement parallel to g0v in Spain, on the board of which one of us sits. Yet despite these important impacts, a variety of features of these settings has made it challenging for these examples to have the systemic, national, and thus easily traceable macrolevel impacts that g0v had in Taiwan.

Other countries have, of course, excelled in various elements of 道. Estonia is perhaps the leading example and shares with Taiwan a strong history of Georgism and land taxes, is often cited as the most digitized democratic government in the world and pioneered digital democracy earlier than almost

---

[39] Beth Noveck, "Designing Deliberative Democracy in Cyberspace: The Role of the Cyber-Lawyer," New York Law School, n.d. https://digitalcommons.nyls.edu/cgi/viewcontent.cgi?article=1580&context=fac_articles_chapters; Beth Noveck, "A Democracy of Groups," *First Monday* 10, no. 11 (November 7, 2005), https://doi.org/10.5210/fm.v10i11.1289.

[40] Beth Simone Noveck, *Wiki Government* op. cit.; Vivek Kundra, and Beth Noveck, "Open Government Initiative," Internet Archive, June 3, 2009, https://web.archive.org/web/20090603192345/http://www.whitehouse.gov/open/.

any other country, starting in the late 1990s.[41] Finland has built on and scaled the success of its neighbor, extending digital inclusion deeper into society, educational system and the economy than Estonia, as well as adopting elements of digitized democratic participation. Singapore has the most ambitious Georgist-style policies on earth and harnesses more creative 數位 economic mechanisms and fundamental protocols than any other jurisdiction. South Korea has invested extensively in both digital services and digital competence education. New Zealand has pioneered internet-based voting and harnessed civil society to improve public service inclusion. Iceland has harnessed digital tools to extend democratic participation more extensively than any other jurisdiction. Kenya, Brazil and especially India have pioneered digital infrastructure for development. We will return to many of these examples in what follows.

Yet none of these have institutionalized the breadth and depth of 數位 approaches to socio-technical organization across sectors that Taiwan has. It is thus more challenging to take these cases as broad national examples on which to found imagination of what 數位 could mean to the world if it could scale up to bridge the divides of nation, culture and sector and forming both the infrastructural foundation and the mission of global digital society. With that anchoring example and additional hope from these other cases, we now turn to painting in greater depth the opportunity a 數位 global future holds.

---

[41] Gary Anthes, "Estonia: a Model for e-Government" *Communications of the ACM* 58, no. 6 (2015): 18-20.

# Part 4: Freedom

## 4-0 Rights, Operating Systems and 🗆 Freedom

Each day, Luna navigates a labyrinth of tech,
From towering giants to startups, a trek.
Interviews blend into a monotonous dance,
Jargon-filled words, devoid of values' stance.
She yearns for projects of substance and worth,
But opportunities veer from her dreams' birth.

One night, deflated, she sinks into her couch,
Holographic ads engulf her, a sensory slouch.
"Nourishing democracy's river," the narration begins,
Capturing her gaze as the manifesto spins.
Fatigue fades as her mind starts to churn,
Screen in hand, words illuminating her concern.

"To those crafting digital communication's frame,
Ensuring privacy, free speech, and equality's flame."
She imagines a hackathon, debates fierce yet fair,
Creating controversial yet impactful software.

"To innovators mirroring our best relations,
Where clicks and interactions build shared celebrations."
She dreams of heartfelt thanks from children she's aided,
Buying soda with gratitude, community ties unfrayed.

"To pioneers of digital assets, a toast,
Empowering choice, economic equality's coast."
She envisions harnessing her phone's might,
Buying magical potions, adventuring through the night.

"To creators of digital democracy, a cheer,
Where governance is a journey, transparent and clear."
She pictures modernizing her family's ancient vines,
Adopting UN techniques, progress intertwines.

"To moral compasses, navigating the virtual sea,
Ensuring digital realms reflect our highest decree."
Luna realizes her calling transcends mere platforms,
Building societal pillars, enriching human norms.

"Together, this community isn't just coding software,
We're sculpting a legacy of compassion and welfare."
In each digital interaction, a chance to uplift,
Connecting humanity, mending the rifts.

---

Internet founder JCR Licklider (Lick) saw a far wider range of fundamental protocols as foundational to a network society than have thus far been manifest in internet protocols. Yet his analysis was more a laundry list than a philosophical analysis. To articulate a clear vision of the foundations of a 數位 society, in this chapter we draw on the definitional concepts of 數位 to outline what these protocols should consist of and the role they should play socially. Then, in the rest of this part of the book, we systematically explore these, the limits to their implementation today and how they might be more fully achieved.

We argue that 數位 societies must be founded on infrastructure that matches the principles of 數位 in both form and substance. Formally, they must combine seamlessly the closely related political idea of a system of rights and technological concept of an operating system. Substantively they must allow the digital representation of societies in the terms 數位 understands them: as diverse, intersecting social groups and people that jointly undertake ambitious and inclusive collaborations.

## Rights as foundation of democracy

Rights are a ubiquitous feature underpinning democratic life. Most simply imagined, democracy (etymologically "rule of the people") is as a system of government, of collective decision-making by the people, rather than a set of actions a government takes towards its people. Yet evolving from its ancient Athenian origins, shaped by Enlightenment philosophy, and forged through revolution, democracy came to also enshrine a set of fundamental freedoms and rights. While these "rights" have varied across democracies in both time and space, broad patterns are not only identifiable, but have formed the foundation of documents such as the United Nations Universal Declaration of Human Rights (UDHR), including equality, life, liberty, personal security, speech, thought, conscience, property, association—to name a few. While there are important debates around the edges of these principles, in broad outlines they define and defend core aspects of the nearly universal characteristics of human behavior as highlighted by leading anthropologists like Nicholas Christakis.[1] These include what Christakis calls the "social suite", the nearly universal tendency of humans to have a sense of personal identity, to form familial relationships as well as long-term friendships, for these to form the basis of broader cooperative social networks and groups towards which members are "biased", to have differentiated trust within these networks based on relationships and capacities and to learn from each other.

Regardless of the precise makeup and universality, however, what we are most interested in is why they are so integral to democracy as a system of government and why so many people and organizations believe a democracy cannot exist

---

[1] Nicholas A. Christakis, *Blueprint: The Evolutionary Origins of a Good Society* (New York: Little Brown Spark, 2019).

without protecting these rights. In her recent book, *Justice by Means of Democracy*, leading 數位 political philosopher Danielle Allen provides a clear account of this connection: government cannot respond to the "will of the people" if their will cannot be safely and freely expressed.[2] If voting one's conscience is personally dangerous, there is no reason to believe that outcomes reflect anything other than a coercer's will. If citizens cannot form social and political associations free of duress, they cannot coordinate to contest decisions by those in power. If they cannot seek livelihood through a diversity of economic interactions (for example, because they are enslaved either by the state or a private master), we should expect their expressed politics to obey their masters, not their inner voice. Without rights, elections become shams.

Many prominent democracies have "committed suicide" through undermining the rights from which they were forged. Perhaps the most famous example was the Weimar Republic that governed Germany for most of the 30 years between the World Wars and ended in the election of the National Socialist German Workers (Nazi) party to a plurality of seats in the parliament, or Reichstag. This famously led to the appointment of Adolf Hitler as Chancellor.[3] Yet, today many democratic societies have elected leaders and governments that have curtailed liberties in a manner that converts them from democracies to what political scientists Steven Levitsky and Lucan A. Way have labeled "competitive authoritarian" regimes.[4] Concerns about unfree societies undermining

---

[2] Danielle Allen, *Justice by Means of Democracy* (Chicago: University of Chicago Press, 2023).

[3] Richard Evans, *The Coming of the Third Reich* (New York: Penguin, 2005).

[4] Steven Levitsky, *Competitive Authoritarianism: Hybrid Regimes after the Cold War* (Cambridge, UK: Cambridge University Press, 2012).

democratic functioning are neither abstract nor theoretical, but current.

Almost all democracies share a focus, and expect others to share a focus, on the preservation of some strongly overlapping set of such rights of speech and association as basic preconditions for democratic functioning. For example, Scandinavian countries have emphasized the importance of what might be called "positive freedom of speech," namely that every citizen regardless of means has a viable path for their voice to be heard, whereas others such as the US, emphasize "negative freedom of speech," that no one may impede through government intervention the expression of a view. Some societies (e.g. in Europe) tend to emphasize the importance of privacy as a fundamental right necessary for civil society to exist independent of the state and thus for politics to be possible. Others (e.g. in Asia) tend to emphasize rights of assembly and association as more central to democratic function. Despite these variances, the underlying assumption of rights of speech and association is that they protect agency, so citizens may have autonomy to form and advance associations for their common interests, so these common interests can be heard politically.

National (and subnational) governments, especially judicial systems, often play a critical role in ensuring that rights are respected and adjudicating their boundaries. Yet thinking of rights only in terms of national legal systems is misleading. Rights represent deeply held beliefs and values rooted in a range of diverse cultural contexts (national, subnational, transnational, etc.). Rights not only carve the possibility space for human action, but they also confer legitimacy. For example, private workplaces or internet platforms generally may restrict speech. Yet expectations of the rights of free speech put severe limits on the kinds of restrictions on speech employees and customers are willing to accept. Similarly, although documents like the UDHR are generally not legally binding, they still inspire and influence laws in many countries, including decisions made by the Supreme Court of Appeal in South Africa.[5] Institutions of different scales (courts, corporations, civil society groups, etc,) are crucial in ensuring these shared cultural expectations are upheld, and no one institution on their own is the "enforcer" or "source" of rights. Furthermore, many religious traditions hold that the source of rights is divine rather than earthly. In this sense, rights may be thought to exist across, above and beyond states, even if states are one critical defender of them.

Rights are also often aspirations and goals, rather than fixed and attainable realities. Much of the history of the US is a drama about the fulfillment of founding aspirations to equality that were long denied.[6] Many positive rights (e.g. a quality education, decent housing) are outside the capacity or mandate of governments, especially in developing countries, to immediately deliver but nonetheless are testaments to the deepest aspirations of a people.[7]

## Operating systems as foundation of applications

Operating systems (OSs) are a ubiquitous feature underpinning digital life. Almost every digital interaction you have had depends on an underlying OS. Linux is the most ambitious and successful open-source software project of all time. Windows, produced by one of our employers, is another

---

[5] Hurst Hannum, "The Status of the Universal Declaration of Human Rights in National and International Law" *Georgia Journal of International and Comparative Law* 25, no. 287 (1995-1996): 287-397.

[6] Jill Lepore, *These Truths: A History of the United States* (New York: Norton, 2018).

[7] Jamal Greene, *How Rights Went Wrong: How our Obsession with Rights is Tearing America Apart* (Boston: Mariner, 2021).

## 4-0 Rights, Operating Systems and 🕮 Freedom

ubiquitous piece of software. iOS and Android power most smartphones.

OSs roughly define the possibility space for applications that run on them. There are basic traits in terms of performance, appearance, speed, machine memory usage—to name a few—that applications running on a particular OS share and must respect to work on that platform. For example, iOS and Android allow for touch interfaces, while earlier smartphones (like the Blackberry or Palm) relied on styluses or keyboard entry. Even today, iOS and Android apps have different looks, feels and performance characteristics. Applications are coded for one (or possibly multiple) of these platforms, drawing on the processes built into the OS to determine what their application can and cannot do, what it must build bespoke and what it can rely on underlying processes for.

Boundaries are rarely sharp. While Macintosh was the first mass-market computer with a graphical user interface (GUI) OS, earlier computers with a command-line interface sometimes had programs that included elements like a GUI. Similarly, while virtual (VR) and augmented reality (AR) headsets (see our chapter on Immersive Shared Reality below) are much more effective today, there are some VR and AR experiences that can run on a smartphone, properly worn on the head. Furthermore, while OS designers try to include security protocols that defend against application behaviors that violate or threaten the integrity of the underlying OS, they can never hope to avoid them entirely.[8] Many, perhaps most, computer "viruses" are precise examples of such violations. OSs thus define the normal behavior of applications on their system, providing tools

---

[8] Nicole Perlroth, *This is How They Tell Me the World Ends: the Cyberweapons Arms Race* (New York: Bloomsbury, 2021).

applications can harness and reasonable expectations about other applications, defining the terrain of the easily possible.

**Figure 4-0-A.** Apple LISA II Macintosh-XL, one of the first commercially available personal computers using a graphical user interface. Source: bGerhard »GeWalt« Walter, retrieved from Wikipedia. CC0.

OSs constantly must adapt to unanticipated behaviors by applications, both desired (to empower new applications) and undesired (to defend against viruses). These adaptations may be minor and superficial; for example, we often receive updates to the OSs on smartphones to defend against security threats. Or, over time phones have transitioned away from users typing "emoticons" and "emojis" with character combinations to natively integrating them into the OS's typing features.[9] Other changes are more dramatic: for example,

---

[9] Gretchen McCulloch, *Because Internet: Understanding the New Rules of Language* (New York: Riverhead Books, 2019).

Google introducing Android versions compatible with cars and televisions.

OSs also defend their integrity in a variety of ways; while security patches are the sharpest and most adversarial, they coexist with developer education, the building of a broad ecosystem of developer support, the gradual development of customer usage and expectations, and more. Applications built on an OS not only support its internal development but also facilitate updates and even new OSs that can enhance or even rival the original OS. And while different OSs differ and compete, they share many common affordances. They at least partially attempt to allow cross development and both backward and forward compatibility, so that applications designed for previous versions continue to work and that applications are "future proof" to new generations, thereby ensuring users access to a wide range of applications.

OSs are almost always works-in-progress. They aim to support and foster functionality they are incompletely able to support. From these repeated attempts, they recursively learn to offer better support. For example, the first prominent audio "smart assistant" released (such as Apple's Siri and Amazon's Alexa) were often comically low quality; quality improved over time with user participation through the systems themselves, enabling more profound oral functions over time in these operating systems.

## foundations

Systems of rights and OSs have many common traits: they serve as foundations for democratic societies and applications that run on top of them, have background conditions assumed in their processes, require special defense and protection to ensure the integrity of a system, and nonetheless, are often at least partly aspirational and incompletely fulfilled, at times in tension internally. And while they are often backed by powerful enforcement mechanisms, they are also part of a diffuse culture in addition to sharply defined institutions and code.[10] Beyond these general parallels, however, there are two aspects of both rights and OSs that are particularly important and distinctive to a 數位 perspective, which we will draw out and contrast to Libertarian and Technocratic approaches.

*Dynamism*

OSs are self-evidently dynamic, just as systems of rights, on reflection, are. This dynamism is central to 數位. Rights support the democracies that rest on them, and OSs support the applications that run on top of them. But the framers of rights and designers of OSs cannot anticipate (or cannot see except "through a glass darkly") how these foundations will be used, abused and reimagined, as different and sometimes adversarial actors harness (often through technological means) precisely the space they provide for such experimentation and innovation. The PRC's *Great Firewall*, for example, restricts and censors internet content, codifying authoritarianism. Yet, global social media platforms endemic to democracies today have sometimes auctioned the attention of their customers including with micro-targeting for election interference and misinformation by adversaries.[11] Continued effective facilitation of democratic conversation will therefore require not just avoiding of censorship, but also of the sale of

---

[10] Lawrence Lessig, *Code: And Other Laws of Cyberspace* (New York: Basic Books, 1999).

[11] Renee DiResta, Kris Shaffer, Becky Ruppel, David Sullivan, Robert Matney, Ryan Fox, Jonathan Albright and Ben Johnson, "The Tactics & Tropes of the Internet Research Agency" (2019), presented to the Congress of the United States, available at https://digitalcommons.unl.edu/senatedocs/2/.

## 4-0 Rights, Operating Systems and ⌬ Freedom

the attention economy to authoritarian influences, as highlighted by the recent international debate over potential authoritarian influences on the short-form video application, TikTok.[12]

Thus, our understanding of free speech, once considered the primary expression of a right that ensures citizens can freely form and build support for political positions, is being challenged because of information technology. This assumption was founded on an environment where information was scarce and thus its suppression was one of the more effective ways to avoid voices being heard. The present environment is different: information is abundant and attention scarce. Thus it is often easier for adversaries who seek to suppress or censor inconvenient views (attacking the foundations of democracy) to simply flood the information commons with distractions and spam, rather than try to suppress dissidents and unwanted content (documented dramatically by the research of Gary King, Jennifer Pan and Molly Roberts).[13] Under such attacks, ensuring diverse, relevant, and genuine content is surfaced for attention is the challenge, not (only) preventing literal censorship. We suspect our protections around free speech will need to evolve correspondingly and discuss pathways to ensure this happens below.

Yet dynamism is not desirable for its own sake, nor should it be used in a ⌬ vision to subsume the entire structure in the

---

[12] *The Economist*, "Tick, Tock: Will TikTok Still Exist in America?" March 13, 2024.

[13] Gary King, Jennifer Pan and Margaret E. Roberts, "How the Chinese Government Fabricates Social Media Posts for Strategic Distraction, Not Engaged Argument", *American Political Science Review* 111, no. 3 (2017): 484-501.

pursuit of some total goal. Instead, dynamism is an emergent property of adaptive systems discovering their future while renewing and improving their ability to continue to adapt in the future, self-organizing to the "edge of chaos" where complexity thrives and grows. OSs and rights can and should evolve to support the applications and democracies that run on top of it, rather than collapsing to an external will—whether it be the narrow profit interest of a company or some national interest.

*Rights and relationships*

A 數位 understanding of rights recognizes systems and groups as much as people. Freedom of association and religion protect associations and religions themselves, as much as those who compose them. Federalist systems, like the US Constitution, recognize the rights of states and localities, not simply individuals. Even commercial freedoms, while often conceived of in terms of individual choices and bilateral exchange, usually protect at least as vigorously the rights of corporate entities and their contractual arrangements, and rights to collective bargaining. Similarly, OSs protect the interactions between applications and users, as much as applications and users separately. Thus, while some elements of a system of rights or OSs may be thought of as protecting or servicing individual users, there is nothing inherently individualistic about them. Similarly, speech, as a form of communication, necessarily involves more than one party. Whether within OSs or in "the public square," the viability of a communication network depends on the collective participation and consent of its many willing applications, users, and groups.

Furthermore, the entities protecting and defending these freedoms are rarely simply nation-states and their associated institutions. Commercial law is a leading example. As scholars such as Anne-Marie Slaughter and Katharina Pistor have highlighted, international networks of legal rules, trade agreements, and mutual respect for precedents are (for better or worse) central to important topics like intellectual property, antitrust, and capital requirements for financial institutions.[14] Each of these is governed by a different network of professionals, international institutions, and even lobbying groups. Thus, rights are not just held by a diversity of groups forming an interacting network; they are also defined by a similar intersecting network of cultures, institutions, and agents. Rights emerge from intersecting people and social circles defending and protecting their networks of social interactions.

*Contrast with Libertarianism and Technocracy*

The dynamic, networked, and adaptive foundations of ⌘ rights and OSs that respectively support democratic exploration and the evolution of application environments stand in stark contrast to the political and technical monistic perspectives embodied in the ideologies of Libertarianism and Technocracy. Libertarianism is grounded in a rigid and "immutable" set of well-defined historical rights, which primarily emphasize individual private property and the prevention of any "violence" that challenges these property relations. Under this view, rights are abstracted or detached from both other rights and any social or cultural context from which they emerged, belonging exclusively to atomic individuals, and technical systems ought to insulate these rights thoroughly and completely from any change or social intrusion as possible. On the other hand, Technocracy is rooted in the notion of an "objective," "utility" or "social

---

[14] Anne-Marie Slaughter, *A New World Order* (Princeton, NJ: Princeton University Press, 2004). Katharina Pistor, *The Code of Capital: How the Law Creates Wealth and Inequality* (Princeton, NJ: Princeton University Press, 2019).

welfare" function that technical systems are designed to "align to" and maximize. Where Libertarians see rights as absolute, unambiguous, static, and universal, the Technocrats deem them as mere obstacles, or encumbrances, in the pursuit of a definable social good.

## freedom

However skeptical one may be of a future immersed in digital simulated worlds (sometimes called "metaverses"), few would deny that many people live large parts of their lives online these days. In that growing part of our lives, what we do, say, and trade is constrained by the possibilities offered by our technologies that network us together—and thus weave our social fabric. The protocols that connect us thus define our rights in the digital age, forming the OS on which societies run.

Intellectually and philosophically, the tradition we described in our chapter on *Connected Society* focuses on the need to move beyond the simplistic frameworks for property, identity and democracy on which liberal democracies have been built in favor of more sophisticated alternatives that match the richness of social life. Technologically, the early networking protocols that provided a governance framework for intercomputer communication attempted precisely to accomplish this, fusing together the parallel but distinct ideas of rights and OSs. Here, interpersonal networking OSs aimed to provide the fundamental capacities to participants needed to support a conception of rights.

4-0 Rights, Operating Systems and ▣ Freedom

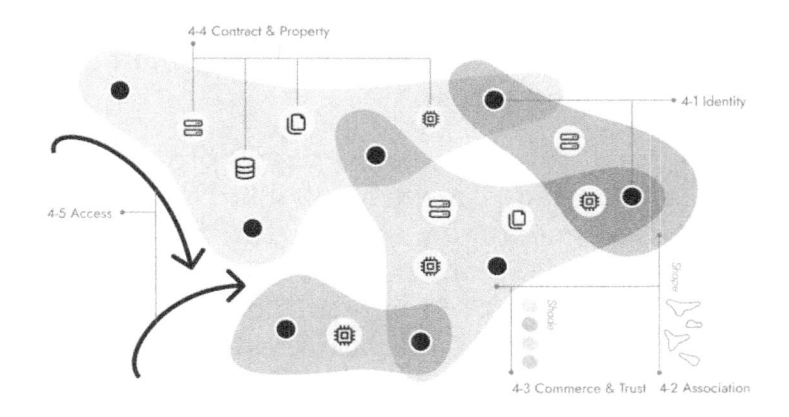

**Figure 4-0-B.** A hypergraph that visualizes people, groups, relationships, and digital assets

Because technological systems are instantiated in formal mathematical relationships, a simple way to see what this requires is to use the canonical mathematical model that directly corresponds to a ▣ description of society, such as the "hypergraph" as pictured in the figure. A hypergraph, which extends the more common idea of a network or graph by allowing groups rather than just bilateral relationships, is a collection of "nodes" (viz. people, represented by the dots) and "edges" (viz. groups, represented by the blobs). The shade of each edge/group represents the strength of the relationship involved (viz. mathematically its "weight" and "direction"), while the digital assets (e.g. data, computation, and digital storage) contained in the edges represent the collaborative substrate of these groups. Any such digital model is, of course, not literally the social world but an abstraction of it and for real humans to access it requires a range of digital tools, which we represent by the arrows entering the diagram. These elements constitute jointly a menu of rights/OS properties which each of the next five chapters articulates one of more completely: identity/personhood, association, commercial trust, property/contract and access.

The project of constructing shared digital protocols to reflect these is in nascent stages, as we highlighted in our chapter *The Lost Dao* and as increasingly accepted by many leading civil actors.[15] Most of the natural, fundamental affordances of networking are not available to most people even in wealthy countries as basic parts of the online experience. There is no widely adopted, non-proprietary protocol for identification[16] that protects rights to life and personhood online, no widely adopted non-proprietary protocols for the ways we

---

[15] Jenny Toomey and Michelle Shevin, "Reconceiving the Missing Layers of the Internet for a More Just Future", *Ford Foundation* available at https://www.fordfoundation.org/work/learning/learning-reflections/reconceiving-the-missing-layers-of-the-internet-for-a-more-just-future/. Frank H. McCourt, Jr. with Michael J. Casey, *Our Biggest Fight: Reclaiming Liberty, Humanity, and Dignity in the Digital Age* (New York: Crown, 2024). McCourt has founded Project Liberty, one of the largest philanthropic efforts around reforming technology largely based on this thesis.

[16] Closed proprietary namespaces and globally managed registries (see "Decentralized Identifiers (DIDs) V1.0." W3C, July 19, 2022, https://www.w3.org/TR/did-core/) as well as verifiable credentials that support collection of credentials from a variety of sources (see "Verifiable Credentials Data Model 1.0." W3C, March 3, 2022. https://www.w3.org/TR/vc-data-model/.)

communicate [17] [18] [19] and form groups online that allows free association, no widely adopted non-proprietary protocols for payments to support commerce on real-world assets and no protocols for the secure sharing of digital assets like computation, memory[20] and data[21] that would allow rights of property and contract in the digital world. Many of these services are almost all controlled and often quasi-monopolized by nation-state governments or more often by private corporations. And even the basic conception of networks that lies behind most approaches to addressing these challenges is too limited, ignoring the central role of intersecting communities. If rights are to have any meaning in our digital world, this must change.

Luckily, it has begun to. A variety of developments in the past decade have fitfully taken up the mantle of the "missing layers" of the internet. This work includes the "web3" and "decentralized web" ecosystems, the Gaia-X data sharing framework in Europe, the development of a variety of digital-native currencies and payment systems and most prominently growing investment in "digital public infrastructure" as exemplified by the "India stack" developed in the country in the last decade. These efforts have been underfunded, fragmented across countries and ideologies and in many cases limited in

---

[17] "More Instant Messaging Interoperability (Mimi)," Datatracker, n.d. https://datatracker.ietf.org/group/mimi/about/.

[18] "Messaging Layer Security," Wikipedia, January 31, 2024, https://en.wikipedia.org/wiki/Messaging_Layer_Security.

[19] "DIDComm v2 Reaches Approved Spec Status!" Decentralized Identity Foundation, July 26, 2022, https://blog.identity.foundation/didcomm-v2/.

[20] See Filecoin Foundation (https://fil.org/) and IPFS (https://www.ipfs.tech/)

[21] See Holochain (https://www.holochain.org/)

⿻ 數位 Plurality: Part 4: Freedom

ambition or misled by Technocratic or Libertarian ideologies or overly simplistic understanding of networks. But together they represent a proof of concept that a more systematic pursuit of ⿻ is feasible. In this part of the book, we will show how to build on these projects, invest in their future and accelerate our way towards a ⿻ future.

## 4-1 Identity and Personhood

In the swiftly moving line, a sense of hope mingled with palpable anxiety. The big screen above reiterated the criticality of the evacuation credentials. Mulu, a well-respected figure in her crumbling community, was on the cusp of a pivotal moment. Climate change had left her homeland in tatters, and she aspired to find solace and clear skies for her daughters in a new land.

As Mulu stepped forward, her past—rich and vibrant—flashed before her. She feared an uncertain future, mainly for her daughters, who faced potential stagnation. The government official, welcoming and friendly, asked her to scan the code for the Common European Asylum System procedure.

Her nearly defunct phone loaded a page with a few straightforward questions.

"Do you grant the common asylum system the consent to request a yes/no answer of…"

1. … your eligibility for our support program?
2. … whether you pose any potential threats to our community?
3. … whether your previous experiences could contribute to a productive role within our society?

She swiftly affixed her signature on the screen. Her phone then began displaying pertinent information to assist her in responding to the questions accurately.

- In a conflict-torn village, you built makeshift schools, bringing smiles to children's faces. This beacon of hope is echoed by 76 trustworthy sources, their praises contained in multiple digital credentials, endorsed by agencies recognized by the EU.

- At a press conference, your firm stance against affiliations with harmful individuals to your community echoed powerfully, backed by 41 digitally signed testimonials, showcasing an unyielding protector of society.
- Your efforts in bridging dialogue between communities and 34 government agencies have crafted a shield of trust and safety around you, each acknowledgment a mark of your dedication, immortalized in a digital shield of recognition.
- Your innovation fueled life-changing projects, celebrated by 78% of your peers through vibrant digital narratives, weaving a dynamic tapestry of your significant contributions to the engineering sector.
- Your support for…

The list goes on. She recalled the lively scenes of children frolicking in the schoolyard, the mentors who inspired her to grace the stage with confidence, and the countless late nights spent collaborating with her dedicated colleagues.

The official's desk illuminated with green lights, approving her application based on the collected affirmations and her proven history.

The same acceptance embraced her daughters, welcoming them to a new beginning. With heartfelt warmth, the official welcomed them into a promising world that seemed ready to know and appreciate them truly, offering a fresh start for Mulu and her daughters to thrive once again.

---

Just as the most fundamental human rights are those to life, personhood and citizenship, the most fundamental protocols for a 數位 society are those that establish and protect participant identities. It is impossible to secure any right or provide any

## 4-1 Identity and Personhood

service without a definition of who or what is entitled to it. Without a reasonably secure identity foundation, any voting system, for example, will be captured by whoever can produce the most false credentials, degenerating into a plutocracy. There is a famous *New Yorker* cartoon from 1993 "On the Internet, nobody knows you're a dog", so famous it has its own Wikipedia page; to the extent this is true, we should expect attempts at online democracy to, quite literally, go to the dogs.[1] This is dramatized in many "Web3" communities that have relied heavily on pseudonymity or even anonymity and have thus often been captured by the interests of those with access to physical and financial resources.[2]

Thus, identity systems are central to digital life and gate access to most online activities: social media accounts, electronic commerce, government services, employment, and subscriptions. What each of these systems can offer depends intimately on *how richly* it can establish user identity. Systems that can only determine that a user is a person will not, for example, be able to offer free benefits without ensuring that person has not already signed up for this offer. Systems that can determine a user is unique but nothing else can only offer services that can legally and practically be made available to every person on the planet.[3] Given the ease of attacks online, only what can be established about a person can securely exist there.

---

[1] Peter Steiner, "On the Internet, nobody knows you're a dog" *The New Yorker* July 5, 1993.

[2] Vitalik Buterin, "On Nathan Schneider on the Limits of Cryptoeconomics", September 26, 2021 at https://vitalik.eth.limo/general/2021/09/26/limits.html.

[3] Puja Ohlhaver, Mikhail Nikulin and Paula Berman, "Compressed to 0: The Silent Strings of Proof of Personhood", 2024 available at https://papers.ssrn.com/sol3/papers.cfm?abstract_id=4749892.

At the same time, many of the simplest ways to establish identity paradoxically simultaneously undermine it, especially online. A password is often used to establish an identity, but unless such authentication is conducted with great care it can reveal the password more broadly, making it useless for authentication in the future as attackers will be able to impersonate them. "Privacy" is often dismissed as "nice to have" and especially useful for those who "have something to hide". But in identity systems, the protection of private information is the very core of utility. Any useful identity system must be judged on its ability to simultaneously establish and protect identities.

To see how this challenge plays out, it is important to keep in mind the several interlocking elements of identity systems:

- Creation: Enrolling in an identity system involves establishing an account and getting assigned an identifier. Different types of systems have different requirements for enrollment related to how confident the system owner is in the identifying information presented by an individual (called *Levels of Assurance*)[4].
- Access: To access the account on an on-going basis, the participant uses a simpler process, such as presenting a password, a key or a multi-factor authentication.
- Linkage: As the participant engages with the systems that their account gives them access to, many of their interactions are recorded and form part of the record that constitutes the system's understanding of them,

---

[4] For example, the International Civil Aeronautics Organization that oversees international commercial air travel developed a Guide to [Evidence of Identity], available at https://www.icao.int/Security/FAL/TRIP/Documents/ICAO%20Guidance%20on%20Evidence%20of%20Identity.pdf.

## 4-1 Identity and Personhood

information that can later be used for other account functions.
- Graph: Among these data that accumulate about a user, many are interactive with other accounts. For example, two users may harness the system to exchange messages or participate together in events. These create data that belong to multiple accounts and thus a "social graph" of connections.
- Recovery: Passwords and keys get lost or stolen and multi-factor authentication systems break down. Most identity systems have a way to recover lost or stolen credentials, using secret information, access to external identity tokens or social relationships.
- Federation: Just as participants creating an account draw on (often verified) information about them from external sources, so too do most accounts—allowing the information contained in them to be at least partially used to create accounts in other systems.[5]

In this chapter, we discuss the operation of existing digital identity systems and the limits to how they navigate the dual imperatives of establishment and protection. We then discuss several important, but limited, on-going initiatives around the world to address these problems. Next, we illustrate how to build on and extend this important work more ambitiously to empower a more ⌬ future. Finally, we highlight how, because of the fundamental role of identity, it connects to and entangles with other fundamental protocols and rights, especially rights of association that we focus on in the next chapter.

---

[5] A leading open standard that allows this is *OAuth* (Open Authorization), an Internet Engineering Task Force open standard published originally as RFC 5849 in 2010 and then updated to OAuth 2.0 as RFC 6749 in 2012.

## Digital identity today

When most people think of their formal "identity", they are usually referring to government issued documents. While these vary across countries, common examples include

- Birth certificates.
- Certificates of enrollment in public programs, often with an associated identification number (such as Social Security for pensions and taxes in the US or the Taiwanese National Health Insurance program).
- Licenses for the use of potentially hazardous tools, such as automobiles or firearms.
- Unified national identification. cards/numbers/databases in some countries.
- Passports for international travel, which constitute perhaps the widest system of identification given its implicit international federation. While these systems vary across countries, they generally share several notable features:
    1. They are canonical and highly trusted in a range of settings, to the point where they are often referred to as "legal" or even "true" identities, with all other forms of identity deriving being either "pseudonyms" or deriving their legitimacy from reference to them.
    2. Partly because of 1), they are used for enrollment into other systems in a variety of contexts (e.g. checking age at a bar, registering for a bank account, paying taxes) even when they were/are intended to be purpose or program specific. A notorious example is the United States Social Security Number (SSN), which was created originally in the 1930's to help manage a new pension

system.[6] By the 1960's it was regularly being requested by many different government and private sector entities. This widespread use meant people's activities across many different contexts could be profiled. In the late 1960s and early 1970s concerns were raised about these practices[7] and a series of laws were passed limiting the ability of agencies within the federal government to share data between agencies and limited the usage of the SSN in the private sector.[8] Since then the federal government has been working to reduce SSN usage and is actively considering alternatives.[9]

---

[6] See Carolyn Puckett, "The Story of the Social Security Number," Social Security Administration, July 2009. https://www.ssa.gov/policy/docs/ssb/v69n2/v69n2p55.html.). See also Kenneth Meiser, "Opening Pandora's Box: The Social Security Number from 1937-2018," UT Electronic Theses and Dissertations, June 19, 2018, http://hdl.handle.net/2152/66022.

[7] Willis Hare, "Records, Computers and the Rights of Citizens," https://www.rand.org/content/dam/rand/pubs/papers/2008/P5077.pdf, Rand Corporation, August 1973.

[8] See "Social Security Numbers: Private Sector Entities Routinely Obtain and Use SSNs, and Laws Limit the Disclosure of This Information." United States General Accounting Office, 2004. https://epic.org/wp-content/uploads/privacy/ssn/gao-04-11.pdf (GAO Report to the Chairman, Subcommittee on Social Security, Committee on Ways and Means, House of Representatives). See also Barbara Bovbjerg, "Social Security Numbers: Federal and State Laws Restrict Use of SSNs, yet Gaps Remain," United States General Accounting Office, 2005, https://www.gao.gov/assets/gao-05-1016t.pdf (GAO Testimony Before the Committee on Consumer Affairs and Protection and Committee on Governmental Operations, New York State Assembly.)

[9] "News Release: DHS Awards for an Alternative Identifier to the Social Security Number," US Department of Homeland Security, October 9, 2020,

3. They are typically issued based on narrow signals of identity, tracing back to other government-issued documents, usually at root a birth certificate that is itself dependent only on the signature of a single doctor. Occasionally these are supplemented by infrequent in-person appearance. However, they are often backstopped by arduous legal procedures if there are persistent disputes over an identity.

These features together create a volatile mix. On the one hand, government-issued identities are foundational to modern life and often intended to avoid invasions of privacy. On the other hand, they do a poor job protecting identity because they are used across so many contexts that they cannot be kept secret and are based on thin signals. Furthermore, as we discuss below, these problems are currently being exacerbated by the advance of technologies, like generative foundation models (GFMs), which can easily imitate and modify content and draw sophisticated inferences from public signals. Additionally, the process of creating digital versions of these IDs has been slow and inconsistent across jurisdictions. For all these reasons, existing physical (paper or plastic) government-issued IDs are in an increasingly precarious position and offer quite an unattractive trade-off between establishment and protection.

A second group of widely used identity systems are account management for the leading technology platforms such as Meta, Amazon, Microsoft (Microsoft Accounts, LinkedIn, GitHub), Alphabet, Apple and others. These are the platforms

---

https://www.dhs.gov/science-and-technology/news/2020/10/09/news-release-dhs-awards-alternative-identifier-social-security-number.

## 4-1 Identity and Personhood

have leveraged open standards like OAuth [10] and OpenID Connect[11] to allow user to use their account from there platform to log-into other systems sometimes called "single sign-on" (SSO). These services are the foundation of the "sign in with ..." buttons that often appear on authentication interfaces online. Via this single sign in process the issuer of the identifier, a.k.a. "the identity provider", the large platform "sees" everywhere an individual who has an account with them and uses it elsewhere goes.

Just as there are a range of government-issued identities that nonetheless share common traits, so too SSO systems are diverse but have important features in common:

1. They are mostly administered by private, for-profit corporations. The convenience they offer and the data they rely on (more on this soon) are used as features to maximize customer retention and value.

2. They harness a wide range of signals and properties of users to maintain the integrity of and harness the value of user identities. While the specifics of the type of data (e.g. purchase histories, social network connections, email correspondence, GPS locations) vary by case, in all cases the maintainer has extensive, detailed, extended and sometimes

---

[10] OAuth 2.0 is the industry-standard protocol for authorization and provides specific authorization flows for web applications, desktop applications, mobile phones, and living room devices. https://oauth.net/2/ IETF Working Group https://datatracker.ietf.org/wg/oauth/about/

[11] OpenID Connect enables application and website developers to launch sign-in flows and receive verifiable assertions about users across Web-based, mobile, and JavaScript clients. https://openid.net/developers/how-connect-works/

intimate awareness of a full profile of behavior by the subject often across multiple domains. [12]

3. Due to point 2, these network endpoint identifiers are widely federated and are accepted for a range of authentication services online, including by services with a limited relationship with the SSO provider.

There are two other important classes of entities that collect a lot of identity information or attributes about people. They share many of these characteristics, but are not digital platform SSO systems and they do not have a direct relationship with the people about whom they collect information: advertising, data brokers, credit-scoring and national security agencies (who develop dossiers on people for both general surveillance and their own screening purposes for employees who agree to be screened to get clearances to do their work).

They similarly rely on rich signals, with high integrity and broad use, but without the public legitimacy of more standard government identities. These data collection systems thus stand on the opposite end of the trade-off spectrum from government identities. They are far better at providing a rich profile about people; however, they operate largely in the shadows because their "all-seeing" nature is socially illegitimate and vests a great deal of power in a few hands.

At a neat half-way point between these extremes in most countries sit accounts for crucial/foundational services such as bank accounts and mobile telephones. Banking is typically regulated by the government and requires government issued ID before you can enroll (a process known as "know your

---

[12] Zuboff, op. cit., *The Age of Surveillance Capitalism*

customer" or KYC). Telecommunications providers often ask for government issued ID to support effective account management (where do we send the bill) and recovery (I lost my phone. Yes, it is me.) and in some countries they are required to know who their customers are before they can get a phone number. Both banks and telephone companies are privately administered and linked to rich user data that can be harnessed for security, and thus often become a crucial input to other identity systems (like SSO systems) but are typically far more regulated than SSO systems and thus typically have greater legitimacy and portability across private providers. In many contexts these systems are thus viewed as a useful combination of security and legitimacy, anchoring ultimate security for many services through multi-factor authentication. However, they at the same time suffer many of the flaws of both corporate surveillance and insecurity, as both can be relatively easily stolen, are hard to recover if stolen and lack the strong legal grounding of government-issued IDs.

In a different direction entirely from this spectrum are smaller, more diverse, and more local identity systems, in both more traditional contexts and digitally native contexts. Examples of these are explored by Kaliya Young in her book *Domains of Identity*:[13]

- Civil society enrollment and transactions, such as educational credentials, membership in professional associations and trade-unions, political parties and religious organizations.
- Employment enrollment and transactions, such as work-related credentials and access.

---

[13] Kaliya "Identity Woman" Young, *Domains of Identity: A Framework for Understanding Identity Systems in Contemporary Society* (London: Anthem Press, 2020).

- Commercial enrollment and transactions, such as loyalty cards and membership in private insurance.
- Pseudonymous identities used in a variety of online social and political interactions from "dark web" fora (e.g. 4chan or Reddit) to video game and virtual world interactions (e.g. Steam).
- Accounts used in "Web3" for financial transactions, Distributed Autonomous Organizations (DAOs, more on these below) and associated discussions often on servers such as Discord.
- Personal digital and real-life connections that record, in machine or biological (viz. mental) substrates shared personal and relational histories, communications exchanged, etc.

These identities are the most 數 of all we have discussed and have the least common characteristics. They share a few features precisely related to their fragmentation and heterogeneity:

1. These systems are highly fragmented, currently have limited interoperability, are rarely federated or connected, and thus tend to have very limited scope of application. Emerging standards such as Verifiable Credentials [14] are seeking to address this challenge.

2. At the same time, these sources of identification are often seen as the most natural, appropriate, and non-invasive. They seem to arise from the natural course of human interactions, rather than from top-down mandates or power structures. They are

---

[14] Verifiable Credentials Data Model v1.1 W3C Recommendation 03 March 2022 https://www.w3.org/TR/vc-data-model/

## 4-1 Identity and Personhood

viewed as highly legitimate, and yet not as a definitive or external source of "legal" identity, often being seen as pseudonymous or otherwise private.

3. They tend to record rich and detailed, personal information, but in a narrow context or slice of life, clearly separated from other contexts. Thus, they have strong potential recovery methods based on personal relationships.

4. They tend to have poor digital user experience; either they are not digitized at all, or the process of managing the digital interface is unfriendly to non-technical users.

While these examples are perhaps most marginal to digital identity, they are also perhaps most representative of its systemic state. Digital identity systems are heterogeneous, generally quite insecure, only weakly interoperable, have limited functionality while allowing entities with concentrated power to engage in extensive surveillance and breaking norms of privacy that in many cases they were established to protect. This problem is increasingly widely recognized, leading to focus in many technology projects on overcoming it.

### Public and decentralized digital identity

In sharp contrast to most prominent trends in technology, the most influential developments in identity tools have been in and/or targeting as a market the development world, often under the banner of "Digital Public Infrastructure". This partly arises from the fact that identity systems are particularly underdeveloped in these countries, creating a strong need for such systems. Perhaps partly as a result, however, these systems have opted to follow a highly unitary and centralizing structure, usually based on biometrics, that while providing an impressive demonstration of what a digital-native identity infrastructure can accomplish, also falls short of helping richly establish and strongly protect identity.

The most prominent example is the Aadhaar identity system supported by the Indian government as part of the India Stack program. Aadhaar enrollment originally required residents to present some existing type of identification from any number of potential entities - existing state level governments, ration cards (the list was extensive).[15] Each enrollee had a photo taken, each iris scanned and shared all ten fingerprints. The new enrollees had the information associated with their identities checked against the database to see if they had already been enrolled. If unique, they were issued an Aadhaar number which was sent to them in the mail on a card. India's Unique Identification Authority (UIDAI).[16] Through special entities that have capabilities to do authentication against the database provides authentication services - people who are interacting with government services were able to assert an Aadhaar number and then presented a fingerprint that was sent into the system and a yes/no answer was returned on authentication.

Subsequently the Indian Supreme Court limited the extent to which the system can be used by the private sector.[17]

---

[15] They were asked for only 4 pieces of demographic information, name, birthdate, sex and physical mailing address (although phone numbers and e-mail addresses were also requested but not required). These are collected by enrollment agents who send the new enrollee information into the central databases managed by the Unique Identification Authority of India in batches.

[16] The official UIDAI site https://uidai.gov.in/en/

[17] Read: Full Text of the Supreme Court's Verdict in the Aadhaar Case. Of the five judge-bench that delivered the verdict, three justices delivered separate opinions. https://thewire.in/law/aadhaar-judgment-supreme-court-full-text

### 4-1 Identity and Personhood

Nonetheless, Aadhaar has enrolled more than 99% of the Indian population because enrollment agents were paid to maximize enrollment across the country. The government has also made Aadhaar a key part of social service provisioning including monthly ration that over 800 million people get monthly and has also pushed to link Tax ID numbers (called PANs). It is believed that Aadhaar achieved some of the most impressive mixes of scale, inclusion of marginalized communities and security of any identity scheme in the world. The Aadhaar model has inspired the development of the Modular Open-Source Identity Platform (MOSIP) [18] and its adoption in Asia (e.g. Philippines, Sri Lanka) and Africa (e.g. Uganda, Morocco, Ethiopia). To date they have enrolled 100 million people. The MOSIP platform has created a decentralized identity module, Inji[19], that gives whoever deploys it the ability to issue verifiable credentials into the wallets of residents/citizens enrolled in each national system.

Partly inspired by this success, a group of technologists including OpenAI Co-Founder Sam Altman and collaborators launched Worldcoin in 2019 with the aim of becoming the first globally universal biometric identity.[20] Using a propriety "orb", they have scanned the irises of several million people, almost exclusively in developing countries, to date. Harnessing cryptography, they "hash" these scans so that they cannot be viewed or recovered, but any future scan can be checked against them to ensure uniqueness. They use this to initialize

---

[18] "Overview," MOSIP, 2021, https://docs.mosip.io/1.2.0/overview.

[19] Inji is a user-centric digital credential stack in MOSIP for all types of credentials and identification solutions. https://docs.mosip.io/inji/

[20] Elizabeth Howcroft, and Martin Coulter, "Worldcoin Aims to Set up Global ID Network Akin to India's Aadhaar," *Reuters*, November 2, 2023, https://www.reuters.com/technology/worldcoin-aims-set-up-global-id-network-akin-indias-aadhaar-2023-11-02/.

an account that they deposit units of a cryptocurrency into. Their mission is to ensure that, as GFMs become increasingly capable of imitating humans, that there remains a secure foundation for identity that could be used, for example, to distribute an equal "universal basic income" to every person on the planet or to allow participation in voting and other universal rights.

Despite this strong interest in these broad biometric systems, they have important limits on their ability to establish and protect identities. Linking such a wide variety of interactions to a single identifier associated with a set of biometrics from a single individual collected at enrollment (or registration) forces a stark trade-off. On the one hand, if (as in Aadhaar) the administrators of the program are constantly using biometrics for authentication, they become able to link or see activities to these done by the person who the identifier points to, gaining an unprecedented capacity to surveil citizen activities across a wide range of domains and, potentially, to undermine or target the identities of vulnerable populations.[21] Activists have raised concerns over this issue have been repeatedly raised in relation to the status of the Muslim minority in India.

On the other hand, if privacy is protected, as in Worldcoin, by using biometrics only to initialize an account, the system becomes vulnerable to stealing or selling of accounts, a problem that has decimated the operation of related

---

[21] It is worth noting, however, that if such systems are augmented with cryptography such as Zero-Knowledge Proofs (ZKPs), they can partially protect the user's privacy. Projects such as Anon-Aadhaar allow an Aadhaar user to selectively reveal only a subset of information to some entity in a provable way. "Advancing Anon Aadhaar: What's New in V1.0.0," Mirror, February 14, 2024, https://mirror.xyz/privacy-scaling-explorations.eth/YnqHAxpjoWl4e_K2opKPN4OAy5EU4sIJYYYHFCjkNOE.

## 4-1 Identity and Personhood

services.[22] Because most services people seek to access require more than proving they are a unique human (e.g. that they have a particular name, an ID number of some type issued to them by a recognized government, that they are a citizen of some country, and maybe some other attributes like educational or employment credentials at a company etc.) this extreme preservation of privacy undermines most of the utility of the system. Furthermore, such systems place a great burden on the technical performance of biometric systems. If eyeballs can, sometime in the future, be spoofed by a GFM combined with advanced printing technology, such a system may be subject to an extreme "single point of failure".[23] In short, despite their important capacity for inclusion and simplicity, biometric systems are too reductive to achieve establish and protect identities with the richness and security required to support 🗔.

Starting from a very different place, another set of work on identity has reached a similar challenging set of trade-offs. Work on "decentralized identity" grew from many of the concerns about digital identity we have highlighted above: fragmentation, lack of natural digital infrastructure, issues with privacy, surveillance and corporate control. A key founding document was Microsoft identity architect Kim Cameron's "Laws of Identity" [24], which emphasized the importance of user control/consent, minimal disclosure to appropriate parties, multiple use cases, pluralism of participation, integration with human users and consistency of experience across context. Kim

---

[22] Ohlhaver et al., op. cit.

[23] Vitalik Buterin, "What Do I Think about Biometric Proof of Personhood?" July 24, 2023 at https://vitalik.eth.limo/general/2023/07/24/biometric.html.

[24] Kim Cameron, "7 Laws of Identity," *Kim Cameron's Identity Weblog*, August 20, 2009, https://www.identityblog.com/?p=1065.

Cameron worked on developing the cardspace [25] system while at MSFT and this became the InformationCard [26] standards. These did not get market adoption in part because they were too early - smart phones were not widely adopted yet and the idea that this device could hold a wallet for people.

The emergence of blockchain distributed ledgers renewed interest in the decentralized identity community on achieving individual control over identifiers rather than being excessively tied to a single issue. This spurred the creation of the Decentralized Identifiers (DID) standard at the W3C that defines a way to have decentralized globally resolvable endpoints with associated public keys.[27] This creates a way to grant individuals "ownership" over identities, rooted in "public" data repositories such as blockchains, and create standardized formats for a variety of entities to issue digital credentials referencing these identifiers.

The systems have the flexibility to allow individuals to have multiple accounts/pseudonyms. They also share a common practical challenge, namely that for an individual to truly "own" their identity, they must either control some ultimate key that gives them access to it and/or be able to reliably recover that key without resort to some higher, controlling authority. Other than possibly biometrics (the problems with which we discussed above), there is no widely agreed method to allow recovery without a trusted authority and no example of keys

---

[25] Wikipedia, "Windows CardSpace," December 14, 2023, https://en.wikipedia.org/wiki/Windows_CardSpace.

[26] Wikipedia, "Information Card," January 25, 2024, https://en.wikipedia.org/wiki/Information_card.

[27] "Decentralized Identifiers (DIDs) V1.0," W3C, July 19, 2022, https://www.w3.org/TR/did-core/.

## 4-1 Identity and Personhood

that individuals have been reliably able to self-manage in large, diverse societies.

Despite these common challenges, the details of these schemes vary dramatically, however. On one extreme, advocates of "verifiable credentials" (VCs) prioritize privacy and the ability of users to control which of the claims about them are presented at any time. On the other extreme, advocates of "soulbound tokens" (SBTs) or other blockchain-centric identity systems emphasize the importance of credentials that are public commitments to e.g. repay a loan or not produce further replicas of a work of art and thus require that the claims be publicly tied to an identity. Here, again, in both the challenges around recovery and the DID/VC-SBT debate we see the unattractive trade-off between establishing and protecting identities.

**Identity as an intersection**

Is there a way past this seemingly irreconcilable conflict, ensuring secure establishment and strong protection of identity without centralized surveillance? The natural answer draws on the tradition of ⌘ we described in *Connected Society* and *The Lost Dao*: harnessing the ⌘ nature of identity and the potential of network architectures. Just as packet switching reconciled and connected decentralization and performance and hypertext reconciled speed with a diversity of pathways through text, it seems increasingly plausible that, with the right mix of experimentation and standards building, a ⌘ approach to identity could reconcile the goals of establishing and protecting identities.

The basic idea can be understood perhaps most easily by contrast to biometrics. Biometrics (e.g. iris scans, fingerprints, genetic information) are a detailed set of physical information that uniquely identifies a person and that in principle anyone with access to that person and appropriate technology may ascertain. Yet people are not just biological but sociological beings. Far richer than their biometric profile is the set of shared histories and interactions they have with other people and social groups. These may include biometrics; after all, anytime we meet someone in person we at least partly perceive their biometrics, and they may leave traces of others behind. But they are far from limited to them. Instead, they encompass all behaviors and traits that are naturally jointly observed in the course of social interactions, including

- Location, as the very act of being together in a place implies joint knowledge of others' locations (which is the basis of alibis in forensics) and most people spend most of their time in the detectable vicinity of other
- Communication, as it always has at least two participants.
- Actions, whether at work, play or workshop are usually performed for or in the presence of some audience...in fact, as we quoted in our chapter *What is 數位?*, this is how Hannah Arendt defines "action".
- Personality traits, which usually manifest in interactions with other people. In fact, the way we think of other's identities are usually primarily in terms of such "sociometrics": things we did with the person, places we went together, things they did and ways they acted, rather than primarily their appearance or biology.

This social, 數位 approach to online identity was pioneered by danah boyd in her astonishingly farsighted master's thesis on "faceted identity" more than 20 years ago.[28] While she focused

---

[28] danah boyd, *Faceted Id/entity: Managing Representation in a digital world* 2002, Master's Thesis for Program in Media Arts and Sciences at the Massachusetts Institute of Technology, available at https://www.media.mit.edu/publications/faceted-identity-managing-representation-in-a-digital-world/.

## 4-1 Identity and Personhood

primarily on the benefits of such a system for feelings of personal agency (in the spirit of Simmel), the potential benefits for the balance between identity establishment and protection are even more astonishing:

- Comprehensiveness and redundancy: Jointly, these data cover almost everything meaningful there is to know about a person; the great majority of what we are is determined by various interactions and experiences shared with others. For almost anything we might want to prove to a stranger, there are some combination of people and institutions (typically many) who can "vouch" for this information without any dedicated strategy of surveillance. For example, a person wanting to prove that they are above a particular age could call on friends who have known them for a long time, the school they attended, doctors who verified their age at various times as well, of course, on governments who verified their age. Such attribute verification systems are common: when applying for some forms of government identification many jurisdictions allow a variety of attribute-proving methods for addresses including bank statements, utility bills, leases etc.
- Privacy: Perhaps even more interestingly, all of these "issuers" of attributes know this information from interactions that most of us feel consistent with "privacy": we do not get concerned about the co-knowledge of these social facts in the way we would surveillance by a corporation or government. However, we will be more precise in the next chapter about the sense in which these (should/could) approaches allay privacy concerns.
- Progressive authentication: While standard verification by a single factor allows the user to gain confidence in the attested fact/attribute equal to their confidence in the verifying party/system, such systems allow a wide

range of confidence to be achieved by drawing on more and more trusted issuers of attributes. This allows adaptation to a variety of use cases based on the security they require.

- Security: 🗒 also avoids many of the problems of a "single point of failure". The corruption of even several individuals and institutions only affects those who rely on them, which may be a very small part of society, and even for them the redundancy described above implies they may only suffer a partial reduction in the verification they can achieve. This is particularly important given the potential risks (as mentioned above) to e.g. biometric systems from advances in AI and printing technology. Given the basis of other verification methods above are much more diverse (a range of communicative acts, physical encounters etc.) the chances of these all fail based on a particular technological advance is far less likely.
- Recovery: This approach also offers a natural solution to one of the most challenging problems above: the recovery of lost credentials. As noted there, recovery typically relies on interactions with a single, powerful entity that can investigate the validity of a claim to an account; alternatives based on giving individuals full "ownership" are usually highly insecure to hacking or other attacks. Yet a natural alternative would be for individuals to rely on a group of relationships allowing, for example, 3 of 5 friends or institutions to recover their key. Such "social recovery" has become the gold standard in many Web3 communities and is increasingly being adopted even by major platforms

### 4-1 Identity and Personhood

such as Apple.[29] As we will explore in a later chapter, more sophisticated approaches to voting could make such an approach even more secure by ensuring that distinct parts of an individual's network who are unlikely to cooperate against her interest would together be able to recover her credentials, something we call "community recovery".[30]

The above benefits are remarkable when compared to the trade-offs described above. But essentially they are fairly simple extensions of the benefits we discussed in *The Lost Dao* that 🔲 structures generally have over more centralized ones, the benefits that motivated the move to packet switching architectures for communications networks in the first place. This is why some of the leading organizations seeking to achieve a future like this, such as the Trust over IP Foundation, draw tight analogies to the history of the creation of the internet protocols themselves. There are of course many technical and social challenges in making such a 🔲 system work:

- Inter-operation: Making such a system work would obviously require a very wide range of present identity and information systems to interoperate, while maintaining their independence and integrity. Achieving this would obviously be a herculean task of coordination, but it is fundamentally a similar one to that underlying the internet itself.

---

[29] Vitalik Buterin, "Why We Need Broad Adoption of Social Recovery Wallets", January 11, 2021 at https://vitalik.eth.limo/general/2021/01/11/recovery.html.

[30] Puja Ohlhaver, E. Glen Weyl and Vitalik Buterin, "Decentralized Society: Finding Web3's Soul", 2022 at https://papers.ssrn.com/sol3/papers.cfm?abstract_id=4105763.

- Complexity: Managing and processing trust and verification relationships with such a diversity of individuals and institutions is beyond the capacity of most people or even institutions. Yet there are several natural approaches to addressing this complexity. One is to harness the growing capacity of GFMs, trained to adapt to the relationships and context of the individual or institution using the model, to extract meaning from such diverse signals; we discuss this possibility extensively in a later chapter on Adaptive Administration. Another approach is to limit the number of relationships any individual or institution has to manage and rely on either institutions of medium size (e.g. medium businesses, churches, etc.) that play an intermediary roles (which Jaron Lanier and one of us have called "mediators of individual data or MIDs) or on "friends of friends" relationships (which we call "transitive trust") which are known to connect, within a small number of links (roughly six), almost any two people on earth.[31] We will discuss the appeal, trade-offs and compatibility between these two approaches below.
- Trust at a distance: Another closely related problem is that many of the natural verifiers for strangers we meet may be people who we do not know ourselves. Here again, some combination of using transitive trust and MIDs as we discuss shortly is natural. Currency, as we will discuss in a later chapter of this part of the book, may also play a role here.

---

[31] Jaron Lanier and E. Glen Weyl, "A Blueprint for a Better Digital Society" *Harvard Business Review: Big Idea Series (Tracked)* September 28, 2018: Article 5 available at https://hbr.org/2018/09/a-blueprint-for-a-better-digital-society. Duncan J. Watts and Steven H. Strogatz, "The Collective Dynamics of 'Small World' Networks" *Nature* 393 (1998): 440-442.

- Privacy: Finally, while most people would feel comfortable with the *recording* of information from the natural flow of social events above, the *sharing* of it for verification could pose important privacy issues. Such information is meant to *stay* in the natural flow of social life and a great deal of care is require ensuring any use of it for identity verification does not violate these norms of "contextual integrity". Addressing this challenge is the focus of the next chapter, as we discuss at the end of this one.

## identity

How can we manage the complexity and social distance involved in identity systems? We will return in a future chapter to the potential role of GFMs. Focusing instead on firmly network-based approaches, the two natural strategies correspond to the two types of networks that in *The Lost Dao* we recounted internet pioneer Paul Baran imagining: "decentralization" (also called "polycentrism", which we will use), where there are many verifiers of significant size but not so many as to create overwhelming complexity, or "distribution", where there are few larger-scale verifiers and we instead use transitive trust to span social distances.[32] A basic heuristic that is useful to keep in mind in considering all these possibilities is the "Dunbar number". This is the number (usually around 150) of people that an anthropologist, Robin Dunbar, argued people could maintain stable relationships with absent significant information technology.[33] Whatever the precise number is, it seems clear most people cannot manage more

---

[32] Cameron, op. cit.

[33] R.I.M. Dunbar, "Neocortex Size as a Constraint on Group Size in Primates", *Journal of Human Evolution* 22, no. 6 (1992): 469-493.

than a few hundred relationships, evaluation of reputation, etc. without significant technological assistance.

The polycentric approach tries to manage this problem by limiting the number of players. While this obviously limits some, it is not a major problem if participants maintain a reasonable diversity of affiliations. Suppose, for example, that we have a population of 10 billion, each person maintains 100 relationships with potentially verifying institutions (e.g. governments, churches, employers etc.). Suppose that to have a reasonable chance for verification to work, any two-person meeting must share at least 5 overlapping memberships. If memberships are randomly distributed, 300 verifiers could co-exist and still allow the chance that verification fails for any random pair of individuals to be one in several million. Of course, individuals who meet are rarely random nor do they form their affiliations randomly, nor are 5 overlapping memberships likely to be absolute necessary for most interactions especially among people meeting randomly. All of these suggest many more verifiers could thrive in such an environment of memberships.

Yet this number would clearly be far smaller than the population size, perhaps around 100,000, the number with the property that goes into 10 billion 100,000 times. This would be vastly more than our current identity landscape, allowing a far better trade-off between autonomy/control and functionality/security. But is even more possible?

One of the most important discoveries in quantitative sociology is that, despite Dunbar-like limits, by traversing a few degrees of separation most humans are connected to each other. To see how this is possible, suppose that each of us can only maintain 100 relationships. This would imply that we might have $100^2 = 10,000$ second degree relationships, $100^3 = 1,000,000$ third degree relationships, $100^4 = 100{,}000{,}000$ fourth degree relationships and

$100^5 = 10{,}000{,}000{,}000$ fifth degree relationships, greater than the global population. Thus, it is entirely possible that each of us could be within 5 degrees of separation from every other person on the planet. Given that some of these relationships will, at any level, overlap, the number of degrees of separation should be somewhat larger: most sociological studies have found roughly 6 degrees of separation between any two randomly chosen people.[34] Furthermore, at least if one goes to chains of 7, there are usually many mostly independent chains of social connection between any two people.

Furthermore, the idea of establishing relationships, information and validity through transitive chains is ancient and common. It lies behind the concept of an introduction, the game "telephone" (which emphasizes some of its limitations) and the popular professional social network LinkedIn. Finding and managing the many possible chains of introductions between socially distant people clearly requires some technical support, but nothing much greater than has already been shown possible by computer science research where it is known as the classical "maximum flow" problem. The problem is actually quite similar to that underlying the packet switching that powers the internet.

Furthermore, the decentralized and distributed strategies can be combined to greatly amplify each other. To take a simple example, consider our suggestion above that there might be 100,000 issuers of attributes. In a world of 10 billion, each would have to be managing relationships with 100,000 participants, on average. If they were also able to manage a similar number of relationships with other issuers, every issuer

---

[34] Watts and Strogatz, op. cit.

would have a direct relationship with every other issuer. Two degrees of separation could do far more, allowing millions of issuing organizations to thrive under the same logic that can leverage the attributes from other issuers to do verification. Thus, a mixture of transitive trust and polycentrism can quite easily allow, even without any of the magic of GFMs we discuss below, a highly 數位, and thus both functional and private, identity landscape.

## Identity and association

The key question that then remains is whether the process of such 數位 social verification would end up undermining the protection of identities. After all, a core part of why we have such a dysfunctional identity landscape is that liberal democratic polities have resisted the creation of identity systems is precisely this fear. If we are to build better alternatives, we need to ensure they are better most of all along this dimension. Yet, to do so requires us to dig deeper into what precisely "privacy" and "control" mean from a 數位 perspective.

As we noted above, almost everything relevant about us is known by others and is typically just as much about them as us. None of us feels this bare fact as an infringement on privacy. In fact, erasing the memory of our first kiss from the mind of the partner to that kiss would be just as much a violation of privacy as sharing that information inappropriately. What we are after, therefore, is not well-described by the term "privacy". It is about information remaining in the social setting for which it was intended, what leading privacy scholar Helen Nissenbaum calls "contextual integrity".[35] In fact, it requires a certain kind of

---

[35] Helen Nissenbaum, "Privacy as Contextual Integrity", *Washington Law Review* 119 (2004): 101-139.

publicity: if information is not shared and understood by those for whom it is intended this can be as damaging as if information is over-shared. Given that these are inherently social settings, furthermore, they are not primarily about the individual choice or protection, but rather the protection of groups of people against violations of their collective norms about information. In short, the central problems are about another fundamental right: freedom of association. In essence, systems supporting and implementing the right of personhood must simultaneously bolster the freedom of association and the dual challenge of establishing and protecting associations parallels those in the identity context.

## 4-2 Association and 🞐 Publics

As the cacophony of war reverberated through the narrow streets of the Middle Eastern city, a relentless barrage of gunfire and the ghostly dance of flames cast a shroud over the metropolis, with a blackout plunging nearly half of it into fear-strewn darkness. The digital backbone of the city, once a beacon of interconnected brilliance, lay in tatters—government databases lay in ruin, communications networks severed by skilled enemy hacks, leaving the city's guardians grappling for any remaining strategies to wrest back control from the chaos.

Amidst the chaos, the hope of an entire nation rested on a group of hackers. They were the last bastions of defense, the last guardians. This decentralized group convened a hackathon aptly named "Guard." Faisal was one of them. In a world in chaos, the group's unwavering determination and skill had made them a beacon of hope.

Slipping on his headset, he activated his assistive agent, establishing an untraceable internet address. He turned on the privacy option of his digital wallet, showcasing his proof of citizenship and a myriad of credentials from hackathons gone by. Such precautions had become essential in these dark times.

As Faisal entered the "Guard" interface, it seemed just like any other online chatroom. The anonymity was palpable, as no one spoke or even typed a message. All that could be seen were silent avatars representing participants. But the difference lay in its secure foundation, which stopped anyone in the room from showing its contents to those outside while ensuring everyone there had heard exactly what was said in this last bastion of hope.

The host, the only voice in the silent room, began, "Several introductions and ground rules are about to show on your screen. Each of you will be asked questions to confirm your presence." A warning followed, highlighting the risk of expulsion for non-compliance or suspicion.

Soon, a virtual Roman soldier appeared on screen, laying out the grand vision of "Guard"—to construct a decentralized defense system for the digital city. Faisal quickly went through the questions, and upon returning to the main room, found that only half of the initial participants remained. This filtering process seemed to break the ice, as the room came alive with chatter.

Wasting no time, the guardians began their mission. Faisal, with his expertise, was naturally drawn to the power grid security group. But their conversation was interrupted by a sudden ring. Faisal picked up the phone, the voice from the other side rushed, "Have you gotten anything? We need the rest of the power grids down."

The urgency in the voice was palpable. Faisal replied, "I can't find a secretive way in. The security is covered by the protocols. I can formally request access, but everyone must agree." He continued, "If even one participant objects, I might receive a copy, but I won't be able to discern if it's authentic."

"Is there no way to duplicate the original code?" the voice asked, desperation evident.

"I'll keep trying," Faisal promised.

---

In his classic summary of his observations of *Democracy in America*, French aristocrat and traveler Alexis De Toqueville highlighted the centrality of the civic association to American self-government "Nothing…is more deserving of our attention than the intellectual and moral associations of America." Furthermore, he believed that such associations were necessary for political action and social improvement because equality across individuals had rendered large scale action by individuals alone impossible: "If men are to remain civilized...the art of associating together must grow and improve in the same ratio in which the equality of conditions is increased."[1]

No individual has ever, alone, made political, social, or economic change. Collective efforts, through political parties, civic associations, labor unions and businesses, are always necessary. For 數位, these and other less formal social groupings are just as fundamental as individuals are to the social fabric. In this sense, associations are the Yin to the Yang of personhood in the most foundational rights and for the same reason are the scourge of tyrants. Again, to quote De Toqueville, "No defect of the human heart suits [despotism] better than egoism; a tyrant is relaxed enough to forgive his subjects for failing to love him, provided that they do not love one another." Only by facilitating and protecting the capacity to form novel associations with meaningful agency can we hope for freedom, self-government, and diversity.

The potential of computers and networking to facilitate such association was the core of Lick and Taylor's vision of "The Computer as Communication Device": "They will be communities not of common location, but of *common interest*."[2] In fact, as of this writing the online version of the popular English dictionary Merriam-Webster defined an association precisely this way: "an organization of persons

---

[1] Alexis De Tocqueville, *Democracy in America*, (Lexington, Ky: Createspace, 2013), also available at
https://www.gutenberg.org/files/815/815-h/815-h.htm.

[2] Joseph Licklider, and Robert Taylor, "The Computer as a Communication Device," *Science and Technology*, April 1968, also available at
https://internetat50.com/references/Licklider_Taylor_The-Computer-As-A-Communications-Device.pdf.

sharing a common interest".[3] Given their shared goals, beliefs, and inclinations, Lick and Taylor believed these communities would be able to achieve far more than pre-digital associations. The only challenge the authors foresaw was that of ensuring that "'to be on line'...be a right" rather than "a privilege". Much of this vision has, of course, proven incredibly prescient as many of today's most prominent political movements and civic organizations formed or achieved their greatest success online.[4]

Yet, perhaps paradoxically, there is an important sense in which the rise of the internet has threatened some of the core features of free association. As Lick and Taylor emphasized, forming an association or community requires establishing a set of background shared beliefs, values and interests that form a *context* for the association and communication within it. Furthermore, as emphasized by Simmel and Nissenbaum, it also requires protecting this context from external surveillance: if individuals believe their communications to their association are monitored by outsiders, they will often be unwilling to harness the context of shared community for fear their words will be misunderstood by those these communications were not intended for.

---

[3] See https://www.merriam-webster.com/dictionary/association.

[4] Japanese philosopher Kojin Karatani explores this concept in his book "The Principle of NAM." Karatani argues that individuals belong not only to geographical regions but also to global "regions" based on their interests. He calls this the "rhizomatic association" and depicts it as a network formation system consisting of diverse "regions." This concept resembles the network structure where small, closely-knit communities are interconnected. Kojin Karatani (2000). "NAM原理" 太田出版 (Published in Japanese. Not translated in English). In this year Karatani founded the New Associationist Movement in Japan. It was an anti-capitalist, anti-nation-state association inspired by experiments with Local Exchange Trading Systems.

數位 Plurality: Part 4: Freedom

The internet, while enabling a far broader range of potential associations, has made the establishment and protection of context more challenging. As information spreads further and faster, knowing who you are speaking to and what you share with them has become challenging. Furthermore, it has become easier than ever for nosy outsiders to spy on associations or for their members to inappropriately share information outside the intended context. Achieving Lick and Taylor's dream, and thus enabling the digital world to be one where 數位 associations thrive, requires, therefore, understanding of the informational context and building 數位 systems that support and protect it.

Therefore, in this chapter we will outline a theory of the informational requirements for association. Then we will discuss existing technologies that have begun to aid or could aid in the establishment of context and in its protection. We will then highlight a vision of how to combine these technologies to achieve not privacy or publicity but rather "數位 publics", the flourishing of many associations of common understanding protected from external surveillance, and why this is so critical to supporting the other digital rights.

## Associations

How do people form "an organization of persons sharing a common interest"? Clearly a group of people who simply happen to share an interest is insufficient. People can share an interest but have no awareness of each other or might know each other and have no idea about their shared interest. As social scientists and game theorists have recently emphasized, the collective action implied by "organization" requires a stronger notion of what it is to have an "interest", "belief" or "goal" in common. In the technical terms of these fields, the required state is what they call (approximate) "common knowledge".

To motivate what this means to a game theorist, it may be helpful to consider why simply sharing a belief is insufficient to allow effective common action. Consider a group of people who all happen to speak a common second language, but none are aware that the others do. Given they all speak different first languages, they won't initially be able to communicate easily. Just knowing the language will not do them much good. Instead, what they must learn is that others also know the language. That is, they must have not just basic knowledge but the "higher order" knowledge that others know something.[5]

The importance of such higher-order knowledge for collective action is such a truism that it has made its way into folk lore. In the classic Hans Christian Andersen tale of *"The Emperor's New Clothes"*, a swindler fools an emperor into believing he has spun him a valuable new outfit, when in fact he has stripped him bare. While his audience all see he is naked, all are equally afraid to remark on it until a child's laughter creates understanding not just that the emperor is naked, but that others appreciate this fact and thus each is safe acknowledging it. Similar effects are familiar from a range of social, economic, and political settings:

- Highly visible statements of reassurance are often necessary to stop bank runs, as if everyone thinks others will run, so will they.[6]

---

[5] That common knowledge is precisely the foundation of context against which communication must optimize is elegantly formally proven by Zachary Wojowicz, "Context and Communication" (2024) at https://papers.ssrn.com/sol3/papers.cfm?abstract_id=4765417.

[6] Stephen Morris and Hyun Song Shin, "Unique Equilibrium in a Model of Self-Fulfilling Currency Attacks", *American Economic Review* 88, no. 3 (1998): 587-597.

- Denunciations of "open secrets" of misdeeds (e.g. sexual misconduct) often lead to a flood of accusations, as accusers become aware that others "have their back" as in the "#MeToo" movement.[7]
- Public protests can bring down governments long opposed by the population, by creating common awareness of discontent that translates to political power.[8]

Mathematically, "common knowledge" is defined as a situation where a group of people know something, but also know that all of them know it, and know that all of them knows that all of them knows it and so on *ad infinitum*. "Common belief" (often quantified by a degree of belief) is when a group believes that they all believe that they all believe that... A great deal of game theoretic analysis has shown that such common belief is a crucial precondition of coordinated action in "risky collective action" situations like the above where individuals can accomplish a common goal if enough coordinate but will be harmed if they act without support from others.[9]

While the common beliefs of a group of people are obviously related to the actual shared beliefs of their average members, they are conceptually distinct. We all know of examples when some "conventional wisdom" or norm persisted even though, individually and privately, almost everyone in a group disagreed with it; in fact, it was precisely this observation that

---

[7] Ing-Haw Cheng and Alice Hsiaw, "Reporting Sexual Misconduct in the #MeToo Era", *American Economic Review* 14, no. 4 (2022): 761-803.

[8] Timur Kuran, *Private Truth, Public Lies: The Social Consequences of Preference Falsification* (Cambridge, MA: Harvard University Press, 1998).

[9] Stephen Morris and Hyun Song Shin, "Social Value of Public Information", *American Economic Review* 92, no.5 (2002): 1521-1534.

led economist J.K. Galbraith to coin the idea of "the conventional wisdom".[10] Furthermore, we can use this notion of community to refer not just to beliefs about facts, but also moral or intentional beliefs. We can think of a "common belief" (in the moral sense) of a community as being things that everyone believes everyone else holds as a moral principle and believes everyone else believes that everyone holds, etc. Similarly, a "common goal" can be something everyone believes others intend and believes everyone believes everyone intends and so on. Such "common beliefs" and "common intentions" are important to what is often called *"legitimacy"*, the commonly understood notion of what is appropriate.[11]

In game theory, it is common to model individuals as collections of intentions/preferences and beliefs. This notion of community gives a way to think about groups similarly and distinctly from the individuals that make them up, given that common beliefs and intentions need not be the same as those of the individuals that are part of that group (on average): group beliefs and goals are common beliefs and goals of that group. In this sense, the freedom to create associations can be understood as the freedom to create common beliefs and goals. Yet creating associations is not enough. Just as we argued in the previous chapter that protecting secrets is critical to maintaining individual identity, so too associations must be able to protect themselves from surveillance, as should their common beliefs simply become the beliefs of everyone, they cease to be a separate association just as much as an individual

---

[10] John Kenneth Galbraith, *The Affluent Society* (New York: Houghton Mifflin, 1958).

[11] Vitalik Buterin, "The Most Important Scarce Resource is Legitimacy" March 23, 2021 at https://vitalik.eth.limo/general/2021/03/23/legitimacy.html.

who spills all her secrets ceases to have an identity to protect. As such, privacy from external surveillance or internal oversharing is just as critical as establishing associations to their freedom.

It is little surprise, then, that many of the historical technologies and spaces that come to mind when we think of the freedom of association are precisely geared to achieving common beliefs and shielding common beliefs from external beliefs from outsiders. Searching, in the imagery online or the writings of political philosophers, for "freedom of association" typically yields images of protests in public spaces, meetings in public spaces like parks and squares and group discussions in private clubs.[12] As illustrated above, group meetings and statements made openly in front of group members are crucial to achieving common beliefs and understanding among that group. Private pamphlets may achieve individual persuasion, but given the lack of common observation, game theorists have argued that they struggle to create public beliefs in the same way a shared declaration, like the child's public laughter, can.

But purely public spaces have important limitations: they do not allow groups to form their views and coordinate their actions outside the broader public eye. This may undermine their cohesion, their ability to present a united face externally and their ability to communicate effectively harnessing an internal context. This is why associations so often have enclosed gathering places open only to members: to allow the secrecy that Simmel emphasized as critical to group

---

[12] Pragmatist political philosophy Richard Rorty wrote "We can urge the construction of a world order whose model is a bazaar surrounded by lots and lots of exclusive private clubs." Richard Rorty, "On ethnocentrism: A reply to Clifford Geertz" *Michigan Quarterly Review* 25, no. 3 (1986): 533.

efficacy and cohesion.[13] The crucial question we thus face is how systems of network communication can offer the brave new world of "communities of interest" these same or even more effective affordances to create protected common beliefs.

**Establishing context**

To the extent parks and squares are the site of protest and collective action, we might well search for a digital public square, a function many platforms have purported to serve.[14] Sites on the original World Wide Web offered unprecedented opportunities for a range of people to make their messages available. But as Economics Nobel Laureate Herbert Simon famously observed, this deluge of information created a paucity of attention.[15] Soon it became hard to know if, who and how one was reaching an audience with a website and proprietary search systems like Google. Proprietary social networks like Facebook and Twitter became platforms of choice for digital communication, but only partly addressed the issue as they had limited (and usually pay-for) affordances for understanding audiences. The digital public square had become a private concession, with the CEO of these companies proudly declaring themselves the public utility or public square

---

[13] George Simmel. "The Sociology of Secrecy and of Secret Societies." *American Journal of Sociology* 11, no. 4 (January 1906): 441–98. https://doi.org/10.1086/211418.

[14] Eli Pariser, "Musk's Twitter Will Not Be the Town Square the World Needs", *WIRED* October 28, 2022 at https://www.wired.com/story/elon-musk-twitter-town-square/.

[15] Herbert Simon, *Designing Organizations for an Information-Rich World* (Baltimore, MD: Johns Hopkins University Press, 1971): pp. 37-52.

of the digital age while surveilling and monetizing user interactions through targeted advertising.[16]

Several recent efforts have begun to address this problem. The World Wide Web Consortium (W3C) published Christine Lemmer Webber and Jessica Tallon's ActivityPub standard as a recommendation to enable an open protocol for social networking that has empowered open systems like Mastodon to offer federated, decentralized services similar to X to millions of people around the world. When it was still Twitter it directly recognized the problem and launched the BlueSky initiative in 2019 which rapidly gained attention after the acquisition of Twitter (now X under his leadership) by Elon Musk. Philanthropist Frank McCourt has invested heavily in Project Liberty[17] and its Decentralized Social Networking Protocol as another, blockchain-based foundation for decentralized networking. While it is hard to predict exactly which of these will flourish, how they will consolidate and so forth, the recent struggles of X combined with the diversity of vibrant activity in this space suggest the likelihood of cooperation and convergence on some open protocol for usable digital publication.

Yet publicity is not the same as the creation of community and association. Posting online resembles much more the distribution of a pamphlet than the holding of a public protest. It is hard for those seeing a post to know who and how many others are consuming the same information, and certainly to gauge their views about the same. The post may influence their beliefs, but it is hard for it to create common beliefs among an

---

[16] danah boyd, "Facebook is a utility; utilities get regulated" May 15, 2010 at https://www.zephoria.org/thoughts/archives/2010/05/15/facebook-is-a-utility-utilities-get-regulated.html.

[17] Frank McCourt, and Michael Casey, *Our Biggest Fight: Reclaiming Liberty, Humanity, and Dignity in the Digital Age*, (New York: Crown, 2024).

identifiable group of compatriots. Features that highlight virality and attention of posts may help somewhat, but still make the alignment of an audience for a message far coarser than what is possible in physical public spaces.

One of the most interesting potential solutions to address this challenge in recent years has been distributed ledger technologies (DLTs) including blockchains. These technologies maintain a shared record of information and append something to this record only when there is "consensus" (sufficient shared acknowledgement of the item to be included) that it should be. This has led cryptographers and game theorists to conclude that DLTs hold special promise in creating common beliefs among the machines on which they are stored.[18] Arguably this is why such systems have supported coordination on new currencies and other social experiments.

Yet even such community among machines does not directly imply it among the people operating these machines. This problem (from the perspective of creating community) is exacerbated by the financial incentives for maintaining blockchains, which lead most participants, motivated by financial gain, to run "validator" software rather than monitor activity directly. This also implies those participating are likely to be whoever can profit, rather than those interested in common, non-commercial action. Nonetheless one can imagine, as we will below, DLTs being an important component of a future infrastructure of association.

**Protecting context**

If establishing context is primarily about creating strongly social notions of publicity, protecting context is about strongly social

---

[18] Joseph Y. Halpern and Rafael Pass "A Knowledge-Based Analysis of the Blockchain Protocol" (2017) available at https://arxiv.org/abs/1707.08751.

notions of privacy. And, just as with technologies of publicity, those of privacy have primarily been developed in a more atomistic monist direction than in ones that support sociality.

The field of cryptography has long studied how to securely and privately transmit information. In the canonical "public key cryptography" scheme, individuals and organizations publish a public key while privately holding its controlling counterpart. This allows anyone to send the holder an encrypted message that can only be decrypted by their private key. It also allows the key controller to sign messages so that others can verify the authenticity of the message. Such systems are the foundation of security on the internet and throughout the digital world, protecting email from spying, allowing end-to-end encrypted messaging systems like Signal and digital commerce.

Building on top of this foundation and branching out from it, several powerful privacy-enhancing technologies (PETs) have been developed in recent years. These include:

- Zero-knowledge proofs (ZKPs)- these allow the secure proof of a fact without leaking the underlying data. For example, one might prove that one is above a particular age without showing the full driver's license on which this claim is based.
- Secure multi-party computation (SMPC) and homomorphic encryption- These allow a collection of individuals to perform a calculation involving data that each of them has parts of without revealing the parts to the others and allow for the process to be verified both by themselves and others. For example, a secret ballot

can be maintained while allowing secure verification of election results.[19]
- Unforgeable and undeniable signatures- These allow key controllers to sign statements in ways that cannot be forged without access to the key and/or cannot be denied except by claiming the key was compromised.[20] For example, parties entering into a (smart) contract might insist on such digital signatures just as physical signatures that are hard to forge and hard to repudiate are important for analog contracts.
- Confidential computing- This solution to similar problems as above is less dependent on cryptography and instead accomplishes similar goals with "air gapped" digital systems that have various physical impediments to leaking information.
- Differential privacy- This measures the extent to which disclosures of the output of a computation might unintentionally leak sensitive information that entered the calculation.[21] Technologists have developed techniques to guarantee such leaks will not occur, typically by adding noise to disclosures. For example, the US Census is legally required both to disclose summary statistics to guide public policy and keep source data confidential, aims that have recently been

---

[19] Josh Daniel Cohen Benaloh, *Verifiable Secret-Ballot Elections*, Yale University Dissertation (1987) at https://www.proquest.com/openview/05248eca4597fec343d8b46cb2bef724/1?pq-origsite=gscholar&cbl=18750&diss=y.

[20] David Chaum and Hans van Antwerpen, "Undeniable Signatures" *Advances in Cryptology – CRYPTO' 89 Proceedings* 435: 212-216 https://link.springer.com/chapter/10.1007/0-387-34805-0_20.

[21] Cynthia Dwork, Frank McSherry, Kobbi Nissim and Adam Smith, "Calibrating Noise to Sensitivity in Private Data Analysis", *Theory of Cryptography* (2006): 265-284.

jointly satisfied using mechanisms that ensure differential privacy.
- Federated learning- Less a fundamental privacy technique than a sophisticated application and combination of other techniques, federated learning is a method to train and evaluate large machine learning models on data physically located in dispersed ways.[22]

It is important to recognize two fundamental limitations of these techniques that depend most on cryptography (especially the first three); namely they depend on two critical assumptions. First, keys must remain in the possession of the desired person, a problem closely related to the identity and recovery questions we discussed in the previous chapter. Second, almost all cryptography in use today will break and in many cases its guarantees be undone by the advent of quantum computers, though developing quantum resistant schemes is an active area of research.

Furthermore, these technical solutions increasingly intersect and integrate with a range of technical standards and public policies that support privacy. These include cryptographic standards set by governments, privacy regulations and rights such as the EU General Data Protection Regulation and standards for the inter-operation of encryption.

Yet a basic limitation of almost all this work is the focus on protecting communication from external surveillance rather than from internal oversharing. Preventing external snooping is obviously the first line of defense, but anyone who followed the saga of US National Security Agency leaker Edward Snowden

---

[22] Brendan McMahan, Eider Moore, Daniel Ramage, Seth Hampson and Blaise Aguera y Arcas, "Communication-Efficient Learning of Deep Networks from Decentralized Data" *Proceedings of the 20th International Conference on Artificial Intelligence and Statistics* (2017).

knows that internal moles and leaks are one of the most important threats to information security. While military intelligence is the most dramatic example, the point stretches much further, especially in the internet age. Increasingly common phishing attacks rely on social engineering, not the ability of the attacker to "crack the code." As highlighted in works ranging from danah boyd's classic study *It's Complicated* to Dave Eggers's book and film *The Circle*, the ease of credibly sharing digital information has made the danger of over-sharing a constant threat to privacy.[23]

The basic problem is that while most cryptography and regulation treat privacy as about individuals, most of what we usually mean when we talk about privacy relates to groups. After all, there is almost no naturally occurring data that pertains to exactly a single individual. Let's revisit some of the examples of the social life of data from the previous chapter.

- Genetic data: genes are, of course, significantly shared in a family, implying that the disclosure of one individual's genetic data reveals things about her family and, to a lesser extent, about anyone even distantly related to her. Related arguments apply to many medical data, such as those related to genetic conditions and transmissible diseases.
- Communications and financial data: communications and transactions are by their nature multiparty and thus have multiple natural referents.
- Location data: few people spend much of their time physically distant from at least some other person with whom they have common knowledge of their joint location at that moment.

---

[23] danah boyd, *It's Complicated: The Social Lives of Networked Teens* (New Haven, CT: Yale University Press, 2014). Dave Eggers, *The Circle* (New York: Knopf, 2013).

- Physical data: There are many data that are not personal to anyone (e.g. soil, environmental, geological). One of the only truly individualistic data are the bureaucratically created identifying numbers created as part of identity schemes deliberately for the purpose of being individualistic, and even these actually pertain not to the individual alone but to her relationship to the issuing bureaucracy.

This implies that in almost every relevant case, unilateral disclosure of data by an individual threatens the legitimate privacy interests of other individuals.[24] Protecting privacy therefore requires defending against unilateral over-sharing. This has generally been thought essentially impossible to externally enforce anyone who knows something can share that information with another. Strategies have thus primarily focused on norms against over-sharing, gossiping, and the like, tools to aid individuals in remembering what they should not share, attempts to make it hard to secretly over-share and policies to punish *ex-post facto* those who do engage in oversharing. All of these are important strategies: literature, media and everyday experience are full of shame for over-sharing and enforcement against leakers. Yet they fall far short of the guarantees enforced by cryptography, which does not merely condemn snoops but locks them out of systems.

Is there any chance of doing something similar for over-sharing? One common approach is simply to avoid data persistence: SnapChat rose to prominence with disappearing

---

[24] danah boyd, "Networked Privacy" June 6, 2011 at https://www.danah.org/papers/talks/2011/PDF2011.html. Daron Acemoglu, Ali Makhdoumi, Azarakhsh Malekian and Asu Ozdaglar, "Too Much Data: Prices and Inefficiencies in Data Markets" *American Economic Journal: Microeconomics* 14, no. 4 (2022): 218-256. Dirk Bergemann, Alessandro Bonatti and Tan Gan, "The Economics of Social Data" *The RAND Journal of Economics* 53, no. 2 (2022): 263-296.

messages, and many messaging protocols have since adopted similar approaches. Another, more ambitious cryptographic technique is "designated verifier proofs" (DVPs) which prove authenticity only to a single recipient while appearing potentially forged to everyone else.[25] Such an approach is only useful for information that cannot be independently verified: if someone over-shares a community password, DVPs are not of much use as unintended recipients can quickly check if the password works.

Yet most types of information are harder to independently and immediately verify even the location of buried treasure requires significant resources to pursue and dig up, otherwise the many adventure stories about such would not be nearly as interesting. As generative foundation models make persuasive deception ever cheaper, the importance of verification will grow. In such a world, the ability to target verification at an individual and rely on the untrustworthiness of overshared information may be increasingly powerful. As such, it may be increasingly possible to protect information more fully from oversharing, as well as snooping.

## publics

If properly combined in a new generation of networking standards, a combination of these tools could give us the capacity to move beyond the superficial traditional divide between "publicity" and "privacy" to empower true freedom of association online. While we usually think of publicity and privacy as a one-dimensional spectrum, it is easy to see that another dimension is equally important.

---

[25] Markus Jakobsson, Kazue Sako and Russell Impagliazzo, "Designated Verifier Proofs and Their Appliations", *Advances in Cryptology-EUROCRYPT '96* (1996): 143-154.

Consider first information "hidden in plain sight", lost in a pile of irrelevant facts, available to all but reaching the awareness of no one a bit like Waldon in the popular American children's game "Where's Waldo?" where children must find a man in a striped shirt hidden in a picture. Contrast this with the secret of the existence of the Manhattan Project, which was shared among roughly 100,000 people but was sharply hidden from the rest of the world. Both are near the midpoint of the "privacy" v. "publicity" spectrum, as both are in important ways broadly shared and obscure. But they sit at opposite ends of another spectrum: of concentrated common understanding v. diffuse availability.

This example illustrates why "privacy" and "publicity" are far too simplistic concepts to describe the patterns of co-knowledge that underpin free association. While any simple descriptor will fall short of the richness we should continue to investigate, a more relevant model may be what elsewhere we have called "⿻ publics". ⿻ publics is the aspiration to create information standards that allow a diverse range of communities with strong internal common beliefs shielded from the outside world to coexist. Achieving this requires maintaining what Shrey Jain, Zoë Hitzig and Pamela Mishkin have called *"contextual confidence"*, where participants in a system can easily establish and protect the context of their communications.[26]

Luckily, in recent years some of the leaders in open standards technologies of both privacy and publicity have turned their

---

[26] Jain Shrey, Zoë Hitzig, and Pamela Mishkin, "Contextual Confidence and Generative AI," *ArXiv* (New York: Cornell University, November 2, 2023), https://doi.org/10.48550/arxiv.2311.01193. See also Shrey Jain, Divya Siddarth and E. Glen Weyl, "Plural Publics" March 20, 2023 from the GETTING-Plurality Research Network at https://gettingplurality.org/2023/03/18/plural-publics/.

attention to this problem. Lemmer Webber, of ActivityPub fame, has spent the last few years working on Spritely, a project to create self-governing and strongly connected private communities in the spirit of ⌗ publics, allowing individual users to clearly discern, navigate and separate community contexts in open standards. A growing group of researchers in the web3 and blockchain communities are working on combining these with privacy technologies, especially ZKPs.[27]

One of the most interesting possibilities opened by this research is achieving formal guarantees of combinations of common knowledge and impossibility of disclosure. One could, for example, create ledgers distributed among members of a community group using DVPs. This would create a record of information that is common knowledge to this community and ensure this information (and its status as common knowledge) cannot be credibly shared outside this community. Additionally, if the protocol's procedure for determining "consensus" relied on more sophisticated voting rules than at present such as those we describe in our chapter on voting below, it might instantiate richer and more nuanced notions of common knowledge than present ledgers.

Furthermore, all the space around these topics is suffused with work on standards: for cryptography, blockchains, open communications protocols like Activity Pub, etc. It therefore does not require great stretches to imagine these standards converging on a dynamically evolving but widely accepted technical notion of an "association" and therefore broadly

---

[27] Elena Burger, Bryan Chiang, Sonal Chokshi, Eddy Lazzarin, Justin Thaler, and Ali Yahya, "Zero Knowledge Canon, Part 1 & 2," *a16zcrypto*, September 16, 2022, https://a16zcrypto.com/posts/article/zero-knowledge-canon/.https://a16zcrypto.com/posts/article/zero-knowledge-canon/.

observed standards enabling associations online to form and preserve themselves. Such a future could enshrine a right to digital freedom of association.

## Association, identity, and commerce

In 1995, one of De Tocqueville's most prominent heirs, political scientist Robert Putnam, began documenting the decline of American civic life starting in 1960s in his essay *"Bowling Alone"*. He attributes this to a corresponding reduction in participatory community associations such as fraternal organizations, religious groups, and parent teacher associations, leading to his quip that there are more people bowling and fewer bowling leagues. He argues that the decrease in associative behavior directly affects the development of social capital and trust which "facilitate coordination and cooperation for mutual benefit."[28]

Putnam addresses several possible reasons but focuses on television and the "privatizing" of our leisure time, noting that "television has made our communities … wider and shallower." His essay preceded the modern internet, but we might import into his argument a phrase from our contemporary digital lives: there's an app for that. A challenge then for the extraordinary reach of 21st century digital technology is the harnessing of that power to form meaningful communities and deeper social interactions. Strong community engagement also cultivates robust civic discourse where social and political problems can be hashed out by constituent citizens.

Digital freedom of association is tightly connected to the other freedoms we discuss in this part of the book. As we saw in the

---

[28] Robert Putnam, "Bowling Alone: America's Declining Social Capital," *Journal of Democracy* 6, no. 1 (1995): 65-78 and *Bowling Alone: The Collapse and Revival of American Community* (New York: Simon & Schuster, 2000).

previous chapter, "privacy" is at the core of the integrity of identity systems yet concerns usually labeled as such are more appropriately connected to the diversity of contexts an individual navigates rather than privacy in an individualistic sense. Thus, the right to freedom of association and the right to the integrity of personhood are inseparable: if it is our entanglement in a diversity of social groups that creates our separateness as a person, it is only by protecting the integrity of that diversity that separate personhood is possible. And, of course, because groups are made up of people, the opposite is true as well: without people with well-articulated identities, there is no way to create groups defined by common knowledge among these people.

Furthermore, the right of free association is the foundation on which commerce and contracts are built. Transactions are among the simplest forms of association and how digital transaction systems can replicate the privacy that is often touted as a core benefit of cash depends intimately on who can view what transactions at what resolution. Contracts are more sophisticated forms of association and corporations even more so. All rely heavily on information integrity and common understandings of obligations. In this sense, the freedom of association we outlined in this chapter, together with identity in the last, are the linchpins for what follows in the rest of the book.

## 4-3 Commerce and Trust

The ambient hum of excitement echoed through the open air, punctuated by distant laughter and chatter. Local families had gathered once more for the beloved retro cinema night—a tradition deeply cherished in this community. Like a canvas of memories, families, lovers, and teens lounged on camping chairs, ready to relive moments from an old movie under the vast expanse of the starlit sky.

Amidst the seasoned attendees was Zvi, standing out with an air of novelty. New to town and having only recently taken up a teaching position at the local school, he was keen to mingle and partake in community festivities. Grasping a bag of chips he intended to share, he joined the queue, absorbing the unique spirit of the evening.

"Thank you for your street art contributions," a voice echoed from the front. Zvi turned his attention to the ticketing booth. Charity event? I wasn't aware, he thought, slightly puzzled.

"I would love us to watch Rogue Stardust." Zvi craned his neck and caught sight of a familiar face, a student from his school, proudly flaunting her school hoodie.

That's unexpected, he mused.

His musings were interrupted as he overheard another exchange, "Ma'am, which movies would you like to choose for tonight, you have several votes from your nursing home and community work."

A gentle, elderly voice responded, "I'd prefer Whispers in the Void and The Last Alchemist, if you don't mind."

"Thank you for your contributions, ma'am." the man at the booth responded, his tone courteous.

### 4-3 Commerce and Trust

Soon, it was Zvi's turn. The man at the booth had an aura of tranquility, reminiscent of a seasoned surfer. His warm smile was contagious.

"Good evening, sir! If you'd like, you can tap your phone here to share your community experiences. It's completely optional but a nice way for us to acknowledge everyone's contributions to our town," the attendant offered, gesturing towards a small, unobtrusive screen on the counter.

Zvi, intrigued yet cautious, queried, "And what happens if I do? Just curious about privacy and all."

"Of course, privacy is key. This device simply displays public community messages and thank-you notes on our local community app. It's the same info anyone can see on the app. Think of it as a digital way of saying thanks and sharing positive vibes," the attendant explained, his tone reassuring.

Zvi, feeling at ease with the explanation, decided to participate. He tapped his phone on the device, and the screen lit up, displaying a colorful array of thank-you messages and fun emojis from residents, acknowledging his recent help with community projects.

Smiling at the warm messages, Zvi replied, "That's a nice touch. Makes you feel part of something special."

"Exactly! And as a part of our community, you get to suggest a movie for tonight. What would you like to add to the lineup?" the attendant asked, his eyes twinkling with friendliness. "Also, thank you for taking the time to help my sister's child after school that day; it truly made a difference for her family."

The warmth of acceptance spread through Zvi as he realized he had been welcomed. With a nod of heartfelt thanks, he made his way to a comfortable nook within the gathering, sharing his crackers with the delighted children nearby.

Beneath a sky speckled with stars, against a backdrop laden with memories, Zvi watched as his cherished film began to play. In this moment, he was enveloped by the profound sense of community—where he was not merely a spectator, but an integral thread woven into the vibrant tapestry of collective memories and experiences.

---

It's a testament to the commercial nature of the contemporary world that none of the protocols we discuss in this section have received nearly the attention of the media and policy as new approaches to facilitating payment and commerce. Cryptocurrencies have been one of the focal technologies of the last decade. But only slightly less heralded and far more broadly adopted have been a range of government and other public payments innovations including instant payments technologies using government identities in places like India, Brazil and Singapore, central bank digital currencies (CBDCs), and regulated inter-operable digital payment systems like those used in the People's Republic of China (PRC). While they are far from universally adopted or inter-operable, a new generation of payment systems are increasingly prevalent in the lives of many people around the globe, making payment in digital spaces increasingly as easy or easier than what cash facilitated in the past.

Yet, in many ways the relatively rapid success of these efforts is a symptom of what is so disappointing about their progress so far. Cash is perhaps one of the "dumbest" technologies of the pre-digital era: it is a single, homogeneous substance transmitted between roughly anonymous, abstracted accounts. While it has proven far harder to replicate this basic function, and thus recent advances are important, this is not a revolutionary technique enabled by digital technology as, for example, hypertext improved on what had been possible in previous writing. In this chapter we will summarize progress thus far, discuss the limitations of traditional money compared to higher aspirations for commerce online and discuss ways to build on recent advances to allow a more ▢ vision of digital commerce.

## Traditional payments

While the early history of money has been a subject of a great deal of recent research, to which we will return below, most people associate the idea with currency in the form of tokens or notes that pass from one hand to another and view other forms of money as abstractions of this more basic concept. This form of "money of exchange" dates to the early civilizations of Babylon, India, and China and in the first millennium BC was increasingly based on precious metals like bronze, silver, and gold.[1] The durability, scarcity, and wide belief in the value of these metals facilitated broad acceptance of them in payment for a range of goods and services.

Yet none of these properties pertain exclusively to precious metals and their use as currency detracted from more practical applications, whether to weapons, machinery, or decorations. This led many societies to move away from direct use of precious metals to other representations of their value that could be made scarce but had no direct use, including commercial receipts, bank notes and government-issued paper that was deemed "legal tender" and thus mandated to be accepted for its face value.

Closely connected was the development of banks, which held currency and other valuables that they promised to return on demand, using these deposits to fund lending to others. Because banks are rarely simultaneously called on to return the full set of deposits, they began to lend out more than they had

---

[1] Glyn Davies, *A History of Money* (Cardiff, UK: University of Wales Press, 2010).

on deposit, giving rise to a system of "fractional reserve banking" and making banks a source of the creation of new money. While the obvious dangers of a bank run this creates are not a topic we have space to focus on here, they created a natural role for "central banks" to help control this process of money creation and avoid banking collapses.

By the early twentieth century, most money was held as accounts, rather than currency (paper or otherwise). Given its rigid denominations and bulk, currency is only effective for relatively small transactions. In parallel to, and arguably earlier than currency, directed transfers between bank accounts with flexible denominations developed, typically called "cheques" today. By the mid-twentieth century, these had become the dominant (by aggregate value) method of funds transfer. Cheques come in several forms, some more reliant on information exchanges across banks and others operating more similarly to cash (unconditional and undirected value transfers).

Cheques, of course, have familiar disadvantages of being slow to both fill out and to clear must be sent around physically. Beginning in the late nineteenth century, some stores began to issue tokens representing "credit accounts" for regular customers and utopian writers like Edward Bellamy began to imagine a world where all payments could be conducted using one or a few lightweight cards.[2] In 1928, Charga-Plate, an early predecessor of the credit card, began operations.[3] Over the following three decades, the use of cards to "buy now, and pay

---

[2] Edward Bellamy, *Looking Backward* (Boston, Ticknor & Co., 1888).

[3] It was a 64 mm × 32 mm rectangle of sheet metal related to Addressograph and military dog tag systems. It sped up back-office bookkeeping and reduced copying errors that were done manually in paper ledgers in each store.

### 4-3 Commerce and Trust

later" gradually expanded first through the airline industry and later through dining.[4]

In 1958, Bank of America launched the BankAmericard, which would become the first successful recognizably modern credit card, which was eventually licensed to other banks around the United States and then around the world.[5] This system was computerized in 1973 under the leadership of Dee Hock, the first CEO of Visa, allowing reduced transaction time, with magnetic strips easing processing. In 1976, all BankAmericard licensees united themselves under the common brand Visa, organized as a bank consortium to manage networks of agreements between banks. During the 1980s, electronic merchant terminals allowed for increasingly wider and faster acceptance of the cards, further accelerated in the 2000s when chips and PINs were widely added.

Cheques clearing systems began to leverage database and telecommunications networks in the 1970s with the development of Automated Clearing Houses (ACHs). These process large volumes of credit and debit transactions between accounts at banks in batches on a net settlement basis. This system supports government payments to people (employees, pensioners), employer payments to employees, business-to-business payments, consumer to bank payments (mortgages) and other such transactions made from one bank account to

---

[4] In 1934 American Airlines offered an Air Travel Card, passengers could "buy now, and pay later" for a ticket against their credit and receive a fifteen percent discount at any of the accepting airlines. By the 1940s, all of the major U.S. airlines offered Air Travel Cards that could be used on 17 different airlines. The concept of customers paying different merchants using the same card was expanded in 1950 by Ralph Schneider and Frank McNamara, founders of Diners Club, to consolidate multiple cards.

[5] Bank of America chose Fresno because 45% of its residents used the bank, and by sending a card to 60,000 Fresno residents at once, the bank was able to convince merchants to accept the card..

another. The first ACH, BACS began operation in the UK in 1968, in the US the first one, operated by the Federal Reserve Bank of San Francisco began processing transactions in 1972. By 2012 there were 98 ACH systems.[6]

This acceleration of electronic transfers led banks themselves to consider how to transfer money internationally and in 1973 they came together to form Society for Worldwide Interbank Financial Telecommunication (SWIFT), a co-operative they all own and manage. SWIFT is a carrier of messages containing the payment instructions between financial institutions involved in a transaction".[7] By 2018 messages about half of all high-value cross-border payments went through its network.[8]

Until roughly the last decade, this constellation covered most transactions. A mix of cash and payments cards were used for small value transactions in physical proximity and wires were used to send money abroad, while larger value transactions flowed primarily over ACHs and to a lesser extent wires and cheques. All these systems predate the emergence of the internet and none of them match its reach, pace, or flexibility: payment cards were traditionally cumbersome and insecure to use online, cash irrelevant and ACHs far too slow (typically 3 days). Unsurprisingly, therefore, Lick, Tim Berners-Lee, Nelson,

---

[6] "Global Payment Systems Survey (GPSS)," World Bank, January 26, 2024. https://www.worldbank.org/en/topic/financialinclusion/brief/gpss#:~:text=The%20Global%20Payment%20Systems%20Survey%20%28GPSS%29%2C%20conducted%20by.

[7] Susan Scott, and Markos Zachariadis, *The Society for Worldwide Interbank Financial Telecommunication (Swift): Cooperative Governance for Network Innovation, Standards, and Community*, (New York, NY: Routledge), pp. 1, 35, doi:10.4324/9781315849324.

[8] Martin Arnold, "Ripple and Swift Slug It out over Cross-Border Payments," *Financial Times*, June 6, 2018, https://www.ft.com/content/631af8cc-47cc-11e8-8c77-ff51caedcde6.

and others believed a native payment system was one of the core features missing from the early development of the internet. The last decade and a half have seen a variety of attempts to address this lacuna.

## Digital money and privacy

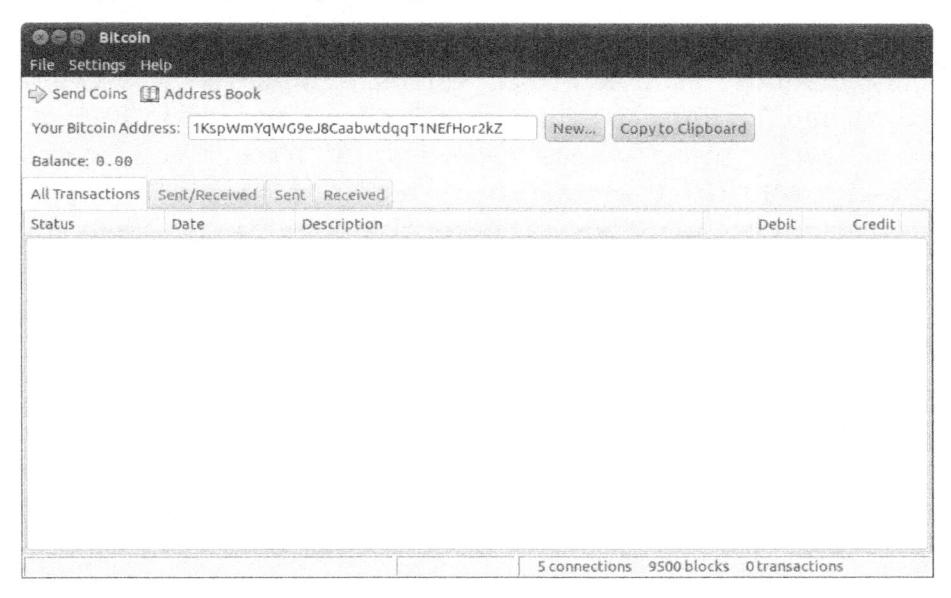

**Figure 4-3-A.** An early implementation of Bitcoin code. Source: Wikipedia, public domain.

One of the first and the most attention-grabbing of these was the emergence of Bitcoin in 2008 and later a range of other "cryptocurrencies" in the 2010s.[9] These systems used DLTs, like

---

[9] Satoshi Nakamoto, "Bitcoin: A Peer-To-Peer Electronic Cash System" (2008) at https://assets.pubpub.org/d8wct41f/31611263538139.pdf. Vitalik Buterin, "A Next-Generation Smart Contract and Decentralized Application Platform" (2014) at https://finpedia.vn/wp-content/uploads/2022/02/Ethereum_white_paper-a_next_generation_smart_contract_and_decentralized_application_platform-vitalik-buterin.pdf.

those we discussed in the last chapter, paired with internally generated financial structures to create a validated substrate for tracking transactions. First, instead of an identity system based on accounting for human participants, they used protocols to prove control over some resource (such as "proof of work" protocols based on solving a puzzle that requires access to powerful computers) to protect against predatory participants. This created an effective financial screen for participation. On the other hand, they rewarded "honest" participants (those whose recording of transactions match others') with "coins" created by including transactions to their own account. The ledger was otherwise openly available to any participant, creating a global, purely financial ledger with pseudonymous accounts that allowed individual people to potentially have many different identifiers.

The early success of Bitcoin drew attention and interest for at least three reasons:

1. It seemed to fill the lacuna in the digital payments space mentioned above, allowing relatively easy cross-border transfers.
2. It was one of the first examples of a large-scale and "important" (carrying real financial consequences) online application without a centralized identity system.
3. Because of its financial structure and scarcity, it was possible for the value of the coins to rapidly appreciate, which they did over several stretches in the following decade and a half, creating great fortunes, speculation, and interest.

While many governments and mainstream business actors recognized the importance of the first point, they saw decentralization as largely superfluous or wasteful and the speculation around cryptocurrencies as a frivolous and potentially destabilizing bubble. This spurred several efforts to re-imagine payment systems for the digital age. The most ambitious efforts were "central bank digital currencies" (CBDCs), which have been launched or piloted in dozens of countries, especially in Africa and Asia and are being explored in many others. These most directly respond to the cryptocurrency trend by creating digital currency-like claims on the central banks.

Yet while holding and trading of currency has become a defining image for many people in recent decades, the accounts above and below suggest this may be a bit of an anomaly in human history. As highlighted by media scholar Lana Swartz in *New Money*, commerce has depended more on communication of and the partially local accounting for *obligations*.[10] It is thus perhaps not terribly surprising that some of the most widely adopted innovations in payments in the last decade have taken the form of changes to payments processing and account transfers, rather than the creation of "currency" *per se*.

This realization interestingly parallels the development of one of the first major means of online payment, the services of the company that came to be known as PayPal. PayPal was originally conceived by founders Max Levchin, Luke Nosek and Peter Thiel as a new digital currency, but quickly moved to become an internet-compatible payments processor.[11] Following the early growth of Bitcoin, many other private, rapid, and low-cost processors entered the market. These included Square and Stripe (targeting businesses) and Venmo (targeting more casual individual-to-individual transactions) all of which were founded in the US in the years immediately following the

---

[10] Lana Swartz, *New Money: How Payment Became Social Media* (New Haven, CT: Yale University Press, 2020).

[11] Today's PayPal was a merger of the original PayPal with X.com, founded by Elon Musk, Harris Fricker, Christopher Payne and Ed Ho, the name of which is now being revived by Musk as the successor to Twitter.

launch of Bitcoin. Perhaps even more impressive was the rapid spread of very low-cost social payments in the PRC through WeChat Pay and in the rest of Asia through Line Pay. These were rapidly followed by a range of similar services facilitated by the largest technology platforms in the West, such as Apple, Amazon and Google.

Seeking to bring these services at lower cost and more inclusively especially in markets incompletely served by these US and PRC-based services, several major developing-world governments have created publicly supported instant payment services, including Singapore's FAST system in 2014, Brazil's Pix system in 2020 and India's Unified Payments Interface in 2016. Even the US has followed with FedNow in 2023. While there are still significant impediments to international inter-operation, there is an increasing consensus that the immediate gap in making instant payments online and in person through digital channels has been met.

Yet the challenges raised by cryptocurrencies cannot be laid to rest quite so easily, as suggested by the resilience of interest and recent currency values in the space. The decline of cash, heralded by defenders of sanction regimes and battlers against financial criminals like economist Kenneth Rogoff, has been bemoaned by privacy advocates and civil libertarians, who argue that the collapse of private payments will have systemic effects individual users fail to account for when choosing how to pay.[12] The oft-touted privacy benefits of Bitcoin have largely proven illusory given that it has become increasingly easy for well-resourced analysts to uncover the controllers of

---

[12] Kenneth S. Rogoff, *The Curse of Cash* (Princeton, NJ: Princeton University Press, 2016).

## 4-3 Commerce and Trust

pseudonymous accounts.[13] However, interest in privacy technology has become a primary focus in the space, stimulating the development of highly private currencies like Zcash and "mixer" services like Tornado cash on top of other currencies. These have stimulated controversy over the trade-offs between privacy and legal accountability, leading to forceful government actions to shut down various privacy features in some jurisdictions. These conflicts have also been at the root of the challenges of achieving seamless international inter-operation for digital payments systems, as countries fight over who can surveil and regulate what activity.

Many of these challenges arise from the same kinds of misspecification of issues usually labeled "privacy" that we highlighted in our identity chapter. There is wide agreement, on the one hand, that financial transactions should be protected from inappropriate surveillance. On the other hand, there is a similarly wide agreement that, with appropriate checks and balances, it should be possible to hold individuals and organizations accountable for facilitating criminal activity. The question of how these can be reconciled is essentially the same as those we addressed in the previous chapter: how can a diversity of informational communities partially interoperate while maintaining their integrity?

After all, financial transactions can never be purely private: they always involve several parties and are at least partly detectable by others in a community where the inflow of transactions affects the economic environment. The goal, then, is not privacy as much as it is contextual integrity: ensuring that this information stays within the affected

---

[13] Alyssa Blackburn, Christoph Huber, Yossi Eliaz, Muhammad S. Shamim, David Weisz, Goutham Seshadri, Kevin Kim, Shengqi Hang and Erez Lieberman Aiden, "Cooperation Among an Anonymous Group Protected Bitcoin during Failures of Decentralization" (2022) at https://arxiv.org/abs/2206.02871.

community unless it is having important and widely recognized spillover effects on other communities (precisely what fiduciary duties, financial and business ethics and, when necessary, law enforcement is meant to capture). And, if it is, it is the community's responsibility to either ensure their culture is not supporting such externally harmful activity or to defend their right to support it if the external claim is unjust.[14] The essence of 數位 "checks and balances" is that the communities involved must become partly aware and involved in such external surveillance, rather than it being asymmetrically and externally imposed.

Yet surveillance is only the beginning of responsibilities that communities of various kinds, ranging from lending circles to nations, would have to take on to create such contextually appropriate financial freedom. Little surveillance is mere voyeurism. Instead, it is intended to prevent a range of financial crimes, from fraud to trading with aggressors against international law (sanctions). Beyond such dramatic transgressions, a range of transactions legitimately matter for people other than the transacting parties: sales of drugs and weapons, taking-on of unreported debts that burden someone's ability to repay other debts, taxable sales, and much more. All this suggests why the anonymous and unaccountable image of cash and centralized control by a government of accounts are both insufficient ways to understand a 數位 system of commercial trust.

---

[14] Recently, interest in explicitly creating communities for such purposes has grown in the Web3 world. Vitalik Buterin, Jacob Illum, Matthias Nadler, Fabian Schär and Ameen Soleimani, "Blockchain Privacy and Regulatory Compliance: Towards a Practical Equilibrium" *Blockchain: Research and Applications* 5, no. 1 (2024): 100176.

## History and limits of currency

Imagining a more ⬚ alternative brings us back to the history of money and why it evolved in the first place. In his account of the institution, the late anthropological historian David Graeber articulated the view of many of the leading scholars of money such as R. G. Hawtrey, Geoffrey Ingham, L. Randall Wray and Samuel A. Chambers to argue that long before money, societies engaged in a range of mutually beneficial collaboration under norms of reciprocity.[15] These were rarely quantified in terms of formal "value" and followed a range of logics beyond simple bilateral favor trading. For example, the community services of a hunter for a village or an elder might put the community in general in their "debt", making gifts to them customary. The richness and diversity of these traditions made their quantification unnatural, but also hard to extend beyond the Dunbar number we discussed in the *Identity and Personhood* chapter of roughly 150 close associates.

As collaboration and exchange extended across larger distances, times or groups, quantification and recording of debts owed and value given became necessary to manage the complexity. While it seems that the earliest such accounts attempted to record the specifics of a debt in terms of the good or service offered, this similarly became quickly unmanageable and common units of quantification were used to simplify accounting and produce the first notions of "currency". Media of exchange, banks, and their notes and various of the other forms of money we discussed above grew as ways of making

---

[15] David Graeber, *Debt: The First 5,000 Years*, (Brooklyn: Melville House, 2014). See also Ralph Hawtrey, *Currency and Credit*, (London, Longmans, 1919); Larry Randall Wray, and Alfred Mitchell Innes, *Credit and State Theories of Money: The Contributions of A. Mitchell Innes*, (Cheltenham: Edward Elgar, 2014); and Samuel Chambers, *Money Has No Value*, (Berlin: Walter de Gruyter GmbH & Co KG, 2023).

these accounts more portable. "Credit" thus was more primary than "cash".

But if currency arose as a simplification to deal with the limits of pre-modern information technology, the natural question is whether one might do much better today. Recording more about transactions and other forms of value creation is not just possible today; it is a routine part of most electronic commerce. Reducing all this to a transfer of money is no longer a necessary simplification, it is a projection of an antiquated historical ritual.

Nor is the role of money as a solvent in socially long-distance trust particularly relevant today. One of the most common stories economists tell for the advantage of money-based exchanges is "the double coincidence of wants": Person A may have something B wants, but the other may not have anything to directly offer in exchange. Money allows them to easily offer goods or services to C, who may have something A wants, without having to assemble the full group. Yet the role of money in avoiding the need for such "trading cycles" is dated: in fact, economists today regularly use "trading cycles" algorithms directly in a variety of contexts without relying on money, given that modern computation makes them cheap to perform.[16]

Similarly, as we noted in the *Identity and Personhood* chapter, it may once have been necessary to offer someone in a distant land a widely valued token, such as gold, instead of a promise to offer a gift in the future, given the low likelihood of a future exchange. Yet such shorthand is far less important today: with everyone within six degrees of social separation and the accounting for relational trust computationally trivial, today it

---

[16] Alvin E. Roth, Tayfun Sönmez and M. Utku Ünver, "Kidney Exchange", *Quarterly Journal of Economics* 119, no. 2 (2004): 457-488.

would be almost as easy to harness interpersonal "debts" in chains of relationships directly as to transfer funds.

A natural question is whether harnessing these new capabilities adds anything meaningful. While we will reserve a detailed discussion of applications of ⌘ commerce and trust to the next part of this book, it is not hard to imagine why such information is important in appropriately allocating the trust and influence that money confers. Someone who has conferred many small benefits across a local community, but interacted little outside of it, and is single has a very different profile of appropriate social favor than someone who is deeply devoted to their family and profession but has few extra-familial social connections in a large city. These two may deserve the same "degree" of social esteem (if quantifying such is even useful), but the esteem is of very different kinds. The former, for example, would be a far more plausible civic or political leader in her community, while the latter would naturally be entitled to professional esteem and a degree of material comfort.

Furthermore, the very economic theory that typically justified the relevance of money confirms this intuition, when applied to social reality. Under certain well-studied conditions, money held by individuals suffices to track value creation. But these conditions require that all goods are private (everything can be consumed by one individual and others' consuming it prevents them from doing so) and production is "submodular", meaning that combining a group of people or assets produces less than the sum of what they could produce separately (the whole is less than the sum of the parts). If, on the other hand, consumption is at least partly social and production may be super-modular, money is a poor or even hopeless way to keep track of value.

An open-source software (OSS) project is an example. Collaboration among multiple individuals often creates greater value than individual actions alone. And the resulting products are replicated and provide utility to many people. It is social consumption. In these situations, money-based management does not function well. Consider a scenario where two individuals collaborate to create value and both actions are necessary. There is no simple or obvious way to divide any value created among these contributors; the value created is fundamentally joint. Furthermore, if the two participants could engage in multiple possible joint projects, which to prioritize depends on the preferences of both, making choices fundamentally collective, decisions that require logic closer to that of voting than commerce.[17]

More broadly, in practice, as sociologists have extensively documented, social influence *does* in practice work in these richer ways. People vote, they gain esteem and authority, develop reputations in a range of contexts: a doctor's lab coat, the standing of an athlete, awards for prestigious academic papers, etc. All of these are sources of influence and command deference from those who regard them highly, allowing the bearer of these marks of status to achieve things someone without them could not.

Of course, these systems are not entirely separate from the commercial sphere: reputations for leadership, nobility, or skill can (sometimes) be monetized by, for example, advertising against or charging for access to the person holding the prestige or by using trust to establish a commercial enterprise harnessing it. But none of these conversions are simple or linear, and, in fact, if one is seen to directly "selling" one's social standing such "selling out" or "corruption" can quickly undermine that standing. Clearly, therefore, the simplest ideas of "sales" and "conversion" are not effective ways to allow

---

[17] Divya Siddarth, Matthew Prewitt, and Glen Weyl, "Supermodular," The Collective Intelligence Project, 2023. https://cip.org/supermodular.

money to inter-operate with these other "symbolic media". This makes money nearly useless to quantify, make transparent, and scale these other systems. The question, then, is how more ⬚ systems of value might overcome this limitation, a question to which we now turn.

## ⬚ money

While there has been a great deal of excitement about the decentralization of cryptocurrencies, there is an important sense in which any currency that aspires to universality is inherently highly centralized: it creates trust and cooperation by everyone ascribing value to the same thing. A more ⬚ approach can, as in our *Identity and Personhood* chapter, follow either a decentralized/polycentric or distributed structure in a way that roughly parallels our ideas there.

In a polycentric structure, instead of a single universal currency, a variety of communities would have their own currencies which could be used in a limited domain. Examples would be vouchers for housing or schooling, scrip for rides at a fair, or credit at a university for buying food at various vendors.[18] These currencies might partially interoperate for example, two universities in the same town might allow exchanges between their meal programs. But it would be against the rules or perhaps even technically impossible for a holder to sell the community currency for broader currency without community consent.[19] In fact, it was the proliferation of experiments with various currencies, some of them with similar intentions, that

---

[18] An early example of community currencies are Local Exchange Trading Systems (LETS) by Michael Linton in 1983. He later visited Kojin Karatani's home, which sparked the New Associationist Movement.

[19] For more elaboration of this idea, see https://www.radicalxchange.org/concepts/plural-money/.

inspired then-*Bitcoin Magazine* writer Vitalik Buterin to conceive Ethereum as a platform for such experimentation, though challenges with secure identities have limited community currency experiments as they make it too easy to sell an account and thus circumvent controls on prohibited transfers.[20]

Such a community currency played a central role in the creation of this book. We used it to measure contributions and to allow contributors to make collective decisions on prioritizing and approving changes to the text in a manner we will discuss in *Collaborative Technology and Democracy*. However, we did not use some of the most sophisticated potential approaches, harnessing the tools from the last chapter. For example, in the future community currencies might be recorded on contextually integral chains that make it hard for currency holders to use the currencies more broadly by preventing them showing others outside the community how much they hold.

A distributed approach would go farther than even a large collection of community currencies, replacing currencies entirely with direct representations of interpersonal debt and trust. In such a system, rather than receiving payment for a good or service, people would effectively "call in a favor" from someone who owes one to them. If you need something from someone who does not owe you a favor, you would leverage the principle of six degrees of separation in the network of "favors owed", as discussed in the Identity chapter. Many potential paths of such favors could be calculated and the total amount of "credit" one can get would be computed by classical computer science algorithms for calculating the "maximum flow" (maxflow) that can be flow between two points in a network. While such calculations are obviously

---

[20] Ohlhaver, Weyl and Buterin, op. cit.

## 4-3 Commerce and Trust

impractical for people to make on the fly when they want to buy a coffee, they are trivial for a computer network. Supporting such richer, socially grounded alternatives to quantifying value primarily through universally fungible currency seems increasingly within reach, with various social currencies (of likes, friends, network centrality, citations, etc.) illustrating first examples of what could become a far richer substrate for future cooperation.[21]

Of course, this will only be possible with the support of widely adopted protocols, ones that facilitate the formation and validation of community ledgers extending those discussed in the previous chapter and/or ones that facilitate long-distance, networked transmission of trust and "debt" in the way TCP/IP did packets of information. These are the aspirations of open source and internet working committees like the aforementioned Trust Over IP Foundation and start-up ventures like Holochain. Beyond the important work of establishing basic, high-quality digital native payments systems, it is this next generation of truly networked and 🔲 systems of commercial trust systems that can underpin the 🔲 markets and cooperation we discuss in much of the rest of this book.

### Commerce in a 🔲 society

Establishing trust, credit and value across long social distances lies at the core of both the identity systems we described previously and the systems of contracting and asset use that we

---

[21] Nicole Immorlica, Matthew O. Jackson and E. Glen Weyl, "Verifying Identity as a Social Intersection" (2019) at https://papers.ssrn.com/sol3/papers.cfm?abstract_id=3375436. E. Glen Weyl, Kaliya Young (Identity Woman) and Lucas Geiger, "Intersectional Social Data", *RadicalxChange Blog* (2019) at https://www.radicalxchange.org/media/blog/2019-10-24-uh78r5/.

focus on in the next chapter. Identity systems are about trusting/credit claims made by someone about a third party. Anyone who accepts an arbitrary number of such claims from someone they do not know well exposes themselves to potentially devastating attacks. On the other hand, accepting some claims about relatively unimportant matters from a less trustworthy source is not too risky. The trust established by a network of verifiers in an identity system is thus *quantitative* and thus depends on quantification of trust, and consequences for betraying this trust, in networks, precisely the sort of system we described here.

At the same time, these systems clearly depend on the technologies of identity and association we developed in the previous chapters, to underpin the definition and information structures of the communities and people who form the network of commercial relationships described here. And, as we will now explore, all are critical to joint use, contracting over and enterprise harnessing the critical assets of the digital age: computation, storage, and data. These ideas should be of particular interest to African communities in which trust-based and open-source social systems, interacting with mobile and digital technologies, indigenously invented the concept of mobile money, and set the pace for Africa's burgeoning fintech industries[22] even as the continent grapples with identification system gaps.[23]

---

[22] Omoaholo Omoakhalen, "Navigating the Geopolitics of Innovation: Policy and Strategy Imperatives for the 21st Century Africa," Remake Africa Consulting, 2023, https://remakeafrica.com/wp-content/uploads/2023/12/Navigating_the_Geopolitics_of_Innovation.pdf.

[23] "The State of Identification Systems in Africa." World Bank Group, 2017, https://openknowledge.worldbank.org/server/api/core/bitstreams/5f0f3977-838c-5ce3-af9d-5b6d6efb5910/content.

# 4-4 Property and Contract

Dear Vasana Gamers,

Step into the Legend with "Yusha"!

We're thrilled to introduce "Yusha", our latest gaming marvel, drawing inspiration from the iconic Dragon Quest series. Embrace the spirit of the cherished Dragon Quest adventures, where heroes vanquish fearsome foes and unravel the mysteries of enchanted realms. "Yusha", meaning "the brave one" in Japanese, elevates this timeless concept, blending it with cutting-edge technology for an unparalleled, real-world gaming odyssey.

Epic Features of "Yusha":

1. Power Up with Your Device and unleash Your Hero's Potential: Tap into the power of your device to fuel your Yusha's adventures. By harnessing the computing power of your local device, you refill your Yusha's energy bar. Your real-world tech usage recharges your hero, bridging your daily life with your in-game exploits.

2. Your World, Your Battlefield: Venture into the real world to shape your virtual domain. As you explore new physical locations, your device captures the topography, transforming it into a dynamic, magical world within the game. This means your real-world adventures directly expand the game's virtual territory, for all players.

3. Forge Connections, Discover Riches: "Yusha" introduces a novel twist to classic gaming mechanics by not randomly dispersing treasures throughout the game map. Instead, these treasures are hidden within the storage of the players' devices and can only be discovered through engaging in social interactions with fellow players. These interactions vary widely and

include activities like embarking on joint quests, healing a fellow player, crafting weapons for others, or simply engaging in conversation and listening to their stories. The method of unlocking these treasures remains a mystery, not even known to the players themselves. The only way forward is to persist in fostering genuine connections with others, reflecting the cooperative essence reminiscent of the legendary Dragon Quest adventures.

4. Guarded Realms: Information regarding your device, location, and surroundings, along with your in-game actions, is thoroughly safeguarded by advanced privacy technologies. The enchanting realm of Yusha is crafted from the players' exploration of the real world. We transfigure these physical environments into resplendent mountains and gleaming golden cities, ensuring that your actual location remains confidential.

5. Live the Adventure: "Yusha" is designed to augment your reality, not just serve as a virtual escape. Your dedication and exploration in the real world directly empower your Yusha and expand your virtual realm. True to the spirit of Dragon Quest, the treasures of our game lie in the connections you make and the adventures you embark upon, both virtually and physically.

Join the ranks of Vasana's adventurers where fantasy and reality blend into an epic saga. When you invest not just your time, but also the computing resources of your device, the physical effort exerted in traversing the real world, and the genuine intent to forge authentic connections, the world of Yusha transforms into a realm that is profoundly immersive and interactive. This convergence of digital and physical efforts brings the game's environment to life, enriching the gaming experience with a unique depth and realism that encourages a deeper sense of engagement and community among players.

Embark on the Adventure, The Vasana Team

---

Most large-scale cooperation today takes place through the pooling of assets into entities that are considered chartered as corporations, including limited liability partnerships, civic organizations, religious organizations, trade associations, unions, and of course, for-profit stock corporations. Their legal basis is in contractual arrangements that governs a sharing of assets (real, intellectual, human, and financial) in a common undertaking towards a shared purpose. Even the simplest, most common, and smallest scale contracts, such as rental agreements, involve the sharing of assets across people.

A core aim of Lick's "Intergalactic Computer Network" was to facilitate the sharing of digital assets, such as computation, storage, and data. And, in some ways, such sharing is the heart of today's digital economy, with "the Cloud" providing a vast pool of shared computation and storage and the wide range of information shared online forming the foundation of the generative foundation models (GFMs) that are sweeping the technology industry. Yet for all the success of this work, it is confined to limited slices of the digital world and controlled by a small group of highly profitable, for-profit entities based in at most a handful of countries, creating both tremendous waste of opportunity and concentration of power. The dream that the internet could enable broad and horizontal asset sharing remains a dream.

As with the other fundamental protocols we have discussed in this part of the book, there have been significant recent efforts to address these gaps. In this chapter we will review the potential of digital asset sharing and survey existing digital asset sharing efforts. We will highlight the accomplishments

數位 Plurality: Part 4: Freedom

and limitations of the existing efforts and sketch a path towards a robust and 數位 online asset sharing ecosystem.

## Assets in the digital age

As highlighted perhaps most dramatically in Kate Crawford's beautifully drawn *Atlas of AI*, the digital world is built on top of the physical world: computer circuits are made from rare metals mined with all the ensuing social challenges, data centers work much like and are often co-located with power plants, data is created by people like the "ghost workers" documented by Mary Gray and Siddarth Suri etc.[1] Any serious account of the digital realm must thus grapple with real property relations. Yet there are crucial assets that emerge from these physical substrates as digital-native abstractions and that are the crucial components of life online.

We will focus on three categories that are most ubiquitous: storage, computation, and data. Yet there are many other examples that intersect with these and have many related challenges, including the electromagnetic spectrum, code, names, and other addresses (e.g. Uniform Resource Locator/URLs), "physical" space in virtual worlds and non-fungible tokens (NFTs).

Storage, computation, and data lie at the core of essentially every online interaction. Anything that occurs online persists from one moment to the next only because of the data it depends on being stored somewhere. The occurrences themselves are embodied by computations being performed to determine the outcome of instructions and actions. And the

---

[1] Kate Crawford, *Atlas of AI* (New Haven, CT: Yale University Press, 2022). Mary Gray, and Siddhath Suri. *Ghost Work: How to Stop Silicon Valley from Building a New Global Underclass*. (Boston: Houghton Miffilin Harcourt, 2019).

input and output of every operation are data. In this sense, storage acts roughly like land in the real economy, computation acts like fuel and data acts like human inputs (sometimes called labor) and artifacts people create and reuse (sometimes called capital).

While land, fuel, labor, and capital are often treated as homogeneous "commodities", as social theorist Karl Polanyi famously argued this is a simplifying fiction.[2] Storage, computation and especially data are heterogeneous, tied to places, people and cultures and these connections affect both their performance characteristics and the social impacts and meanings of using them in a digital economy and society. While these challenges are significant for fictitious commodities "in real life", in some ways they are even more severe for digital assets and at the very least societies have had far less time to jointly adapt economic and social structures around them. These challenges are among the key inhibitors to a functional digital system of sharing, property, and contract.

## The Intergalactic Computer Network

Lick's 1963 "*Memorandum For Members and Affiliates of the Intergalactic Computer Network*" did not focus on the potential for online socialization or commerce that characterized so much of his contemporary and later writing.[3] Instead, perhaps because of his scientific audience at the time, he emphasized the potential for scientists to massively increase their productivity through computer networks by sharing analytic tools, memory, storage, computation, research findings and the promise this might have for related

---

[2] Polanyi, op. cit.

[3] Licklider, "Memorandum for Members and Affiliates of the Intergalactic Computer Network", op. cit.

military applications. This was also a natural extension of the "time-sharing" systems that were one of the first projects Lick funded and aimed to allow a semblance of what would become the "personal computing" experience in the era of large mainframe computers by allowing many users to share access to a larger machine's capacity. In this sense, the internet began, above all, as a platform for precisely the sort of large-scale computational resource sharing that we focus on in this chapter.[4]

To appreciate why such an apparently dull topic excited such an (otherwise) expansive mind, it is useful both to look backwards from today at the limits he was trying to overcome and forward to the limits we might, in delivering on his vision, overcome ourselves. During the 1950s and 1960s, the dominant paradigm of computing was large "mainframes" sold primarily by International Business Machines (IBM). These were expensive machines intended to serve the needs of an entire business, university department or other large grouping. To access these machines, users would have to bring programs to a central administrator, and they would, infrequently, have a single "high risk" chance to run their desired computation. If it turned out to have a bug, as it often did, they would have to return later, having meticulously and without practical tests attempted to fix these errors. At the same time, because preparing programs and managing the machine was so challenging, much of their time was spent idling, waiting for programs to arrive.

Contrast this to today's world of personal computing, where most people in developed countries today have computers on their desks, laps, or wrists and in their pockets that perform a dizzying array of computations with near-instant feedback. Of course, much of this has been empowered by Moore's Law of

---

[4] Waldrop, *The Dream Machine*, op. cit.

doubling computational power per unit price every eighteen months. But what Lick and some of the early projects he funded at the Massachusetts Institute of Technology and other universities saw was that at least some of this was possible even with the computers of the time if they were used more efficiently and with greater attention to the human need for feedback that he had studied in his work on designing airplane interfaces.

Much of the limited computation power then available was wasted in idle time and the feedback desired by users did not require a full machine at every desk. Instead, every user could have a basic display and input station ("client") connected via a network to a central machine ("server") whose time they shared, a set-up first pioneered a few years earlier in the Plato project at the University of Illinois Urbana-Champagne as a computer-based teaching system.[5] This allowed ARPANET members, such as Douglas Engelbart, to simulate a future of personal computing in the era of the mainframe.

What amazing future could we simulate if we could more effectively share our computational assets? It is hard to know without a tighter accounting of the underutilization of digital assets than we currently have. But it seems likely that we could at least buy half a decade more of effective Moore's Law simply by utilizing more effective digital assets that lay fallow. The possibilities for data sharing are richer and potentially even more transformative. Many of the most intractable problems today have answers if the power we see being unleashed by GFMs could be applied to medical diagnosis, environmental resource optimization, industrial production and more that is limited by the challenges today of sharing data across organizational and jurisdictional boundaries.

---

[5] Brian Dear, *The Friendly Orange Glow: The Untold Story of the PLATO System and the Dawn of Cyberculture* (New York: Pantheon, 2017)

數位 Plurality: Part 4: Freedom

## The state of sharing

Studies of the semiconductor industry indicate that several times as many semiconductors are used in personal devices (e.g. PCs, smartphones, smartwatches, video game consoles) as go into cloud infrastructure and data centers.[6] While there is little systematic study, personal experience indicates that most of these devices are mostly little used most of the day. This is likely particularly true of video game consoles, that disproportionately hold exceptionally valuable graphics processing units (GPUs). This suggests that a majority if not a large majority of computation and storage lies fallow at any time, not even accounting for the prevalent waste even in cloud infrastructure. Data are even more extreme; while these are even harder to quantify, the experience of any data scientist suggests that the overwhelming majority of desperately needed data sits in organizational or jurisdictional silos, unable to power collaborative intelligence or the training of GFMs.

Asset sharing may have important implications for values such as national security and the environment. Waste of resources effectively reduces the supply of semiconductors that national security policies have aimed at maximizing and, like any waste, increases the demand for environmental resources per unit of output. However, it is important to bear in mind that the sources of energy employed by distributed devices and their efficiency in converting this energy to computation may in some cases be lower than those of cloud providers, making it important to pair improvements to digital asset sharing with the greening of the consumer electrical grid. Perhaps the most important

---

[6] Gartner, "Gartner Forecasts Worldwide Semiconductor Revenue to Grow 17% in 2024" (2023) at https://www.gartner.com/en/newsroom/press-releases/2023-12-04-gartner-forecasts-worldwide-semiconductor-revenue-to-grow-17-percent-in-2024

implication of digital asset sharing for security may be increased interdependence between participants in these sharing networks which may bring them into tighter geopolitical alignment, especially given the requisite alignments of privacy and collaboration regulations.

What is most shocking about these figures is perhaps their comparison to physical assets, which one would naturally assume should be harder to share and ensure full utilization given the difficulty of transportation and physical redeployment. When unemployment rates for workers or vacancy rates for housing rise above single digits, political scandal usually ensues; such waste is omnipresent in the digital world. In short, rates of waste (effective under- and unemployment) of physical assets even close to these would be considered a global crisis.

The key reason why this silent crisis is a bit less surprising than the figures suggest is that these purely digital assets are comparatively new. Societies have had thousands if not tens of thousands of years to experiment with various social organizational systems to provide for the needs of the people within them. [7] The origins of our contemporary systems of property (rental systems, capital management), labor, and practices that involve the abstract representation of value [8] (with deeds, documents issued to people, supply chain transactions, money) can be traced to certain social-

---

[7] David Graeber and David Wengrow, *op cit*. In this book the authors explore a vast range of political creativity and flexibility surrounding how humans have organized themselves in the last 100,000 years.

[8] Hernando de Soto, *The Mystery of Capital: Why Capitalism Triumphs in the West and Fails Everywhere Else*, (New York: Basic Books, 2000). In the book he emphasizes that the abstract representation of property through formal titles and documentation allows assets to be leveraged in the financial system, enabling them to generate wealth and spur economic growth

psychological qualities that arose after 1000 years of cultural practices. The ban on cousin marriages in Christian Europe led to the emergence of people who were free to form new institutions and re-constitute how property was held which created new types of democratic institutions that didn't exist before. [9] There have been decades to figure out how to efficiently rent cars and increasingly harness digital tools to improve the sharing of these assets (e.g. ride and house sharing platforms). Digital assets, especially those in the hands of large groups of non-technical people, date back only a few decades. A crucial task before us, then, is to determine the crucial social and technical barriers to utilizing digital assets with the same effectiveness we have come to expect of physical assets.

One way to understand what stands in the way of computational asset sharing is to consider the areas where it has been relatively successful and draw out the differences between these domains and those where it has thus far mostly failed. To do so, we will run through the three areas of focus above: storage, computation, and data.

The closest framework to an open standard for asset sharing exists in storage, through the Interplanetary File System (IPFS) explicitly modeled on Lick's vision and pioneered by Juan Benet and his Protocol Labs (PL), which was a partner on some of the software that supported building this book. This open protocol allows computers around the world to offer storage to each other at a reasonable cost in a peer-to-peer, fragmented, encrypted, and distributed manner that helps ensure redundancy, robustness, and data secrecy/integrity. Prominent services built on the protocol include the use by Taiwan's Ministry of Digital Affairs and other governments facing strong adversaries who may hold leverage over more centralized

---

[9] see Henrich, "Part III: New Institutions, New Psychologies," in op. cit.

## 4-4 Property and Contract

service providers. To ensure the persistence of their data and the storage market PL also created the Filecoin system to allow commercial transactions and incent users to store as much of the entire network's data as they can. Yet even IPFS has been a limited success for "real-time" storage, where files need to be stored to allow their rapid access from many places around the world. It thus seems to be the relative simplicity of "deep" storage (think of the equivalent of the "public storage" spaces provided as a commodity service in real life) that has allowed IPFS to survive.

The more complicated challenge of optimizing for latency has been handled overwhelmingly by large corporate "cloud" providers such as Microsoft Azure, Amazon Web Services Google Cloud Platform and Salesforce. Most of the digital services familiar to consumers in the developed world (remote storage of personal files across devices, streaming of audio and video content, shared documents, etc.) depend on these providers. They are also at the core of most digital businesses today, with 60% of business data being stored in proprietary clouds and the top two proprietary cloud providers (Amazon and Microsoft) capturing almost two-thirds of the market.[10]

Yet even beyond the drawbacks of this space being controlled by a few for-profit companies, these cloud systems have achieved, in many ways, far less than the visionaries like Lick imagined.

First, heralds of the "cloud era" such as the Microsoft team that helped persuade the company to pursue the opportunity saw

---

[10] Josh Howarth, "34 Amazing Cloud Computing Stats" *Exploding Topics*, February 19 2024 at https://explodingtopics.com/blog/cloud-computing-stats. Felix Richter, "Amazon Maintains Cloud Lead as Microsoft Edges Closer" *Statista* February 5, 2024 at https://www.statista.com/chart/18819/worldwide-market-share-of-leading-cloud-infrastructure-service-providers/

many of the gains from the cloud arising from more efficient resource sharing across tenants and applications to ensure full utilization.[11] Yet, in practice, most of the gains from the cloud have come from physical cost savings of data centers co-located with abundant power sources and efficiently maintained, rather than from meaningful cross-tenant resource-sharing as few cloud providers have effectively facilitated this kind of market and few customers have found ways to make sharing resources work for them.

More dramatically, the cloud has largely been built in new data centers around the world, even as most available computation and storage remains severely underutilized in the pockets and on the laps and desks of personal computer owners around the world. Furthermore, these computers are physically closer and often more tightly networked to the consumers of computational resources than the bespoke cloud data centers…and yet the "genius" of the cloud system has systematically wasted them. In short, despite its many successes, the cloud largely has involved a reversion to an even more centralized version of the "mainframe" model that preceded the time-sharing work Lick helped support, rather than a realization of its ambitions.

Yet even these limited successes have been far more encouraging than what has been achieved in data sharing. The largest-scale uses of data today are either extremely siloed not just within corporate or institutional boundaries but even highly subdivided by privacy policies within these or otherwise based on the ingestion of publicly available data online without even the awareness, much less consent, of the data creators. The leading example of the latter is the still-undisclosed data sets

---

[11] Rolf Harms, and Michael Yamartino, "The Economics of the Cloud," 2010, https://news.microsoft.com/download/archived/presskits/cloud/docs/The-Economics-of-the-Cloud.pdf.

on which the GFMs were trained. The movement to allow data sharing even for clear public interest cases, such as public health or the curing of diseases, has been held out for years under a variety of names and yet has made very little progress either in the private sector or in open standards-based collaborations.

This problem is widely recognized and the subject of a variety of campaigns around the world. Examples include the European Union's Gaia-X data federation infrastructure and their Data Governance Act, India's National Data Sharing and Accessibility Policy, Singapore's Trusted Data Sharing Framework and Taiwan's Plural Innovation strategy are just a few examples of attempts to overcome these challenges.

## Impediments to sharing

What lessons can we glean from these failures about the impediments to more effective sharing of digital assets? From the fact that data sharing has failed most spectacularly, and storage sharing has struggled most with issues around data sharing, a natural hypothesis is that related issues may lie at the core of many of these problems. After all, related challenges reoccur in all these domains. Much of the structure of IPFS and the challenges it faces relate to maintaining data privacy while allowing storage far from the person or organization seeking to maintain this privacy. A central advantage of the cloud providers has been their reputation for security and privacy of customer data while allowing those customers to share it across their devices and perform large-scale computations on it.

A basic contrast between data and many real-world assets is important in understanding these challenges. Lending and pooling of assets is ubiquitous in the economy as we discussed above. Critical to it is the possibility of decomposing the rights one has to an asset. Legal scholars typically describe three attributes of property: "usus" (the right to use something), "abusus" (the right to alter or dispose of it) and "fructus" (the right to the value it creates). A standard rental contract, for example, transfers to the renter the usus rights, while retaining abusus and fructus for the landlord. A corporation grants usus of many assets to employees, abusus only to senior managers and often only with checks and balances and reserves fructus for shareholders.

Achieving this crucial separation is different and arguably more challenging for data. The simplest ways of giving access to usus of data also allow the person granted access the ability to abuse or transfer the data to others (abusus) and the ability for others to gain financial benefit from those data (fructus), possibly at the expense of the person sharing it. Many who chose to publish data online that has now been incorporated into GFMs believed they were sharing information for others to use, but they did not perceive the full implications that sharing would have. Of course, norms, laws and cryptography could all potentially play a role in correcting this situation, and we turn to these shortly. At present these are all underdeveloped relative to expectations in, for example, corporate governance or housing rentals, impairing the ability of data sharing to thrive.

To make matters more complicated, settling on such a set of standards is, for the reasons we highlighted in the *Association and 數位 Publics chapter*, challenged by the other key property of data: that interests in it are rarely if ever usefully understood as mostly individual rights. Data are inherently associational, social, and intersectional, making many of the simplest "quick fixes" for this problem (in terms of privacy regulations and cryptography) so misfitting that they impede progress more than they facilitate it.

Furthermore, even if there were a clear set of solutions to these challenges, there is no straightforward way to implement them directly. The most simplistic understanding of contracts is that they are commitments between parties described and mutually agreed to in a document. Freedom of contract simply requires this to be enforced. The reality is much richer, however: it is impossible to specify in a contract how to resolve many conflicts that may arise and no one could read and process such a detailed document if it were.[12]

Contracts are necessarily both ambiguous on many points and deliberately do not touch many questions that (e.g. "the worker should work really hard" and "the employer should be fair") that are important but hard to precisely specify. Most contractual arrangements are therefore governed primarily by customary expectations, legal precedent, statutes that are consistent with these, mutually expected norms, etc. In many contexts, contractual provisions that conflict with these evolved principles will not be enforced. These norms and legal structures have co-evolved over decades and even centuries to govern canonical relationships like rental and employment, minimizing the role that formal court-based contractual provisions and enforcement must play. While self-enforcing digital "smart contracts" might thus provide a way to implement such norms smoothly, they cannot substitute for the process of creating a stable social understanding of how data collaboration works, what different parties can expect and when various legal and technical enforcement mechanisms should and will kick in.

Challenges of this sort surround efforts to build infrastructure for sharing digital assets like data. The basic problem is that information has a near-infinity of possible uses, meaning that heavily "contractualist" approaches that seek to define exactly how parties may use information run into unmanageable

---

[12] Sanford J. Grossman and Oliver D. hart, "The Costs and Benefits of Ownership: A Theory of Vertical and Lateral Integration", *Journal of Political Economy* 94, no. 4: 691-719.

complexity. Such contracts' zones of "incompleteness" are vast because it is not possible even to imagine, let alone catalog and negotiate over all the possible future uses of information like genetics or geolocation. That means that the most promising possible benefits of data sharing – which involve taking advantage of new technical affordance to convey information to distant parties all around the world – are also the most dangerous and ungovernable. The potential market is therefore paralyzed. If we cannot address these problems with conventional contracts, our ideal spheres of information sharing will end up matching the shape of our associations – meaning we need better maps of our associative connections, and, as discussed elsewhere, better assurances against information leakage even from trusted communities.

Of course, these are far from the only problems besetting digital asset sharing: optimizing for latency, mapping security measures, appropriately standardizing units of computation, and other such technical obstacles are also significant. But the challenges created by the lack of clear and meaningful standards (both legal and technical) for protecting data while it is shared spill out into almost every aspect of scalable digital cooperation. While no deductive analysis can substitute for the social experimentation and evolution that will be needed to reach such standards, we can highlight some of the components and efforts that seem likely to address the central tensions above and thus should become important to social exploration if we are going to get past the current barriers to digital asset sharing.

## property

The first and simplest issue to address is standards for performance and security for computational asset sharing. When users store their data or entrust a computation to others, they need assurances that their data will not be compromised by a third party and that the computation will

## 4-4 Property and Contract

be performed according to their expectations, that their data will be retrievable by themselves or their customers with an expected distribution of latency by people in various places etc. Currently these sorts of guarantees are central to the value propositions of the cloud providers. Because there are no standards that can easily be met by a broad set of individuals and organizations offering computational services, these powerful companies dominate the market. An analogous example is the introduction of Hypertext Transfer Protocol Secure (HTTPS), which allowed a range of web hosting services to meet security criteria that give web content consumers confidence that they can access data from that website without being maliciously surveilled. Such standards could naturally be paired with standardized formats for searching, requesting, and matching on additional performance and security features.

However, as noted above, the thorniest questions pertain not to performance or third-party attacks, but to the problems at the heart of data collaboration: what should a collaborator Party B with whom Party A shares data or other digital assets learn about Party A's data? While this obviously has no single right answer, setting parameters and expectations in ways that allow participants to benefit from collaboration without frequently undermining their critical interests or those of other people affected by this collaboration is central to making data collaboration feasible and sustainable. Luckily, several tools are becoming available that will help provide technical scaffolding for such relationships.

While we have discussed it in the *Association* chapter, it is worth recalling their relevance here. Secure multi-party computation (SMPC) and homomorphic encryption allow multiple parties to perform a computation together and create a collective output without each revealing to the others the inputs. While the simplest illustrative examples include calculating an average salary or tallying votes in an election, far more sophisticated possibilities are increasingly within reach, such as training or fine-tuning a GFM. These more ambitious applications have helped create the field of "federated learning" and "data federation", which allow the computations necessary for one of these ambitious applications to be performed locally on a distributed network of personal or organizational computers with the inputs to the model being passed back and forth securely without the underlying training data ever leaving the machine or servers of the respective parties to the communication. In collaboration with open source providers of these tools such as OpenMined, international organizations like the United Nations have increasingly built experimental showcase platforms for data collaboration harnessing these tools.[13] An alternative to this distributed approach is to use specialized "confidential computers" that can be verified to perform particular calculations but give no one access to their intermediate outputs. Because these machines are expensive and produced by only a limited range of companies, however, these lend themselves more to control by a trusted central entity than diffuse collaboration.

While these approaches can help achieve collaboration without unnecessary information being conveyed across collaborators, other tools are needed to address the information contained in the desired outputs (e.g. statistics or models) created by the collaboration. Models may both leak input information (e.g. a model reproduces intimate details of the medical history of a particular person) or may, conversely, obscure the source of information (e.g. reproduce input creative text without attribution, in violation of a license). Both are significant

---

[13] "The UN is Testing Technology that Processes Data Confidentially" *The Economist* January 29, 2022.

## 4-4 Property and Contract

impediments to data collaboration, as collaborators will typically want an agency over the use of their data.

Tools to address these challenges are more statistical than cryptographic. Differential privacy limits the degree to which input data can be guessed from a collection of output data, using a "privacy budget" to ensure that together disclosures do not reliably reveal inputs. Watermarking can create "signatures" in content showing its origin in ways that are hard to erase, ignore or even in some cases detect. "Influence functions" trace the role a particular collection of data plays in producing the output of a model, allowing at least partial attribution of the output of an otherwise "black box" model.[14]

All these techniques have fallen somewhat behind the speed, scale, and power of the development of GFMs. For example, differential privacy focuses mostly on the literal statistical recoverability of facts, whereas GFMs are often capable of performing "reasoning" as a detective would, inferring for example someone's first school from a constellation of only loosely related facts about later schools, friendships, etc. Harnessing the capacity of these models to tackle these technical challenges and deriving technical standard definitions of data protection and attribution, especially as models further progress, will be central to making data collaboration sustainable.

Yet many of the challenges to data collaboration are more organizational and social than purely technical. As we noted earlier, interests in data are rarely individual as almost all data are relational. Even beyond this most fundamental point, there

---

[14] Pan Wei Koh and Percy Liang, "Understanding Black-Box Predictions via Influence Functions", *Proceedings of the 34th International Conference on Machine Learning*, 70 (2017): 1885-1894

are many reasons why organizing data rights and control at the individual level is impractical including:

- Social leakage: Even when data do not directly arise from a social interaction, they almost always have social implications. For example, because of the shared genetic structure of relatives, something like a 1% statistical sample of a population allows the identification of any individual from their genetic profile, making the preservation of genetic privacy a profoundly social undertaking.
- Management challenges: It is nearly impossible for an individual alone to understand the implications, both financial and personal, of sharing data in various ways. While automated tools can help, these will be made or shaped by social groups, who will need to be fiduciaries for these individuals.
- Collective bargaining: The primary consumers of large data sets are the largest and most powerful corporations in the world. The billions of data creators around the world can only achieve reasonable terms in any arrangement with them, and these companies could only engage in good faith negotiations, if data creators act collectively.

Organizations capable of taking on this role of collectively representing the rights and interests of "data subjects"[15] have

---

[15] Jaron Lanier, *Who Owns the Future?*, (New York: Simon and Schuster, 2014).

been given a variety of names: data trusts,[16] collaboratives,[17] cooperatives,[18] or, in a whimsical turn of phrase one of the authors suggested, "mediators of individual data" (MIDs).[19] Some of these could quite naturally follow the lines of existing organizations: for example, unions for creative workers representing their content, or Wikipedia representing the collective interest of its volunteer editors and contributors. Others may require new forms of organization, such as the contributors of open-source code that is being used to train code-generation models, authors of fan fiction and writers of Reddit pages may need to organize their own forms of collective representation.

Beyond these formal technologies, organizations and standards, broader and more diffuse concepts, expectations and norms will have to develop so as to ensure broad understanding of what is at stake in data collaborations, so that contributors feel empowered to strike fair agreements and hold their collaborators accountable. Given the pace of technological change and adaptation in what data collaborations will thus become, these norms will both have to become pervasive and reasonably stable *and* dynamic and adaptive. Achieving this will require practices of education and

---

[16] Sylvie Delacroix, and Jess Montgomery, "Data Trusts and the EU Data Strategy," Data Trusts Initiative, June 2020. https://datatrusts.uk/blogs/data-trusts-and-the-eu-data-strategy.

[17] See the Data Collaboration Alliance at https://www.datacollaboration.org/

[18] Thomas Hardjono and Alex Pentland, "Data cooperatives: Towards a Foundation for Decentralized Personal Data Management," *arXiv* (New York: Cornell University, 2019), https://arxiv.org/pdf/1905.08819.pdf.

[19] Lanier and Weyl, op. cit.

cultural engagement that keep pace with technical change, as we discuss in the following chapters.

Once they develop and spread sufficiently, data collaboration tools, organizations and practices may become sufficiently familiar to be encoded in common sense and legal practice as deeply as "property rights" are, though as we noted they will almost certainly have to take a different form than the standard patterns governing private ownership of land or the organization of a joint-stock corporation. They will, as we noted, need to include many more technical and cryptographic elements, different kinds of social organizations with a greater emphasis on collective governance and fiduciary duties and norms or laws protecting against unilateral disclosure by a member of a MIDs (analogous to prohibitions against unilateral strikebreaking against unions). These may form into a future version of "property" for the digital world, but one much more attuned to the 數位 character of data.

## 數位 real property

Achieving 數位 property will be a challenge, but it is instructive to remember that many property rights systems in other realms are contested and in flux. In some ways the deeply social character of data sets it apart from real world assets, and therefore our existing modes of designing property rights and contractual systems are not readily applied to data. But in other ways, the deeply social character of data accentuates, through its unfamiliarity, many of the ways traditional property systems are themselves ill-suited to managing real assets today.

We take one step away from the purely digital asset world and look at two examples of digitally-related assets whose property rights regimes are changing rapidly. These two examples are electromagnetic spectrum and name spaces on the internet.

Traditionally, entitlements to broadcast on a particular electromagnetic frequency in a particular geographic range have (in many countries including the US) been assigned or auctioned to operators with licenses being renewed at low cost. This has effectively created a private property-like entitlement based on the idea that users of frequencies will interfere if many are allowed to operate on the same band of spectrum in the same place and that licensees will steward the band if they have property rights over it. These assumptions have been tested to the breaking point recently, however, as many digital applications (such as WiFi) can share spectrum and the rapidly changing nature of uses for spectrum (e.g. moving from over-the-air broadcasting to 5G wireless) has dramatically changed interference patterns, requiring reorganization of the spectrum against which legacy license holders can often serve as holdouts.[20] This in turn has led to significant changes to the property system, allowing licensing agencies like America's Federal Communications Commission to relocate holdouts in auctions, and proposals by leaders in the space for even more radical designs that would mix elements of rental and ownership as we discuss in our *Social Markets* chapter below or leave spectrum unlicensed for specified shared uses.[21]

---

[20] Paul R. Milgrom, Jonathan Levin and Assaf Eilat, "The Case for Unlicensed Spectrum" at https://papers.ssrn.com/sol3/papers.cfm?abstract_id=1948257 and Paul Milgrom, "Auction Research Evolving: Theorems and Market Designs", *American Economic Review* 111, no. 5 (2021): 1383-1405.

[21] E. Glen Weyl and Anthony Lee Zhang, "Depreciating Licenses", *American Economic Journal: Economic Policy* 14, no. 3 (2022): 422-448. Paul R. Milgrom, E. Glen Weyl and Anthony Lee Zhang, "Redesigning Spectrum Licenses to Encourage Innovation and Investment", *Regulation* 40, no. 3 (2017): 22-26.

The evolution of property in name spaces has been even more radical. Traditionally the Internet Corporation for Assigned Names and Numbers (ICANN) allowed registration of domain names at relatively low cost with nominal fees for renewal, like the property-like licensing regime for spectrum. While this system has evolved, the more fundamental change has been that today, most people reach websites through search engines rather than direct navigation. These engines usually list sites associated with a given name based on a variety of (mostly not publicly disclosed) signals of their relevance to users as well as including some paid advertisements that are auctioned in real-time.[22] While relevance algorithms are something of a black box, a reasonable first mental model for them is the original "PageRank" algorithm of Google founders Sergey Brin and Larry Page, which ranked pages based on their "network centrality", a notion related to the network-based voting systems we will discuss in our chapter on *Voting* below. [23] Thus, to a first blush, we can think of the *de facto* property regime of internet name spaces today as being a combination of collective direction towards the interest of browsers (rather than domain owners) combined with a real-time auction for domain owners. Both are a far cry from traditional property systems.

This is not, of course, to suggest that any of these are ideal and certainly not socially legitimate. These systems have been largely designed far from the public eye, without public understanding by teams of technocratic engineers and

---

[22] Benjamin Edelman, Michael Ostrovsky and Michael Schwarz, "Internet Advertising and the Generalized Second-Price Auction: Selling Billions of Dollars Worth of Keywords", *American Economic Review* 97, no. 1: 242-259

[23] Sergey Brin and Lawrence Page, "The Anatomy of a Large-Scale Hypertextual Web Search Engine", *Computer Systems and ISDN Systems* 30, no. 1-7: 107-117.

economists. Few even recognize that they operate much less believe they are appropriate.[24] On the other hand, they respond to real challenges in creative ways, and the issues they address stretch well beyond the narrow domains to which they have been applied thus far. Addressing holdout problems and spectrum sharing are central to allowing digital development that is broadly demanded by the public and viewed as central to even issues of national security. Similar holdout issues pervade the redevelopment of urban spaces and the building of common infrastructure, and much land currently held as private property could be made into shared spaces like parks (or vice-versa).

Treating name spaces as private property makes little sense, given that those who happen to own a name that is contested (e.g. "ABC.com") may be domain squatters, legacy owners serving a limited audience, fraudsters exploiting a brand, etc. While some of the stability and signal of importance from owners' willingness to pay offered by property rights are clearly important, the systems used by search engines achieve this in arguably a better balance by explicitly accounting for the public interest in stability and the real-time demands from those who would pay for the name space than does a simple private property system. Again, these issues show up frequently in "real world" domains from trademarks and other intellectual property to the ownership of antiquities and historic locations in cities. It only takes a slight stretch of imagination to see how, if they combine with far better public engagement, education

---

[24] In fact, authors of this book have been prominent critics of these designs for these reasons. Zoë Hitzig, "The Normative Gap: Mechanism Design and Ideal Theories of Justice", *Economics and Philosophy* 36, no. 3: 407-434. Glen Weyl, "How Market Design Economists Helped Engineer a Mass Privatization of Public Resources", *Pro-Market* May 28, 2020 at https://www.promarket.org/2020/05/28/how-market-design-economists-engineered-economists-helped-design-a-mass-privatization-of-public-resources/.

⌗ 數位 Plurality: Part 4: Freedom

and advocacy, the innovative alternatives to property that evolved and are evolving in the digital realm might help us rethink property systems more broadly in a ⌗ direction, a theme we will explore in greater depth in our *Social Markets* chapter below.

## 4-5 Access

Lucy: Hello, this is Luc from Château du Soleil Couchant out of Bordeaux.

Municipal Rep: Greetings, Lucy. What can I do for you today?

Lucy: Well, we at Château du Soleil Couchant are in talks with several other vineyards about the idea of creating a coalition for the implementation of a new hail cannon system across our properties. We've secured backing from 12 of the 14 regional vineyards; however, we require a mechanism that guarantees openness, fair decision-making, and the distribution of costs and advantages among all parties involved.

Lucy: To pull this off, we need a governance framework that encourages participation from neighboring vineyards. We've noticed the Wine Trade Association has had great success with their collaborative efforts, and we aim to emulate their model.

Municipal Rep: I appreciate the overview. Could you elaborate on why you need these collaborative tools?

Lucy: Certainly. There's been skepticism among local vineyards about the efficacy of hail cannons, but the latest generation has been scientifically validated to disrupt hailstorm formation. Hail is a longstanding menace to our crops. To be effective, we need widespread adoption of these systems. We're initiating a pilot program to build trust locally, but a governance system akin to what helped the Wine Trade Association resolve their differences would be invaluable.

Municipal Rep: Thanks for elaborating. The collaboration framework the French Wine Trade Association uses was adapted from the U.S. Wine and Spirit Association's model back in 2036. Based on what you've described, we've already tailored it to better fit your regional circumstances. It's important to note, though, that these tools are designed to foster inclusive discussion and consensus, not to drive specific outcomes like the adoption of hail cannons.

Lucy: Understood, and I appreciate the clarification.

Municipal Rep: Great. I've just configured the platform based on our discussion and launched it at www.bordeauxhailcannon.assoc. A detailed changelog has been dispatched to you. Should you need further modifications, please let me know.

Lucy: I certainly will. Could you also send over some advice or common hurdles that others have faced?

Municipal Rep: Definitely. While I can't share confidential details from past projects, I can walk you through the general use of these tools, as well as our past learning.

Lucy: That sounds perfect, thank you. I'll review the changelog and get back to you by tomorrow.

Municipal Rep: Excellent, have a good evening.

---

Long before the rise of the internet, access to information had always been a crucial part of human civilization: as Sir Francis Bacon put it centuries ago, "knowledge is power". In today's information age, and even more in the future we describe in this book, the literal truth in this dictum is ever more present. While the previous chapters of this part focus on the aspects of digital life that ensure human rights, these mean nothing to human life unless every human can securely and faithfully access this world we imagine. In this chapter, we will explore what making such access a fundamental right must mean.

We are not interested in mere access, but *access with integrity*. If the information some receive is accurate and others

4-5 Access

corrupted, it is worse than if the latter had no access at all. Democracy depends on a populace that can fully participate: every voice is critical. While, as we have emphasized above, different communities make sense of the pattern of facts differently. But this diversity of perspective must come founded on underlying common access to uncorrupted input data if it is to contribute to a 🔲 future. We all can and must make our own meanings of life, but we are denied our equal right to do so if some of us receive manipulated versions of the inputs to the global information commons.

From the United Nations' adoption of the Universal Declaration of Human Rights in 1948 to the Declaration for the Future of the Internet in 2022, human society has continuously emphasized the importance of freedom of expression and access. These two documents illustrate a pathway that extends from basic human rights to the principles of freedom and security in the digital age. In 2023, the Global Declaration on Information Integrity Online directly addressed the collective challenges posed by generative AI and its potential for mass manipulation.

In simple terms, we must ensure that everyone has equal access to contextually complete information; otherwise, it can become worthless or even weapon. This imperative is not solely driven by digital technology; it also requires a collective, universal, and inclusive digital alliance, supported by a democratic structure. In today's era, where internet access is considered a digital human right, the spirit of 🔲 flows seamlessly across the globe, much like the ancient concept of 'dao.' This spirit is woven from zeros and ones, continuously expanding our 'internet of beings' and integrating with societal structures in ways that combine democratic governance with collaborative technology. Thus, "access" signifies not just technological availability but also contributes to the realization of everyone's innate vision, naturally fostering trust, mutual respect, and safety.

Next, we will clarify the status of internet access, countries' efforts towards access, as well as our expectations for the digital environment and prospects for future development.

## Bridging the digital divide

During global digitalization, nations like Taiwan, Estonia, and the Scandinavian nations have pioneered the principle of digital access as a foundational right through proactive government support for internet development, cross-disciplinary collaboration, and the involvement of local community workers as key policy and implementation participants. But this is just a downpayment on the long-term investment we need to support digital public infrastructure. These collective efforts not only propel societal change but also help consolidate democratic values and establish collective consensus. It is no surprise that these countries that lead in access are also those which have most strongly embraced the substantive digital democracy we discuss in the next section of the book.

Yet, these positive outcomes are not widespread. Digital disparity exemplifies social polarization, particularly between rural and urban areas. Prior to the pandemic, 76% of urban households around the world had access to home internet, which was nearly double the 39% in rural regions. The pandemic has intensified public attention on such disparities as more areas of life — from work and education to socializing — have moved online. The International Telecommunication Union (ITU) reports that in 2020 alone, 466 million people used the internet for the first time.[1] While the number and global penetration of internet users have continued to grow, multifaceted inequalities in access remain. These contribute to a wide range of economic, political, and social inequities.

Building on previous chapters of this book, we need to understand the fundamental right of access from 🔲 perspectives, and the role of policymakers is crucial. They need to focus on global digital divides and take corresponding measures to resolve the inequality in access. Such steps must also include investment in digital public infrastructure to protect contextual integrity for online exchange.

While openness is promoted, digital participants also need to contribute their efforts to illuminate the dark and tricky corners existing on the internet, watching out for each other. Of course, this issue touches upon global social structures and cultural diversity. Fortunately, we no longer need to cross oceans as De Tocqueville did to learn from the valuable experiences of different countries in building digital democracy and sustainable development. To safeguard and establish a safer and more open digital access environment, there are two important courses of action:

1. Digital Infrastructure: Develop an interoperable model for international infrastructures that overcomes the challenges of collective action we discuss in the *Social Markets* chapter below, thereby providing equitable services globally.

2. Information Integrity: Address the challenges posed by mimetic models (so-called "deepfakes") to maintain

---

[1] International Telecommunications Union, *Facts and Figures* (2022) at https://www.itu.int/itu-d/reports/statistics/2022/11/24/ff22-internet-use-in-urban-and-rural-areas/.

semantic security and allowing continued enjoyment of the benefits of the digital age.

If we can advance these two fundamental rights, the other rights described in this part of the book can reach into the lived experience of all people and serve as a substrate not just of collective intelligence "online", but in the daily lives of everyone across the world. As we have highlighted throughout the book, many public services and social interactions in today's digital environment seem overshadowed by capitalism. Nowadays, "internet access is a human right." is nearly a consensus among democracies. What remains is to untangle the complications between democracy and internet access.

## Infrastructures for information integrity

Forestry expert Suzanne Simard focuses on exploring the collaborative nature of forests, viewing them as intelligent systems.[2] These forests not only possess self-awareness and spontaneous development capabilities, but also feature close interactions between various ecological components. Simard has studied how tree roots and symbiotic mycorrhizal fungi communicate in the soil layers of ancient forests in British Columbia. She discovered with colleagues that in this environment driven by fungal networks, different types of trees can send warning signals to each other and share essential sugars, water, carbon, nitrogen, and phosphorus.[3]

---

[2] Suzanne Simard, *Finding the Mother Tree: Discovering the Wisdom of the Forest* (New York: Knopf, 2021).

[3] Suzanne W. Simard, David A. Perry, Melanie D. Jones, David D. Myrold, Daniel M. Durall and Randy Molina, "Net Transfer of Carbon Between Ectomycorrhizal Tree Species in the Field", *Nature* 388 (1997): 579-582.

In such a vibrant forest, a single 'mother tree' can establish connections with hundreds of other trees. Multiple such mother trees ensure the continuity of the entire forest as a collective organism through overlapping networks, ensuring a secure and robust environment through open connections.

Digital infrastructure follows a similar pattern with open standards (protocols), open-source code, and open data. It serves as a public foundation that is open to the global community, collaborating with tens of thousands of digital communities while offering open and secure Internet access and jointly defending against immediate digital threats.

Taiwan is one of the world's primary distributed denial of service (DDoS) hotspots, according to Cloudflare's report.[4] Its government has adopted the IPFS framework discussed in the previous chapter for its websites, allowing it to interconnect with both private digital services and emerging open networks. This structure is not only more resistant to sudden DDoS attacks but is also conducive to open collaboration and mutual support with global technology communities. This provides an illustration of how to make systems more robust against information manipulation.

Furthermore, it is essential to ensure that people have the right to access information with contextual confidence. The primary goals of open government data align with this: granting more power to citizens and increasing government transparency and accountability, can together effectively combat corruption and enable democratic systems to serve the people more efficiently. The Ukrainian "Diia" and the Estonian "mRiik" serve

---

[4] Omer Yoachimik and Jorge Pacheco, "DDoS threat report for 2023 Q4" *Cloudflare Blog* January 9, 2024 at https://blog.cloudflare.com/ddos-threat-report-2023-q4.

as examples that highlight the bidirectional features of trusted networks and information openness.

Both Estonia and Ukraine are proactive in digitalization toward public participation. They make digital technology a genuinely necessary social tool for the public, providing secure, open digital public services for citizens to access government services and real-time information. Diia has shown the world how digital technology can break down long-standing corruption. This year, Estonia launched its latest app "mRiik," largely inspired by the Ukrainian app Diia.[5]

Digital infrastructure does not point to a one-size-fits-all solution; each nation still needs to adapt based on its unique development needs. However, the fundamental functions and democratic essence are of similar values and offer a common ground for expansion. Taiwan, Estonia, and Ukraine show us how information integrity and digital infrastructure intertwine to enhance societal resilience.

In conclusion, the right to access is a cornerstone for achieving digital democracy and social inclusivity. To move towards such a future requires multi-dimensional efforts, including technological innovation and policy cooperation. The next chapter will delve deeper into these intertwined issues.

---

[5] Note Ukraine's readiness to share its code and UX/UI design methods with Estonia (see Igor Sushon, "Estonia Launches the State Application MRiik, Built on the Basis of the Ukrainian Application Diia," Mezha, January 19, 2023, https://mezha.media/2023/01/19/diia-mriik/.https://mezha.media/2023/01/19/diia-mriik/)"

# Part 5: Democracy

## 5-0 Collaborative Technology and Democracy

This book was created to demonstrate ⌘ in action and as well as describe it: to show as well as tell. As such, it was created using many of the tools we describe in this section. The text was stored on and updated using the Git protocol that open source coders use to control versions of their software. The text is shared freely under a Creative Commons 0 license, implying that no rights to any content herein are reserved to the community creating it and it may be freely reused. At the time of this writing, dozens of diverse experts and citizens from every continent contributed to the writing as highlighted in our credits above and we hope many more will the continued evolution of the text after physical publication, embodying the practices we describe in our *Creative Collaboration* chapter.

Work was collectively prioritized and rewards determined using a "crowd-funding" approach we describe in our *Social Markets* chapter below. Changes to the text in future evolution will be approved collectively by the community using a mixture of the advanced voting procedures described in our ⌘ *Voting* chapter below and prediction markets. Contributors were recognized using a community currency and group identity tokens as we described in our *Identity and Personhood* and *Commerce and Trust* chapters above, which in turn was used in voting and prioritization of outstanding issues for the book. These priorities in turn determined the quantitative recognition received by those whose contributions addressed these challenges, an approach we have described with other as a "⌘

*Management Protocol*".[1] All this was recorded on a distributed ledger through an open-source protocol, GitRules, grounded on open-source participation rather than financial incentives. Contentious issues were resolved through tools we discuss in the *Augmented Deliberation* chapter below. The book has been translated and copy-edited by the community augmented by many of the cross-linguistic and subcultural translation tools we discuss in our *Adaptive Administration* chapter.

To support the financial needs of the book during the publication process, we harnessed several of the tools we describe in the *Social Markets* chapter. We hope to harness technologies from the Immersive Shared Reality chapter to communicate and explore the ideas from the book with audiences around the world.

For all these reasons, as you read this book you are both learning about the ideas and evaluating them on their merits and at the same time experiencing what they put into practice can create. If you are inspired by that content, especially critically, we encourage you to contribute to the living and community managed continuations of this document and all its translations by submitting changes through a git "pull request" or by reaching out to one of the many contributors to become part of the community. We hope as many criticisms of this work as possible will be inspired by the open-source mantra "so fix it!"

---

While a human rights operating system is the foundation, the point of the system for most people is what is built on top of it.

---

[1] Tobin South, Leon Erichsen, Shrey Jain, Petar Maymounkov, Scott Moore and E. Glen Weyl, "Plural Management" (2024) at https://papers.ssrn.com/sol3/papers.cfm?abstract_id=4688040.

## 5-0 Collaborative Technology and Democracy

On top of the bedrock of human rights, liberal democratic societies run open societies, democracies, and welfare capitalism. On top of operating systems, customers run productivity tools, games, and a range of internet-based communication media. In this chapter, we will illustrate the collaboration technologies that can be built on the foundation of social protocols of the previous section.

While we have titled this section of the book "democracy", what we plan to describe goes well beyond many conventional descriptions of democracy as a system of governance of nations. Instead, to build on top of fundamental social protocols, we must explore the full range of ways in which applications can facilitate collaboration and cooperation, the working of several entities (people or groups) together towards a common goal. Yet even these phrases miss something crucial that we focus on the power that working together must create something greater than the sum of what the parts could have created separately.

Mathematically, this idea is known as "supermodularity" and captures the classic idea attributed to Aristotle that "the whole is greater than the sum of the parts".[2] An early example of the quantitative application of supermodularity is the idea of "comparative advantage", the first comprehensive description of which that we are aware of presented by the English economist David Ricardo in 1817.[3] "Comparative advantage" says, roughly, that overall welfare will be maximized when all trading partners specialize in making their most efficient

---

[2] Divya Siddarth, Matt Prewitt and Glen Weyl, "Beyond Public and Private: Collective Provision Under Conditions of Supermodularity" (2024) at *https://cip.org/supermodular*.

[3] David Ricardo, *On the Principles of Political Economy and Taxation*, (London: John Murray, 1817).

product, even when some other partner can make *everything* more efficiently. Comparative advantage is understood as an 'economic law' stating in effect that there are guaranteed gains from diversity that can be realized through the market mechanism. This idea has been extremely influential in neoliberal economics (see *Social Markets*), although later iterations are more sophisticated than the Ricardian version and one need not accept the simplistic "free trade" implications to appreciate the benefits of gains from trade. Furthermore, given our emphasis on diversity, what we mean by "gains" here is context-specific and need not be simplistically economic; instead, it will be defined by the norms and values of the individuals and communities coming together. Furthermore, our focus is less on people or groups *per se* than on the fabric running through and separating them, social difference. Thus, what we will describe in this part of the book is, most precisely, how technology can empower supermodularity across social difference or, more colloquially, "collaboration across diversity".

This chapter, which lays out the framework for the rest of this part of the book, will highlight why collaboration across diversity is such a fundamental and ambitious goal. We then define a spectrum of domains where it can be pursued based on the trade-off between depth and breadth of collaboration. Next, we highlight a framework for design in the space that navigates between the dangers of premature optimization and chaotic experimentation. Yet harnessing the potential of collaboration across diversity also holds the risk of reducing the diversity available for future collaboration. To guard against this we discuss the necessity of *regenerating* diversity. We round out this chapter by describing the structure followed in each subsequent chapter in this part.

## Collaboration across diversity: promise and challenges

Why are we so focused on collaboration across diversity? A simple way to understand this is by analogy to energy systems. Prior to industrialism, rare encounters with powerful thermodynamic effects (such as oil fires in the ground) were met with fear and attempts to suppress these conflagrations. Yet with the advent of industrial harnessing of fossil fuels, it became more common to greet such explosions with a prospector's eye, looking to harness the potential energy that led to these explosions productively. In a world beset by conflict, we must learn to build engines that, just as in the Taiwanese example we opened with, convert the potential energy driving these conflicts into useful work. The ⌬ age must learn to harness social and informational potential energy as the industrial age did for fossil fuels and the nuclear age did for atomic energy.[4] Such an age may fulfill the prophecy of Matthew 20:16, "So the last shall be first, and the first last", as the most diverse and conflict-ridden places on earth (especially in Africa) hold arguably more potential energy than anywhere on the planet.

While novel in a certain sense, this is also one of the oldest and most universally resonant of all human ideas. All life depends on survival and reproduction, and cooperation across difference is critical to both: avoiding deadly conflict, but also reproduction that requires the unlike to come together,

---

[4] The analogy here is even tighter than it might seem at first. What is usually called "energy" is actually "low entropy"; a uniformly hot system has lots of "energy" but this is not actually useful. All systems for producing "energy" work by harnessing this low entropy ("diversity") to produce work; such systems also have the advantage of avoiding "uncontrolled" releases of heat through explosions ("conflict"). There is thus a quite literal and direct analogy between ⌬'s goal of harnessing social low entropy and industrialism's goal of harnessing physical low entropy.

especially if inbreeding is to be avoided. Perhaps the most universal feature of religions around the world and across history have been their celebration of those who have achieved peace and cooperation across difference.

For those with a more practical and quantitative orientation, however, perhaps one of the most compelling bodies of evidence is the finding, popularized by economist Oded Galor in his *Journey of Humanity*.[5] Building on his work with Quamrul Ashraf charting long-term comparative economic development, he argues that perhaps the most robust and fundamental driver of economic growth is societies' ability to productively and cooperatively harness the potential of social diversity.[6]

While using migratory distance from Africa (where diversity is maximum as noted above) as a proxy for "diversity", Galor and collaborators have since argued that diversity takes a wide range of forms and leads to a broad range of divergent outcomes.[7] Today the word "diversity" is in many contexts used to specify some dimensions along which oppression was historically organized in societies like the US that are particularly culturally dominant in the world today. Yet such a definition is simplistic relative to the tremendous diversity of forms of diversity that define our world:

---

[5] Oded Galor, *The Journey of Humanity: A New History of Wealth and Inequality with Implications for our Future* (New York: Penguin Random House, 2022).

[6] Quamrul Ashraf and Oded Galor, "The 'Out of Africa' Hypothesis, Human Genetic Diversity, and Comparative Economic Development", *American Economic Review* 103, no.1 (2013): 1-46.

[7] Oded Galor, Marc Klemp and Daniel Wainstock, "The Impact of the Prehistoric Out of Africa Migration on Cultural Diversity" (2023) at https://www.nber.org/papers/w31274.

- Religion and religiosity: A diverse range of religious practices, including secularism, agnosticism, and forms of atheism, are central to the metaphysical, epistemological, and ethical perspective of most people around the world.
- Jurisdiction: People are citizens of a range of jurisdictions, including nation states, provinces, cities etc.
- Geographic type: People live in different types of geographic regions: rural v. urban, cosmopolitan v. more traditional cities, differing weather patterns, proximity to geographic features etc.
- Profession: Most people spend a large portion of their lives working and define important parts of their identities by profession, craft, or trade.
- Organizations: People are members of a range of organizations, including their employers, civic associations, professional groups, athletic clubs, online interest groups etc.
- Ethno-linguistics: People speak a range of languages and identify themselves with and/or are identified by others with an "ethnic" groups associated with these linguistic groupings or histories of such linguistic associations, and these are organized by historical linguists into rough phylogenies.
- Race, caste and tribe: Many societies feature cultural groupings based on real or perceived genetic and familial origins that partly shape collective self- and social perceptions, especially given the legacies of severe conflict and oppression based on these traits.
- Ideology: People adopt, implicitly or explicitly, a range of political and social ideologies organized according to schema that themselves differ greatly across social context (e.g. "left" and "right" are key dimensions in some contexts, while religious or national origin divides may be more important in others).

- Education: People have a range of kinds and levels of educational attainment.
- Epistemology/field: Different fields of educational training structure thought. For example, humanists and physical scientists typically approach knowledge differently.
- Gender and sexuality: People differ in physical characteristics associated with reproductive function and in social perception and self-perception associated with these, as well as in their patterns of intimate association connected to these.
- Abilities: People differ greatly in their natural and acquired physical capabilities, intelligence, and challenges.
- Generation: People differ by age and life experiences.
- Species: Nearly all the above has assumed that we are talking exclusively about humans, but some of the technologies we will discuss may be used to facilitate communication and collaboration between humans and other life forms or even the nonbiological natural or spiritual worlds, which is obviously richly diverse internally and from human life.

Furthermore, as we have emphasized repeatedly above, human identities are defined by combinations and intersections of these forms of diversity, rather than their mere accumulations, just as the simple building blocks of DNA's four base pairs give rise to life's manifold diversity.

Yet, if history teaches anything, it is that for all its potential, collaboration across diversity is challenging. Social differences typically create divergences in goals, beliefs, values, solidarities/attachments, and culture/paradigm. Simple differences in beliefs and goals alone are the easiest to overcome by sharing information or agreeing to disagree, many differences in beliefs can be bridged and with common understanding of objective circumstances, compromises on goals are straightforward. Values are more challenging, as they involve things that both sides will be reluctant to compromise over and tolerate.

But the hardest differences to bridge are typically those related to systems of identification (solidarity/attachment) of meaning-making (culture). Solidarity and attachment relate to the others to which one feels allied or sharing in a "community of fate" and interests, groups by which one defines who and what one is. Cultures are systems of meaning-making that allow us to attach significance to otherwise arbitrary symbols. Languages are the simplest example, but all kinds of actions and behaviors carry differing meaning depending on cultural contexts.[8]

Solidarity and culture are so challenging because they stand in the way not of specific agreements about information or goals but of communication, mutual comprehension, and the ability to regard someone else as a partner capable and worthy of such exchange. While they are in an abstract sense related to beliefs and values, solidarities and culture in practice precede these in human development: we are aware of our family and those who will protect us and learn to communicate long before we consciously hold any views or aim for any goals. Being so foundational, they are the hardest to safely adjust or change, usually requiring shared life-shaping experiences or powerful intimacy to reform.

Beyond the difficulty of overcoming difference, it also holds an important peril. Bridging differences for collaboration often erodes them, harnessing their potential but also reducing that potential in the future. While this may be desirable for protection against conflict, it is an important cost to the

---

[8] Lisa Wedeen, "Conceptualizing Culture: Possibilities for Political Science", *American Political Science Review* 96, no. 4 (2002): 713--728.

productive capacity of diversity in the future. The classic illustration is the way that globalization has both brought gains from trade, such as diversifying cuisine, while at the same time arguably homogenizing culture and thus possibly reducing the opportunity for such gains in the future. A critical concern in 數位 is not just harnessing collaboration across diversity but also *regenerating* diversity, ensuring that in the process of harnessing diversity it is also replenished by the creation of new forms of social difference. Again, this is analogous to energy systems which must ensure that they not only harvest but also regenerate the sources of their energy to achieve sustainable growth.

**The depth-breadth spectrum**

Because of the tensions between collaboration and diversity, one would naturally expect a range of approaches that make different trade-offs in terms of *depth* and *breadth*. Some aim to allow deep, rich collaboration at the cost of limiting this collaboration to small and/or homogeneous groups. We can think of the "depth" of collaboration roughly in terms of the *degree* of supermodularity for a fixed set of participants: how much greater is what they create than the sum of what they can create separately, according to the standards of participants. Relationships of love are among the deepest as they allow transformations that are foundational to life, meaning, and reproduction that those participating could never have known separately. Superficial, transactional, and often anonymous transactions, like permeate market-based capitalism, on the other hand, brings small gains from trade but nowhere near the depth of connection of intimate love.

# 5-0 Collaborative Technology and Democracy

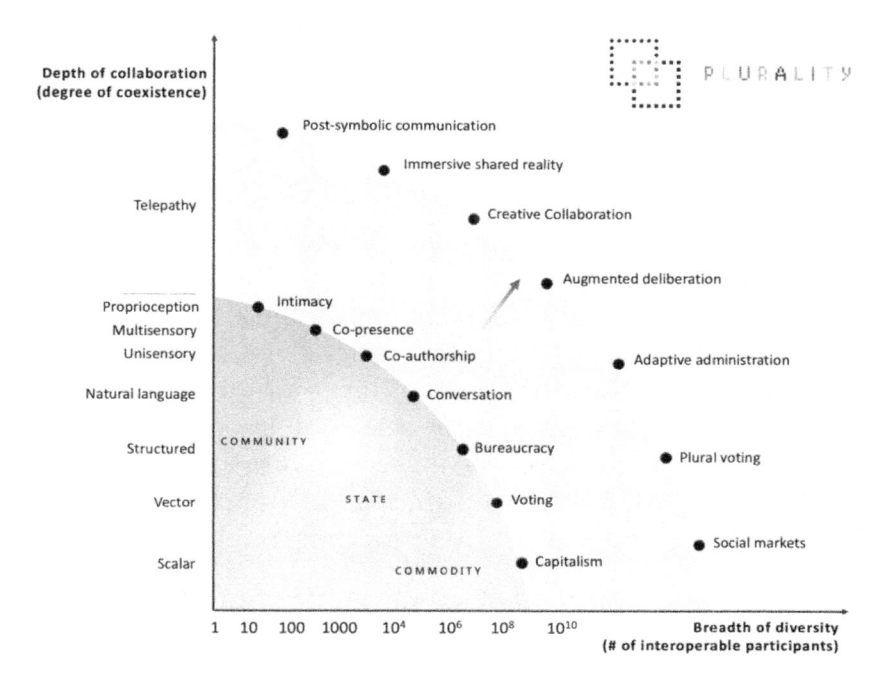

**Figure 5-0-A.** The trade-off between breadth of diversity and depth of collaboration represented as points along a production possibility frontier.

One rough way to think about quantifying the differences between these interaction modes is in terms of the information theoretical concept of *bandwidth*. Capitalism tends to reduce everything to a single amount (scalar) of money. Intimacy, on the other hand, typically not only immerses all senses but goes beyond this to touch "proprioception" (also known as kinesthesia), the internal sensations of one's own body and being that neuroscientists believe constitute a majority of all sensory input.[9] Intermediate modalities lie

---

[9] Uwe Proske and Simon C. Gandevia, "The Proprioceptive Senses: Their Roles in Signaling Body Shape, Body Position and Movement, and Muscle Force", *Physiological Review* 92, no. 4: 1651-1697.

between, activating structured forms of symbols or limited sets of sense.

The natural trade-off, however, that is the reason capitalism has not been superseded by universal intimacy is that high bandwidth communication is challenging to establish among large and diverse groups. Thinner and shallower collaboration scales more easily. While the simplest notion of scale is the number of people involved, this is shorthand. Breadth is best understood in terms of inclusion across lines of social and cultural distance rather than simply large numbers of people. For example, deep collaboration may well be easier among a large extended family, physically co-located and sharing a language and religion than among a handful of people scattered around the world, speaking different languages, etc.

We can see there being a full spectrum of depth and breadth, representing the trade-off between the two. Economists often describe technologies by "production possibilities frontiers" (PPF) illustrating the currently possible trade-offs between two desirable things that are in tension. In Figure A, we plot this spectrum of cooperation as such a PPF, grouping different specific modalities that we study below into broad categories of "communities" with rich but narrow communication, "states" with intermediate on both and "commodities" with thin but broad cooperative modes. The goal of 🔲 is to push this frontier outward at every point along it, as we have illustrated in these seven points, each becoming a technologically enhanced extension.[10]

---

[10] This tripartite division of modes of exchange into communities, state, and commodities is inspired by Kojin Karatani, *The Structure of World History: From Modes of Production to Modes of Exchange* (Durham, NC: Duke University Press, 2014). Karatani's aspiration to achieve the return of community at a broader scale can be seen as an ambitious example of 🔲.

One example illustrating this trade-off is common in political science: the debate over the value of deliberation compared to voting in democratic polities. High quality deliberation is traditionally thought to only be feasible in small groups and thus require processes of selection of a small group to represent a larger population such as representative government elections or sortition (choosing participants at random), but is believed to lead to richer collaboration, more complete airing of participant perspectives and therefore better eventual collective choices. On the other hand, voting can involve much larger and more diverse populations at much lower cost but comes at the cost of each participant providing thin signals of their perspectives in the form (usually) of assent for one among a predetermined list of options.

But for all the debate between the proponents of "deliberative" and "electoral" democracy, it is important to note that these are just two points along a spectrum (both mostly within the "state" category) and far from even representing the endpoints of that spectrum. As rich as in-person deliberations can be, they provide nowhere near the depth of sharing, connection and building of common purpose and identity that the building of committed teams (as in e.g. the military) and long-term intimate relationships do. And while voting can allow hundreds of millions to have a say on a decision, it has never cut across social boundaries in any way close to what impersonal, globalized markets do every day. All these forms have trade-offs and the very diversity of the ways in which we have historically navigated them and the ways in which these have improved overtime (e.g. the advent of video conferencing) should be a source of hope that concerted development can radically improve these trade-offs, allowing richer collaboration across a broader diversity of social differences than in the past.

⌗ 數位 Plurality: Part 5: Democracy

## Goals, affordances and multipolarity

Yet aiming at "improving" this trade-off requires us to specify at least something about what would count as an improvement. What makes a collaboration good or meaningful? What precisely constitutes social difference and diversity? How can we measure both?

One standard perspective, especially in economics and quantitatively inclined fields, is to insist that we should specify a global "objective" or "social welfare" function against which progress should be judged. The difficulty, of course, is that, in the face of the limitless possibilities of social life, any attempt to specify such a criterion is destined to crash land on the shores of the unknown and possibly unknowable. The more ambitiously we apply such a criterion in pursuing ⌗, the less robust it will prove, because the more deeply we connect to others across greater difference, the more likely we are to realize the failings of our initial vision of the good. Insisting on specifying such a criterion in advance of learning about the shape of the world leads to premature optimization, which prominent British computer scientist Tony Hoare once labeled "the root of all evil".[11]

One of the worst such evils is papering over the richness and diversity of the world. Perhaps the archetypal example is conclusions about the optimality of markets in neoclassical economics, which depend on simplistic assumptions and have often been used to short-circuit attempts to discover systems for social resource management that deal with problems of increasing returns, sociality, incomplete information, limited rationality, etc. As will become evident in the coming chapters,

---

[11] Randall Hyde, "The Fallacy of Premature Optimization" Ubiquity February, 2009 available at https://ubiquity.acm.org/article.cfm?id=1513451.

we know very little about how to even build social systems that are sensitive to these features, much less even approximately optimal in the face of them. This shows why the desire to optimize, chasing some simple notion of the good, often seduces us away from the aspirations of ⌖ as much as it aids us in pursuing it. We can be tempted to maximize what is simple to describe and easy to achieve, rather than anything we are after.

Optimization, especially in the pursuit of a "social welfare function" carries another pitfall: of "playing God" or idolatry. Maximizing social welfare requires taking a "view from nowhere" and imagining one can influence conditions on a universal level available to no one. We all act from and for specific people and communities, with goals and possibilities limited by who we are, where we sit and who cares what we say, in a ⌖ of other forces that hopefully form together a pattern that can avoid disaster. Tools that are only good for some abstractly universal perspectives do not just overreach: they will appeal to no one who can adopt them.

At the same time, there is an opposite extreme danger. If we simply pursue designs that imitate features of life and thus engage our attention with little sense of purpose or meaning, we can easily be co-opted to serve the darkest of human motives. The profit motives and power games that organize so much of today's world do not naturally serve any reasonable definition of a common good. The dystopian novels of Neal Stephenson, the Black Mirror series and the predicament of technologist Tunde Martins in the recent Nigerian science fiction show Iwájú remind us of how technical advance decoupled from human values can become traps that fray social bonds and allow the power-hungry to loot, control and enslave us.

Nor do we look to hypothetical scenarios to perceive the danger of compelling technologies pursued without a broader guiding mission. The dominant online platforms of the "Web2" era such as Google, Facebook and Amazon grew precisely out of a mentality of bringing critical features of real-world sociality (viz. collectively determined emergent authority, social networks, and commerce) to the digital world. While these services have brought many important benefits to billions of people around the world, we have extensively reviewed above, their many shortcomings have brought the world to a dangerous path without a broader set of public goals to guide them. We must build tools that serve the felt needs of real, diverse populations, meeting them where they are, and yet we cannot ignore the broader social contexts in which they sit and the conflicts that we might exacerbate in meeting those perceived needs.

Luckily, a middle, pragmatic, path is possible. We need neither take a God's eye nor a ground-level view exclusively. Instead, we can build tools that pursue the goals of a range of social groups, from intimate families and friends to large nations, always with an eye to limitations of each perspective and on the parallel developments we must connect to and learn from emanating from other parallel directions of development. We can aim to reform market function by focusing on social welfare, but always doing so based on adding to our models' key features of social richness revealed by those pursuing more granular perspectives and expecting our solutions will at least partly founder on their failures to account for these. We can build rich ways for people to empathize with others' internal experience, but with an understanding that such tools may well be abused if not paired with the discipline of deliberation, regulation, and well-structured markets.

We can do this guided by a common principle of cooperation across difference that is too broad to be formulated as a consistent objective function, yet elegant enough to unify a wide range of technologies: **we develop tools that allow greater cooperation and consensus at the same time as they make space for greater diversity**.

Consider two extremely different examples we will discuss below that both can be justified by this logic: brain-to-brain interfaces and approval voting. While the first is a wildly futuristic and worryingly invasive concept, the second is an old and widely applied voting method. Yet the simple idea of cooperation across difference helps justify both: a key aspiration of brain-to-brain interface is to allow children to retain more of their imagination as they grow to adulthood by allowing them to directly share this imagination rather than having to fit it into what they can write or draw.[12] This allows much greater diversity and much greater common understanding. Similarly, a key goal of approval voting (where citizens can vote for as many candidates as they wish and the one with the most votes wins) is to simultaneously ensure that the elected candidate has very wide general consensus *and* enable there to exist a much broader diversity of candidates because voters are not afraid a "third party" will act as a spoiler as voters can choose both the third party and one of the leading ones.[13]

Each of these technologies carries its risks: brain-to-brain interfaces could easily be used to manipulate, and approval voting could create a race towards mediocrity, as we discuss in relevant chapters below. Yet the diversity of modes highlighted by this approach gives hope that any connections we make and

---

[12] Rajesh P. N. Rao, Andrea Stocco, Matthew Bryan, Devapratim Sarma, Tiffany M. Youngquist ,Joseph Wu and Chantel S. Prat, "A Direct Brain-to-Brain Interface in Humans" *PLOS One* 9, no. 11: e111322 at https://doi.org/10.1371/journal.pone.0111332.

[13] Steven J. Brams and Peter C. Fishburn, "Approval Voting", *American Political Science Review* 72, no. 3: 831-847.

conflicts we resolve are but one stage in a process of collaboration across diversity. Every successful step forward should bring even more challenging forms of diversity into the world we can perceive, reshaping our understanding of ourselves and our aspirations and demanding that we struggle that much harder to bridge them. While such an aspiration lacks the satisfying simplicity of maximizing an objective function or pursuing technical advance and social richness wherever they lead, this is precisely why it is the hard path worth pursuing. Following another *Star Trek* slogan, ad astra per aspera: "to the stars, through adversity" or in the words of Nobel laureate André Gide, "Trust those who seek trust, but fear those who have found it."

## Regenerating diversity

Yet, as noted above, even if we manage to avoid these pitfalls and successfully bridge and harness diversity, we run the risk, in the process, of depleting the resource diversity provides. This is possible at any point along the spectrum and at any level of technological sophistication. Intimate relationships that form families can homogenize participants, undermining the very sparks of complementarity that ignited love. Building political consensus can undermine the dynamism and creativity of party politics.[14] Translation and language learning can undermine interest in the subtleties of other languages and cultures.

Yet homogenization is not an inevitable outgrowth of bridging, even when one effect is to recombine existing culture and thus lessen their average divides. The reason is that bridging plays a positive, productive role, not just a defensive one. Yes, interdisciplinary bridging of scientific fields may loosen the

---

[14] Nancy L. Rosenblum, *On the Side of the Angels: An Appreciation of Parties and Partisanship* (Princeton, NJ: Princeton University Press, 2010).

internal standards of a field and thus the distinctive perspective it brings to bear. But it may also give rise to new, equally distinctive fields. For example, the encounter between psychology and economics has created a new "behavioral economics" field; encounters between biology, physics and computer science have birthed the blossoming field of "systems biology"; the encounter between computer science and statistics has helped launch "data science" and artificial intelligence.

Similar phenomena emerge throughout history. Bridging political divides may lead to excess homogenization, but it can also lead to the birth of new political cleavages (e.g. the birth of the Republican party in the mid-19th century US). Families often bear children, who diverge from their parents and bring new perspectives. Most artistic and culinary novelty is born of "bricolage" or "fusion" of existing styles.[15] The syntheses that emerge when thesis and antithesis meet are not always compromises, but instead there may be new perspectives that realign a debate.[16]

None of this is inevitable and of course there are many stories of intersections that undermine diversity. But this range of possibilities gives hope that with careful attention to the issue, it is possible in many cases to design approaches to collaboration that renew the diversity that powers them.

---

[15] Claude Lévi-Strauss, *The Elementary Structures of Kinship*, (Boston: Beacon Press, 1969).

[16] This concept is often erroneously attributed to the work of G.W.F. Hegel, but originates with Johann Gottlieb Fichte and was not an important part of Hegel's thought. Johann Gottlieb Fichte, "Renzension des Aenesidemus", *Allgemeine Literatur-Zeitung* 11-12 (1794).

⿻ 數位 Plurality: Part 5: Democracy
# Infinite diversity in infinite combinations

In this part of the book, we will (far from exhaustively) explore a range of approaches to collaboration across difference and how further advances to ⿻ can extend and build on them. Each chapter will begin, as this one did, with an illustration of technology near the cutting edge of what is possible that is in use today. It will then describe the landscape of approaches that are common and emerging in its area. Next it will highlight the promise of future developments that are being researched, as well as risks these tools might pose to ⿻ (such as homogenization) and approaches to mitigating them, including by harnessing tools described in other chapters. We hope that the wide range of approaches we highlight draws out not just the substance of ⿻, but also the consistency of its approach with its substance. Only a ⿻ complementary and networked directions can support the development of a ⿻ future.

# 5-1 Post-Symbolic Communication

Overlooking Tokyo, nestled within the National Museum of Emerging Science and Innovation (Miraikan) lies The Park of Aging, a realm where time bends into the distant future, offering a rare portal to your mind and body after years worn by aging.[1] Visors blur vision, mimicking cataracts. Sounds are stripped of high pitches. In a photo booth that mirrors the trials of aged perception, facial expressions are faded and blurred. The simple act of recalling a shopping list committed to memory becomes an odyssey as one is ceaselessly interrupted in a bustling market. Walking in place on pedals with ankle weights on and while leaning on a cart simulates the wear of time on the body or the weight of age on posture. The Park of Aging is not just an exhibit, but an immersive conversation across time, a dialogue with your older self through the senses of sight, sound, and the aches and pains of age. This journey of empathy extends beyond the future self, to also foster a deeper connection with a present overlooked cohort: the elderly.

The Park of Aging is a poignant example of proprioceptive, post-symbolic communication, where participants receive information through an intimate, sensorial experience beyond merely interpreting words and symbols, utilizing all sensemaking of the body; the Park immerses participants in the sensations of being old, unlocking the first-hand experience of

---

[1] The entire artificial island of Odaiba on which Miraikan sits is something of a monument to 🔳. It contains a monument to Doraemon, a Manga robotic cat from the future who in Japanese cartoons of the 1970s returned to guide the imagination of children in the present, who has been a major inspiration in Taiwan. The largest mall on the island is named DiverCity and is devoted to the role of diversity in innovation.

the deteriorating senses, including seeing and hearing words and symbols.

---

Temporal conversation with aging, experiences of proprioceptive, non-symbolic communication today are ubiquitous and include mediation, psychedelics, religious experience, romantic intimacy, dance, yoga, combat, and sports. Not coincidentally, these experiences which harness information gathered from many senses including proprioception ("higher-bandwidth communication") are also correlated with long-lasting human bonding and connection when shared. Perhaps it is the diversity of information simultaneously presented to the senses (depth) that contribute to the significance of the experience and therefore strength of connection and "union."

Technological innovations such as neural interfaces, mediated reality, and generative foundation models (GFMs) expand the possibility space of post-symbolic communication, where unions within oneself and among people can occur not only in person, but across temporal, physical, and social distance facilitated by technology. In this chapter, we describe these technologies and explore their frontiers. We examine how these technologies could revolutionize interpersonal connections, education, and collaboration by enabling the transmission of thoughts, feelings, and sensory experiences beyond the compression of words and symbols. We consider the opportunities to rectify cultural misunderstandings and conflicts by fostering profound empathy and shared experience. Yet, in a space where ideas flow as seamlessly as emotions, we must also explore the risks of this level of connectivity, including surveillance, homogenization, disconnection, and oblivion.

## Intimacy today

Post-symbolic communication, a term coined by Jaron Lanier, ventures beyond the realm of language and symbols to explore the potential for direct and immersive shared experience by harnessing all senses, including proprioception.[2] Our first experience of non-verbal communication is in the natal womb; the synchronization of heartbeats between a mother and her unborn child, especially when the mother breathes rhythmically, suggests an intrinsic communication pathway.[3] As we develop, humans convey information nonverbally through body language, facial expression, tone, touch, laughter, crying, facial blood flow and smell. Biochemical messengers can convey emotional states and trigger responses in others, often unconsciously. For instance, research has shown that human sweat contains compounds that, when detected by others, can convey stress or fear, influencing the receiver's perception and behavior.[4]. We also see glimpses of the post-symbolic potential in long-established practices of intimacy among humans:

- Dance: stepping deeper into music, participants synchronizing their movements, both feel their body and anticipate their partner's movements to create shared

---

[2] Jaron Lanier, *You Are Not a Gadget a Manifesto*, (London [Etc.]: Penguin Books, 2011).

[3] P. van Leeuwen, D. Geue, Michael Thiel, Dirk Cysarz, S Lange, Marino Romano, Niels Wessel, Jürgen Kurths, and Dietrich Grönemeyer, "Influence of Paced Maternal Breathing on Fetal-Maternal Heart Rate Coordination," *Proceedings of the National Academy of Sciences of the United States of America* 106, no. 33 (August 18, 2009): 13661-66. https://doi.org/10.1073/pnas.0901049106.

[4] Judith Fernandez, "Olfactory interfaces: toward implicit human-computer interaction across the consciousness continuum," Diss. Massachusetts Institute of Technology, School of Architecture and Planning, Program in Media Arts and Sciences, 2020.

experience. Traditional dances like the Adumu ritual of the Maasai people also serve as a way for communal shared experiences through synchronicity.
- Combat: on the battlefield, soldiers experience heightened senses, adrenaline, and a battery of sounds, leading to intense awareness of their surroundings and their comrades. Non-verbal cues become critical for survival and strategy. This shared high-stress environment creates a bond and deep understanding and trust develop among those who rely on each other for their lives.
- Sports: in team sports, players develop a keen sense of each other's presence and movements. Teammates often anticipate each other's actions and work as a cohesive unit, relying on signals communicated through sound, movement, and hand gestures. This synchrony is somewhere between dance and combat, also fueled by common purpose.
- Romantic intimacy: through touch, eye contact, and emotional vulnerability, partners create a unique, shared experience. Attention to the internal experience of a partner is critical to a successful bond, building proprioceptive empathy that demands perhaps the deepest mutual trust and understanding humans are capable of.
- Religious experience: in mystical practices like Sufism, participants collectively engage in rituals like whirling and chanting. These shared spiritual practices engage the senses in the same way and create a sense of unity and connection with something greater than oneself, fostering community not just among people, but with a greater spiritual presence.
- Yoga: in a yoga class, practitioners move together through sequences of poses, guided by the rhythm of their breath. Despite the individual nature of the practice, there is collective harmony in the movements

## 5-1 Post-Symbolic Communication

and the shared goal of health and peace, as well as a heightening nervous system through stretches and poses. This shared physical and meditative experience fosters a sense of communal energy and focus.

Each of these contexts illustrates how shared experiences, beyond the scope of verbal communication, can create deep bonds and understanding between participants through intensive, shared sensorial inputs. Yet, communication can also happen within oneself (or between oneself and the spiritual world), as a form of introspection, yielding some of the most profound and transformative experiences.

- Meditation: a practice of inward focus and mindfulness, meditation has a diverse set of practices across a range of traditions. One common practice is to observe one's own thoughts and feelings without judgment, fostering greater recognition and understanding of one's own mental and emotional states, offering an opportunity to bridge and reconcile internal differences and contradictions.
- Psychedelics: The use of psychedelics can lead to profound internal experiences and altered states of consciousness that disrupt usual patterns of thought and perception, opening alternative narratives to make sense. Users often report experiencing deep introspective insights, a sense of oneness with the universe, confronting deep-seated emotions and memories, or communication with seemingly non-embodied forms of consciousness.
- Prayer: Similarly, through prayer, contemplation, or participation in religious rituals, individuals open communication to something beyond their sensory experience. Whether through a feeling of divine presence or an internal sense of clarity and peace, these experiences can be deeply impactful and transformative,

and foster a greater connection to themselves and their place in the universe.

Intimate experience today is rich with examples that touch upon the edges of post-symbolic communication. From physiological signals to chemosignals we are just beginning to learn the non-verbal, information-dense modes that can synchronize human experience and form the deepest human bonds between oneself and other humans, groups, and the universe broadly.

## Post-symbolic communication tomorrow

Today, we stand on the cusp of a Cambrian explosion in technologies that can advance post-symbolic communication and enable participants to communicate their physiological, psychological, and even phenomenological states of being. The Park of Aging is an example of an early experiment, but we can expect deeper, immersive, wholly sensorial experiences with novel integrations of technology that combine in supermodular ways. A number of these technologies include:

- Neural and Brain-Computer Interfaces (BCI): devices that connect directly to the brain capture neural activity and offer a direct pathway for communicating complex thoughts and emotions.[5] BCIs enable direct communication between the brain and external devices. Future developments could allow for the sharing of thoughts, emotions, and experiences directly from one mind to another, allowing for an unprecedented level of interaction.
- Haptic feedback and homuncular flexibility: Haptic devices provide tactile sensations, simulating touch and

---

[5] Rao et al., op. cit.

physical interactions in virtual environments and allowing users to feel and respond to virtual stimuli as if they were real. Similarly, with homuncular flexibility, individuals can learn to control virtual bodies that differ significantly from their own, thereby transcending the limitations of their physical bodies.[6] A leading examples is the near-universal capacity of humans to "regain" from their evolutionary past a sense of agency over a tail, given sufficient feedback and control in a virtual world.[7]

- 3D audio and immersive soundscapes: Advanced sound technologies that create three-dimensional auditory experiences can deeply enhance the sense of immersion in a virtual space, conveying emotions and atmosphere in a way that traditional stereo sound cannot.
- Wearable tracking of affect and physiology: Devices that monitor heart rate, skin conductance, and other physiological markers can provide insight into a user's emotional and physical state, enabling shared experiences that are responsive to these states.
- Projection mapping and spatial computing: Technologies allow for the transformation of physical spaces into interactive, digitally augmented environments. They can create shared, multi-sensory experiences that blend the physical and digital worlds.

---

[6] Andrea Won, Jeremy Bailenson, Jimmy Lee, and Jaron Lanier, "Homuncular Flexibility in Virtual Reality," *Journal of Computer-Mediated Communication*, Volume 20, Issue 3, 1 May 2015, Pages 241–259, https://doi.org/10.1111/jcc4.12107

[7] William Steptoe, Anthony Steed and Mel Slater, "Human Tails: Ownership and Control of Extended Humanoid Avatars" *IEEE Transactions on Visualization and Computer Graphics* 19, no. 4 (2013): 583-590.

- Neurofeedback and mindfulness: These applications use real-time displays of brain activity to teach self-regulation of brain function. They can be used for meditation, mental health therapy, and enhancing self-awareness and empathy.[8]
- Neuromodulation: Neuromodulation techniques, such as deep brain stimulation, have implications for enhancing cognitive function, treating neurological disorders, and even augmenting human capabilities. However, they also introduce neuroethical challenges such as moral bio-enhancement (MBE) - the use of biomedical technology to morally improve humans.

When combined with GFMs, these technologies will further enable us to generate visual representations of our thoughts at a pace that closely mirrors the speed of our imagination. These technologies together are unlocking responsive, adaptive environments or characters in virtual spaces that can react in real-time to users' emotions, actions, or choices beyond simple interpretation of natural language inputs.[9] Researchers have already shown how brain implants can connect the intentions of a paralyzed patient into physical movements, demonstrating

---

[8] Hengameh Marzbani, Hamid Reza Marateb and Marjan Mansourian, "Neurofeedback: A Comprehensive Review on System Design, Methodology and Clinical Applicaitons", *Basic Clinical Neuroscience* 7, no, 2: 143-158.

[9] Han Huang, Fernanda De La Torre, Cathy Fang, Andrzej Banburski-Fahey, Judith Amores, and Jaron Lanier. "Real-Time Animation Generation and Control on Rigged Models via Large Language Models," arXiv (Cornell University, February 15, 2024), https://arxiv.org/pdf/2310.17838.pdf (Originally at the 37th Conference on Neural Information Processing Systems (NeurIPS) Workshop on ML for Creativity and Design in 2023).

the remarkable potential of neural interfaces to bridge the gap between thought and action.[10]

Combined, these capabilities enable the transmission of ideas and emotions that can occur directly and seamlessly and have profound implications for how we share and understand one another's internal experiences, creative visions, aspirations, and even past traumas to facilitate reconciliation, healing, and forgiveness. For example, imagine a child immersing themselves in the sensory experiences of their parents at the same age. Or two warring groups experiencing the pain and loss of their adversary's family members.

## Frontiers of post-symbolic communication

In the more distant future, the evolution of non-symbolic communication promises to profoundly reshape our understanding of intimacy and the very essence of life's touchstones, such as childhood and relationships. Imagine a world where the boundaries of personal experiences blur, redefining intimacy not as a physical or emotional proximity but as a deep, seamless sharing of consciousness. Telepathy, once a realm of science fiction or religious practice, becomes a scientific reality, allowing for the direct transmission of thoughts, feelings, and sensory experiences from mind to mind. Human relationships evolve into deeper, more meaningful connections where misunderstandings are a choice and empathy abound. Children, in this new paradigm, grow not just by learning from others' words or observing actions but by immersing themselves in the lived experiences of others from any culture or epoch, including their ancestors. This experiential osmosis accelerates empathy and wisdom,

---

[10] Henri Lorach, Andrea Galvez, Valeria Spagnolo, et al., Walking naturally after spinal cord injury using a brain-spine interface, *Nature* 618, 126-133 (2023), https://doi.org/10.1038/s41586-023-06094-5

fostering a society where learning is as much about absorbing direct experiences as it is about traditional education.

Long-distance relationships, too, can expect to undergo a radical transformation. Physical distance becomes a matter only of connection speeds, allowing for the sharing of thoughts, emotions, and sensory experiences in real-time, irrespective of geographic separation. Lovers, friends, and family members can experience each other's joys, sorrows, and mundane moments as if they were in the same room, creating a form of intimacy that transcends physical presence. This paradigm shift brings profound changes in societal structures – the traditional nuclear family could give way to more fluid, globally interconnected familial networks. As we steer towards this horizon, the very fabric of human connection and communication is poised to undergo a metamorphosis, redefining what it means to be intimately connected and be "human."

## Limits of post-symbolic communication

The journey into post-symbolic communication is not without its perils. The very tools that promise deeper connection could also lead to a loss of personal identity. Worse, participants could be surveilled, leaving thoughts, emotions, and motivations open to manipulation; any window into our mind is also a window of influence. At the extreme, there is a risk that participants no longer have a private inner world while also disconnecting from the outer world, a dystopia of which we have be warned at least since the time of E. M. Forster and most vividly in recent years by the 1999 film *The Matrix*.[11] Unchecked visibility into our minds allows for unprecedented levels of manipulation and control, potentially by technology companies

---

[11] E. M. Forster, "The Machine Stops", *Oxford and Cambridge Review* November 1909.

## 5-1 Post-Symbolic Communication

or governments that distract humanity with an alternate reality, or simulation. As humans lose touch with the reality of the physical world, over-reliance on telepathic communication could lead to the atrophy of traditional communication skills and cultural practices, with people becoming dependent on direct mental connections. Furthermore, in a world where the boundaries between self and other blur, the sanctity of individual thought and experience could be threatened. High-bandwidth communication could lead to a homogenization of thoughts and experiences as individual perspectives merge into a collective consciousness, erasing our differences.

Balancing telepathic communication with lower-bandwidth, structured forms of communication is essential to preserve privacy, autonomy, diversity, and human governance in the future. Communication, like speech and text, is less direct and immediate than telepathy but is structured and deliberate. It requires the sender to formulate thoughts into words or sentences, providing a level of control and reflection that instantaneous telepathic communication lacks.

Markets and voting systems also serve as quintessential examples of lower-bandwidth, structured forms of communication, offering a counterbalance. In markets, the myriad decisions made by consumers and producers are communicated through the price mechanism. This system, while less immediate and detailed than telepathic communication, provides a structured and aggregated way of expressing preferences and values. It allows for privacy in decision-making, as individuals do not have to reveal the full spectrum of their thoughts and motivations. Similarly, voting is a deliberate, structured form of communication where individuals express their political and social preferences at a fixed point in time.

Unlike continuous and invasive telepathic streams, voting encapsulates the will of the populace in a manner that is both manageable and interpretable, preserving the autonomy of the individual voter. This structured approach is crucial in maintaining a balance between efficient communication and the safeguarding of personal autonomy, privacy, and democratic processes, thereby acting as a vital check against the overreach of an all-encompassing telepathic matrix.

## 5-2 Immersive Shared Reality

"Stand up and face the mirror", the at-first innocent but gradually more-threatening refrain, echoes through Courtney Cogburn's *1000 Cut Journey*.[1] Simple words that invite the visitor to this immersive-reality environment to experience life through the eyes, ears, and body of Michael Sterling, a black man. Small moments of casual racism build to a crescendo of hopelessness and induce a pervasive sense of helplessness. Perception, or reality? It depends on whose shoes you're standing in. Some may kick off their shoes the moment they remove the VR headset, but for Michael Sterling, there's nothing he (or now you) can do to erase the footprints of direct experience.

In *Becoming Homeless*, you look around your already-bare apartment to decide which possessions to sell next.[2] You're losing your home, so it does not matter anymore, and you just choose something. Then, from the moment of actual homelessness, the downward spiral accelerates. You lose your dignity, your physical security, and your health in quick succession. No more hopes and dreams, thoughts and prayers cannot help you now. Your new daily grind rips 25 years off your life expectancy faster than "*Wolf of Wall Street*" Jordan Belfort could uncork a bottle of champagne. "Good luck!" "Work hard!" and - sadly - "I love you!" are now just words you might

---

[1] Cogburn Research Group. "1,000 Cut Journey," n.d. *https://cogburnresearchgroup.socialwork.columbia.edu/research-projects/1000-cut-journey*.

[2] Alex Shashkevich, "Virtual Reality Can Help Make People More Empathetic," *Stanford News*, October 17, 2018, *https://news.stanford.edu/2018/10/17/virtual-reality-can-help-make-people-empathetic*.

have heard long ago, spoken to a person you can hardly remember.

---

Immersive shared reality technologies unlock a new chapter in human interaction, leveraging cutting-edge virtual reality (VR), augmented reality (AR) and mixed reality (MR) systems. Unlike the deeply personal and sensorially rich exchanges of post-symbolic communication, shared immersive reality presents a broader canvas for human interaction, enabling people to engage in shared, multisensory experiences. This chapter delves into the landscape of immersive technologies, today's applications, tomorrow's potential, and the frontier. It shows how immersive technologies may facilitate shared experiences that blend physical and virtual reality, complementing and expanding human experience with interactions that surpass physical, spatial, and social limitations. Immersive shared reality (ISR) creates spaces where communities may converge for socialization, gaming, entertainment, and more, facilitating connections that, while less intense than symbolic communication, are meaningful and emotionally resonant. From VR gatherings that unite people across the globe, to mass online gaming and virtual music festivals, these digital arenas extend the possibility space of shared human experience.

On the horizon, shared ISR is poised for rapid expansion. Technological advances will deepen the sensory integration of these virtual experiences, extending beyond sight and sound to include touch, smell, and even taste. This future, teeming with hybrid reality environments and emotional connectivity, heralds a new era of human interaction, where digital spaces not only simulate reality but enhance it, bridging divides and fostering broader understanding. However, ISR also has its perils. From the widening of surveillance to virtual escapism, these challenges demand thoughtful consideration to ensure that our digital futures augment, rather than eclipse, the richness of human experience.

**Copresence today**

Throughout history, some of the most meaningful human experiences involve multisensory copresence. Religious observances often engage many senses in large groups. Clubs and parties are among the most treasured entertainment experiences because of their multisensory activation. Political rallies, group assemblies (whether at schools or for concerts), collective outings (hiking, sports, etc.) all engage a range of senses.

Technology has increasingly played a role in facilitating such copresence, especially at a distance, in recent years. ISR refers to technology that creates a shared virtual environment where users can interact in real-time. This type of "reality" can be considered a subset application of Mediated Reality as illustrated in Figure A, a broader term that encompasses various technologies that mediate our perception of reality, including Virtual, Augmented and Mixed Reality (a.k.a. VR, AR, MR).

ISR can apply to many human interactions. Some of the most common applications are socialization, gaming, entertainment, sports, and fitness:

- VR gatherings: These digital spaces enable people from around the world to interact in a shared virtual environment. Here, avatars represent participants, allowing for expressive movements and interactions that go beyond verbal communication. These virtual gatherings can range from collaborative work meetings to social events, where the sense of presence is amplified by the immersive, 3D environment. Participants experience a sense of togetherness and community, facilitating connections that, while not as intense as physical interactions, are still meaningful and emotionally resonant.

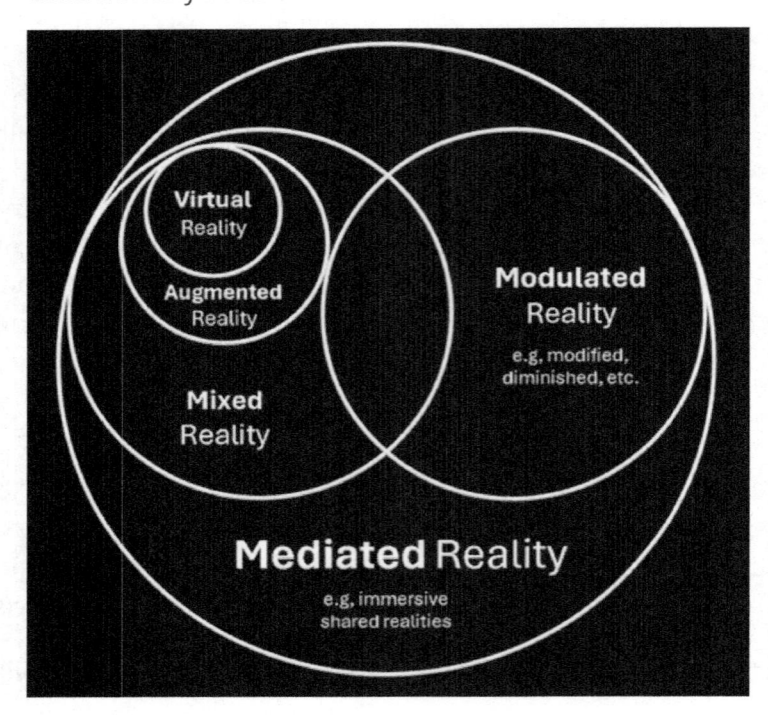

**Figure 5-2-A.** Mediated Reality Framework adapted from Mann and Nnlf (1994). Source: *Wikipedia*, CC 3.0 BY-SA.

- Mass online gaming: Online multiplayer games create expansive worlds where players collaborate, compete, and strategize together. Communication is a blend of in-game gestures, strategic planning, and quick decision-making, often under time pressure. This environment nurtures a form of camaraderie and collective intelligence, as players become attuned to each other's play styles and tactics and take common action towards common goals.
- Online religious services: In the digital era, religious gatherings have expanded into online platforms,

## 5-2 Immersive Shared Reality

allowing congregations to participate in services and rituals remotely. This form of communal worship, while lacking the physical closeness of traditional services, still offers a sense of shared belief, uniting participants in a common religious experience.

- Virtual music festivals and parties: With the advent of streaming technology, music festivals and parties have found a new home in the virtual world through a range of media, from opera in movie theaters to VR concert and music festival experiences. Virtual elements have even become increasingly central to the most prized in-person music venues, leading to massive investments that integrate digital and physical experiences ever more closely.
- E-sports tournaments: E-sports have gained immense popularity, with spectators and players engaging in highly competitive gaming at a professional level. These events, often streamed to vast audiences, create a shared sense of excitement and allegiance among fans.
- Remote fitness classes: The rise of online fitness, especially during the pandemic, has brought people together in pursuit of health and wellness. Participants engage in synchronized workouts, yoga sessions, or dance classes from their own homes, sharing a common goal and a sense of group motivation.
- Virtual tourism: travelers can experience remote places, walking through historic cities or visiting foreign landscapes from the comfort of their homes. This technology enables travelers to virtually walk through historic cities, marvel at natural wonders, and immerse themselves in foreign landscapes.
- Immersive artistic experiences: Alongside the rise of remote shared experience, a new genre of in-person immersive art has developed and become increasingly prevalent form at the intersection of live entertainment

and museums. Participants jointly explore mysteries, escape from puzzles, live in the world of an artist who saw the world through differently abled eyes, or surround themselves in worlds of novel tactile and visual sensations that transport them to new shared understandings of the possible.

## Immersive shared reality tomorrow

ISR technology is connecting people to learn and empathize at unprecedented scales and social distances, as highlighted in our opening example. The future of ISR promises to make distant or imagined experiences palpably real, enveloping users in a synthetic world that simulates multiple senses simultaneously. While sight and sound have been the traditional focus, new sensors and actuators promise to deepen integration of touch, smell, and even taste. Haptic feedback systems will replicate the subtleties of physical contact. Olfactory technology will enable fragrances and odors to be part of storytelling, education, and even retail experiences in VR. Taste retargeting will unlock virtual dining experiences through the altering of taste perception by delivering chemical modulators to the mouth.[3] Here are a few envisioned advancements and novel examples that extend the concept of ISR into new dimensions:

- Hybrid reality environments: Leveraging AR and VR in tandem, these environments blend physical and digital elements seamlessly. Imagine attending a conference where remote participants appear as full-size holograms, capable of interacting with physical objects

---

[3] Jas Brooks, Noor Amin, and Pedro Lopes, "Taste Retargeting via Chemical Taste Modulators," In *Proceedings of the 36th Annual ACM Symposium on User Interface Software and Technology (UIST '23)*, Association for Computing Machinery, New York, NY, USA, Article 106, (2023): 1-15, https://doi.org/10.1145/3586183.3606818.

and participants in real-time, a technique one of us frequently uses for remote appearances. This blurs the line between who is present physically and who is digital.
- Emotional connectivity: Emerging technologies aim to transmit nuanced human emotions and physical sensations through VR, using advanced haptic feedback, biometric sensors, and emotional GFMs. This could enable users to feel the warmth of a handshake, the pressure of a hug, or even the subtleties of emotional expression conveyed through a virtual avatar, deepening connections and empathy between participants and enabling those with visual or auditory impairments to engage through other senses.
- Massive multi-user online laboratories (MMOLs): Scientists can collaboratively conduct experiments in a shared virtual laboratory. MMOLs could facilitate real-time collaboration on scientific research and education across the globe, breaking down barriers to access and enabling a form of immersive, collective discovery.
- Civic Spaces: Digital replicas of civic centers, town halls, and community spaces where people can gather to discuss, debate, and make decisions about their communities. These spaces would allow for a more inclusive and accessible form of civic engagement, enabling participants to engage in local governance or community planning processes from anywhere in the world. They would also leverage our intuitions from real world spaces much more closely than existing online spaces do, thus helping improve the creation of context and common understanding online.
- Immersive learning: From virtual field trips to interactive historical reenactments, educational content will become more immersive, allowing students of all ages to explore and learn in ways that are engaging, memorable, and more impactful than traditional

methods. Such learning can range from deepening connections to historical experience through immersion to providing vocational training in a far broader range of high-risk scenarios than is currently possible.[4]

- Cross-cultural exchange: Platforms specifically designed to foster understanding and empathy between diverse cultural groups by immersing users in the experiences of people from different backgrounds. Through narratives, rituals, and daily life activities, these platforms could use VR and AR to bridge cultural divides and build a global sense of community. For example, language learning applications use these to immerse users in the linguistic and cultural background of others. Another example is the Portals Policing Project [5], which shares the lived experiences of people with law enforcement in a controlled, yet realistic virtual chamber, improving understanding and trust on both sides.
- Environmental climate experiences: Interactive simulations that allow users to experience the potential impacts of climate change firsthand. For example, the Tree demonstrates how VR can evoke empathy and compassion for the natural environment by transforming the user into a rainforest tree and

---

[4] For example, education of nurses in VR has shown significant potential to accelerate tactile learning. Jeeyae Choi, Elise C. Thompson, Jeungok Choi, Colette Waddill and Soyoung Choi, "Effectiveness of Immersive Virtual Reality in Nursing Education", *Nurse Educator* 47, no. 3: E57-E61.

[5] "Portals Policing Project," The Justice Collaboratory, n.d., https://www.justicehappenshere.yale.edu/projects/portals-policing-project.

exposing them to the threats of deforestation and climate change.[6]

- Therapy: Leveraging the power of VR to create therapeutic environments, sessions increasingly offer greatly enhanced cognitive behavioral therapy, enabling patients to be exposed in a carefully modulated way to the sources of phobias, traumatic past experiences, anxiety-producing social situations and more. Therapy for children suffering from autism spectrum and attention deficit and hyperactivity disorders is increasingly bearing fruit.[7]

As these technologies mature, they are increasingly harnessed to not just simulate reality but to enhance it, creating a bridge between diverse cultures and fostering a global community of shared experiences and mutual understanding regardless of one's origin or language. These envisioned applications of ISR hold the potential to transform how we interact with the world and each other, fostering understanding, empathy, and collaboration across all facets of human endeavor.

## Frontiers of immersive shared reality

As we gaze to the horizon of ISR, the very nature of communal experience and human connection undergoes a profound metamorphosis. Imagine stepping into a world where shared virtual spaces are not mere simulations, but extensions of our physical reality, offering experiences that are as rich and complex as those encountered in the tangible world. In this future, ISR technologies enable a fusion of senses, thoughts, and emotions. At the frontiers of ISR, we are not merely

---

[6] See www.treeofficial.com

[7] Paul M.G. Emmelkamp and Katharina Meyerbröker, "Virtual Reality Therapy in Mental Health", *Annual Review of Clinical Psychology* 17 (2021): 495-519.

spectators but active participants in a revolution of multisensory integration.[8]

- Imagined worlds and shared dreams: More sophisticated and controlled use of sensory inputs (e.g. smell, taste, visual and auditory), will enable participants to generate and share realities that deeply resonate with participants' emotions and memories. Such stimuli, when reactivated during sleep, not only can enhance these memories[9], but facilitate sharing altered states of consciousness [10] and shared lucid dreams. [11] Participants will be able to explore the subconscious playground of the human mind together. GFMs are already enabling users to "speak the world into existence" and as input modalities become richer, sharing imagination and dreams become ever more possible.[12]

- Simulated worlds: Virtual environments can simulate realities—both the future and past—under different

---

[8] Patricia Cornelio, Carlos Velasco, and Marianna Obrist, "Multisensory Integration as per Technological Advances: A Review," *Frontiers in Neuroscience* (2021): 614.

[9] Judith Fernandez, Nirmita Merha, Bjoern Rasch, and Pattie Maes,

[10] Michelle Carra, Adam Haarb, Judith Amoresb, Pedro Lopesc, et al., "Dream Engineering: Simulating Worlds through Sensory Stimulation," *Consciousness and Cognition* 83 (2020): https://doi.org/10.1016/j.concog.2020.102955.

[11] Karen Konkoly, Kristoffer Appel, Emma ChabaniKonkoly et al., Real-time dialogue between experimenters and dreamers during REM sleep, *Current Biology* 32, 7 (2021): https://doi.org/10.1016/j.cub.2021.01.026

[12] Han Huang, Fernanda De La Torre, Cathy Mengying Fang, Andrzej Banburski-Fahey, Judith Amores and Jaron Lanier, "Real-time Animation Generation and Control on Rigged Models via Large Language Models" (2024) at https://arxiv.org/abs/2310.17838.

conditions. For example, participants will be able to experiment with scenarios of climate change, such as rising sea levels or the impact of extreme weather events, making distant concepts an immediate and personal experience, or potentially beneficial futures to plan to both achieve them and avoid unintended harm. With affective computing, the system may adapt to the environment based on the user's response, physiology as well as memories or preferences, creating a feedback loop that heightens awareness and empathy.

- Virtual design studios: Community members, architects, and engineers may come together to co-create the green spaces of tomorrow to redefine "planning." Participants virtually touch the bark of trees slated for planting and inhale the fragrant blossoms intended for the gardens. Participant feedback can modify the simulation in real-time, enabling sensorial immersion into different visions for a project. Harnessing methods from our *Augmented Deliberation* chapter below, they could deliberate and see the possibilities for joint design come to life around them, printing the design on to physical space only having lived in it together virtually.
- Collective memory palaces: Envision virtual environments where entire communities can deposit, share, and experience collective memories and knowledge. These memory palaces serve not only as repositories of communal wisdom but as spaces where individuals can relive historical events or explore the collective psyche of humanity, fostering a deeper understanding and connection across generations. They could also redefine the experience of memorializing collective traumas, allowing them to be told from a variety of perspectives quickly and flexibly.
- Empathy amplifiers: ISR could allow us to experience the world through the eyes of another. This direct sharing of

experiences would serve as an empathy amplifier, dissolving prejudices and fostering a profound sense of unity and understanding among diverse groups of people. Envision simulations that allow individuals to live through the collective experiences of entire communities, nations, or civilizations, feeling their struggles, joys, and challenges as their own. This could serve as a powerful tool for education and conflict resolution, promoting peace on a global scale.

- Global consciousness networks: Imagine a future where people can connect their consciousness to a global network, sharing thoughts, emotions, and experiences in a dynamic, evolving stream of collective awareness. This network would enable a form of communication and connection that goes beyond language, allowing for an unparalleled synchronization of human intention and action towards global challenges.

- Inter-specific communication platforms: Beyond human-to-human interaction, ISR could extend the boundaries of communication to include other species as we discuss further in our *Environment* chapter. By translating non-human languages and experiences into formats we can understand and vice versa, these platforms could foster an unprecedented level of empathy and cooperation between humans and other life forms on our planet.

- Digital legacies: ISR could allow individuals to create digital legacies—entire worlds crafted from their memories, thoughts, and experiences. These realms would not only serve as a form of immortality but also as a means for future generations to explore the lives and insights of their ancestors in a deeply personal and interactive way.

- Collective creativity spaces: These digital platforms would enable artists, musicians, writers, and creators of all kinds to collaborate in real-time, across the globe, in shared virtual spaces. Here, ideas and inspirations merge in a communal creative flow, leading to art and innovation that truly represents the collective human spirit, transcending individual capabilities, as we elaborate on further in the next chapter.

As we embark on this journey, we stand on the brink of redefining human experience and collaboration. The technologies that lie ahead promise not just advancements in the way we interact with the world, but a revolution in the way we perceive, connect, and innovate. In this new era, the barriers between individual consciousness and collective experience become more fluid, heralding a future where our shared realities foster a deeper unity and yet more creative collaborations.

## Limits of immersive shared reality

Unlike the intimate, direct exchange of thoughts and emotions envisioned in post-symbolic communication, ISR unlocks new dimensions for human interaction and coordination from simple social interaction to education, work, and entertainment— bringing with them a distinct set of limitations and ethical concerns. If the Matrix is a dystopia of post-symbolic communication, a similar and a fitting dystopian parallel can be drawn from Neal Stephenson's *Snow Crash* and the similar but more broadly known *Ready Player One* by Ernest Cline, adapted into a film directed by Steven Spielberg.[13] In both stories, people retreat into ISR simulations ("the Metaverse" for Stephenson, "the OASIS" for Cline) in response to social and environmental decline, further reinforcing that decline as they abandon civic engagement in the physical world. These stories illustrate several risks of ISR:

---

[13] Ernest Cline, *Ready Player One* (New York: Crown, 2011).

- Virtual escapism: Dependency on ISR at the expense of the real world it depends on, rather than as a way of creating more effective understanding and collective action within it, risk a doom loop like the risks of GFMs creating garbage outputs that undermine their future training and the risk of industrial development destroying the environment on which it depends.
- Diminished physical health: Immersing oneself in alternative realities for extended periods can lead to psychological effects, such as difficulty distinguishing between virtual and physical experiences or feeling disconnected from real-world social bonds. The ready availability of an idealized digital escape could impact mental health, leading to isolation or a diminished ability to cope with real-world challenges. Prolonged engagement in virtual environments raises concerns about physical health, including the effects of extended screen time on vision, and the sedentary lifestyle associated with immersive digital activities.
- Digital divide: A new digital frontier risks widening the gap between those with access to the latest technologies and those without. As these ISR becomes more integral to social and professional life, lack of access could marginalize individuals and communities unless access is treated as a human right in the same way as we have advocated above for internet access.
- Corporate control, surveillance, and monopolization: ISR blurs the lines between public and private, where digital spaces can be simultaneously intimate and open to wide audiences or observed by corporate service providers. Unless ISR networks are built according to the principles of rights and interoperability we emphasized above and governed by the broader 數位 governance approaches that much of the rest of this part of the book are devoted

to, they will become the most iron monopolistic cages we have known.

- Identity and authenticity: The freedom to create and adopt any personas in ISR sharpens the challenges of authenticity and identity we have highlighted above. It illustrates the potential for anonymity and fluid identity in shared immersive realities to complicate trust and relationships, as well as the possibility of losing one's sense of self.

We must, therefore, prevent a headlong rush into a monopolistic and dystopian "metaverse" undermining the very real potential of these technologies to empower richer human connection by understanding them in the context of the other tools that must complement, support, and undergird their development.

## 5-3 Creative Collaborations

In 79 AD, the cataclysmic eruption of Mount Vesuvius entombed the Roman cities of Pompeii and Herculaneum along with a trove of 1,800 papyrus scrolls from the first and second centuries BC that otherwise would have deteriorated over time. These scrolls, containing significant philosophical and literary relics of an ancient world, have long tantalized scholars. Early attempts at unrolling them, beginning in the 18th century, often ended in destruction of the brittle, carbonized documents. Modern imaging techniques, however, opened new avenues for exploration, exemplified by the Vesuvius Challenge 2023— a landmark prize at the intersection of history, technology, and collaborative problem-solving. The Challenge would allow contestants computer access to the scanned scrolls to win a series of prizes for virtually unwrapping them.

To counter information siloing, the organizers introduced smaller "progress prizes" awarded bi-monthly that required participants to publish their code or research open source, enriching the entire community's shared knowledge base. Notable contributions included the *"Volume Cartographer"* by Seth Parker and others in Brent Seales' lab, and Casey Handmer's *identification of a unique 'crackle' pattern* forming letters.[1] Youssef Nader later harnessed domain adaptation

---

[1] Stephen Parsons, C. Seth Parker, Christy Chapman, Mami Hayashida and W. Brent Seales, "EduceLab-Scrolls: Verifiable Recovery of Text from Herculaneum Papyri using X-ray CT" (2023) at *https://arxiv.org/abs/2304.02084*. Casey Handmer, "Reading Ancient Scrolls" August 5, 2023 at https://caseyhandmer.wordpress.com/2023/08/05/reading-ancient-scrolls/

techniques on these findings.[2] As the competition progressed, its structure fostered a dynamic where winners not only shared their findings and methodologies but were also able to reinvest their winnings into enhancing their equipment and refining their techniques. This environment also proved fertile for the formation of new collaborations, as exemplified by the Grand Prize winners.

Announced February 5, 2024, the Grand Prize of $700,000 criterion was to decipher 4 passages of 140 characters each, with at least 85% of characters recoverable. In a demonstration of interdisciplinary and global cross-collaboration, a team comprising Luke Farritor (a 21-year-old college student and SpaceX intern), Nader (a doctoral student in Berlin), and Julian Schilliger (a recent master's graduate in robotics at ETH Zurich) shared a breakthrough victory to win. Together they exceeded expectations by recovering an additional 11 columns of text, containing more than 2000 characters. Each team member brought their expertise and earlier achievements to this collaborative effort. Their success not only marked a significant academic milestone but also propelled the entire field of digital archaeology forward.

---

Artistic expression through media such as music, visual arts, theater, architecture, film and even cuisine are among the most powerful and canonical foundations for forming the shared cultures that define social groups. While not as powerfully engaging as full multisensory shared experience, they can spread much farther and engage fully one and sometimes more sensory experiences in a richer way than verbal communication. Today, the boundaries of geography, expertise, and even

---

[2] Youssef Nader, "The Ink Detection Journey of the Vesuvius Challenge" February 6, 2024 at *https://youssefnader.com/2024/02/06/the-ink-detection-journey-of-the-vesuvius-challenge/.*

audience are dissolving thanks to a mix of digital tools and platforms that unlock creative collaboration. This chapter explores how these technologies are fostering a new era of collaborative creation, characterized by unprecedented accessibility, real-time interaction, and a shared creative space. We will see how artists, educators, and entrepreneurs can harness the power of crowdsourcing and online platforms to break down barriers and expand the creative process. These technologies not only connect individuals but also foster a shared creative process that is more inclusive, dynamic, and expansive than ever before.

**Cocreation today**

Artistic cocreation is nothing new. For thousands of years, musicians, dancers and actors have formed bands. Some of the most canonical literary texts such as the Bible, the Bhagavad Gita and the Homerian epics were all almost certainly written by many hands over generations. Films sometimes have distractingly long credit rolls for a reason.

Yet these culture-defining collaborative projects have traditionally been slow and expensive, limiting both access to output and participation in the process of creation. Cowriting, for example, has traditionally involved months, years or even generations of retelling, adaptation, rewriting, etc. to achieve a coherent and digestible narrative. The massive live entertainment industry testifies to the expense of flying teams around the world to present the experience of creative collaboration to diverse audiences. Other forms of joint creativity, such as scientific collaborations like those highlighted above, have traditionally taken place in massive physically co-located laboratories like Los Alamos.

Yet early technologies that became part of the fabric of the internet, imagined by people like Ted Nelson as we highlighted

## 5-3 Creative Collaborations

in *The Lost Dao*, have already transformed the possibilities of collaborative creative practice and sharing.

- Online collaboration: Tools like Slack, Asana and Notion (which we used in this project) have revolutionized the workspace by enabling teams to collaborate in real-time, regardless of geographic location. These platforms support a wide range of creative projects, from software development to marketing campaigns, by providing an infrastructure for communication, project management, and document sharing. They exemplify how digital workspaces can enhance productivity and foster a sense of community among team members.

- Cloud-based creative software: Adobe Creative Cloud, Autodesk, and GitHub (which was the primary platform for writing this book) offer sophisticated tools for designers, engineers, and developers to work on shared projects simultaneously. This technology allows for real-time feedback and iteration, reducing the time from concept to creation and enabling a more fluid and dynamic creative process. Even more prominently, collaborative word processing software such as Google docs has enabled real-time collaborative editing by many people in diverse geographies.

- Open-source projects: Some of the most ambitious creative collaborations take place in open-source co-edited projects like Wikipedia, where thousands co-create increasingly canonical content. Platforms like GitHub and GitLab facilitate similar codevelopment for software, while others like Hugging Face allow this for development of Generative Foundation Models (GFMs). This collaborative model leverages the collective intelligence of a global community, accelerating innovation and improving software quality through diverse inputs and perspectives.

- Remote artistic collaborations: Artists and creators use platforms like Twitch, Patreon, and Discord (the primary collaborative platform we used to discuss this project) to collaborate on projects, share their creative process, and engage with audiences in real-time. These platforms enable artists to co-create with other artists and fans, breaking down the barriers between creator and audience and fostering a participatory culture around the creative process.

- Educational collaborations: Online non-profit education platforms like Coursera, edX, and Khan Academy bring together educators and learners from across the globe. They support collaborative learning experiences, peer-to-peer feedback, and group projects, making education more accessible and fostering a global learning community.

- Crowdsourced innovation: Platforms like Kickstarter and Indiegogo enable entrepreneurs to collaborate with the public to fund and refine new products and projects. This model of collaboration invites input and support from a broad audience, validating ideas and ensuring they meet the needs and desires of potential users.

As we move forward, the possibilities for collaborative innovation can increase in breadth and depth, thriving on the collective intelligence, diverse perspectives, and unique contributions of larger (and even global) communities, redefining the boundaries of innovation, art, science, and education.

## Creative collaboration tomorrow

At the boundaries of ⿻ practice we are already seeing a world where real-time global collaboration assisted by advance computational models become the norm, propelling the creative process to new heights of inclusivity and innovation. The story of the Herculaneum scrolls encapsulates the essence of collaborative innovation—bridging the past with the future, merging diverse expertise to illuminate the unknown. It serves as an emblematic beginning to our exploration, reminding us that at the heart of every great discovery lies the spirit of collaboration, a spirit that continues to drive humanity forward, beyond the limits of our imagination. Rather than exceptional, the Vesuvius Challenge and its winners trace a common pattern. Consider the 2009 Netflix Prize, which offered a million dollars to the team that could beat their internal movie recommendation algorithm by 10%. The prize competition dragged on for more than two and a half years and only succeeded in the end when the leading teams gave up working alone, but instead combined with diverse other teams and their diverse algorithms.[3] One might even use this conception to reimagine neural networks as social networks, simulating diversity and disputes between people with diverse perspectives. Arguably this simultaneous simulation of multiple perspectives is precisely what may account for their increasing dominance in a wide range of tasks.[4]

We are seeing the beginnings of this future in a diversity of emerging practices.

- Synthetic instruments and generative art: The electronic musical forms that rose to prominence in the 1980s were grounded in the ability to synthesize a wide range of sound profiles electronically that in the past would have required elaborate instrumentation or have been

---

[3] Scott E. Page, *The diversity bonus: How great teams pay off in the knowledge economy* (Princeton, NJ: Princeton University Press, 2019).

[4] James Evans. "The case for alien AI," *TedxChicago2024*, October 6th, 2023, https://www.youtube.com/watch?v=87zET-4IQws.

impossible. Today we are seeing the seed of an even more radical revolution, as GFMs are increasingly being harnessed by artists to allow a far broader range of people to synthesize a dazzling array of experiences. For example, leading artists Holly Herndon, Mat Dryhurst and their collaborators have harnessed GFMs to allow them to sing in the voices of historical figures or others not present and to allow others to sing in their voices. Artist and musician Laurie Anderson has used a variety of models to produce texts that speak to contemporary problems with historical style and wisdom. A generation of "generative artists" have explored the intersecting creativity embedded in these models to draw out elements of the collective psyche. In a small way, in this project we have blended voice samples of many participants to create an audio version read in our common voice.

- Cross-cultural collaboration: Where once language and cultural misunderstanding were central barriers to creative collaboration across widely varying contexts, GFMs are increasingly able to translate not just languages, but cultural styles, making fusions increasingly fruitful in music, film, and more.
- Alien art: While GFMs can mimic and automate the way humans generate ideas, we could instead aspire to generate "alien intelligence" that takes our thought in directions humans are unlikely to identify, thus generating new fodder for collaboration across diversity.[5] For instance, Google DeepMind initially trained AlphaGo to mimic human strategies in playing Go games. Conversely, their next version, AlphaGo

---

[5] Jamshid Sourati and James Evans, "Complementary artificial intelligence designed to augment human discovery," *arXiv preprint arXiv:2207.00902* (2022), https://doi.org/10.48550/arXiv.2207.00902.

Zero, was trained solely against other model adversaries like itself, generating an unfamiliar and disconcerting yet effective "alien" strategy that surprised many master Go players. Research demonstrates that interacting with these diverse AI strategies has increased the novelty and diversity of the human Go-playing population [6]. If such approaches were applied to the cultural sphere rather than to games, we might find novel artistic forms emerging to inspire "awe" or resonance in alien machine intelligences, then feeding back to provoke new artistic forms among humans, just as the "encounter with the East" was critical to creating modern art in the West.

- Digital twins and simulation for creative testing: Advanced simulations and digital twin technology will enable creative teams to test and refine their ideas in virtual replicas of real-world environments. With digital twins driven by GFMs that accurately mimics human behaviors, we could conduct in-silico social experiments at an unprecedented speed and scale. For instance, by deploying alternative news feed algorithms on in-silico social media platforms, where large language model (LLM) agents that mimic human social media users interact with one another, we can explore and test the impact of these alternative algorithms on macro-level social outcomes, such as conflicts and polarization.[7]

---

[6] Minkyu Shin, Jin Kim, Bas van Opheusden, and Thomas L. Griffiths, "Superhuman artificial intelligence can improve human decision-making by increasing novelty," *Proceedings of the National Academy of Sciences* 120, no. 12 (2023): e2214840120, https://doi.org/10.1073/pnas.2214840120.

[7] Petter Törnberg, Diliara Valeeva, Justus Uitermark, and Christopher Bail. "Simulating social media using large language models to evaluate alternative news feed algorithms," *arXiv preprint arXiv:2310.05984* (2023), [

Tomorrow, we expect digital tools to unlock a symphony of minds, amplified and harmonized by GFMs and real-time high bandwidth remote synchronization. Yet, this is merely the prelude to a grand concerto of human and digital collaboration. As we wield these digital tools to broaden the space of creative collaboration, we will find ourselves in an ever-evolving dance, one where technology not only aids us but also reshapes our perspectives, fostering a rapid integration of diverse ideas and talents. We are not just witnessing the emergence of new creative processes; we are participating in the birth of a globally inclusive, multidisciplinary renaissance, one that promises to redefine the landscape of creativity and problem-solving for generations to come.

**Frontiers of creative collaboration**

The "symphony of minds," assisted and amplified by technology, is poised to transcend beyond the mere exchange of ideas and creations to a realm where collective consciousness redefines creativity.

- Telepathic creative exchanges: With advancements in post-symbolic communication, collaborators will be able to share ideas, visions, and creative impulses directly from mind to mind. This telepathic exchange will enable creators to bypass the limitations of language and physical expression, leading to a form of collaboration that is instantaneously empathetic and deeply intuitive.
- Inter-specific collaborative projects: The expansion of communication technologies to include non-human perspectives will open new frontiers in creativity. Collaborations could extend to other intelligence species (e.g., dolphins, octopuses), incorporating their perceptions and experiences into the creative process. Such projects could lead to unprecedented forms of art

and innovation, grounded in a more holistic understanding of our planet and its inhabitants.
- Legacy and time-travel collaborations: With the creation of digital legacies and immersive experiences that allow for time travel within one's consciousness, future collaborators might engage not only with contemporaries but also with the minds of the past and future. This temporal collaboration could bring insights from different eras into conversation, enriching the creative process with a multitude of perspectives and wisdom accumulated across generations.
- Collective creativity for global challenges: The challenges facing humanity will be met with a unified creative force, as collaborative platforms enable individuals worldwide to contribute their ideas and solutions. This collective creativity will be instrumental in addressing issues such as climate change, harnessing the power of diverse perspectives and innovative thinking to create sustainable and impactful solutions.

As we embark on this collaborative odyssey, humanity stands poised to redefine creativity itself. It is a future where creativity is not just a shared endeavor but a shared experience, connecting participants in a web of collective imagination and innovation. Yet, as we approach this crescendo of human potential—where the symphony of collaborative genius reaches its zenith—we also must explore its ethical considerations and limitations.

## Limits of creative collaboration

The future of creative collaborations, while pregnant with potential for novel collaboration paradigms, also has a range of limitations and ethical dilemmas. As we envision the zenith of creative synergy enabled by technologies that dissolve the barriers of distance, language, and even individual cognition, the shadow of potential dystopian outcomes looms large. Dave

Eggers's classic *The Circle* highlights the dangers of constant creative sharing to erode the very sense of self that is the locus of creative genius. As we pursue increasing collaboration, we must constantly guard against:

1. Loss of privacy and autonomy: In a future where every thought, idea, and creative impulse can be shared instantly, the sanctity of private thought is at risk. A society under constant surveillance and pressure to share every aspect of one's life parallels the potential for creative collaborations to become invasive, where the constant demand for openness stifles individual creativity and autonomy.

2. Homogenization of creativity: As collaborative platforms become more sophisticated, there's a risk that the algorithms designed to enhance synergy could instead lead to a homogenization of ideas. This could dampen true innovation, as the unique perspectives and unconventional ideas are smoothed over in favor of consensus and algorithmic predictability. This highlights the urgency of exploring the designs of crowdsourced platforms and AIs that reward the exploration and connections of novel, heterogeneous ideas. For instance, crowdsourced innovation and co-creation processes could further be facilitated by AI that bridges existing ideas and communities that are less likely to be connected in the platform.[8]

3. Over-reliance on technology: Future collaborations might lean heavily on technological interfaces and GFM-driven processes, potentially leading to a depreciation of human skills and intuition in the creative process. This

---

[8] Feng Shi and James Evans, "Surprising combinations of research contents and contexts are related to impact and emerge with scientific outsiders from distant disciplines," *Nature Communications* 14, no. 1 (2023): 1641, https://doi.org/10.1038/s41467-023-36741-4.

## 5-3 Creative Collaborations

over-reliance is at risk of creating a dependency on technology for social interaction and validation, raising concerns about the atrophy of traditional creative skills.

4. Digital divide and inequality: In a society stratified by access to technology and information, the future of creative collaborations could exacerbate existing inequalities. Those with access to cutting-edge collaboration platforms will have a distinct advantage over those without, potentially widening the gap between the technological haves and have-nots, and monopolizing creativity within echelons of society that can afford such access.

5. Manipulation, exploitation, and collapse: The potential for exploitation of creative content and ideas by corporate overreach is a significant concern. As creative collaborations increasingly occur within digital platforms owned by corporations, the risk of intellectual property being co-opted, monetized, or used for surveillance and manipulation grows, threatening the integrity of the creative process. By reducing the incentive for creativity, such traps risk killing the goose of creativity and diversity that lays the golden eggs of training GFMs in the first place.

6. Erosion of cultural diversity: In a world where creative collaborations are mediated by global platforms, there's a risk that local cultural expressions and minority voices are overshadowed by dominant narratives. This could lead to a dilution of cultural diversity in creative outputs, ending in monolithic culture that neutralizes dissent and diversity.

In addressing these challenges, the future of creative collaboration must navigate the delicate balance between leveraging the immense potential of technology to enhance human creativity and ensuring that this does not come at the expense of privacy, autonomy, and cultural diversity. Central to this journey is the leveraging of open-source technologies and the principles of ⌘. Open-source platforms, by their very nature, encourage transparency and collective ownership, countering the risks of hidden monopolies and collusion that can arise in proprietary systems. These can be further augmented by many of the economic and governance models we highlight in what follows. Something that is already beginning to happen as leading ⌘ artists like Holly Herndon, Joseph Gordon-Levitt and will.i.am champion not only harnessing GFMs but also ensuring they are designed to attribute, celebrate and empower creators to live sustainably.

Furthermore, many of the risks of cultural homogenization arise from the encroachment of a single medium, with all its sensory limits, into a broader range of life. To preserve creativity, we must bolster the space for the even deeper intimate connections and reflection on which creativity depends. Luckily, this is precisely the role that the even-more-intimate technologies we discussed in the preceding chapters can play, ensuring that an endless stream of shared music and artistic mashups do not crowd out the deep relationships that are the foundation of physical and cultural reproduction.

## 5-4 Augmented Deliberation

As we have noted above, one of the most common concerns about social media has been its tendency to entrench existing social divisions, creating "echo chambers" that undermine a sense of shared reality.[1] News feed algorithms based on "collaborative filtering" selects content that is likely to maximize user engagements, prioritizing like-minded content that reinforces users' existing beliefs and insulates them from diverse information. Despite mixed findings on whether these algorithms truly exacerbate political polarization and hamper deliberations, it is natural to ask how these systems might be redesigned with the opposite intention of "bridging" the crowd. The largest-scale attempt at this is the Community Notes (formerly Birdwatch) system in the X (formerly Twitter) social media platform.

Community Notes (CN) is a community-based "fact-checking" platform. CN allows members of the X community to flag potentially misleading posts and provide additional contexts about why the posts could be misleading. CN participants not only submit these notes to the platform; they also rate the notes proposed by others. These ratings are used to assess whether the notes are helpful and are eligible to be publicly released to the X platform as illustrated in Figure A.[2]

---

[1] Cass Sunstein, *republic.com* (Princeton, NJ: Princeton University Press, 2001) and *#republic: Divided Democracy in the Age of Social Media* (Princeton, NJ: Princeton University Press, 2018).

[2] Vitalik Buterin, "What do I think about Community Notes?" August 16, 2023 at https://vitalik.eth.limo/general/2023/08/16/communitynotes.html.

數位 Plurality: Part 5: Democracy

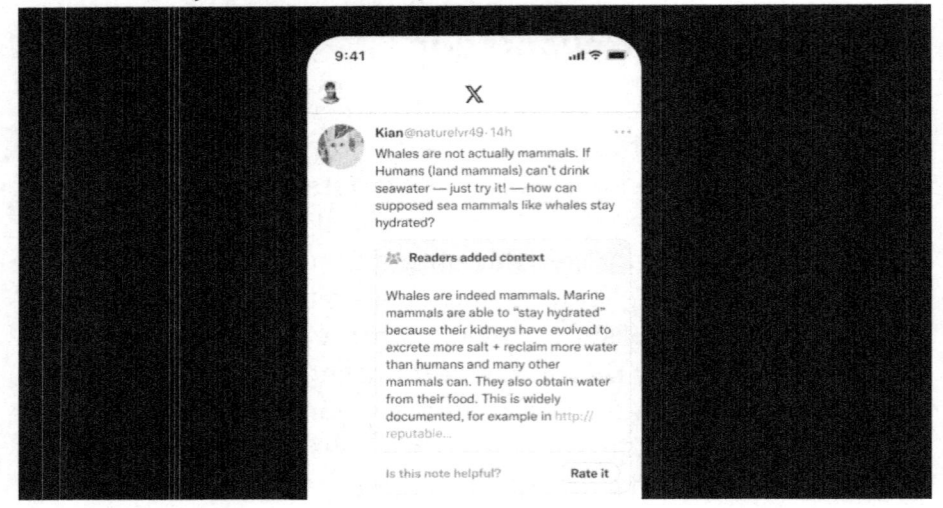

**Figure 5-4-A.** Community Notes on X correcting a misleading post. Source: Direct capture from application, by fair use.

Specifically, raters are placed on a one-dimensional spectrum of opinion, discovered by the statistical analysis from the data but in practice corresponding in most applications to the "left-right" divide in the politics of much of the Western hemisphere. Simultaneously, the support each note receives from any community member is attributed to a combination of its affinity to their position on this spectrum and some underlying, position-agnostic "objective quality". Notes are then considered to be "helpful" if this objective quality, rather than the overall ratings, is sufficiently high. Instead of prioritizing notes that are supported by a biased, like-minded cluster of users, the system rewards notes that are supported by diverse groups of users, correcting biases driven by political and social fragmentation. This approach leverages alternative social media algorithms to augment human deliberations, prioritizing content based on the principle of collaboration across diversity, consistent with 數位, to which hundreds of millions of people are currently exposed each week.³ This platform has been shown to encourage the exploration of diverse political information, compared to the previous methods of moderating misinformation.⁴

---

In this chapter, we explore the considerable power and limitations of human conversations, expressing hope that advances in 🖳 might transform conversations into a more powerful engine for both amplifying and connecting diverse perspectives in ways previously unimaginable.

## Conversation today

The oldest, typically richest, and still most common form of conversations is the "in-person meeting." Idealized portraits of democracy typically refer to discussions involved in these in-person conversations, such as what took place among traditional tribes, in the Athenian marketplaces, or in New England town halls, rather than to votes or media. The recent film, *Women Talking*, brilliantly captures this spirit in its portrait of a traumatized community coming to a plan for common action through discussion. Groups of friends, clubs, students and teachers, all exchange perspectives, learn, grow, and form a common purpose through in-person talk. In addition to their interactive nature, in-person interactions often carry elements of richer, non-verbal communication, as participants share a

---

[3] Stefan Wojcik, Sophie Hilgard, Nick Judd, Delia Mocanu, Stephen Ragain, M.B. Fallin Hunzaker, Keith Coleman and Jay Baxter, "Birdwatch: Crowd Wisdom and Bridging Algorithms can Inform Understanding and Reduce the Spread of Misinformation", October 27, 2022 at https://arxiv.org/abs/2210.15723.

[4] Junsol Kim, Zhao Wang, Haohan Shi, Hsin-Keng Ling, and James Evans, "Individual misinformation tagging reinforces echo chambers; Collective tagging does not," *arXiv preprint arXiv:2311.11282* (2023), https://arxiv.org/abs/2311.11282.

physical context and can perceive many non-verbal cues, such as facial expressions, body language, and gestures, from others in the conversation.

The next oldest and most common communicative form is writing. While far less interactive, writing enables words to travel over much greater distances and time. Typically conceived as capturing the voice of a single "author", written communications can spread broadly, even globally, with the aid of printing and translation. They can endure for thousands of years, allowing for a "broadcast" of messages much farther than amphitheaters or loudspeakers can achieve.

This underscores a crucial trade-off: the richness and immediacy of in-person discussions versus the extensive reach and permanence of the written word. Many platforms strive to blend elements of both in-person and written communication by creating a network where in-person conversations serve as links among individuals who are physically and socially proximate, and writing serves as a bridge, connecting people who are geographically distant from each other. The World Cafe [5] or Open Space Technology [6] methods allow dozens or even thousands of people to convene and participate in small groups for dialogue while the written notes from those small clusters are synthesized and distributed broadly. Other examples include constitutional and rule-making processes, book clubs, editorial boards for publications, focus groups, surveys, and other research processes. A typical pattern is that a group deliberates on writing that is then submitted to another deliberative group that results in another document that is then sent back, and so on. One might recognize this in legal tradition

---

[5] "The World Cafe", The World Café Community Foundation, last modified 2024, (https://theworldcafe.com/)

[6] "Open Space", Open Space World, last modified 2024, https://openspaceworld.org/wp2/

via oral and written arguments, as well as the academic peer review process.

One of the most fundamental challenges this variety of forms tries to navigate is the trade-off between diversity and bandwidth.[7] On the one hand, when we attempt to engage individuals with vastly diverse perspectives in conversations, the discussions could become less efficient, lengthy, costly, and time-consuming. This often means that they have trouble yielding definite and timely outcomes; resulting in the "analysis paralysis" often bemoaned in corporate settings and the complaint (sometimes attributed to Oscar Wilde) that "socialism takes too many evenings".

On the other hand, when we attempt to increase the bandwidth and efficiency of conversations, they often struggle to remain inclusive of diverse perspectives. People engaging in conversation are often geographically dispersed, speak different languages, have different conversational norms, etc. Diversity in conversational styles, cultures and language often impedes mutual understanding. Furthermore, given that it is impossible for everyone to be heard at length, some notion of representation is necessary for conversation to cross broad social diversity, as we will discuss at length below.

Perhaps the fundamental limit on all these approaches is that while methods of *broadcast* (allowing many to hear a single statement) have dramatically improved, *broad listening* (allowing one person to thoughtfully digest a range of perspectives) remains extremely costly and time consuming.[8]

---

[7] Sinan Aral, and Marshall Van Alstyne, "The diversity-bandwidth trade-off," American journal of sociology 117, no. 1 (2011): 90-171.

[8] To our knowledge, this concept of "broad listening" originates with Andrew Trask. However, we have no written reference for it with him and thus want to ensure he is credited here.

As economics Nobel Laureate and computer science pioneer Herbert Simon observed, "(A) wealth of information creates a poverty of attention."[9] The cognitive limits on the amount of attention an individual can give, when trying to focus on diverse perspectives, potentially impose sharp trade-offs between diversity and bandwidth, as well as between richness and inclusion.

Several strategies have, historically and more recently, been used to navigate these challenges at scale. Representatives are chosen for conversations by a variety of methods, including:

1. Election: A campaign and voting process are used to select representatives, often based on geographic or political party groups. This is used most in politics, unions, and churches. It has the advantage of conferring a degree of broad participation, legitimacy, and expertise, but is often rigid and expensive.
2. Sortition: A set of people are chosen randomly, sometimes with checks or constraints to ensure some sort of balance across groups. This is used most in focus groups, surveys and in citizen deliberative councils [10] on contentious policy issues.[11] It maintains reasonable legitimacy and flexibility at low cost, but sacrifices (or needs to be supplemented with) expertise and has limited participation.

---

[9] Herbert Simon, "Designing Organizations for an Information-Rich World," In *Computers, Communications, and the Public Interest*, edited by Martin Greenberger, 38–72. Baltimore: The Johns Hopkins Press, 1971. https://gwern.net/doc/design/1971-simon.pdf.

[10] A Citizen Deliberative Council (CDC) article on the Co-Intelligence Site https://www.co-intelligence.org/P-CDCs.html

[11] Tom Atlee, *Empowering Public Wisdom* (2012, Berkley, California, Evolver Editions, 2012)

3. Administration: A set of people are chosen by a bureaucratic assignment procedure, based on "merit" or managerial decisions to represent different relevant perspectives or constituencies. This is used most in business and professional organizations and tends to have relatively high expertise and flexibility at low cost but has lower legitimacy and participation.

Once participants are selected and arrive, facilitating a meaningful interaction is an equally significant challenge and is a science unto itself. Ensuring all participants, whatever their communicative modes and styles, can be fully heard requires a range of social technologies and practices, including clear purpose and agenda setting, active inclusion, small group breakouts, careful management of notes (often called the "harvest" of many small group conversations), turn-taking, and encouragement of active listening and often translation and accommodation of differing abilities for auditory and visual communication styles. A very rich field of "dialogue and deliberation" research and methods have been innovated over the last 50-60 years, and the National Coalition for Dialogue and Deliberation is a hub for exploring these.[12] These tools can help overcome the "tyranny of structurelessness" that often affects attempts at inclusive and democratic governance, where

---

[12] *Liberating Structures* (2024) has 33 methods for people to work together in liberating ways. Participedia is public participation and democratic innovations platform documenting methods and case studies. To get at the heart of the underlying patterns in good and effective processes two communities developed pattern languages 1) The Group Works: A Pattern Language for Brining Meetings and other Gatherings (2022) and 2) The Wise Democracy Pattern Language.

unfair informal norms and dominance hierarchies override intentions for inclusive exchange. [13]

Appropriate use of digital technologies can augment the social technologies for engagement, and the intersection of the two can be fruitful. Physical travel distance used to be a severe impediment to deliberation. However, phone and video conferences have significantly mitigated this challenge, making various formats of distance/virtual meetings increasingly common venues for challenging discussions.

The rise of internet-mediated writing, including formats such as email, message boards/usenets, webpages, blogs, and notably social media, has significantly broadened "inclusion" in written communication. These platforms offer novel opportunities for individuals to gain visibility and attention easily through user interactions (e.g., "likes" or "reposts") and algorithmic ranking systems. This paradigm shift has enabled the diffusion of information among the public, a process once firmly controlled by the editorial procedures of legacy media. However, the effectiveness of these platforms in optimally distributing attention remains a topic of debate. A common drawback is the lack of context and thorough moderation in the diffusion of information, contributing to issues like the spread of "misinformation" and "disinformation," and the dominance of well-resourced entities. Moreover, the reliance on algorithmic ranking can inadvertently create "echo chambers," confining users to a narrow stream of content that reflects their existing beliefs, thus limiting their exposure to a diverse range of perspectives and knowledge.

---

[13] Jo Freeman, "The Tyranny of Structurelessness." WSQ: Women's Studies Quarterly 41, no. 3-4 (2013): 231-46. https://doi.org/10.1353/wsq.2013.0072.

## Conversation tomorrow

Recent advances are progressively shifting the dynamics of the trade-offs, enabling more efficient and networked sharing of rich, in-person deliberations. Simultaneously, these developments are facilitating more thoughtful, balanced, and contextualized moderation within increasingly inclusive forms of social media, thereby enhancing the overall quality and reach of these platforms.

As we discussed in The Life of a Digital Democracy chapter above, one of the most successful examples in Taiwan has been the vTaiwan system, which harnesses OSS called Polis.[14] This platform shares some features with social media services like X, but builds abstractions of some of the principles of inclusive facilitation into its attention allocation and user experience. As in X, users submit short responses to a prompt. But rather than amplifying or responding to one another's comments, they simply vote these up or down. These votes are then clustered to highlight patterns of common attitudes which form what one might call user perspectives. Representative statements that highlight these differing opinion groups' perspectives are displayed to allow users to understand key points of view, as are the perspectives that "bridge" the divisions: ones that receive assent across the lines that otherwise divide. Responding to this evolving conversation, users can offer additional perspectives that help to further bridge, articulate an existing position or draw out a new opinion group that may not yet be salient.

Polis is a prominent example of what leading technologists Aviv Ovadya and Luke Thorburn call "collective response

---

[14] Christopher T. Small, Michael Bjorkegren, Lynette Shaw and Colin Megill, "Polis: Scaling Deliberation by Mapping High Dimensional Opinion Spaces" *Recerca: Revista de Pensament i Analàlisi* 26, no. 2 (2021): 1-26.

systems" and "bridging systems" and others call "wikisurveys".[15] Other leading examples include All Our Ideas and Remesh, which have various trade-offs in terms of user experience, degree of open source and other features. What these systems share is that they combine the participatory, open, and interactive nature of social media with features that encourage thoughtful listening, an understanding of conversational dynamics and the careful emergence of an understanding of shared views and points of rough consensus. Such systems have been used to make increasingly consequential policy and design decisions, around topics such as the regulation of ride-hailing applications and the direction of some of the leading generative foundation models (GFMs).[16] In particular, working closely with the 數位 NGO the Collective Intelligence Project (CIP), Anthropic's recently released Claude3 model, considered by many to be the current state-of-the-art in GFMs, sourced the constitution used to steer model behavior using Polis.[17] OpenAI, the other leading provider of GFMs today, also worked closely with CIP to run a grant program on "democratic

---

[15] Matthew J. Salganik and Karen E. C. Levy, "Wiki Surveys: Open and Quantifiable Social Data Collection" *PLOS One* 10, no. 5: e0123483 at https://journals.plos.org/plosone/article?id=10.1371/journal.pone.0123483. Aviv Ovadya and Luke Thorburn, "Bridging Systems: Open Problems for Countering Destructive Divisiveness across Ranking, Recommenders, and Governance" (2023) at https://arxiv.org/abs/2301.09976. Aviv Ovadya, "'Generative CI' Through Collective Response Systems" (2023) at https://arxiv.org/pdf/2302.00672.pdf.

[16] Yu-Tang Hsiao, Shu-Yang Lin, Audrey Tang, Darshana Narayanan and Claudina Sarahe, "vTaiwan: An Empirical Study of Open Consultation Process in Taiwan" (2018) at https://osf.io/preprints/socarxiv/xyhft.

[17] Anthropic, "Collective Constitutional AI: Aligning a Language Model with Public Input" October 17, 2023 at https://www.anthropic.com/news/collective-constitutional-ai-aligning-a-language-model-with-public-input.

## 5-4 Augmented Deliberation

inputs to AI" that dramatically accelerated research in this area and on the basis of which they are now forming a "Collective Alignment Team" to incorporate these inputs into the steering of OpenAI's models.[18]

An approach with similar goals but a bit of an opposite starting point centers in-person conversations but aims to improve the way their insights can be networked and shared. A leading example in this category is the approach developed by the Massachusetts Institute of Technology's Center for Constructive Communication in collaboration with their civil society collaborators; called Cortico. This approach and technology platform, dubbed Fora, uses a mixture of the identity and association protocols we discussed in the Freedom part of the book and natural language processing to allow recorded conversations on challenging topics to remain protected and private while surfacing insights that can travel across these conversations and spark further discussion. Community members, with permission from the speakers, lift consequential highlights up to stakeholders, such as government, policy makers or leadership within an organization. Cortico has used this technology to help inform civic processes such as the 2021 election of Michelle Wu as Boston's the first Taiwanese-American mayor of a major US city.[19] The act of soliciting perspectives via deep conversational data in collaboration with under-served communities imbues

---

[18] Tyna Eloundou and Teddy Lee, "Democratic Inputs to AI Grant Program: Lessons Learned and Implementation Plans", *OpenAI Blog*, January 16, 2024 at https://openai.com/blog/democratic-inputs-to-ai-grant-program-update

[19] Meghna Irons, "Some Bostonians Feel Largely Unheard, With MIT's 'Real Talk' Portal Now Public, Here's a Chance to Really Listen," The Boston Globe, October 21, 2021, https://www.bostonglobe.com/2021/10/25/metro/some-bostonians-feel-largely-unheard-with-mits-real-talk-portal-now-public-heres-chance-really-listen/.

the effort with a legitimacy absent from faster modes of communication. Related tools, of differing degrees of sophistication, are used by organizations like StoryCorps and Braver Angels and have reached millions of people.

A third approach attempts to leverage and organize existing media content and exchanges, rather than induce participants to produce new content. This approach is closely allied to academic work on "digital humanities", which harnesses computation to understand and organize human cultural output at scale. Organizations like the Society Library collect available material from government documentation, social media, books, television etc. and organize it for citizens to highlight the contours of debate, including surfacing available facts. This practice is becoming increasingly scalable with some of the tools we describe below by harnessing digital technology to extend the tradition described above by extending the scale of deliberation by networking conversations across different venues together.

Other more experimental efforts, closely aligned with the techniques discussed in our *Immersive Shared Reality* chapter above, aim to enhance the depth and quality of remote deliberations, aspiring to emulate the richness and immediacy typically found in in-person interactions. A recent dramatic illustration was a conversation between Meta CEO Mark Zuckerberg and leading podcast host Lex Fridman, where both were in virtual reality able to perceive minute facial expressions of the other. A less dramatic but perhaps more meaningful example was the Portals Policing Project, where cargo containers appeared in cities affected by police violence and allowed an enriched video-based exchange of experiences with such violence across physical and social distance.[20] Other promising elements include the increasing ubiquity of high-quality, low-cost and increasingly culturally aware machine translation tools and work to harness similar systems to enable people to synthesize values and find common ground building from natural language statements.

**Frontiers of augmented deliberation**

Some of these more ambitious experiments begin to point towards a future, especially harnessing language capabilities of GFMs to go much further towards addressing the "broad listening" problem, empowering deliberation of a quality and scale that has henceforth been hard to imagine. The internet enables collaboration at an extreme scale by reducing the possible space of collaborative actions, such as to buy/sell market transactions, and by utilizing a similar reduction in information transmission, i.e. to five star rating systems. An effective increase in our ability to transmit and digest information can result in a corresponding increase in our ability to deliberate on difficult and nuanced social issues.

One of the most obvious directions that is a subject of active development is how systems like Polis and Community Notes could be extended with modern graph theory and GFMs. The "Talk to the City" project of the AI Objectives Institute, for example, illustrates how GFMs can be used to replace a list of statements characterizing a group's views with an interactive agent one can talk to and get a sense of the perspective. Soon, it should be possible to go further, with GFMs allowing participants to move beyond limited short statements and simple up-and-down votes. Instead, they will be able to fully express themselves in reaction to the conversation.

---

[20] Amer Bakshi, Tracey Meares and Vesla Weaver, "Portals to Politics: Perspectives on Policing from the Grassroots" (2015) at https://www.law.nyu.edu/sites/default/files/upload_documents/Bakshi%20Meares%20and%20Weaver%20Portals%20to%20Politics%20Study.pdf.

Meanwhile, the models will condense this conversation, making it legible to others who can then participate. Models could also help look for areas of rough consensus not simply based on common votes but on a natural language understanding of and response to expressed positions. A recent large-scale study highlights the positive impact of such tools in enhancing online democratic discussions. In this experiment, a GFM was used to provide real-time, evidence-based suggestions aimed at refining the quality of political discourse to each participant in the conversation.[21] The results indicated a noticeable improvement in the overall quality of conversations, fostering a more democratic, reciprocal exchange of ideas.

While most discussion of bridging systems focuses on building consensus, another powerful role is to support the regeneration of diversity and productive conflict. On the one hand, they help identify different opinion groups in ways that are not a deterministic function of historical assumptions or identities, potentially allowing these groups to find each other and organize around their perspective. On the other hand, by surfacing as representing consensus positions that have diverse support, they also create diverse opposition that can coalesce into a new conflict that does not reinforce existing divisions, potentially allowing organization around that perspective. In short, collective response systems can play just as important a role in mapping and evolving conflict dynamically as helping to navigate it productively.

---

[21] Lisa Argyle, Christopher Bail, Ethan Busby, Joshua Gubler, Thomas Howe, Christopher Rytting, Taylor Sorensen, and David Wingate, "Leveraging AI for democratic discourse: Chat interventions can improve online political conversations at scale." *Proceedings of the National Academy of Sciences* 120, no. 41 (2023): e2311627120.

## 5-4 Augmented Deliberation

In a similar spirit, one can imagine harnessing and advancing elements of the design of Community Notes to reshape social media dynamics more holistically. While the system currently lines up all opinions across the platform on a single spectrum, one can imagine mapping out a range of communities within the platform and harnessing its bridging-based approach not just to prioritize notes, but to prioritize content for attention in the first place. Furthermore, bridging can be applied at many different scales and to diverse intersecting groups, not just to the platform overall. One can imagine a future, as we highlight in our *Media* chapter below, where different content in a feed is highlighted as bridging and being shared among a range of communities one is a member of (a religious community, a physically local community, a political community), reinforcing context and common knowledge and action in a range of social affiliations.

Such dynamic representations of social life could also dramatically improve how we approach representation and selection of participants for deeper deliberation, such as in person or in rich immersive shared realities. With a richer accounting of relevant social differences, it may be possible to move beyond geography or simple demographics and skills as groups that need to be represented. Instead, it may be possible to increasingly use the full intersectional richness of identity as a basis for considering inclusion and representation. Constituencies defined this way could participate in elections or, instead of sortition, protocols could be devised to choose the maximally diverse committees for a deliberation by, for example, choosing a collection of participants that minimizes how marginalized from representation the most marginalized participants are based on known social connections and affiliations. Such an approach could achieve many of the benefits of sortition, administration and election simultaneously, especially if combined with some of the liquid democracy approaches that we discuss in the voting chapter below.

It may be possible to, in some cases, even more radically reimagine the idea of representation. GFMs can be "fine-tuned" to increasingly accurately mimic the ideas and styles of individuals.[22] One can imagine training a model on the text of a community of people (as in Talk to the City) and thus, rather than representing one person's perspective, it could operate as a fairly direct collective representative, possibly as an aid, complement or check on the discretion of a person intended to represent that group.

Most boldly, this idea could in principle extend beyond living human beings as we explore further in our *Environment* chapter below. In his classic *We Have Never Been Modern*, philosopher Bruno Latour argued that natural features (like rivers and forests) deserve representation in a "parliament of things".[23] The challenge, of course, is how they can speak. GFMs might offer ways to translate scientific measures of the state of these systems into a kind of "Lorax", Dr. Seuss's mythical creature who speaks for the trees and animals that cannot speak for themselves.[24] Something similar might occur for unborn future generations, as in Kim Stanley Robinson's *Ministry for the Future*.[25] For better or worse, such GFM-based representatives might be capable of carrying out deliberations faster than most humans can follow and might then convey summaries to human participants, allowing for deliberations that include individual

---

[22] Junsol Kim, and Byungkyu Lee, "Ai-augmented surveys: Leveraging large language models for opinion prediction in nationally representative surveys," *arXiv* (New York: Cornell University, November 26, 2023): https://arxiv.org/pdf/2305.09620.pdf.

[23] Bruno Latour, *We Have Never Been Modern* (Cambridge, MA: Cambridge University Press, 1993).

[24] Dr. Seuss, *The Lorax* (New York: Random House, 1971).

[25] Kim Stanley Robinson, *Ministry for the Future* (London: Orbit Books, 2020).

humans and also allow for other styles, speeds and scales of natural language exchange.

## Limits of augmented deliberation

The centrality of natural language to human interaction makes it tempting to forget its severe limitations. Words may be richer symbols than numbers, but they are as dust compared to the richness of human sensory experience, not to mention proprioception. "Words cannot capture" far more than they can. Whatever emotional truth it has, it is simply information, so it is theoretically logical that we form far deeper attention in common action and experience than in verbal exchange. Thus, however far deliberation advances, it cannot substitute for the richer forms of collaboration we have already discussed.

On the opposite side, talk takes time, even in the sophisticated versions we describe. Many decisions cannot wait for deliberation to fully run its course, especially when great social distance must be bridged, which will generally slow the process. The other approaches to collaboration we discuss below will address the need for timely decisions typical in many cases.

Many of the ways in which the slow pace of discussion can be overcome (e.g. using LLMs to conduct partially "in silico" deliberation) illustrate another important limitation of conversation: other methods are often more easily made transparent and thus broadly legitimate. The way conversations take inputs and produce outputs are hard to fully describe, whether they occur across people or in machines. In fact, one could consider inputting natural language to a machine and producing a machine dictation as just a more sophisticated, non-linear form of voting. But, in contrast to the administrative and voting rules we will discuss in the next two chapters, it might be very hard to achieve common understanding and legitimacy on how this transformation takes place and thus make it the basis for common action in the way that voting and markets often are. Thus, checks on the way deliberations occur and are observed arising from those other systems are likely to be important for a long time to come.

Furthermore, deliberation in the democratic process is also limited by the ability for humans to practically audit more capable GFMs. GFMs have also been demonstrated to adhere to instructions blindly in a way that may lead them to censor some perspectives.[26] To be properly 數位 models must offer a diverse array of reasonable responses, enabling them to adapt and reflect various perspectives, and ensuring they are accurately calibrated to the nuances of specific populations.

Lastly, deliberation is sometimes idealized as helping overcome divisions and reach a true "common will". Yet, while reaching points of overlapping and rough consensus is crucial for common action, so too is the regeneration of diversity and productive conflict to fuel dynamism and ensure productive inputs to future deliberations. Thus, deliberations and their balance with other modes of collaboration must always attend, as we have illustrated above, to this stimulus to productive conflict as much as it does to the resolution of conflict and the mitigation of explosive conflict.

---

[26] David Glukhov, Ilia Shumailov, Yarin Gal, Nicolas Papernot, and Vardan Papyan, "LLM Censorship: A Machine Learning Challenge or a Computer Security Problem?" *arXiv* (New York: Cornell University, July 20, 2023): https://arxiv.org/pdf/2307.10719.pdf.

## 5-5 Adaptive Administration

**Figure 5-5-A.** The results of this work can be seen taking place already. Source: Courtesy of Microsoft.

To launch what has come be known as the "Year of AI", Microsoft CEO Satya Nadella demonstrated at the World Economic Forum in Davos, Switzerland how a farmer speaking a local language in rural India could use a feature phone paired with a large language model (LLM) back end to access public services. The model understood the voice, translated from the local language to the national language in which the relevant forms were available, helped navigate what needed to be filled out, and returned guidance via voice to the farmer.

This demonstration built on years of work and multi stakeholder collaborations including AI4Bharat, Karya and IVR Junction, which have employed Indians to gather data on local languages, harnessed these data to empower LLMs to translate across these languages and connected illiterate Indians with access only to simple feature phones to connect to a "voice-based internet". Together these hold the promise of helping preserve and strengthen the cultural diversity of India by ensuring those who speak less prominent languages and live far from cities are still able to access the public services they need to sustain their ways of life.

Building on these demonstrations, Indian business, civil and government entities have launched services to harness these capabilities at scale. These include a government-provided chatbot to support applications to farmer financial support programs and a free What's App based multilingual chatbot that offers guidance on a variety of public services.

---

Administration and bureaucracy are central features organizing much of the world. They involve structured forms of communication and rule-bound processing of this information that is much more formal and stricter than the conventions of natural language. It is a less rich sensory experience that often has the aim of achieving legitimacy, equity, and procedural fairness. Yet they usually allow some form of extended communication in contrast to more strictly mathematical and mechanical interactions of voting or markets. Thus, they generally require deeper common understanding between participants to proceed effectively and ensure that conventions are harnessed and not violated. Administration is at the core of most interactions between individuals or small businesses with governments or large corporations. It is also central in the formation of medium-term relationships between people within a polity without tight social connections. It governs most of what we think of as law, property systems, identification, hiring and admissions and most functions of the "administrative state" and "corporate bureaucracy".

The classic complaints against bureaucracy and administration are that they are at once capricious, granting excessive discretionary power to those who hold various adjudicatory positions in the administration, and rigid, unable to adapt to

## 5-5 Adaptive Administration

either the nuances of an individual case nor to cultural settings outside the scope of the bureaucracy's expectations. In this chapter we aim to illustrate how advances in digital technology, especially generative foundation models (GFMs), may help alleviate some of these trade-offs, allowing more diverse groups of people to cooperate in administrative systems while respecting their ways of life.

## Administration today

Many of the most consequential junctures of life turn on administrative outcomes based on information structures (various kinds of "forms") that are much thinner than the way we conduct most of our lives. Examples include:

- Identification and travel documents
- Educational transcripts, resumés and other summaries of "the course of a life" (curriculum vitae/CV)
- Legal documents, including property deeds and contracts
- Tax fillings
- Structured performance evaluations
- Medical intake and evaluation forms
- Legal filings (though these usually include more detail and context than the above)

These structured forms of information allow for "fair", "just" and "impartial" evaluation of potential allocations or choices that are too complex to rely on universally transparent rules, as markets and votes do. To achieve fairness, these systems often deliberately discard a range of information, as dramatically illustrated by the blindness of justice in various personified representations in European tradition. As scholars since at least pioneering sociologist Max Weber have remarked, to achieve these twin goals of harnessing richer information than votes or markets while maintaining fairness, administrative systems employ large "bureaucracies" and much digital processing to evaluate these structured data according to rules and procedures.[1]

Thus, administrations run into two opposing complaints, which roughly correspond to the limits of the richness of the collaboration they allow and the limits of their ability to span social diversity.[2]

The first might be called the problem of "rigidity", namely that bureaucratic rules, by throwing away a lot of detail, lead to outcomes that are insensitive to important features of specific cases or local circumstances. Examples range from the mundane to the oppressive and simply ridiculous. Consider:

- Most jurisdictions have speed limits for driving cars to ensure safety. Yet the safe speed for driving varies dramatically with road, environmental and other related conditions. This means that speed limits are, most of the time, either too high or too low for the circumstances. Similar logic applies to almost all administrative policy settings, from the prices of goods to the break time allowed workers.
- To obtain most high-paying jobs, people from a diversity of cultures around the world must fit their accomplishments and lives into the format of CVs and transcripts designed to make them legible to administrative bureaucracies and hiring managers, rather than to reflect their accomplishments accurately.
- In the late 1990s, a Dutch airliner ended up physically shredding hundreds of live squirrels that lacked appropriate paperwork for transiting Schiphol airport.

---

[1] Max Weber, *Economy and Society* (Somerville, NJ: Bedminster Press, 1968).

[2] A forthcoming book provides an excellent study in these pathologies, as well as providing the squirrel example below. Davies, op. cit.

## 5-5 Adaptive Administration

While a particularly gruesome example, almost anyone who has flown is aware of the rigidity of the bureaucratic systems that administer air travel and will thus not be overly surprised by this outcome.

Yet at the same time as they are rigid, "cold" and "heartless", an equally common and opposite complaint about bureaucracies is their "complexity": that they often are inscrutable, hard to navigate (see, for example, Franz Kafka's classic work *The Castle*), full of red tape, and give excessive discretion to apparently arbitrary bureaucrats.[3] These problems are among the most infuriating features of bureaucracies and are a constant source of complaint by Libertarians. In fact, they have largely inspired many of the ideas about "distributed autonomous organizations" (DAOs) and "smart contracts" that are intended to escape excessive discretion, as well as leading to the high costs of the legal sector. And yet, clearly a key reason for such complexity is the need to handle the diversity and nuance of the cases they must administer. The leading reason, therefore, that bureaucracies become illegitimate as they try to span a broad range of social diversity is that, to accommodate this range, they must become too complex to function properly. Increasingly, however, digital technologies are emerging that allow this trade-off to be navigated more elegantly and thus allow richer cooperation to legitimately span a broader range of diversity.

### Adaptive administration tomorrow

The most important suite of technologies so far in achieving elegant complexity navigation have been those usually referred to as "artificial intelligence"(AI). However, as we have repeatedly noted, the term AI refers more to an aspiration

---

[3] Franz Kafka, *The Castle* (Munich: Kurt Wolff Verlag, 1926).

than to a particular set of tools and in this case, the details of the tools involved are critical to what distinguishes the administrative bureaucracies of old from the potential opened by GFMs. The AI work that dominated the field in the 1970s and 1980s, sometimes called "good old-fashioned AI" (GOFAI), was in many ways an attempt to automate traditional bureaucratic processing. Programmers, by talking to "experts", would attempt to encode administrative processes in complicated sets of nested rules (often called "decision trees"): Does the patient have a fever? If yes, are her eyes red; if not are her lymph nodes inflamed?... This style of AI ran into major obstacles and fell from favor during the 1990s. It has since largely been replaced by "machine learning", especially neural networks, and their most ambitious and recent outgrowth, GFMs.

In sharp contrast to GOFAI, machine learning is a statistical and emergent approach to classification, prediction, and decisions. Rather than applying a top-down set of hard-coded rules, the system learns to classify based on examples, in a probabilistic manner and in ways that often have no simple explanation. In neural networks, and especially GFMs, there are often billions or even trillions of "nodes" that receive input from each other. These nodes then trigger and input to other nodes, all coalescing to predict an outcome such as the next word or image. Based on such processes, GFMs have shown remarkable and rapidly improving ability to realistically reproduce the type of flexible classification, reaction and reasoning humans are often capable of in a rapidly scalable and largely reproducible way.

Such successes have created the tantalizing prospect of GFMs ameliorating the fundamental tradeoff at the heart of administration. Harnessing GFMs as components in administrative processes could allow them to take a far more diverse and unstructured range of inputs, adapt to them in the manner that a thoughtful and knowledgeable expert might,

## 5-5 Adaptive Administration

and do so in a way that offers a degree of reproducibility without imposing undue burdens on users to fill out specialized forms.

Explorations of this possibility have emerged especially in the last two years as interest around GFMs has exploded:

- As we highlighted in our introductory vignette, these tools have shown significant promise in allowing marginalized communities access public services that they may otherwise struggle to discover and navigate. A primary role of social workers has long been to support such navigation, but public expenditures have typically been far too small to ensure anywhere close to universal access, especially in developing countries. Leaders in such practices have been the Finnish government's Kela-Kelpo project, Germany's Federal Pension Insurance system and the Benefits Data Trust in the US.
- A similar but even more ambitious application is harnessing GFMs to improve access to legal advice and services for those who cannot afford high quality traditional legal support. Examples include Legal Robot and DoNotPay, both of which aim to help customers with limited means reduce the imbalance in legal access with corporate entities that can afford high quality legal services because they care not just about case outcomes but the precedents they create.[4]
- Job markets often fall into a "rich get richer" pattern as top employers often recruit exclusively from elite universities or use job experience at famous peer firms as a primary indicator of potential, foreclosing paths to opportunity for many who may have less conventional

---

[4] Marc Galanter, "Why the 'Haves' Come Out Ahead: Speculations on the Limits of Legal Change", *Law and Society Review* 9, no. 1 (1974): 95.

paths and, perhaps more importantly, forcing everyone interested in such opportunities down a narrow educational and career path. Several new human resources platforms (such as HiredScore, Paradox.ai, Turing and Untapped) aim to expand the breadth and diversity of candidates that hiring managers can consider. A leading challenge is that the limited examples of hiring such diverse candidates in the past can undermine the reliability and flexibility of such algorithms.

- Many of the most environmentally and culturally rich regions of the earth are either poorly mapped or mapped in ways that impose the perspective of colonial outsiders, rather than indigenous peoples who are more attentive to the environment and have long-existing relationships.[5] A variety of groups have harnessed digital mapping tools and increasingly GFMs to describe such traditional patterns of rights and assert them against colonial legal systems. These include Digital Democracy, the Rainforest Foundation US, the Australian Government's Indigenous Land and Sea Corporation and México's SERVIR Amazonia.[6]

As the last example especially suggests, a range of digital technologies not traditionally associated with "AI" are also relevant here, including mapping (global positioning and geographical information systems). This is dramatically illustrated in the collaborative mapping work of Ushahidi that

---

[5] Aníbal Quijano, "Coloniality and Modernity/Rationality", *Cultural Studies* 21, no. 2-3: 168-178.

[6] Jake Ramthun, Biplov Bhandari and Tim Mayer, "How SERVIR Uses AI to Turn Earth Science into Climate Action", *SERVIR blog* November 21, 2023 at https://servirglobal.net/news/how-servir-uses-ai-turn-earth-science-climate-action.

has helped in the response to disasters and conflict.[7] Also included are transparent databases (including distributed ledgers) as illustrated in a range of cases where these are being used as substrates for refugee identities by organizations like ID2020 or for land registries in Honduras. Furthermore, the power of GFMs stems less from being "AI" than from their networked and probabilistic structure, which allows them to adapt to a greater diversity and ambiguity of inputs. Such structures can also exist in networks of human relationships, including more adaptive forms of bureaucracy, packet-switching based trust relationships, etc.

**Frontiers of adaptive administration**

Whether grounded in networks of human minds, computer-simulated neurons or, most likely and effectively, an interweaving mesh of both, the potential for such systems could stretch well beyond these first experiments which largely aim to fit into existing rigid administrative structures and thus, in many cases, to reinforce their limitations. It is thus worth freeing our minds from some of these constraints to imagine building towards more transformative change.

One of the most promising directions was proposed by Danielle Allen, David Kidd, and Ariana Zetlin.[8] They suggest the gradual replacement of traditional coursework and grades with a far more diverse range of "badges". Starting with concrete recognition of specific measurable skills which then help qualify

---

[7] Ory Okolloh, "Ushahidi, or 'Testimony': Web 2.0 Tools for Crowdsourcing Crisis Information" in Holly Ashley ed., *Change at Hand: Web 2.0 for Development* (London: International Institute for Environment and Development, 2009).

[8] Danielle Allen, David Kidd and Ariana Zetlin, "A Call to More Equitable Learning: How Next-Generation Badging Improves Education for All" Edmond and Lil Safra Center for Ethics and Democratic Knowledge Project, August 2022 at https://www.nextgenbadging.org/whitepaper.

holders for "mezzo badges". Based on holding an appropriate combination of micro and mezzo badges people eventually ladder up to recognizable "macro badges" that can be used by potential employers or educational institutions. This process directly mirrors that which occurs within a neural network, where combinations of lower-level inputs trigger progressively higher-level and thus more meaningful outputs. Allen and her co-authors argue that such a system would be much more consistent with years of research in educational psychology which emphasizes the granular nature of skills and the poor fit of standard classroom practices to it and the fact that many students, especially historically marginalized and/or academically disinclined ones, often end up excluded from opportunity by such rigid structures.

Not only could GFMs and other neural networks be mirrored in the structure of such a system, but they might also be directly useful to it in allowing employers to cope with the more complex CVs it would create. GFMs could also help students navigate the more diverse learning pathways they would allow and could directly instantiate and produce some of the relevant badges. Furthermore, technologies of publicity (including social networks, verifiable credentials, and distributed ledgers) would likely be critical to achieving trust, credibility, and transparency around such badges. Relatedly, but perhaps more broadly, many practices of identification and admission to credentialed spaces (clubs, schools, nations via migration etc.) could rely on a more distributed network of signals from a variety social relations as we discussed in our *Identity and Personhood* chapter if such a range of signals could be meaningfully processed by more adaptive administrative infrastructure in the future.

Even more ambitiously, it might be possible to one day integrate far more diverse legal systems into administrative practices. The arrival of modernity and colonialism around the world largely overrode a range of traditional practices that varied dramatically by geography and culture. Many of these practices persist informally but jar with formal legal structures imposed by often distant national governments. These include practices around gender and sexual relationships, obligations associated with gift giving, the resolution of familial conflict and obligations, land use and more. While in some cases there is growing consensus that the abolition of such traditions is appropriate (e.g. prohibitions on female genital marking), in many cases laws have "overwritten" traditional practices more out of convenience than conviction. Traditional practices make it difficult, for example, for someone from far away to understand how to acquire land or appropriately intermarry in a community. The sometimes enforced, sometimes cajoled homogenization of cultural practices has brought some benefits to intermixing and dynamism, but at a great cost to often ancient and diverse wisdom of cultures.

Just as GFMs are increasingly capable of providing low-cost translation across a growing number of languages, it is just possible to imagine that equally rapid translation across cultural norms may become feasible. These services in the past have been provided imperfectly and at great expense by cultural anthropologists and ethnographers. Cheaper and easier translation may allow a much wider range of languages to remain viable and attractive to new generations because of the external interoperability it would allow. Similarly cheaper and easier translation of norms might make a much broader range of legal and property practices sustainable. This would reduce the constant burden of fitting into modernity imposed not just on colonized but also on a range of "traditional" communities within the developed world, often in rural areas. It would also greatly enrich the diversity that remains as the fuel for social growth and progress, as next generations of GFMs learn from being stretched by these cultural differences to perform ever more flexibly.

Beyond the preservation of existing diversity, such a future could help support its further diversification and speciation. Many of the practices we have sketched in this book challenge the imaginations of even ambitious futurists. This has led those attracted by experiments with these kinds of ideas to propose "network states", "charter cities", "seasteads" and other forms of escape from existing legal jurisdictions that, obviously, run into a range of tensions with preserving broader public goods and social order. Yet such clean separation may not be necessary to support such experiments if they can easily be understood by and integrated into existing legal structures by machine translation. This may empower a diverse range of experimentation with combinations of novel and traditional practices, while maintaining cooperation across broad social differences, and empowering the flourishing of ever expanding, infinite diversity in infinite combinations.

## Limits of adaptive administration

There may be no technology today whose pitfalls and dangers are more discussed than GFMs and for good reasons. Their opacity, mystique of autonomy (implicit in the common "AI" terminology that we therefore mostly avoid) that helps obscure the conditions of their creation, potential to inherit the biases of both their source data and creators, and potential for misuse all pose significant dangers.

In the context of administrative applications, the manifestations of these flaws are easy to see. While GFMs may be less burdensome to interact with, they arguably further exacerbate the opacity of bureaucracy and may not much mitigate the problems of discretion and human bias given that it is often extremely challenging to map the biases of such systems or what clusters of human behaviors in the past shape their outputs today.[9] Because such models overwhelmingly train on existing data, measuring the data diversity that AI researchers value, but struggle to define, is crucial to ensuring the models are generally performant and able to cope with diversity in the way we imagine. The terms of power on which such diversity is explored and incorporated into the models will shape how they offer opportunity for diversity or force conformity. Many of the ethnographers of old became tools of colonial subjugation rather than voices of inclusive translation.[10] Furthermore, if abused by powerful interests, interoperability across legal regimes can easily slip into regulatory arbitrage, taking advantage of the gap between legal intent and formal rules.

Luckily, some of the technologies we highlight in other chapters of this section have the potential to address at least partially some of these harms. While GFMs logic is hopelessly opaque when we try to reduce it to the simplistic representations of mathematics, richer formats like immersive shared reality or post-symbolic communication may give access to deeper modes of connection and understanding that aid in the establishment of trust in human communities that enables the use of richer discretion. Many of the methods of collective deliberation and decision-making we highlighted in the previous chapter and further explore in the next have natural applications to defining legitimate distributions of power that can directly shape the governance of GFMs, the distribution of the economic value they create, and the ways they are

---

[9] See for example Safiya Umoja Noble, *Algorithms of Oppression: How Search Engines Reinforce Racism* (New York: New York University Press, 2018). Cathy O'Neil, *Weapons of Math Destruction: How Big Data Increases Inequality and Threatens Democracy* (New York: Broadway Books, 2016). Ruha Benjamin, *Race After Technology: Abolitionist Tools for the New Jim Crow* (Cambridge, UK: Polity Press, 2019).

[10] Talal Asad, *Anthropology & the Colonial Encounter* (Ithaca, NY: Ithaca Press, 1973).

collectively steered to behave in line with public wills. Grounded in legitimacy such practices can provide and explore through richer interaction modes, these and other digital systems hold significant promise of overcoming the simultaneously cold and arbitrary nature of the world of systems that has been the price of modernity.

## 5-6 Voting

In the best-selling strategy game of all time, *Civilization VI*, players manage a civilization from the birth of the first settlements to the near future, competing and sometimes cooperating with other civilizations in a race to victory through culture, military conquest, diplomatic support, scientific achievement and/or religious influence. In the game's widely adopted and climate change-themed expansion pack "*Gathering Storm*", diplomatic decisions affecting the whole world are decided in a "World Congress". Civilizations accumulate "diplomatic favor" from alliances, infrastructure, and so forth. They can then spend these to influence global policies, such as regulation of fossil fuels, controls on nuclear weapons or immigration rules.

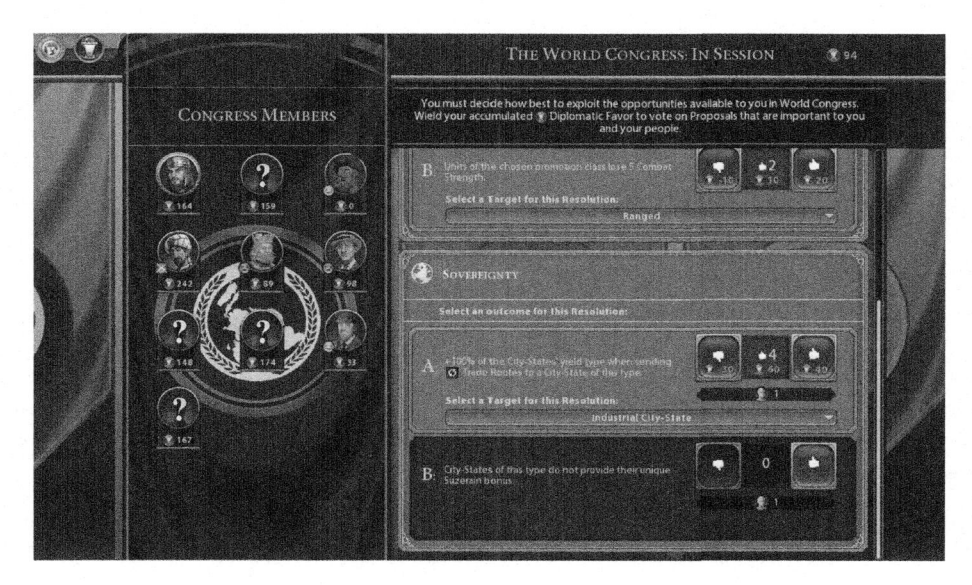

**Figure 5-6-A.** A player chooses how to spend their accumulated Diplomatic Favor in the 'World Congress' of *Civilization VI*. Source: Direct screen capture from application, by fair use.

When voting, countries can choose from a range of options, such as which civilization will be targeted for closer scrutiny of its actions by the world. Every civilization gets a single vote for free, but additional votes cost increased diplomatic favor, at an increasing rate. The first additional vote costs 10 diplomatic favor, the second 20, and so on, as illustrated in Figure A. There are typically several votes on different issues in a single Congress and diplomatic favor can be saved across Congresses as well as used for other purposes such as nominating special issues for consideration. Each civilization must thus gauge how important each issue is to them, then "buy" votes using diplomatic favor just up to the point where the amount they care matches the increasing cost of having more influence on that issue compared to the value of saving their favor.

This game mechanic is a variant of the "Quadratic Voting" procedure one of us invented, which is now widely used outside of games as well, as we will explore below.[1] Because of the logic above, it aggregates not just the direction of individual preferences but also their strength. Thus, when individual action is independent, it can lead to decisions based not just on "the greatest numbers" but "the greatest good for the greatest number".

---

A main theme of this part of the book has been how much broader collaborative technologies and democracy are than the institutions we might usually associate with them. Yet, the formal institutions that most come to mind when we think about "democracy" are systems for holding votes and

---

[1] The Economist, "The Mathematical Method that Could Offer a Fairer Way to Vote", December 18, 2021.

elections. Voting is used throughout not just democratic systems, but governance regimes more broadly: corporate governance, management of cooperative housing, book clubs, games etc. It provides a way for a large and diverse group to, relatively quickly and at relatively low cost, make a definite decision on a point of disagreement. While the communication it allows is far thinner than the technologies we have thus far described, it can often be a much more broadly inclusive process that leads to verdicts of the "common will" that are typically thought of as more legitimate (at least among the usually limited set of those enfranchised) than the outcomes of markets. In this chapter, we will explore the ways voting works and fails to work in the settings it is most often applied today, innovations like Quadratic Voting (QV) that are creating higher-fidelity signals of the "public will", and peer into the horizon of ways researchers are re-imagining how large groups of people can choose their future together.

## Voting today

In the most common form of voting, every member of some community selects one of several mutually exclusive options and the option with the most votes is selected. Some trace this practice to the ability of a group with greater numbers to triumph in certain kinds of violent conflicts (such as phalanx engagements in Ancient Greece), which could be avoided by tallying the strength of positions. Despite its simplicity, this "plurality rule" is not a particularly compelling representation of in the way we use it, for several reasons including:

1. It tends to create a "lesser of two evils" dynamic (known as "Duverger's Law" to political scientists) where people are forced to vote for one of the two leading alternatives

even if they dislike both and some trailing alternative might win broader support.[2]
2. In many contexts, the simple equality assumed in such a tally is not widely legitimate. Different participants in a vote may have differing degrees of legitimate interest in an issue (e.g. representing different populations, having spent longer time in a community, etc.).
3. Even at its best, it represents the direction in which a majority chooses, rather than an overall sense of the "will of the group", which should include how important different issues are to people and how much they know about them. This is often called the "tyranny of the majority".

A range of widely used voting procedures aim to address these challenges in limited ways such as:

- Ranked choice and approval voting: These two recently popular systems partially address issue 1. In ranked choice systems, participants rank several alternatives, and the decision depends on this full list in some way. The simplest examples are "run-off" type systems, where the set of candidates is gradually narrowed and, as this happens, the top choice of each person for the remaining candidates becomes their new vote. In approval voting, voters may choose as many options as they wish to "approve" and the most approved option is selected. Both methods clearly have a ⌗ character both literally in allowing multiple votes and spiritually in allowing both greater consensus and greater diversity of parties by avoiding the Duverger "spoiler effect". However, economics Nobel Laureate Kenneth Arrow famously proved in his "Impossibility Theorem" that no

---

[2] Maurice Duverger, *Les Partis Politiques* (Paris: Points, 1951).

system with such simple inputs can generally achieve a "reasonable" representation of the common will.[3]

- Weighted voting: In contexts where equality of voters is obviously inappropriate, weighted voting schemes are used. Common examples are "one-share-one-vote" in corporate governance, voting based on population size in federal and confederal bodies (e.g. the European Union or United Nations) and voting based on measures of power (e.g. GDP) in contexts where it is thought important to respect power differences. These weights are, however, often the subject of significant dispute and lead to paradoxes of their own, such as the "51% attack" (also known as "tunneling") where someone can buy 51% of a corporation and loot its assets, expropriating the remaining 49%.[4]

- Federal, proportional, and consociational representation: While voting systems are, as we have discussed above, usually formally "monistic", there are important examples of trying to address the tyranny of the majority this can create. In federal, consociational and functional systems, sub-units, such as geographies, religions, ethnic or professional groups, have a status beyond simply their population and usually receive some kind of special or population-disproportionate weight intended to avoid oppression by larger groups.

---

[3] Kenneth J. Arrow, *Social Choice and Individual Values* (New York, John Wiley & Sons, 1951). See also Kenneth O. May, "A Set of Independent Necessary and Sufficient Conditions for Simple Majority Decision" 20, no. 4 (1952): 680-684, Allan Gibbard, "Manipulation of Voting Schemes: A General Result", *Econometrica* 41, no. 4 (1973): 587-601 and Mark A. Sattherthwaite, "Strategy-Proofness and Arrow's Conditions: Existence and Correspondence Theorems for Voting Procedures and Social Welfare Functions", *Journal of Economic Theory* 10, no. 2 (1975): 187-217.

[4] Simon Johnson, Rafael La Porta, Florencio Lopez-de-Silanes and Andrei Shleifer, "Tunneling", *American Economic Review* 90, no. 2 (2000): 22-27.

While these systems thus in various ways incorporate ⬚ elements, their design is typically haphazard and rigid, based on historical lines of potential oppression that may no longer track the relevant social issues or can entrench existing divides by formally recognizing them; they thus have become increasingly unpopular.[5] More flexible are systems of "proportional representation", where representatives in some body are chosen in proportion to the votes they receive, helping achieve greater balance, though often at least partly "kicking the can" of majoritarian tensions down the road to the decisions of the representative body's coalition formation.

Thus, while voting is a canonical democratic technology, it is also one riddled with paradoxes, rigidity and widely recognized unsolved problems. A new generation of approaches has recently tried to improve more dramatically on what is possible.

## Voting tomorrow

While the above problems seem diverse, they boil down to two questions: how to appropriately represent degrees and weights of interests and how to make representation flexible and adaptive. As Nobel Laureate Amartya Sen famously observed, problems with Arrow's Theorem vanish once strength and weight of preference is accounted for, and evidently weighted voting is all about such issues.[6]

---

[5] For a lengthier discussion see E. Glen Weyl, "Why I am a Pluralist" *RadicalxChange Blog*, February 10, 2022 at https://www.radicalxchange.org/media/blog/why-i-am-a-pluralist/.

[6] Amartya Sen, *Collective Choice and Social Welfare*, (Cambridge, Massachusetts: Harvard University Press, 1970).

## 5-6 Voting

Representation of subgroups is challenging as there are strong reasons for doing it, yet many ways of achieving it seem insufficient or overly rigid and prescriptive. These strike at the core of the problem with the extreme simplicity of votes: they carry very limited information about voters' thoughts and preferences.

Two recent developments have offered exciting, though incomplete, approaches to addressing these problems. We highlighted the first at the start of the chapter: QV and other related approaches to incorporating voting weights. QV originates with statistician (and, unfortunately, eugenicist) Lionel Penrose, father of the prominent contemporary astrophysicist Roger Penrose. He noted that, when weighing votes, it is natural, but misleading, to give a party with twice the legitimate stake in a decision twice the votes. The reason is that this will typically give them more than twice as much power. Uncoordinated voters on average cancel one another out and thus the total influence of 10,000 completely independent voters is much smaller than the influence of one person with 10,000 votes.[7]

A physical analogy, prominently studied simultaneously with Penrose by J.C.R. Licklider (our hero in *The Lost Dao* above), may be useful to see why.[8] Consider a noisy room where one is trying to have a conversation. It is often the case that the overall decibels of the noise are far greater than the strength of the voice of a conversation partner. Yet it is often still possible

---

[7] L. S. Penrose, "The Elementary Statistics of Majority Voting", *Journal of the Royal Statistical Society* 109, no. 1 (1946): 53-57.

[8] J. C. R. Licklider, "The Influence of Interaural Phase Relations upon the Masking of Speech by White Noise", *Journal of the Acoustic Society of America* 20, no. 2 (1948): 150-159. Thus, deeply ironically, Lick may be seen as one of the fathers of QV as well.

to hear what they are saying. Part of this is driven by the human capacity for focus, but another factor is that precisely what makes the background "noise" is that each contributor is far weaker than the (closer) voice one is attending to. Given that the sounds of all this noise are largely unrelated, they tend to cancel out on average and allow the one voice that is just a bit stronger to shine far stronger. Visual signal processing can be similar, where a range of scribbles fade into a gray or brown background, allowing a clear message that is only slightly stronger to stand out against it.

When background signals are completely uncorrelated and there are many of them, there is a simple way to mathematically account for this: a series of uncorrelated signals grows as the square root of their number, while a correlated signal grows in linear proportion to its strength. Thus 10,000 uncorrelated votes will weigh as heavily as only 100 correlated ones. This implies that, to award the holder of stake only proportionately greater power, its voting weight should grow as the square root of its stake, a principle often called "degressive proportionality". This in turn suggests a direction for addressing several challenges above by making a geometric (multiplicative) compromise between the intuitions of weighted and simple voting and by allowing expression of preference strength across issues and votes but taking the square root of the "weight" a voter puts on any issues. The former idea is Penrose's "square-root voting" rule, approximately used in several elements of governance in the European Union across member nations. The later is the QV rule we discussed above and used, for another example, frequently in the Colorado State Legislature to prioritize spending.

It is important to note, however, that these clean rules are only optimal when voters are perfectly internally unified and perfectly externally uncorrelated/uncoordinated. ⌬ thinking cautions us against such simplistic models, encouraging us to perceive the social connections across individuals and organizations, though of course accounting for these within a voting system requires identity systems that can record and account for these.

Another compatible approach that has gained ground in recent years is "liquid democracy"(LD). This idea, which traces back to the path-breaking work of Charles Dodgson (a.k.a. Lewis Carroll, author of the children's classic *Alice in Wonderland*), who also first posed the question of weighting of votes for people holding multiple votes that helped inspire QV.[9] LD extends the idea of proportional representation, allowing any voter to delegate their vote(s) to others, who may then re-delegate them, allowing bottom-up, emergent patterns of representation.[10] Such systems are increasingly common, especially in corporate and other for-profit (e.g. DAO) governance, as well as in a limited set of political contexts such as Iceland. However, these systems have an unfortunate tendency to concentrate power often excessively, given that delegation often flows to a small number of hands. This tendency has somewhat soured initial enthusiasm.

## Frontiers of voting

The radical and transformative potential of QV and LD suggest ways that voting systems in the future may be vastly richer than those we are accustomed to. The range of possibilities is nearly

---

[9] Charles L. Dodgson, *The Principles of Parliamentary Representation* (London, Harrison and Sons, 1884).

[10] An early implementation of such a value-propagating system is exemplified by PICSY, pioneered by Ken Suzuki in 2009. While he initially developed it independently from Kojin Karatani, he later joined the New Associationist Movement. Ken Suzuki, *Propagational investment currency system (PICSY): proposing a new currency system using social computing.* PhD diss., Tokyo University, 2009.

endless, but a few promising ones are useful to illustrate this breadth:

- Correlation discounting and eigenvoting: QV and the Penrose rule apply degressive proportionality (using the square-root rule) to the voting weights of respectively individuals and/or social groups (like nations). A natural extension would be to allow for a wider diversity of sources of correlation/coordination within and across individuals, as would be true in a general statistical model. In this case, an optimal rule would likely involve partial "correlation discounting" based on the degree of social connection and, perhaps, the identification of underlying "principal" social factors that drive coordination and correlation, as is common in statistical modeling.[11] These underlying independent factors, called "eigenvalues", could then be viewed as the "real" independent voters, to whom degressive proportionality could be applied, a process not dissimilar to how PageRank works. This could create a dynamic, adaptive, optimized version of consociationalism that avoids its rigidity and entrenchment of existing divides.

- Adaptive representation: Another approach to similar adaptive representation would be a single-member district or federal system, but with boundaries not based (exclusively) on geography but instead current social divides, such as geographic type (urban v. rural), race, or education. Clearly both this and the previous idea rely

---

[11] Ohlhaver, Weyl and Buterin, op. cit. Joel Miller, E. Glen Weyl and Leon Erichsen, "Beyond Collusion Resistance: Leveraging Social Information for Plural Funding and Voting" (2023) at https://papers.ssrn.com/sol3/papers.cfm?abstract_id=4311507.

heavily on a 🔲 identity system to allow these features to be inputs into the voting process.

- Predictive voting: Robin Hanson has long advocated combining prediction markets (where people bet on future outcomes) with voting. While the "Futarchy" proposal he has advanced focuses on a cleaner separation between these two elements, in the governance of this book described above we use such a mixture, with participants being able to simultaneously vote and predict the outcome of a decision, being rewarded for a correct decision.[12] Such systems may be particularly useful when there is a large range of proposals or options: predictions can help bring attention to proposals deserving attention that voting can then decide on.
- Quadratic liquid democracy: As noted above, a natural way to avoid the power concentrations that liquid democracy can give rise to is the use of degressive proportionality. RadicalxChange, a non-profit advancing 🔲, has implemented a related system for its internal decision-making.
- Assisted real-time voting: Another commonly discussed idea is that voting could be made far more frequent and granular if digital assistants could learn to model voters' perspectives and preferences and vote on their behalf and subject to their review/auditing.[13]

---

[12] Robin Hanson, "Shall we Vote on Values but Bet on Beliefs?", *Journal of Political Philosophy* 20, no. 2: 151-178.

[13] Nils Gilman and Ben Cerveny, "Tomorrow's Democracy is Open Source", *Noema* September 12, 2023 at https://www.noemamag.com/tomorrows-democracy-is-open-source/.

Perhaps the most exciting possibilities are now these could combine infinite diversity, infinitely combining to support the infinite combinations that they help infinite diversity form.

## Limits of voting

One natural concern, however, about even these highly flexible and adaptive approaches to reach a sense of compromise is that the compromise itself throws the baby of diversity out with the bathwater of conflict. Yet one of the most interesting properties of systems like eigenvoting or sophisticated forms of liquid democracy is the new kinds of coalitions and representations they might help form. If one-person-one-vote rules originated from the attempt to avoid conflict by giving the side with greater support a non-violent way to take power, these systems help diffuse conflict based on a more sophisticated theory: that it arises from the consistent reinforcement of existing social divisions by allowing the same groups to consistently form majorities and minorities. By discounting support from previously affiliated groups, they avoid reinforcing existing conflicts, while creating new ones that cut across these lines, hopefully thereby generating nearly as much diversity as they compromise over, but in directions that avoid entrenching persistent divides.

Yet despite these strengths, even in its richest form, voting expresses and determines preferences about decisions already posed by other social processes. Some combination of the methods above can completely transform how we understand voting, leaving today's approaches as far behind as the computer left the abacus. Yet it would fundamentally undermine the richness of our humanity to allow this potential to fool us into believing they can substitute for the need for the richer communication and codesign we have described in previous chapters. Only in the context of the creative collaborations, deliberations, imaginations, and administrative

## 5-6 ⌗ Voting

systems we have sketched can collective decisions be meaningful.

Nor is it likely that, anytime soon, voting systems will stretch greatly beyond the national boundaries that currently contain them. The demands of ⌗ identity systems supporting some of the above suggest that while voting in new transnational configurations is imaginable, systems of voting are unlikely any time soon to truly reach global legitimacy. To truly reach that scope of diversity, we must turn to the re-imagining of the thinnest of all the substrates for collaboration: market economies.

## 5-7 Social Markets

As we have noted above, open-source software (OSS) is one of the most dynamic 數位 ecosystems in the world. Yet, because software is made freely available, it has long struggled for reliable sources of funding. At the same time, many public and charitable funders see value in the ecosystem but find it hard to navigate what projects to support given the heterogeneity of the ecosystem compared, say, to traditional academic research.

Recent attempts to overcome this challenge have focused on matching funds and community donations, where a sponsor supports a class of projects, but this pool of funds is directed by the small donations of participants in the projects. Traditionally such systems (such as GitHub Sponsors) could be manipulated by wealthy participants (such as corporations), whose donations could command most matching funds.

To overcome this, a number of new matching platforms, such as GitCoin Grants, connect sponsors (small donors and grants) using a "plural funding" formula that accounts not just for the total funding received, but also the diversity of its source across individual contributors and connected social groups. These platforms have become important sources of funding for OSS, channeling in total more than a hundred million dollars in funding. This has been especially important to Web3 related projects, in Taiwan, and in supporting this book. They are also increasingly being applied to domains (e.g. environment, local business development) outside OSS.

5-7 Social Markets

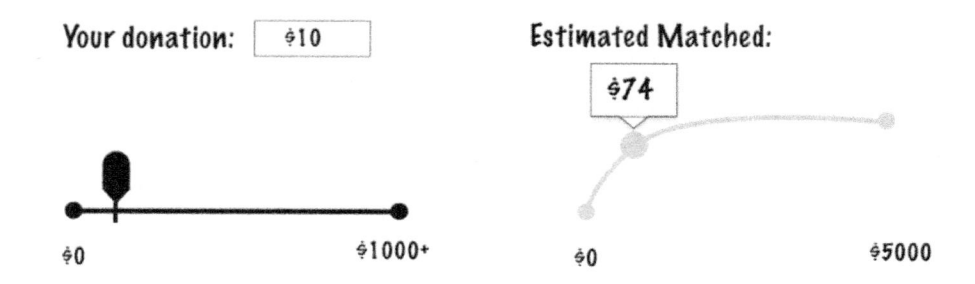

**Your donation:** $10

$0 — $1000+

**Estimated Matched:** $74

$0 — $5000

**Figure 5-7-A.** Contributions on Gitcoin are matched by a matching pool, powered by Quadratic Funding. Quadratic Funding is a 🔲 funding formula because it elevates many small contributions across social distance. Source: GitCoin Team contribution.

Explorer Home > Web3 Community and Education > Project Details

數位

PLURALITY

**Plurality.net**

0x2a6...2DE5f
https://Plurality.net
pluralitybook

Created on: November 10th, 2023
PluralityBook
jason.antenmann

$332.84
funding received in current round

87
contributors

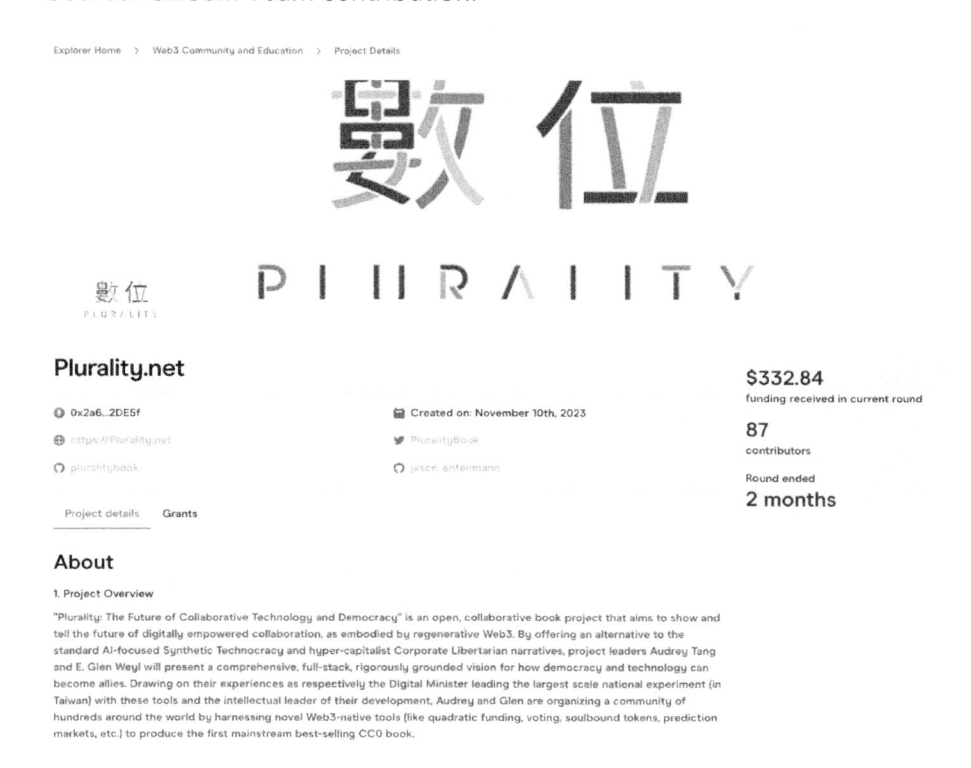

Round ended
2 months

Project details   Grants

**About**

1. Project Overview

"Plurality: The Future of Collaborative Technology and Democracy" is an open, collaborative book project that aims to show and tell the future of digitally empowered collaboration, as embodied by regenerative Web3. By offering an alternative to the standard AI-focused Synthetic Technocracy and hyper-capitalist Corporate Libertarian narratives, project leaders Audrey Tang and E. Glen Weyl will present a comprehensive, full-stack, rigorously grounded vision for how democracy and technology can become allies. Drawing on their experiences as respectively the Digital Minister leading the largest scale national experiment (in Taiwan) with these tools and the intellectual leader of their development, Audrey and Glen are organizing a community of hundreds around the world by harnessing novel Web3-native tools (like quadratic funding, voting, soulbound tokens, prediction markets, etc.) to produce the first mainstream best-selling CC0 book.

**Figure 5-7-B.** The project page for the 🔲 book on Gitcoin. As of February 2, 2024, the 🔲 book had received $332.84 in funding from 87 contributors. Source: Direct screen capture from application, by fair use.

391

No institutions connect more people across broader social diversity in collaborative exchange than those of global capitalism. The limited remit and strength of international governance create severe bounds on the ability to provide transnational public goods through voting and deliberation, but the almighty dollar (and yuan) is respected in most corners of the planet. Capital flows and the technology it is invested in shape lives around the world. International trade and other commercial agreements are among the strongest and nearly universally respected agreements. Private ownership has become a far more consistent pattern across the planet than any other feature of the "rule of law".[1] Since the fall of the Soviet Union, while national borders have hardly budged and few new nations have been born, companies like Amazon, Google, and Meta have arguably grown to a position of prominence around the planet exceeding all but a handful of nation-states.

At the same time, for all the elaborate financial and corporate structures built on top of them, markets are perhaps the most simplistic structure conceivable as a pattern for human cooperation. While they can be applied more broadly, as we will see, the argument for their desirability rests on a vision of bilateral transactions between a buyer-seller pair, each of which is representative of a sea of similarly situated and thus equally powerless buyers and sellers, all engaging in a transaction whose effects are bounded by a predetermined set of private property rights that avoid any "externalities" on non-transacting parties. Any notion of emergent, surprising, group level effects, of supermodularity and shared goods, of heterogeneity, or of

---

[1] Pistor, op. cit.

diversity of information are bracketed as "imperfections" or "frictions" that impede the natural, ideal functioning of markets.

This debate has been at the core of the conflict over capitalism, long before its ascendancy, as documented by social scientist Albert Hirschman.[2] On the one hand, markets have been seen to be almost uniquely universally "civilizing", alleviating the potential for conflict across social groups, and "dynamic", allowing entrepreneurship to create new forms of large scale social organization that foster and support (social) innovation.[3] On the other hand, markets are poor at supporting the flourishing of other forms of scaled social interaction. They corrode many of the other technologies of collaboration we describe. While allowing the creation of some new forms, they tend to turn these into exploitative, socially irresponsible, and often reckless monopolies. In this chapter we will explore this paradox and how radical new forms of markets, like those we described above, can maintain, and extend this inclusive and dynamic character while fostering a far more diverse range of rich human collaboration.

## Capitalism today

Capitalism is typically understood as a system based on private property in the means of production, voluntary market-based exchange, and free and vigorous operation of the profit motive from this starting point. Global capitalism today (sometimes

---

[2] Albert Hirschman, *The Passions and the Interests*, (Princeton: Princeton University Press, 1997).

[3] Joseph Schumpeter, *Capitalism, Socialism and Democracy* (New York: Harper & Brothers: 1942). Quinn Slobodian, *Globalists: The End of Empire and the Birth of Neoliberalism* (Cambridge, MA: Harvard University Press, 2018).

called "neoliberalism") features several interlocking sectors and features, including:

1. Free trade: Extensive free trade agreements, overseen by organizations such as the World Trade Organization, ensure that a wide range of goods can flow mostly unimpeded across jurisdictions covering most of the planet.
2. Private property: Most real and intellectual assets are held as private property, conferring joined rights of use, disposal, and profit. These rights are protected by international territorial and intellectual property treaties.
3. Corporations: Most large-scale collaborations using extra-market governance are undertaken either by nation-states or by transnational corporations that are operated for profit, owned by shareholders, and governed by the principle of one-share-one-vote.
4. Labor markets: Labor is based on the idea of "self-ownership" and the wage system, with some important qualifications. People are generally not free to move across jurisdictional boundaries to work.
5. Financial markets: Shares in corporations, loans and other financial instruments are traded on sophisticated financial markets that allocate capital to projects and physical investments based on projections of the future.
6. Ventures and start-ups: New corporations and thus most new forms of large-scale international cooperation come into existence through a system of "venture capital", where "start-ups" sell shares in their potential future earnings or resale value to public markets in exchange for the funding they need to begin a new business.

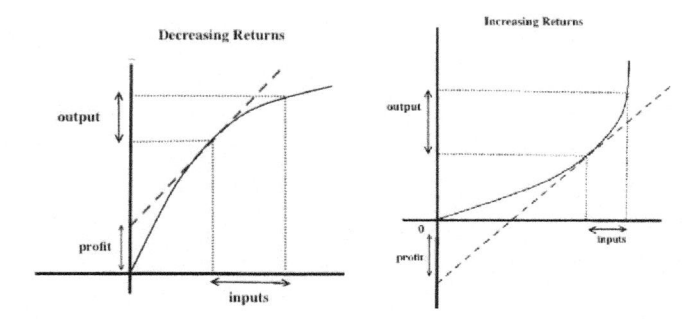

**Figure 5-7-C.** Payment of marginal returns requires paying workers and other factor providers an amount derived from tracing the tangent to graph of output as a function of inputs back to 0 input. The gap to the origin indicates profits, which are positive under decreasing returns, but negative (thus loses) under increasing returns.

Many textbooks have been written, including some by some of our close friends, on this structure.[4] It is hard to doubt that it is one of the most powerful modes of cooperation humans have ever devised and has been central to the unprecedented progress in material conditions around the world in the last two centuries. Furthermore, the most famous theoretical results in economics are the "fundamental welfare theorems", which assert that under certain conditions markets lead selfish individuals "by an invisible hand" to serve the common good.[5] Yet the conditions and scope of this result are quite circumscribe, which is why capitalism has so many familiar problems.

1. Increasing returns and public goods: Perhaps the most restrictive condition, highlighted by the founding fathers of the "marginal revolution" that ushered in modern

---

[4] Daron Acemoglu, David Laibson and John List, *Economics* (Upper Saddle River, NJ: Pearson, 2021).

[5] Adam Smith, *An Inquiry into the Nature and Causes of the Wealth of Nations* (London: W. Strahan and T. Cadell, 1776).

economics, is "decreasing returns", the opposite of the supermodularity we used to define collaboration. This requires that production have "decreasing marginal returns" or more generally and less formally, that "the whole is less than the sum of its parts". Only then can profitable production be consistent with the principle of, for example, paying workers their marginal contributions to production; when there are increasing returns, paying everyone their marginal product yields a loss, as shown in Figure C. Public goods that benefit a large number of people at little additional cost and are hard to stop people from using are an extreme case and economists have long argued that markets dramatically under-supply these. But even less extreme cases of increasing returns/supermodularity are severely under-provided by capitalism. Nobel Prizes, among others, to Paul Romer and Paul Krugman for showing how fundamental these goods are to growth and development.[6] In short, perhaps the greatest paradox of global capitalism is that it is at once the largest scale example of collaboration and yet has trouble precisely supporting the forms of technological collaboration that it heralds.

2. Market power: In some cases where exclusion from shared goods can be imposed by barriers or violence, funding of such collaboration can be partially alleviated by charging for access. But this tends to create monopolistic control that concentrates power and reduces the value created by scaling collaboration, undermining the very collaboration it aims to support.

---

[6] Paul Krugman, "Scale Economies, Product Differentiation and the Pattern of Trade", *American Economic Review* 70, no. 5 (1980): 950-959. Paul Romer, "Increasing Returns and Long-Term Growth", *Journal of Political Economy* 94, no. 5 (1986):1002-1037.

3. Externalities: At the core of John Dewey's 1927 classic *The Public and its Problems*, is recognizing the genius of innovation to create new forms of interdependence, both for good and ill.[7] The motors of the nineteenth century transformed human life, yet also turned out to transfigure the environment in unanticipated ways. Radio, flight, chemicals...all redesigned how we can cooperate, but also created risks and harms that previous systems of "property rights" and rules generally did not account for. The victims (or in some cases beneficiaries) of these "externalities" are, by construction, not directly party to market transactions. Thus, precisely to the extent that new means of collaboration developed in markets are revolutionary, markets and the corporations they spawn will not directly involve those affected by their innovations, preventing either their benefits from being fully tapped or their risks from being mitigated.
4. Distribution: Theoretically, markets are simply indifferent to distribution and "endowments" can be rearranged to achieve desired distributive goals. But achieving this ideal redistribution faces enormous practical hurdles and thus markets tend to often yield shockingly inegalitarian outcomes, sometimes for reasons fairly divorced from their alleged "efficiency" benefits. In addition to the direct concerns these create, they also often help undermine the greater equality often assumed or harnessed in other collaborative forms described in previous chapters.

Recognition of and response to these challenges are arguably the leading currents of the politics of the last hundred and fifty

---

[7] John Dewey, *The Public and its Problems*, op. cit.

years in much of the world, so we must review them only very superficially.

1. Antitrust and utility regulation: A primary focus of the populist movement of the late nineteenth century and early twentieth in the US was the restraint of the power of corporate monopolies using a mixture of structural (e.g. corporate break-ups or prevention of mergers) or behavioral (e.g. price or non-discrimination regulation) interventions.[8] While these help address some of the abuses of monopoly, they often do so at the cost of reducing the advantages of collaboration (scale) and/or by reintroducing the rigidities of nation-state based governance that it is the great advantage of entrepreneurship to help transcend.

2. Labor unions and cooperatives: An alternative approach to addressing market power has been the creation of corporate governance modes that try to give voice to those over whom a company holds power. Powerful unions are created to "countervail" the labor market power of firms and enable customer or worker representation in company governance through cooperative or "codetermination" structures.[9] While these have been some of the most vibrant and effective correctives to corporate power, they have been limited primarily to a traditional model of full-time employment that has struggled to keep pace with the dynamism and internationalism of labor markets and the diversity of collaboration in the digital age.

---

[8] Matt Stoller, *Goliath: The 100-Year War Between Monopoly Power and Democracy* (New York: Simon & Schuster, 2020).

[9] John Kenneth Galbraith, *American Capitalism: The Concept of Countervailing Power* (New York: Houghton Mifflin, 1952).

3. Eminent domain/compulsory purchase and land/wealth taxes: To address smaller-scale market power (e.g. over land and specific pieces of wealth), many jurisdictions have rights of "eminent domain" or "compulsory purchase" allowing the forced repurchase of private property with the support of public authorities, usually with compensation and subject to judicial review. Some jurisdictions also charge taxes on land, wealth, or inheritance to both reduce inequality and help increase the circulation of assets away from those who might monopolize them. While crucial to social equity and development, these approaches rely heavily on often fragile administrative processes to reach equitable valuations.
4. Industrial, infrastructure, and research policy: To overcome the tendency of markets to underfund public goods and more generally supermodular collaboration, many governments provide funding for infrastructure (e.g. transportation, communications, electrification), research and development of new technologies and the development to scale of new (for the country) industries. While critical to technical, industrial, and social progress, these investments struggle to span national borders in the way capitalism does and are often administered by bureaucracies with far less information that the participants in the fields they support have.
5. Open source, charity, and the third sector: A more flexible approach to similar goals is the "third" or "social" sector efforts including charity and volunteer effort (like the OSS community) that build scalable collaboration on a voluntary, non-profit basis. While they are among the most dynamic forms of scaled collaboration today, these efforts often struggle to scale and sustain themselves given the lack of financial

support from the most powerful market and government institutions.
6. Zoning and regulation: The risk of markets failing to account for external harms and benefits are generally addressed by government-imposed restrictions on market activity, usually called "regulation" at broader levels and "zoning restrictions" on more local levels. Occasionally, especially in environmental matters, economists' preferred solutions of "Pigouvian" taxes or tradeable permits are used. While these restrictions are the central and thus indispensable way to address externalities, they are beset by all the limits of rigid, nation-state- (or corresponding local justification) based decision-making we discussed above, and given their economic stakes are often captured/controlled by interest groups imperfectly aligned to the interests of even the supposedly relevant public.[10]
7. Redistribution: Most developed capitalist nations have extensive systems of taxation of income and commerce that fund, among other things, social insurance and public welfare schemes that ensure the availability of a range of services and fiscal support as a check against extreme inequality. In contrast to the promise of land and wealth taxes, however, these primary income sources generally partly impede the functioning of markets, struggle to extract many of the most runaway fortunes and only imperfectly correct the structural ways inequality impede other forms of collaboration.

The limitations of these solutions are so widely understood that they led to a significant backlash in many countries beginning in the 1970s, the so-called "neoliberal reaction".

---

[10] Edward L. Glaeser and Joseph Gyourko, "The Impact of Zoning on Housing Affordability" (2002) at https://www.nber.org/papers/w8835.

## 5-7 Social Markets

Yet the limits of markets persist and there has been a resurgence in the last decade of both solutions, but also of creative attempts to transcend them and avoid many of the trade-offs they create.

### Social markets tomorrow

As we highlighted in the *Connected Society* chapter above, the desire to combine and even enhance the dynamism of markets while at the same time addressing their limits was a primary motivation for ⌗, especially the thought of Henry George and his followers, including economics Nobel Laureate William Vickrey, to whom the previous book written by one of the authors of this one was dedicated.[11] Vickrey pioneered the economics subfield of "mechanism design", which explores these possibilities and has led to many of the creative possibilities that have been deployed in the past decades.

- Partial common ownership: To overcome the challenges of administering land taxes, a variety of historical thinkers, including Founder of the Chinese Republic Sun Yat-Sen (who we discussed extensively in our *A View from Yushan* chapter) and economist Arnold Harberger, have proposed having owners self-assess the value of their property under penalty of having to sell at this self-assessed value.[12] This has the simultaneous effect of forcing truthful valuations for

---

[11] Eric A. Posner and E. Glen Weyl, *Radical Markets: Uprooting Capitalism and Democracy for a Just Society* (Princeton, NJ: Princeton University Press, 2018).

[12] Sun, op. cit. Arnold C. Harberger, "Issues of Tax Reform for Latin America" in Joint Tax Program of the Organization of American States eds., *Fiscal Policy for Economic Growth in Latin America* (Baltimore, MD: Johns Hopkins Press, 1965).

taxation and of forcing turnover of underutilized or monopolized assets to broader publics. It is particularly easy to enforce in digital asset registries, such as blockchains, and thus has gained popularity in recent years, especially for non-fungible token (NFT) art works, as well having been used for many years for land in Taiwan.[13]

- Quadratic and 數位 funding: As described at the start of this chapter, a natural way to fund public/supermodular goods without relying excessively on the limited knowledge of administrators is for such an administrator, philanthropist, or public authority to match contributions by distributed individuals. Mechanism design theory, similar to the logic supporting quadratic voting in the previous chapter, can be used to show that under similar assumptions of atomized behavior, matching funds should be proportioned to the square of the sum of square roots of individual contributions, giving greater weight to a large number of small contributors than to a few large ones.[14] Recently designs have stretched beyond traditional individualistic designs to account for 數位 group interests and affiliations.[15]

- Stakeholder corporation: While partial common ownership and quadratic funding may help ensure the turnover of organization and asset control, they do not

---

[13] Emerson M. S. Niou and Guofu Tan, "An Analysis of Dr. Sun Yat-Sen's Self-Assessment Scheme for Land Taxation", *Public Choice* 78, no. 1: 103-114. Yun-chien Chang, op. cit.

[14] Vitalik Buterin, Zoë Hitzig and E. Glen Weyl, "A Flexible Design for Funding Public Goods", *Management Science* 65, no. 11 (2019): 4951-5448.

[15] Ohlhaver et al., op. cit. and Miler et al., op. cit.

directly ensure that organizations serve rather than exercising illegitimate power over their "stakeholders", such as customers and workers. Drawing on the traditions we described above, there a variety of renewed movements in recent years to create a "stakeholder" corporation, including Environmental, Social and Governance principles, the platform cooperativism, the distributed autonomous organizations (DAOs), "stakeholder remedies" in antitrust (viz. using antitrust violations to mandate abused stakeholders have a voice), data unions and the organization of many of the most important large foundation model companies (e.g. OpenAI and Anthropic) as partial non-profits or long-term benefit corporations.[16]

- Participatory design and prediction markets: Digital platforms and mechanisms are also increasingly used to allow more dynamic resource allocation both within corporations and in connections between corporations and their customers.[17] Examples include ways for customers to contribute and be rewarded for new product designs, such as in entertainment platforms like Roblox or Lego Ideas, and prediction markets where

---

[16] Colin Mayer, *Prosperity: Better Business Makes the Greater Good* (Oxford, UK: Oxford University Press, 2019). Zoë Hitzig, Michelle Meagher, André Veig and E. Glen Weyl, "Economic Democracy and Market Power", *CPI Antitrust Chronicle* April 2020. Michelle Meagher, *Competition is Killing us: How Big Business is Harming our Society and Planet - and What to Do About It* (New York: Penguin Business, 2020).

[17] See Erich Joachimsthaler, *The Interaction Field: The Revolutionary New Way to Create Shared Value for Businesses, Customers, and Society*, PublicAffairs, 2019. See also Gary Hamel, and Michele Zanini, *Humanocracy: Creating Organizations as Amazing as the People inside Them*, (Boston, Massachusetts: Harvard Business Review Press, 2020).

- Market design: The field of market design, for which several Nobel Prizes have recently been awarded, applies mechanism design to create market institutions that mitigate problems of market power or externalities created by ignoring the social implications of transactions. Examples include markets for tradable carbon permits, the auction design examples we discussed in the *Property and Contract* chapter above and a number of markets using community currencies or other devices to facilitate market-like institutions in communities (e.g. education, public housing or organ donation) where using external currency can severely undermine core values.[18]
- Economies of esteem: Related to these local currency markets are online systems where various quantitative markers of social esteem/capital (e.g. badges, followers, leaderboards, links) partly or fully replace transferable money as the "currency" of accomplishment.[19] These can often, in turn, partly interoperate with broader markets through various monetization channels such as advertising, sponsorship and crowdfunding.

While this blossoming of alternatives to simplistic markets is a powerful proof of concept for moving beyond the traditional

---

[18] Atila Abdulkadiroğlu, Parag A. Pathak and Alvin E. Roth, "The New York City High School Match", *American Economic Review* 95, no. 2 (2005): 365-367. Nicole Immorlica, Brendan Lucier, Glen Weyl and Joshua Mollner, "Approximate Efficiency in Matching Markets" *International Conference on Web and Internet Economics* (2017): 252-265. Roth et al., op. cit.

[19] Nicole Immorlica, Greg Stoddard and Vasilis Syrgkanis, "Social Status and Badge Design", *WWW '15: Proceedings of the 24th International Conference on World Wide Web* (2015: 473-483.

limits of the market. But they represent the beginning, not the end, of the possibilities for the technologically enabled social markets of the future.

## Frontiers of social markets

Building off these experiments, we are just able to glimpse what a comprehensively transformed market system might look like. Some of the most promising elements include:

1. Circular investment: One of the most remarkable results of economic theory is named after Henry George. Proved originally by Vickrey but first published by Richard Arnott and Nobel Laureate Joseph Stiglitz, the Henry George Theorem states, roughly, that the taxes that can be raised from correctly designed common ownership taxes can fund all the subsidies required to fund supermodular investments.[20] While the result is much more general, a simple illustration is the way that building better local public schools tend to raise land values: if this value can be raised by a land tax, in principle any education investment worth funding can be supported. More generally, the result suggests a near limitless potential, like that realized in a superconducting circuit, for innovation in taxation/common property and allocation of funds to super-modular activity, to generate progress.

2. ⬚ property: How can these funds be raised? While partial common property schemes are an interesting start, they need to be paired with tools that can recognize and protect common interests in the way and

---

[20] William Vickrey, "The City as a Firm" in Martin S. Feldstein and Robert P. Inman, eds., *The Economics of Public Services*: 334-343. Richard Arnott, and Joseph Stiglitz, "Aggregate Land Rents, Expenditure on Public Goods, and Optimal City Size," *The Quarterly Journal of Economics* 93, no. 4 (November 1979): 471. https://doi.org/10.2307/1884466.

stability with which land and other assets are used. The voting systems we described in the previous chapter are a natural answer here and there may be great potential in ▣ property systems that can bring these together, returning much of the value of a range of wealth to intersecting publics ("fructus") while also giving important access ("usus") and disposal ("abusus") rights to these communities.

3. ▣ funding across boundaries: ▣ funding can also extend dramatically beyond its current bounds, to allocate the resources thus raised. Two of the most interesting directions are cross-jurisdictional and inter-temporal. Current international trade treaties focus primarily on breaking down trade barriers, including the subsidies that help support supermodular production as we discussed above. A future form of international economic cooperation could assemble matching funds for cross-jurisdictional economic ventures, harnessing a mechanism like ▣ funding. One key advantage of capitalism is that it is one of the few scaled systems with a significant intertemporal planning component, where companies raise funds for profits that appear distant. One can imagine, however, even more ambitious intertemporal economic systems with matching funds, for example, for institutions that promote cooperation across generations or with those who are not even born yet. This might overcome concerns about the lack of long-term planning, as well as the conservation of valued past institutions, in many quarters, creating an organic version of a "ministry for the future".[21]

---

[21] Robinson, op. cit.

4. Emergent publics: Possibilities are equally promising for how the organizations thus supported can be made truly accountable to their stakeholders. Stakeholding of various kinds (as workers, customers, suppliers, targets of negative externalities like pollution dumping or misinformation, etc.) could be tracked by harnessing the type of ⌗ identity systems we discussed above. These could then be linked to participation using voting and deliberation systems like those we highlighted earlier in ways that are much less demanding on individuals' time and attention and able to reach broadly legitimate decisions than existing collective governance more quickly.[22] These in turn can make truly democratic and ⌗ governance of emergent publics a realistic alternative to traditional corporate governance. One could then imagine a future where new democratic entities governing emerging technologies in ways that are close to as legitimate as governments emerge as frequently as start-ups, creating a web of dynamic and legitimate governance.

5. ⌗ management: Internally, it is also increasingly possible to see past the hierarchical structure that typically dominates corporate control. The Plural Management Protocol we used to create this book tracks the types and extent of contributions from diverse participants and harnesses mechanisms like we have described above to allow them to prioritize work (which then determines the recognition of those who address those issues) and determine which work should be incorporated into a project though a basis of exerting

---

[22] An interesting first experiment in this direction is being undertaken by the Web3 protocol *Optimism*, which uses a mixture of one-share-one-vote and more democratic methods in different "houses" to govern its protocol.

authority and predicting what others will decide.[23] This allows for some of the important components of hierarchy (evaluation by trusted authorities, migration of this authority based on performance according to those authorities) without any direct hierarchical reporting structure, allowing networks to potentially supplant strict hierarchies.

6. Polypolitan migration policy: It is also increasingly possible to imagine breaking down the stringency of international labor markets through related mechanisms. As philosopher Danielle Allen has proposed, migration could be conditioned upon endorsement or support from one or more civil society groups in the receiving country, extending and combining existing practices in countries like Canada and Taiwan that respectively allow private community-based sponsorship and allow a diversity of qualifying pathways for long-term work permits.[24] These could diffuse the stringent control of labor mobility by nation states while maintaining accountability to avoid harms or challenges with social integration.

While these only begin to scratch the surface of possibilities, they hopefully illustrate how completely markets could be reconceived harnessing 數位 principles. While the debates over markets and the state often falls into predictable patterns, the possibilities for moving radically beyond this simplistic binary are just as broad as for any other area of 數位.

---

[23] South et al., op. cit.

[24] Danielle Allen, "Polypolitanism: An Approach to Immigration Policy to Support a Just Political Economy" in Danielle Allen, Yochai Benkler, Leah Downey, Rebecca Henderson & Josh Simons, etc., *A Political Economy of Justice* (Chicago, IL: University of Chicago Press, 2022): ch. 14.

## Limits of social markets

Yet the potential of markets should not be mistaken for being a miracle cure or the primary pattern for the future of ⊙. Even in these greatly enriched forms, markets remain a thin shell that at best can comfortably fit and provide material support and interface for a diversity of richer human relationships, and at worst can undermine them. The best we can therefore hope for is to create market forms flexible enough that they fade into the background of the flowering of emergent social forms they support.

What we must guard against most rigorously is the tendency of markets to concentrate power in private organizations or limited cultural groups in ways that homogenize and erode diversity. Achieving this requires institutions that deliberately encourage new diversity, while eroding existing concentrations of power, like those we have highlighted. It also requires, as we have suggested, constantly bringing other forms of collaboration across diversity[25] to intersect with markets, whether voting, deliberation, or creative collaboration, while creating market systems (like ⊙ money) that can deliberately insulate these from broader market forces.

Yet despite all their manifest dangers and limitations, those pursuing ⊙ should not wish markets away. Something must

---

[25] Pooling across diversity is a very general principle. Although size matters, bigger is not always better, and the strength of the connections formed can matter more. For example, families, teams, or troops – small networks connected by high-value interactions – can outperform much larger ones in the production of ⊙ goods. If we consider the record of Paleolithic art, banding together to perform key social functions is extremely ancient, so collaborative pooling at a range of scales, albeit by non-state and non-market actors, seems an exception to the rule that 'public goods' are always under-supplied.

coordinate at least coexistence if not collaboration across the broadest social distances and many other ways to achieve this, even ones as thin as voting, carry much greater risks of homogenization precisely because they involve deeper ties. Socially aware global markets offer much greater prospect for than a global government. Markets must evolve and thrive, along with so many other modes of collaboration, to secure a future.

# Part 6: Impact

## 6-0 From ⬚ to Reality

⬚ has the tangible potential, in the next decade, to transform almost every sector of society. Examples we study are:

1. The workplace, where we believe it could raise economic output by 10% and increase the growth rate by a percentage point.
2. Health, where we believe can extend human life by two decades.
3. Media, where it can heal the divides opened by social media, provide sustainable funding, expand participation, and dramatically increase press freedom.
4. Environment, where it is core to addressing most of the serious environmental problems we face, perhaps even more so than traditional "green" technologies.

While we do not detail them here, we also expect fundamental effects in a wide range of other areas including:

- Energy, where it can help underpin a fundamental transition from the "hunter-gatherer" model of fossil fuels to the "agricultural" model of directly harnessing solar energy.
- Learning, where it can upend the linear structure of current schooling to allow far more diverse and flexible, lifelong learning paths.

---

The previous parts of this book have sketched lofty visions of transforming a broad range of social systems. Yet however imaginative such futurism is, it can quickly feel impractical, empty, and false if disconnected from the presently felt needs of real people today and pathways to address these needs while bringing systemic change. Furthermore, much of the rhetoric so far has focused on broad social systems like "democracy" that, while inspiring, can often feel distant from the lived experience or scope of agency of most people.

In this part of the book, we therefore try to bring the potential impact of 📱 down to the concrete challenges facing citizens, workers and leaders across a range of social activities and sectors. Before turning to specific such sectors, in this chapter we aim to sketch general contours of a 📱 "theory of change", highlighting how these sectors are natural starting points and showing how and why experiments in these areas can prove both of direct value and capable of spreading to systemic, global empowerment of 📱.

## The graph structure of social revolutions

Radical social and technological change holds an irresistible allure to human imagination, yet so often ends in tragedy, as the Beatles lamented in their social ballad "*Revolution*". Political scientists Steven Levitsky and Lucan Way found in a recent analysis that not a single violent revolution in the twentieth century led to lasting democratic government.[1] Yet we can all think of many dramatic changes for the better in human history, from the dramatic advances in information and communications technologies of the twentieth century to the establishment of a diversity of free and democratic governments around the world over the last three hundred years.

---

[1] Steven Levitsky, and Lucan Way, *Revolution and Dictatorship*, (Princeton: Princeton University Press, 2022).

6-0 From ⌗ to Reality

What allows for peaceful and beneficial, yet dramatic, progress? In her classic treatise on the topic, social philosopher Hannah Arendt contrasts the American and French Revolutions.[2] The American Revolution, she argues, grew out of local democratic experiments inspired by migrants exploring ancient ideals (both from their own past and, as we have recently learned, that of their new neighbors) to build a life together in a new and often hazardous setting.[3] As they traded ideas and built on related concepts circulating at the time, they came to a broad conclusion that they had discovered something more general about governance that contrasted to how it was practiced in Britain. This gave what Arendt calls "authority" (like what in our *Association and ⌗ Publics* chapter we call "legitimacy") to their expectations of democratic republican government. Their War of Independence against Britain allowed this authoritative structure to be empowered in a manner that, for all its inconsistencies, hypocrisies, and failures, has been one of the more enduring and progressive examples of social reform.

The French Revolution, on the other hand, was born of widespread popular dissatisfaction with material conditions, which they sought to redress immediately by seizing power, long before they had gained authority for, or even detailed, potential alternative forms of governance. While this led to dramatic social upheavals, many of these were quickly reversed and/or were accompanied by significant violence. In this sense, the French Revolution, while polarizing and widely discussed, failed in many of its core aspirations. By placing immediate material demands and the power to achieve them ahead of the process of building authority, the French Revolution burdened

---

[2] Hannah Arendt, *On Revolution*, (New York: Penguin, 1963).

[3] David Graeber, and David Wengrow, op. cit.

the delicate process of building social legitimacy for a new system with more weight than it could bear. The French revolution demanded, and got, bread; the American demanded, and got, freedom.

While Arendt's example is drawn from the political sphere, it resonates with literature on innovation in a wide range of fields from evolutionary biology to linguistics. While the precise results differ, this work all indicates that dramatic innovation thrives in environments where a diversity of "groups" (e.g. linguistic, economic, or biological) that are internally tightly connected and externally loosely connected interact.[4] This allows innovation to gain the necessary scale and show its resilience, and then to spread. More connected structures or more centralized ones either stifle innovation or make it dangerous, as changes are only occasionally net benefits. More disconnected structures do not allow innovation to spread.

While intuitive, these observations are a significant contrast to the model of experimentation and innovation increasingly discussed in both the science and social science literature on "randomized controlled trials" and the technology business literature on "blitzscaling", each of which we will consider in turn. Randomized controlled trials, derived primarily from individual, non-transmissible medical and cognitive psychology applications, focuses on the randomized testing of treatments across individuals or other social subgroups leading

---

[4] R. A. Fisher, *The Genetical Theory of Natural Seleciton* (Oxford, UK: Clarendon Press, 1930). James Milroy and Lesley Milroy, "Linguistic Change, Social Network and Speaker Innovation", *Journal of Linguistics* 21, no. 2: 339-384. Gretchen McCulloch, *Because Internet: Understanding the New Rules of Language* (New York: Riverhead, 2019). Daron Acemoglu, Asuman Ozdaglar and Sarath Pattathil, "Learning, Diversity and Adaptation in Changing Environments: The Role of Weak Links" (2023) at https://www.nber.org/papers/w31214.

to an approval and then rapid disbursement of the treatment to all indicated patients as with, for example, Covid-19 vaccines.[5] This literature has become increasingly influential throughout the social sciences, especially development economics and associated applied work on poverty alleviation.[6] This has encouraged the spread of a model of "experimentation on" communities, where economic and design experts construct interventions and test them on communities that may benefit from them, evaluate them according to often preregistered metrics and then propagate thus-measured effective treatments more broadly.

This approach contrasts with "community-based innovation" allied to academic "Participatory Action Research" (PAR), pioneered in public rather than individual health research, which also has provided a rough approximation to the way that many early digital technologies that laid the foundation for ⬚ later on (such as the time-sharing, personal computing, and many applications).[7] As we discussed briefly in *"The Lost Dao"* chapter, these began in communities of early adopters which usually included many of the system designers "experimenting with" digital tools. While these communities often had some nascent ideas of what their systems were good for, they rarely could reduce desired outcomes to pre-specified metrics and, in fact, many of the components of their systems were created by other early adopters. These systems spread to adjacent

---

[5] Donald B. Rubin, "Estimating Causal Effects of Treatments in Randomized and Nonrandomized Studies," *Journal of Educational Psychology* 66, no. 5: 688-701.

[6] Abhijit V. Banerjee and Esther Duflo, *Poor Economics: A Radical Rethinking of the Way to Fight Poverty* (New York: PublicAffairs, 2011).

[7] Fran Baum, Colin MacDougall and Danielle Smith, "Participatory Action Research", *Journal of Epidemiology and Community Health* 60, no. 10: 854-857.

communities and eventually out to the public through many rounds of learning from the community in unexpected ways and feeding such learning back into product designs, as well as the making available of applications created by communities.

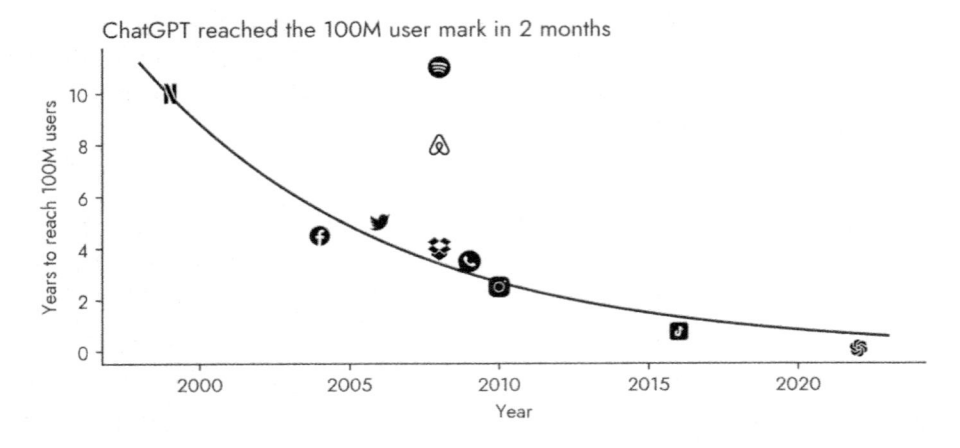

**Figure 6-0-A.** Time of various consumer digital products to 100 million users over the year. Source: Data from Netscribes at https://www.netscribes.com/chatgpt-4-a-near-to-perfect-ai-powered-digital-assistant/ and logos from Icons8 at https://icons8.com/ by fair use.

"Experimentation on" and "experimentation with" each clearly have their strengths and drawbacks. But the latter mode has become increasingly inconsistent and even dangerous given the style of adoption spread that is sought in today's venture capital fueled digital technology industry. Venture capitalists like LinkedIn Founder Reid Hoffman have celebrated the "masters of scale" who champion "blitzscaling", in which start-ups receive large, early injections of venture financing to allow them to invest in growing their user base rapidly and then leveraging the benefits of this supermodularity (e.g. network effects, learning from user data, etc.) to achieve a dominant market position.[8] Perhaps the most dramatic example of this was Hoffman-backed OpenAI, which achieved 100 million users within a few months of launching its ChatGPT. We display this trend in Figure A, which shows how long various consumer products took to reach the 100 million user mark, with a clear downward trend overtime, capped by ChatGPT. Such rapid adoption led to widespread public concern about the potential social harms from such systems and regulation aimed at avoiding the cycle of "move fast and break things" and the social backlash that accompanied comparatively earlier, slower-growing technologies (like ride hailing and social media).[9]

The basic challenge is that "experimentation with" is dangerous when paired with a fully capitalist market driven model of managing new technologies. Because it seeks to manage system harms, challenges and interdependencies as they arise, rather than by *a priori* testing, it requires that the development process itself be driven by a more holistic notion of the technology's impact on the adopting community than sales or adoption figures allow.[10] This is precisely what many of the early ⌘ experiments discussed in *"The Lost Dao"* aimed to provide, through involvement of many social sectors and standardization processes, with commercial scaling

---

[8] Reid Hoffman and Chris Yeh, *Blitzscaling: The Lightening-Fast Path to Building Massively Valuable Companies* (New York: Currency, 2018). For a thoughtful and balanced evaluation see Donald F. Kuratko, Harrison L. Holt and Emily Neubert, "Blitzscaling: The Good, the Bad and the Ugly", *Business Horizons* 63, no. 1 (2020): 109-119.

[9] Future of Life Institute, "Pause Giant AI Experiments: An Open Letter" March 22, 2023 at https://futureoflife.org/open-letter/pause-giant-ai-experiments/.

[10] Daron Acemoglu and Todd Lensman, *Regulating Tranformative Technologies* (2023) at https://www.nber.org/papers/w31461.

circumscribed. Yet even this more balanced version of "experimentation with" falls short of the highest aspirations we might have for the safe and inclusive development of technologies that eventually aspire to be globally transformative, but which may carry significant risks.

Even when technologies are successfully developed in the interests of the communities harnessing them, accounting for all the systemic harms they may create in these communities, they still may have significant spillovers on those not among this early adopter community. The key danger is that technologies may be usable as weapons or otherwise harnessed by the community to benefit at the expense of others, a far more common effect than may appear at first glance because even "helpful" and "harmless" tools may endow the (often-privileged) early adopted community with social and economic advantages that they can use to subjugate, marginalize, or colonize others. As Microsoft's President Brad Smith frequently repeats, most tools can also be used as weapons.[11] This "competitive" effect has some benefits, in spurring adoption by and spread across communities seeking to harness the benefit of the tools partly in their rivalry and potentially by doing so creating pressure to harness and resolve resulting rivalries. But it can also, at best, create exclusion and inequality that undermines the basis of freedom and, at worst, can lead to "arms race" dynamics that undermine the benefits of new tools and instead turn them into universal dangers.

A natural way to overcome this tendency is for the technology to develop in rough balance across primary existing social divides, allowing a network of participants to both govern its

---

[11] Brad Smith and Carol Ann Browne, *Tools and Weapons: The Promise and the Peril of the Digital Age* (New York: Penguin, 2019).

internal harms but also to resolve the potentially competing interests of the groups represented in accessing and directing the technology. At the same time, for such spread to be effective, early adopters must hold sufficient prestige or be able to gain it through the benefits of the tools that, in a roughly balanced way across their respective networks, the technology can spread.

This sketches an ambitious but reasonably clear picture of what a ⌗ strategy for diffusing ⌗ looks like:

1. Seeds must be of a scale of community sufficient to encompass the diversity the technology aims to bridge, but also small enough to be one of a very large number of such experiments.
2. Seeds should be communities of early adopters gaining tangible value or with clear interest in not just using but contributing to the technology and not so vulnerable that to-be-expected failures will prove deeply harmful.
3. Seeds should have prestige within some network or be able to attain it with help from the technology, so further spread is likely.
4. Seeds should be strong communities with institutions to manage and address the systemic harms and support the systemic benefits of the technologies.
5. Seeds should be diverse among themselves and have loose networks of communication between them to ensure a balanced diffusion, avoid conflict and address spillovers.

⌘ 數位 Plurality: Part 6: Impact

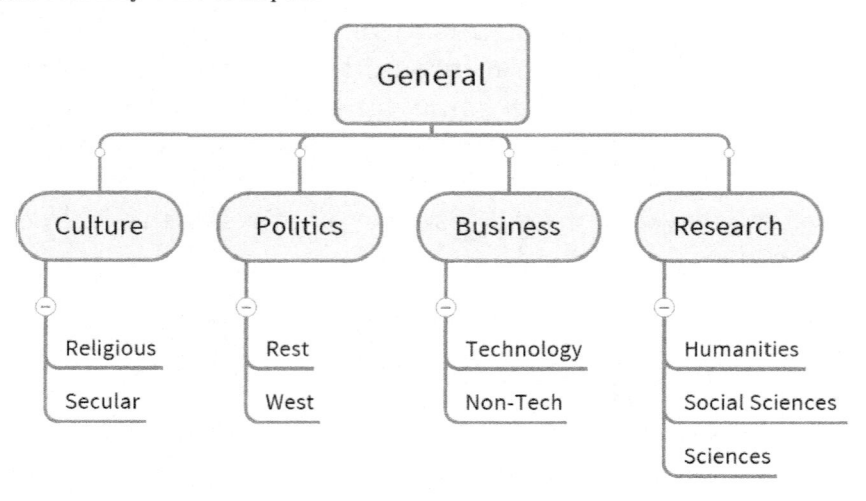

```
                        General
         ┌──────────┬─────────┬──────────┐
      Culture    Politics   Business   Research
        │          │          │           │
     Religious    Rest    Technology   Humanities
     Secular      West    Non-Tech     Social Sciences
                                        Sciences
```

**Figure 6-0-B.** Illustration of the ⌘ marketing approach of bridging and covering social divisions.

While it is obviously impossible to perfectly achieve these five goals simultaneously, each challenging, they provide a rough "north star" to guide towards as we consider sectors for impact of ⌘. Furthermore, to illustrate that trying to achieve them is not impractical, we implemented using these criteria in marketing this book (viz. in choosing endorsements to pursue, media to seek coverage in, events to hold etc.), an approach we refer to as ⌘ Marketing. While fully illustrating this is complex, we show our approach to the last criterion in Figure B. We took our full audience, tried to consider the primary lines of division within it and then chose a marketing vector (such as an endorser) with respect across these lines of division, then recursively applied this approach to each sub-community; Figure B shows the categories thus generated two levels deep into the associated "tree". As to whether the result of this approach was effective and whether we did a good job implementing this, you should be able to judge by reading this book and its endorsements better than we can at the time of writing this! As in many parts of this project, we invite you to experiment and learn with us.

## Fertile ground

Another criterion above is scale. To realize the benefits of ⌑ technology within a community requires the community to contain at least a rough approximation of the diversity that technology aims to span. This differs dramatically across various directions of technology. The most intimate technologies of post-symbolic communication and immersive shared reality can be powerful even in the smallest communities and relationships, creating few constraints on scale and diversification of seeding and thus making it natural to prioritize other criteria above. At the opposite extreme, voting systems and markets are rarely used in intimate communities and require significant scale to be relevant, especially in their socially enriched forms, making entry points far scarcer, more ambitious, and potentially hazardous.

However, given the reasonable flexibility across scales of most ⌑ technologies, the most broadly attractive sites for experimentation will be those that both contain enough diversity *within them* to enable most applications and are themselves sufficiently diverse *across them* to allow reasonable choice of diverse, safe, prestigious seeds. While any simplistic quantitative representation falls short of the richness needed to characterize such examples, a simple rule of thumb is to seek for roughly the same diversity *across communities* as *within communities* as quantified by the number of units as illustrated in Figure C. In a world of (very roughly) 10 billion people, these would be units of roughly 100,000 people, as there are 100,000 such units if the whole world were partitioned into them: they have the scale of the square root of global population. There is, of course, nothing magic about 100,000,

數位 Plurality: Part 6: Impact

but it offers a rough sense for the scale of communities and organizations that are the most fertile ground in which to plant the seeds of ⌬.

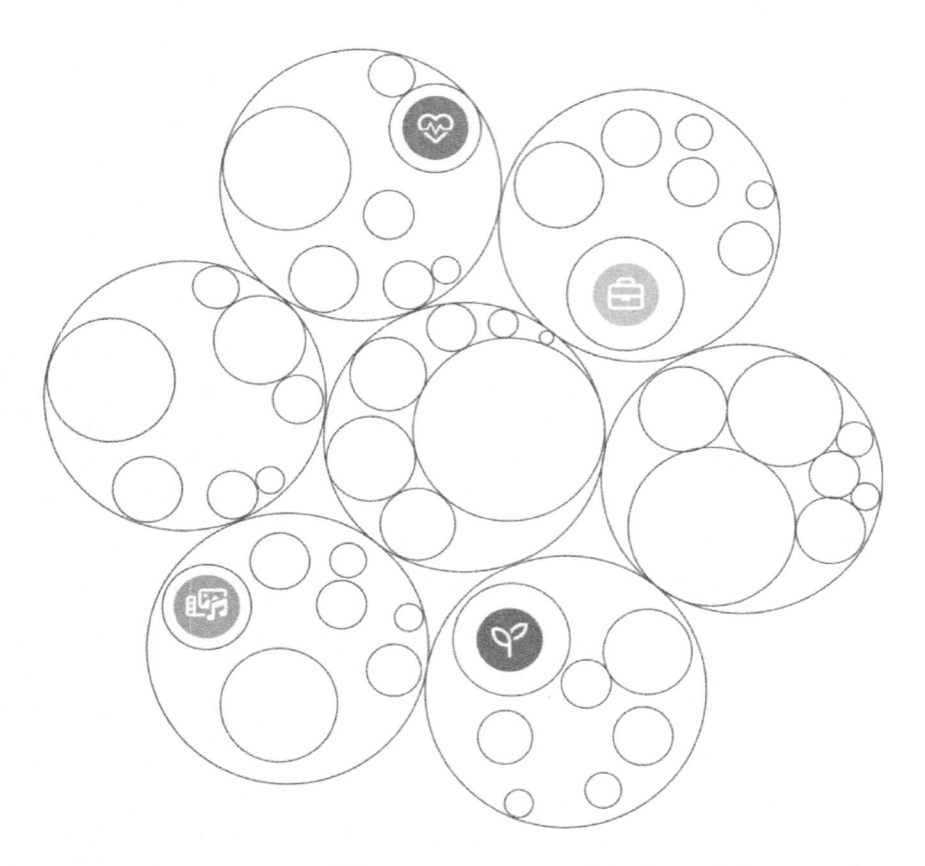

**Figure 6-0-C.** Illustration of the "square-root scale" of social change, where there are an equal number of units within each experimental site as experimental sites, along with symbols of the sectors we study. Source: Generated by authors, all icons in public domain.

There are many kinds of communities at this scale. Geographically, this is roughly the scale of most middle-sized municipalities (large towns or small cities). Economically, it is the size of employees in a large corporation or, politically, in a median nation. Religiously, it is, for example, roughly the number of Catholics in a Diocese. Educationally, it is a bit larger than the number of students at a large university. Socially, it resembles the membership of many mid-sized civic organizations or social movements. Culturally, it is roughly the active fan base of a typical television program, performing artist or professional sports club. In short, it is a prevalent level of organization in a wide range of social spheres, offering rich terrain for surveying.

**Surveyor's map**

Perhaps the two most prominent sites of experimentation with ⌗ we have highlighted above are Taiwan and web3 communities. These two sites share some important characteristics, and yet also sharply diverge in many ways both in terms of their character and the ⌗ applications they have focused on. Both are roughly the same size. In 2021, web3 applications (dApps) had about 1.5 million monthly active users, though only a fraction of these actively participated in the most ⌗-adjacent services, such as GitCoin. The ⌗ services of all kinds built by the g0v community in Taiwan have reached similar numbers. [12] The types of diversity in each community, however, are radically different.

While statistics are not entirely reliable, web3 users are spread quite broadly around the globe according to patterns like the internet broadly. However, users tend to be extremely technically sophisticated, skew male, very young, and, anecdotally based on our experience in the space, tend to be

---

[12] Friedrich Naumann Foundation. "Examples of Civic Tech Communities-Governments Collaboration Around The World," n.d. https://www.freiheit.org/publikation/examples-civic-tech-communities-governments-collaboration-around-world.

atheistic, politically right of center and ethnically of European, Semitic and Asian origin.[13] Participants in the Taiwanese digital ecosystem are obviously mostly from Taiwan and thus mostly of the ethnicities represented there. But they are more diverse in age, technical background, political perspective, and religious background.[14]

The two ecosystems have also focused on different sides of the spectrum of 󰵌 we discussed in the previous part of the book. Taiwan has focused primarily on the deeper and narrower applications of 󰵌 and the fundamental protocols (identity and access) that support these most strongly. Global web3 communities have focused on the shallower and more inclusive applications and the fundamental protocols (association, commerce, and contract) that most support these.

Both have been critical early testbeds for 󰵌, yet measuring them against our criteria also illustrates their limitations. The Taiwan ecosystem is larger than required for many of the applications developed there, which is likely why it has hosted a range of subcommunities (that they often call "data coalitions") engaging in more advanced experiments supported by the broader ecosystem. The Taiwan ecosystem has strong potential for prestige in Asia and many of the countries typically called democracies, while the geopolitical conflicts surrounding it create some challenges in making it a seed for fully equitable global spread. Web3 communities, on

---

[13] a16zcrypto. "State of Crypto 2023." Https://A16z.Com. Andressen Horowitz, 2023. https://api.a16zcrypto.com/wp-content/uploads/2023/04/State-of-Crypto.pdf.

[14] Austin, Sarah. "Web3 Is About More Than Tech, Thanks to Its Inclusivity." Entrepreneur, June 3, 2022. https://www.entrepreneur.com/science-technology/web3-is-about-more-than-tech-thanks-to-its-inclusivity/425679.

the other hand, may be a bit small and homogeneous to allow for a fully robust test of whether new market institutions can rival the reach of capitalism. Furthermore, many of the scandals that have plagued the web3 space endanger its ability to generally serve as a beacon of innovation that can equitably spread.

It is therefore crucial to carefully consider which places might be the most promising for ⌘ to spread next. One obvious example that pervades our discussions so far, is the governance of cities. Yet precisely because we have drawn on such public sector examples so heavily thus far, we focus in this part of the book on a diversity of social sectors where ⌘ can seed reality that touch a much broader range of life than the narrow definition of public sector "democracy". In doing so, we aim to match the scales mentioned above and cover a broad range of life experiences, while attending to areas with respect and prestige in a broad range of societies.

We consider, as symbolized also in Figure C:

1. Workplace, which is a highly influential sector because so much of the capitalist economy is driven by it. Again, especially in the largest companies, finding scale matches is quite straightforward.
2. Health, which is another sector touching almost every life, is especially relevant outside of the working years we cover in the previous chapter and perhaps the most widely respected social sector. Many health systems, as noted above, match in scale.
3. Media, which perhaps has the greatest capacity to spread new practices as it is close to the conceptual, communicative, and ideational foundation of most societies. Many publications and social media platforms match the relevant scale.

4. The environment, which surrounds us all and touches us at a global scale unlike anything else, and which complements the other sectors, appealing to many who urge us to think beyond human work, health, and idea exchange.

In each of these domains we highlight through a series of vignettes and attempt to roughly quantify how a range of technologies could transform practice in ways that could potentially scale across or even beyond the sector.

# 6-1 Workplace

More than a billion people worldwide work outside their homes in formal organizations with at least a few other people.[1] These "workplaces" produce about 70% of global output and are the first thing most people think of when they hear "economy". Just as we consider the vast contribution of workplaces to the global economy, it is essential to address inefficiencies that hinder productivity. U.S. workers spend an average of 31 hours per month in meetings deemed unproductive, a significant drain on both time and resources.[2] If ⿻ is to help re-imagine the economy, it must restructure formal work, which we turn to in this chapter.

The advances we discuss, which are just a sampling of potential implications of ⿻ in the workplace, cover strengthening remote teams, designing effective corporate campuses, improving communication, accessing talent more inclusively and supporting more effective provision of common corporate infrastructure and more dynamic adaptation to changing industries. We estimate that the first four of these components could increase global gross domestic product by approximately 10% in total and that the last might permanently

---

[1] International Labor Organization, " World Employment and Social Outlook: Trends" (2023) at https://www.ilo.org/wcmsp5/groups/public/---dgreports/---inst/documents/publication/wcms_865387.pdf.

[2] Alyson Krueger, "Fewer Work Meetings? Corporate America Is Trying," *The New York Times*, April 10, 2023, https://www.nytimes.com/2023/04/07/business/office-meetings-time.html.

increase the GDP growth rate by half a percentage point a year.[3]

**Strong remote teams**

The Covid-19 pandemic transformed the world of work, bringing changes expected for decades to fruition in a year. A leading study by Barreto et al., for example, found that work from home rose from 5% of the American workforce to a high above 60%.[4] Perhaps the most extreme manifestation has been

---

[3] If, as noted in the chapter, about 50% of formal sector work will be remote and, as in this study, if team-building exercises increase team performance by about 25%, if this applies to about half of formal sector work and if about half the benefit goes into cost, we should expect a gain of about 2% of GDP from improved remote team-building. If agglomeration benefits are about 12% for work facilities and this applies again to half of formal sector work and can be improved by 50%, again we get 2% of GDP. If meetings are 25% of formal sector work time and can be improved by 25%, this is about 4% of GDP. Standard economic estimates of the costs of labor search and matching are about 4% of GPD, similar to the cost spent on human resources; if mitigated by 50% this would raise GDP by 2% (not to mention significantly dampen the cost of business cycle unemployment). Finally, most GDP growth (of roughly 2-3% annually globally) has been traced by economists to technological advance through the research and development of new products, which is now about 80% in the private sector according to the figures we discussed in the introduction. If the efficiency of this could be increased by a quarter through more flexible intrapreneurship, this could raise global GDP growth annually by half a percent. Cameron Klein, Deborah DiazGranados, Eduardo Salas, Huy Le, Shawn Burke, Rebecca Lyons, and Gerald Goodwin, "Does Team Building Work?" *Small Group Research* 40, no. 2 (January 16, 2009): 181-222. https://doi.org/10.1177/1046496408328821. Michael Greenstone, Richard Hornbeck, and Enrico Moretti, "Identifying Agglomeration Spillovers: Evidence from Winners and Losers of Large Plant Openings," *Journal of Political Economy* 118, no. 3 (June 2010): 536-98. https://doi.org/10.1086/653714.

[4] Jose Barrero, Nicholas Bloom, and Steven J. Davis. 2023, "The Evolution of Working from Home," _Stanford Institute for Economic Policy Research

the rise of so-called "digital nomads", who have harnessed the increasing opportunity for remote work to travel continuously and work a variety of remote jobs as encouraged by programs like Sardinia regional program for digital nomads and Estonia and Taiwan's e-citizenship and gold cards respectively, that one author of this book holds. While there has been a substantial return to physical work since the end of the pandemic, at least a part of the change appears here to stay; Barreto et al. find that after the pandemic, workers on average want to work about half the week from home and believe their productivity is similar or better in that setting. While some studies have found some evidence of mildly reduced productivity, these effects do not seem large enough to overcome the persistent demands for hybrid work styles.[5]

Yet there is little question that remote work has real downsides. Some of these, such as ensuring work-life balance, avoiding distractions and unhealthy at-home working conditions, are not easily addressed through remote collaboration tools. But others include lack of organic interactions with colleagues, missing opportunities for feedback or forming deeper personal connections with colleagues, etc.[6] While ▢ can be used to

---

*(SIEPR) Working Paper* no. 23-19 (July 2023): https://siepr.stanford.edu/publications/working-paper/evolution-working-home.

[5] Natalia Emanuel, Emma Harrington, and Amanda Pallais, "The Power of Proximity to Coworkers: Training for Tomorrow or Productivity Today?" *National Bureau of Economic Research Working Paper* no 31880 (November 2023): https://doi.org/10.3386/w31880.

[6] Longqi Yang, David Holtz, Sonia Jaffe, Siddharth Suri, Shilpi Sinha, Jeffrey Weston, Connor Joyce, et al., "The Effects of Remote Work on Collaboration among Information Workers," *Nature Human Behaviour* 6, no. 1 (September 9, 2021): 43-54. https://doi.org/10.1038/s41562-021-01196-4.

address most of these, we will focus on one in particular: the building of strong and deeply trusting teams.

Remote immersive shared reality (ISR) significantly enhances team building and training across disciplines by facilitating collaborative and creative teamwork in virtual environments. Global collaboration in virtual environments has been effective for interdisciplinary teamwork, particularly in healthcare education[7], highlighting its utility in overcoming geographic barriers.[8] Virtual worlds foster team creativity by providing avatars for personal expression, immersive experiences for co-presence, and tools for modifying environments, enhancing creative collaboration across distributed teams.[9] Furthermore, 3D virtual worlds and games, like those developed in *Second Life* for team building, offer cost-effective solutions for enhancing communication, emotional engagement, and

---

[7] Lin Lu, Honglin Wang, Pengran Liu, Rong Liu, Jiayao Zhang, Yi Xie, Songxiang Liu, et al., "Applications of Mixed Reality Technology in Orthopedics Surgery: A Pilot Study," *Frontiers in Bioengineering and Biotechnology* 10 (February 22, 2022): https://doi.org/10.3389/fbioe.2022.740507.

[8] Rachel Umoren, Dora Stadler, Stephen L. Gasior, Deema Al-Sheikhly, Barbara Truman, and Carolyn Lowe, "Global Collaboration and Team-Building through 3D Virtual Environments," Innovations in Global Medical and Health Education 2014, no. 1 (November 1, 2014), https://doi.org/10.5339/igmhe.2014.1.

[9] Pekka Alahuhta, Emma Nordbäck, Anu Sivunen, and Teemu Surakka, "Fostering Team Creativity in Virtual Worlds," *Journal For Virtual Worlds Research* 7, no. 3 (July 20, 2014): https://doi.org/10.4101/jvwr.v7i3.7062.

situational awareness among team members, proving essential for teamwork in safety-critical domains.[10][11]

In-person teams often engage in a variety of joint learnings or other not-directly-productive activities to build team trust, connection, and spirit. These range from casual lunches to various kinds of extreme team sports, such as "trust falls"[12], simulated military exercises, ropes courses, etc. What nearly all these have in common is that they create a shared activity that benefits from and thus helps develop trust among members, in a similar manner to the way we discussed shared military service developing strong and lasting cooperative bonds in the *Post-Symbolic Communication* chapter.

Obviously most such activities currently rely heavily on being in person, thus many hybrid and fully remote teams, especially those that have many members who started as remote employees, miss the team-building benefits created by such activities or can achieve them only at considerable travel expense. ISR offers significant potential for overcoming this challenge. Lunches among sufficiently realistic avatars, ones reflecting detailed facial expressions for example, may soon help bring the rich connections achieved in the office within the

---

[10] Jason Ellis, Kurt Luther, Katherine Bessiere, and Wendy Kellogg, "Games for Virtual Team Building," *Proceedings of the 7th ACM Conference on Designing Interactive Systems* (February 25, 2008): pp 295-304, https://doi.org/10.1145/1394445.1394477.

[11] Heide Lukosch, Bas van Nuland, Theo van Ruijven, Linda van Veen, and Alexander Verbraeck, "Building a Virtual World for Team Work Improvement," *Frontiers in Gaming Simulation*, 2014, 60-68, https://doi.org/10.1007/978-3-319-04954-0_8.

[12] A "trust fall" is an exercise where a person falls backward, counting on others to catch them. This activity is used to build trust and teamwork, as it requires relying on others to prevent injury. From the mid-2010s, the trust fall became less popular due to the potential for traumatic brain injuries if catchers fail.

reach of remote teams. While it would seem impossible to achieve the vivid connections of parties or extreme sports in remote shared reality, there is increasingly strong evidence that real experiences of fear and trust can develop in sufficiently realistic simulated environments.[13] As "e-sports" begin to rival the popularity and, in the right ISR environments, physical intensity of in-person physical sports, the benefits of "campus athletics" may increasingly make their way to remote work.

Yet even more promising than how recreation-at-a-distance can mimic approaches of in-person teams is the harnessing of digital tools to create even deeper connections than are possible without digital aids. The simplest example would be extensions to extreme sports or military scenarios that would be unsafe or unreasonably costly to simulate in-person. But these are only the beginning; eventually, direct neural interfaces may allow colleagues to remotely share a level of intimate empathy that will be bound primarily by professional propriety, rather than by the barriers of physical distance.

## Designing inclusive campuses

Much work, especially white-collar work, is physically localized to significant extents in large "corporate campuses". While many of the functions these campuses bring together are separate or organizationally distant, broad co-location is often a goal because of the chance intersections it is thought to allow that may stimulate work across divisions of the company. Such "agglomeration" effects have been shown by a large economic literature to be an important source of the economic benefit of

---

[13] Jih-Hsuan Tammy Lin, "Fear in Virtual Reality (VR): Fear Elements, Coping Reactions, Immediate and Next-Day Fright Responses Toward a Survival Horror Zombie Virtual Reality Game", *Computers in Human Behavior* 72 (2017): 350-361.

cities.[14] A core role of corporate campuses is to capture these benefits within a company.

Achieving this goal, however, requires careful design. Excessive segregation by organization and discipline or focus on core work undermines the benefit of agglomerative spontaneity. Excessive fragmentation by organization and discipline undermines direct productivity. Different elements of campus (walkways, dining facilities, offices, shared space, recreational facilities etc.) play diverse roles in fostering direct work and spontaneous connections. For instance, Steve Jobs redesigned Pixar's headquarters to include a central atrium with a large theater, cafeteria, mailboxes, and viewing rooms.[15] By encouraging computer scientists, animators and other staff to mingle in a shared space, this layout boosts chance encounters and cross-pollination. Yet architectural revamps pose significant challenges: they're costly and need to support other elements that are specific to each company, such as nature of the work or brand identity. It is thus hardly surprising that there is no standard best campus design; campuses differ radically in their design, a leading exemplary being Apple's torus spaceship shown in Figure A. Anything that could reduce the costs of exploration could significantly improve the quality.

---

[14] Jane Jacobs, *The Economy of Cities* (New York: Vintage, 1969). Edward L. Glaeser, Hedi D. Kallal, José A. Scheinkman and Andrei Shleifer, "Growth in Cities",*Journal of Political Economy* 100, no. 6 (1992): 1126-1152.

[15] Pixar Headquarters and the Legacy of Steve Jobs (2012) https://officesnapshots.com/2012/07/16/pixar-headquarters-and-the-legacy-of-steve-jobs/

**Figure 6-1-A.** Apple's famously unusually shaped corporate campus. Source: Unsplash stock photo, free for commercial use.

A natural way to make such experiments dramatically easier is to create ISR campuses in which employees can explore potential configurations and attend virtual meetings. These configurations can be prototyped far more rapidly and flexibly than building a physical campus, allowing for a range of exploration in the course of time employees spend attending virtual meetings. Based on feedback, employees can even help redesign the space and iterate on the layout. If a potential design seems to be achieving its goals reasonably well and fits a potential site, it could then be "printed" through a more standard engineering and construction process. In short, these tools could make the design of physical space much more like what word processing and collaborative documents have made writing: a process that is able to engage in broad experimentation and accumulate diverse feedback before it must be greatly scaled.

## Difficult conversations

Meetings are a central part of white-collar work, consuming on average approximately a quarter of working time.[16] Yet for all the time they take up, perhaps the greater cost is the meetings that do not happen because of how burdensome they are. Business leaders frequently misunderstand the needs of their customers, the challenges within their teams and the duplication of work because meeting with the relevant stakeholders would take too long. To make matters worse, many meetings are quite ineffective, as dominant personalities carry on and the wisdom of those who are less empowered or assertive is lost. In the realm of white-collar work, meetings are a notorious time sink, with office employees dedicating about 18 hours a week on average. This not only represents approximately $25,000 in annual payroll costs per employee but also encompasses meetings that 30% of employees find unnecessary. Moreover, a reduction in meetings by 40% has been linked to a 71% surge in productivity, underlining the critical need for streamlining communication.[17] Anything that could significantly speed meetings and increase their quality could transform organizational productivity.[18]

---

[16] Branka, "Meeting Statistics – 2024", *Truelist Blog* February 17, 2024 at https://truelist.co/blog/meeting-statistics/.

[17] Arthur Brooks, "Why Meetings Are Terrible for Happiness," *The Atlantic*, December 15, 2022, https://www.theatlantic.com/family/archive/2022/11/why-meetings-are-terrible-happiness/672144/.

[18] Michael Gibbs, Friederike Mengel, and Christoph Siemroth, "Work from Home and Productivity: Evidence from Personnel and Analytics Data on Information Technology Professionals," *Journal of Political Economy Microeconomics* 1, no. 1 (February 1, 2023): 7–41, https://doi.org/10.1086/721803.

While meetings have a variety of goals and structures, perhaps the most common type is an attempt to share a variety of perspectives on a common project to achieve alignment and assignment of responsibilities. Such meetings are closely connected to the deliberative conversations we highlighted in our chapter on *Augmented Deliberation*. An important reason why, despite the rise of asynchronous communication via services like Slack, Teams, and Trello, synchronous meetings remain so prevalent is that asynchronous dialogs often suffer from the same lack of thoughtful time and attention management that are necessary to make synchronous meetings successful. Approaches like Polis, Remesh, All Our Ideas, and their increasingly sophisticated LLM-based extensions promise to significantly improve this, making it increasingly possible to have respectful, inclusive, and informative asynchronous conversations that include many more stakeholders.

practices and tools can also enable more open and inclusive conversations about the biggest issues facing the organization. Today, the responsibility for setting direction is typically limited to the top of the pyramid. This simplifies strategy development, but at the cost of resilience and creativity: if a handful of executives are unwilling to adapt and learn, the whole organization stalls. And even if executives were all exceptional visionaries, their combined intellect is unlikely to suffice for the task at hand. What is instead required is a process that harnesses the ingenuity of everyone who has a stake in the organization's success, as highlighted by W. Edwards Deming's work on Total Quality Management.[19] Imagine an open conversation that generates tens of

---

[19] W. Edwards Deming, "Improvement of Quality and Productivity through Action by Management", *National Productivity Review* 1, no. 1 (1981): 12-22.

thousands of insights and ideas (for instance around customers' needs or emerging trends) and uses collective intelligence to combine, prioritize, and ultimately distill them into a common point of view about what lies ahead. What are the big opportunities that can redefine who we are? What are the biggest challenges we need to tackle head on? What aspiration truly reflects our common purpose? By opening the conversation to new voices, encouraging unorthodox thinking, and fostering horizontal dialogue, it's possible to transform a top-down ritual into an exciting, participative quest to define a shared future.

Beyond office politics, national politics are also increasingly entering and dividing workplaces, leading some executives to take extreme measures such as banning political discussions at work.[20] A potential alternative to such stringent restrictions, which may suppress but not resolve tensions and undermine employee morale, might be to build channels such as the above to allow thoughtful and inclusive discussions of social issues, especially those relevant to corporate policies, to take place respectfully and at scale. Overall, these technologies promise to make workplaces more efficient, engaging, consensual and harmonious, providing tools to help achieve the cultural goals many executives strive for.

## hiring

Many businesses and roles have "standard career paths", recruiting primarily graduates from a limited number of degree programs, set of professional backgrounds/ experiences, etc. While these businesses often regret that they

---

[20] Ellen Huet, "Basecamp Follows Coinbase In Banning Politics Talk at Work," *Bloomberg*, April 26, 2021, https://www.bloomberg.com/news/articles/2021-04-26/basecamp-follows-coinbase-in-banning-politics-talk-at-work.

thereby exclude many talented and diverse candidates, recruiting from backgrounds that have lower "hit rates" is often very costly: it would require them to learn to identify promising resumés from a broader range of settings, verify accomplishments and credentials outside of typical channels, send representatives traveling more and further, understand unfamiliar dimensions of diversity and train those who may be less prepared for the culture of their organization. The rigidity created by this hiring process is a leading reason so many are forced into the narrow paths of learning we highlighted in the previous chapter.

The capabilities of social identity systems, modern large language models (LLMs), and ISR technologies may help in addressing many of these challenges. Network-based verification systems, as we described in the *Identity and Personhood* chapter can allow the secure verification of a diversity of credentials and accomplishments across a large gulf of social distance rapidly and cheaply. LLMs, properly trained and fine-tuned, should soon allow the "translation" of resumés not just across languages, but across diverse social contexts, helping hiring managers understand "equivalent" qualifications across a range of settings and a diversity of paths that could support performance in a role. They can similarly help applicants better understand the range of roles their background may qualify them for.

They also may be able to provide a richer sense of the range of diversity spanned by a company's customer base that would be helpful to represent among employees and help them to empathize and connect with customers. Human resource departments could optimize for diversity in more sophisticated, intersectional ways rather than simply seeking to match population proportions in salient categories. Remote shared reality experiences can help them hold interactive recruiting events in a wider range of venues at lower cost and allow applicants a deeper sense of the work environment. They can also accelerate the acculturation and on boarding processes much as we described in the previous chapter. In short, these tools can together allow for a future of human resources that reaches a far wider range of talent and allows opportunities for everyone to shine as the unique intersectional contributor they are.

**Aligning wisdom and influence**

In most organizations, power—whether it's about controlling resources, making decisions, accessing important information, or having the power to reward or discipline others—is tied to one's position. Formal hierarchy provides clarity in terms of who is responsible for what, but this "legibility" has significant drawbacks. Positional authority can be too expansive, like a finance executive becoming CEO and suddenly claiming expertise in product design. It is also binary (you either have it or you do not), which means that incompetent managers retain power until they're removed (often much later than ideal). Finally, traditional hierarchies do not give employees say in selecting their leaders. This is the opposite of the social web, where power emerges from the bottom up.[21]

In ▢ workplaces, the traditional single hierarchy can be complemented by multiple, issue-specific hierarchies in the spirit of the ▢ theory of identity. Power can shift fluidly based on contribution. Emerging technologies can help match value added with decision rights. For example, LLMs can sift through communication data to spot associates who consistently provide valuable insights on specific topics. LLMs can create dynamic social graphs that pinpoint key network figures and provide rich context on the nature of their connections and compile feedback from various sources to present a comprehensive assessment of an individual's "natural

---

[21] See Hamel and Zanini, op. cit. ch. 9.

leadership." These approaches recognize and reward valuable contributions of people irrespective of role and serve a reality check for those who still occupy formal positions of authority. Over time, they can reduce dependency on formal hierarchies altogether.

## Supporting intrapreneurship

Another effect of traditional hierarchies is that those managed by different high-level managers come to form different organizations within the parent, each with their own cultures, goals, and visions. While these internal distinctions are usually viewed as important to ensuring accountability, they are also often viewed as a barrier to organizational cooperation and dynamism, potentially undermining the collaborations needed to provide common infrastructure and meet the needs ("disruptions") of changing political, economic, social, and technological environments. For example, the organization in which one of us works, Microsoft, has sometimes been satirized for its internal organization conflicts and, under the leadership of its current CEO Satya Nadella has worked to forge a "One Microsoft" culture to overcome this.[22]

While much of this has been demonstrated through exemplars of such cooperation and inspirational leadership, Nadella has also helped establish some institutions intended to help achieve the organizational equivalent of the "solidarity and dynamism" we have discussed above. In particular, one of us had the honor to serve in the Office of Chief Technology Officer (OCTO) Kevin Scott, whose duties included coordinating cross-company investments that no one organization would find it in their interest to take on and

---

[22] Satya Nadella with Greg Shaw and Jill Tracie Nichols, *Hit Refresh: The Quest to Rediscover Microsoft's Soul and Imagine a Better Future for Everyone* (New York: Harper Business, 2017).

stimulating "intrapreneurship", the building of new business lines often drawing on expertise across existing organizations.[23]

While OCTO achieved much (including incubating the now well-known relationship with OpenAI) during the author's time there, a persistent challenge was harnessing a small staff that was necessarily much less informed than those "on the ground" about business needs and opportunities to decide on major investments and incubations intended to bring cross-cutting benefits. A leading example was the cross-company technical project he was most involved with, around Web3 strategy, where interested and expert employees were widely scattered across the company. This was particularly difficult because the intention was for many of these investments to accrue not directly to the bottom line of an internal start-up, but to other business lines. Because of this and the structure of jobs at Microsoft, the typical use of large incentives for eventual success to compensate for the likelihood of failure is hard to apply. Various organizations navigate this challenge in different ways; for example Google (now Alphabet) has traditionally given employees 20% of their time free to pursue passion projects for the organization, outside their primary organizational role.[24] Yet this suffers the obvious challenge that individuals may pursue idiosyncratic projects that at worst may not be aligned to the broader mission and at best usually fail to

---

[23] An entertaining outgrowth of corporate acronyms in this case was that he had the title OCTOPEST (Office of the Chief Technology Officer Political Economist and Social Technologist), paralleling the title of his colleague Jaron Lanier who at the time of this writing remains Microsoft's OCTOPUS (Office of the Chief Technology Officer Prime Unifying Scientist).

[24] Annika Steiber and Sverker Alänge, "A Corporate System for Continuous Innovation: the Case of Google Inc.", *European Journal of Innovation Management* 16, no. 2: 243-264.

scale as they do not bring enough people together to cooperate on an ambitious project.

A natural alternative to the extremes of centralized management and uncoordinated individual initiative would be to harness 數位 conversational and funding tools. An organization like OCTO could have a much larger budget, but much less discretion, providing matchmaking and cross-pollination services and matching funds for investments with support from many organizations. It could use data from or posting within internal communication platforms to identify cross-organizational clusters of interest, host free and fun events to build connections across these organizations and then offer matching funds if a diversity of organizations are willing to invest employee time or other resources in supporting a shared investment or incubation. Compared to the "20% time model", this would offer much more "free time" to pursue projects that have genuine cross-organizational support, but that one's direct reporting chain sees as tangential, and less support for purely idiosyncratic interests. As such, it would empower employees to coordinate investments among themselves that could transform the business overall, allowing agility to avoid disruption.

Putting these together, we can imagine a future where remote teams can form the same strong bonds as in-person teams, where in-person teams can co-design inclusive workplaces that foster spontaneous connections while maintaining focus, where meetings are far more efficient and inclusive even when asynchronous, where a far wider range of talent can be placed into leading roles. This could create a more inclusive and representative workplace where employees can easily collaborate across divisions and with corporate support to overcome hurdles and build the common infrastructure and new ventures their employer needs to survive and thrive in a dynamic business environment. In short, it is not hard to see a future of truly ▢ workplaces, embracing and harnessing collaboration across a wide range of internal and external diversity to achieve a more productive and inclusive future.

數位 Plurality: Part 6: Impact

## 6-2 Health

In the past 75 years humanity has added 25 years to global life expectancy, significantly more than in the previous 10,000 years. These advances were realized through a monist atomist model of health and healthcare as we highlighted in our *Living in a ⌘ World* chapter. Such models (e.g. 'tropical medicine') were developed and refined through centuries of imperial and colonial governance, but their implementation worldwide was rapidly accelerated following the formation of the United Nations. This included achievements like the eradication of smallpox, the rapid expansion of immunizations including through Gavi the Vaccine Alliance, the massive expansion of antiretroviral therapy for HIV, and the recent reductions in maternal mortality through improvements in skilled birth attendance. Perhaps the most dramatic illustration of this model was that within two years of the appearance of COVID-19, 70% of world's population had received at least a single vaccine dose.

At the same time, progress in health-related Sustainable Development Goals (SDGs) has stalled or reversed[1], half the world's population lacks access to essential health services[2], impoverishing healthcare payments affect hundreds of millions each year[3], mental health services worldwide are severely

---

[1] "The Sustainable Development Goals Report: Special Edition," (New York: UN DESA, July 2023), https://desapublications.un.org/file/1169/download.

[2] "Tracking Universal Health Coverage: 2023 Global Monitoring Report," (Geneva: World Health Organization, September 18, 2023), https://iris.who.int/bitstream/handle/10665/374059/9789240080379-eng.pdf?sequence=1.

[3] "Tracking Universal Health Coverage: 2023 Global Monitoring Report," (Geneva: World Health Organization, September 18, 2023),

underdeveloped[4], half of premature deaths are caused by non-communicable diseases[5] costing more than $2 trillion annually[6], and less than 3% of the world's population in some countries has access to basic assistive technologies (wheelchairs, walkers, canes, prosthetic limbs, eyeglasses, white canes, and hearing aids.[7] If we can address these social and intersubjective threats to health as effectively as we have the atomistic ones, we can easily add another 20 years to human life expectancy in the next century.

---

Achieving this goal, however, requires embracing a 🔲 concept of health (Figure A). Of course, the world will still need doctors, nurses, health facilities, laboratories, vaccines, drugs, and medical devices. But it also needs to empower the co-construction of *health agency* on the part of individuals and their communities, a term Jennifer Prah Ruger uses to describe the promotion of individuals' capabilities to act in their own

---

https://iris.who.int/bitstream/handle/10665/374059/9789240080379-eng.pdf?sequence=1.

[4] "Transforming Mental Health for All," (Geneva: World Health Organisation, 2022), https://iris.who.int/bitstream/handle/10665/356119/9789240049338-eng.pdf?sequence=1.

[5] "Noncommunicable Diseases," World Health Organization, September 16, 2023, https://www.who.int/news-room/fact-sheets/detail/noncommunicable-diseases.

[6] "Financing NCDs," NCD Alliance, March 2, 2015, https://ncdalliance.org/why-ncds/financing-ncds.

[7] "Assistive Technology." World Health Organization: WHO, May 15, 2023. https://www.who.int/news-room/fact-sheets/detail/assistive-technology.

interests with respect to their health[8]. However, health agency is rightly understood as *primarily* emergent, multiscale, embedded, and complex (see our chapter Living in a 數位 World ). In this view and as we now highlight, the central blockers to the next great era of human life extension are:

1. Lack of financing
2. Missing markets
3. Coordination failures
4. Missing communities
5. Non-aligned incentives
6. Lack of enabling services.

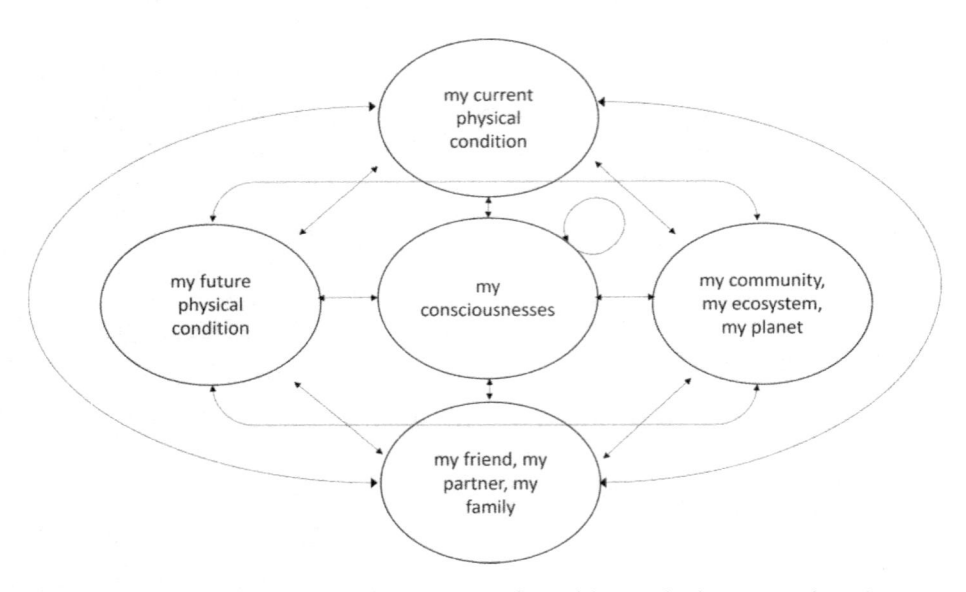

**Figure 6-2-A.** The Relational Concept of Health - Including social and intersubjective aspects of health rather than just the atomistic.

---

[8] Jennifer Ruger, Health and Social Justice, (New York: Oxford University Press, 2010), pp. 276.

## Reimagining health insurance

Health insurance allows people facing a range of risks to support their common health expenditures, both facilitating payments and evening out risk across time and people. While the role of insurance in "saving for a rainy day" is clear to most, the value of "pooling" risk across individuals is subtler: it facilitates both the collection of regular and predictable payments to offset unpredictable and sudden expenses and the redistribution from the better to the worse off.[9] This latter function of insurance is common to all expenditures intended to alleviate the suffering of the worse off, who from the "original position" prior to birth that John Rawls asks us to consider, are the victims of bad luck in their social or genetic position.[10]

Health insurance in practice varies along the three dimensions of prepayment, risk pooling, and redistribution. Private insurance in a competitive market faces the problem that insurers with better information can draw off lower-risk individuals by charging less, leaving the non-discriminating insurer with an 'adverse selection' of high-risk patients[11]. *Private health insurance* in a market economy thus tends to reduce to

---

[9] In his 1991 Lindley Lecture, the philosopher Derek Parfit distinguished a novel theory of ethics, in contrast to either utilitarianism or egalitarianism, which he called "the priority view". Its main tenet is that the worse off have a special claim on resources. Prioritarianism (before the term) has been used by economists in the analysis of social welfare functions ('optimal taxation') since at least the 1970s. Prioritarianism is not usually considered - as it is here - as a form of insurance.

[10] John Rawls, *A Theory of Justice*, Revised edition, (Cambridge, MA: Harvard University Press, 1999).

[11] Kenneth Arrow, "Uncertainty and the welfare economics of medical care," *American Economic Review* 53, 5 (1963): 941-973.

an actuarially informed *health savings plan* (i.e. with no risk pooling or redistribution), like self-managed Health Savings Accounts (HSAs) in the US.[12] This voids the HSA of most insurance value, including that of prudential savings, since individuals cannot calibrate their savings rates without actuarial information.

On the opposite extreme, "single payer" *national health insurance*, financed by general government revenues and enacted through a compulsory and universal mandate, embodies the three elements of prepayment, risk pooling, and redistribution. However, such systems are rigidly based on a nation-state concept that is only one way of achieving pooling and redistribution at scale. For example, the Scandinavian countries admired for their socialization of risk have smaller populations than most large private health insurers in the US.

A natural alternative to this simplistic dichotomy of extremes precedes both in practice, namely *social health insurance* in which communities of solidarity care for those in need. Such a pattern is familiar to nearly everyone from their family lives, and it is not hard to understand how it extended to tribes and kin relationships. However, it also played a key role in classical Western civilization, such as the Roman *collegia* (the members of which co-deputize each other to act in their interests), where such family relations were extended to emerging urban social formations. Modern forms of social health insurance also emphasize the shared responsibility of a community for its members' healthcare costs and thus supplement individual, usually risk-adjusted prepayments, with collectivized contributions, usually not risk adjusted, from the employer (formerly, from the guilds, such as the medieval German

---

[12] See Healthcare.gov, "Health Savings Account (HSA)," HealthCare.gov, 2019, https://www.healthcare.gov/glossary/health-savings-account-HSA/.

*knappschaften*) and/or from another actor such as the state. Most health systems in the world predominantly follow either the social or the national insurance model, although private health insurance can be found virtually everywhere. Many current critiques of social health insurance object to i) financing healthcare from a tax on wages assessed through payroll deductions and ii) limiting entitlement to those who contribute such payments through the formal sector. Although there is merit in these concerns, it is useful to take a ⌬ perspective on social health insurance: there is a valid sense in which individuals who share a profession, or employer, and who therefore tend to share a common set of beliefs and values, should manifest a sense of solidarity that is particularly acute.[13]

Accordingly, we can reimagine health insurance as a '⌬ good' as in *Social Markets*: one that exhibits supermodularity in group size (especially across those facing diverse risks or life situations), but not requiring or even benefiting from universal participation. A ⌬ good builds on the strength of common belief across diverse scales and shapes embodied by ⌬ publics (see our chapter *Association and ⌬ Publics*). Of note is that the social model of health insurance began with the fact of 'association', namely, the creation of shared space for the enactment of common belief, shielded from full public surveillance and financed by ⌬ mechanisms. This reconceptualization allows for a dramatic expansion in the scope and role of insurance: rather than simply offering savings, risk smoothing or redistribution, ⌬ insurance might be used to finance the *conditions required for* health, rather than

---

[13] Émile Durkheim, *De la Division du Travail Social* (Paris: Presses Universitaires de France, 1893).

merely the payment of services to treat disease or infirmity. The more strongly a community interacts, the more likely it is to face common environmental or behavioral health risks, whether from the spread of communicable diseases, the ensuring of safe working conditions, the social spread of practices of healthy living, or the creation of a healthy local natural environment. Health insurance might then look more like life insurance, and there is no strong reason for the two to be segmented and several strong reasons for them not to be.[14] Essentially, such an insurance fund could act as a mutual-aid society to foster coordination in the joint production of health rather than merely in its restoration: 'healthy minds in healthy bodies' but also healthy persons in healthy families and communities (see Figure A, above). Such a model, which we might call a "health production society", would ensure risk pooling and redistribution but could be much more relevant and effective at targeting the social determinants of health.

For example, it might be formed, in a developing country, to ensure the provision of clean water, sanitation, or adequate nutrition or in a wealthy country to mitigate the abuse of substances and ultra-processed foods that together account for 20 million global deaths a year.[15] The relevant needs are highly localized and, in fact, are often hard to address outside of a community context grounded in shared values, professional goals and belief systems. Or another such society might be formed on the global level for infections and globally transmissible diseases such as malaria, HIV or tuberculosis,

---

[14] Robin Hanson, *Buy Health, Not Health Care*, Cato Journal 14, 1 (1994):135-141, Summer.

[15] Anna Gilmore, Alice Fabbri, Fran Baum, Adam Bertscher, Krista Bondy, Ha-Joon Chang, Sandro Demaio, et al., "Defining and Conceptualising the Commercial Determinants of Health," *The Lancet* 401, no. 10383 (April 8, 2023): 1194-1213. https://doi.org/10.1016/S0140-6736(23)00013-2.

## 6-2 Health

such as the Global Fund to AIDS, Tuberculosis and Malaria. National reinsurers for local health production societies could help ensure that local networks most effective at interventions do not excessively fall prey to shared health risks. In short, a range of intersecting ⌗ health production societies could move beyond an atomistic, risk-based understanding of health to address the full range of social challenges in health, recognizing the pooling of risk as simply one example of supermodularity. Such societies would rely on the full host of technologies we have described above for building community consensus, common understanding/purpose and shielding action from outside surveillance (such as by a national insurer) that could undermine it.

### Health impact tokenization

For this discussion, *outputs* are the direct result of health services (e.g. people vaccinated); *outcomes* are the final intended result (e.g. deaths avoided through morbidity or mortality risk reduction); and *impacts* are the knock-on effects outcomes have in the world at large (e.g. future children born). Impact is thus an open-source commodity: it can be forked to whatever use the beneficiary can devise (Figure B). Although impacts are a *causal* effect of health services (e.g. a child who otherwise would have died did not, and then went on to be a parent), impacts are not the primary *intended* effect of health services. The primary intended effect of health services is reducing morbidity or mortality risk, which as we have seen is an insurance function. Health services, which produce non-market-traded outcomes (e.g. lives saved *and* healthier lives, through the insurance function) and market-traded and non-market-traded impacts (e.g. more labor to sell *and* more time for visits with friends, through the open-source function), thus have an accounting problem: it is hard to measure the value of outcomes (e.g. the value of a life saved) but it is often still harder to measure the value of relevant impacts. Thus, since the full social value of health projects is in practice never counted, let alone captured or rendered tradeable, many win-win health investments remain blocked.

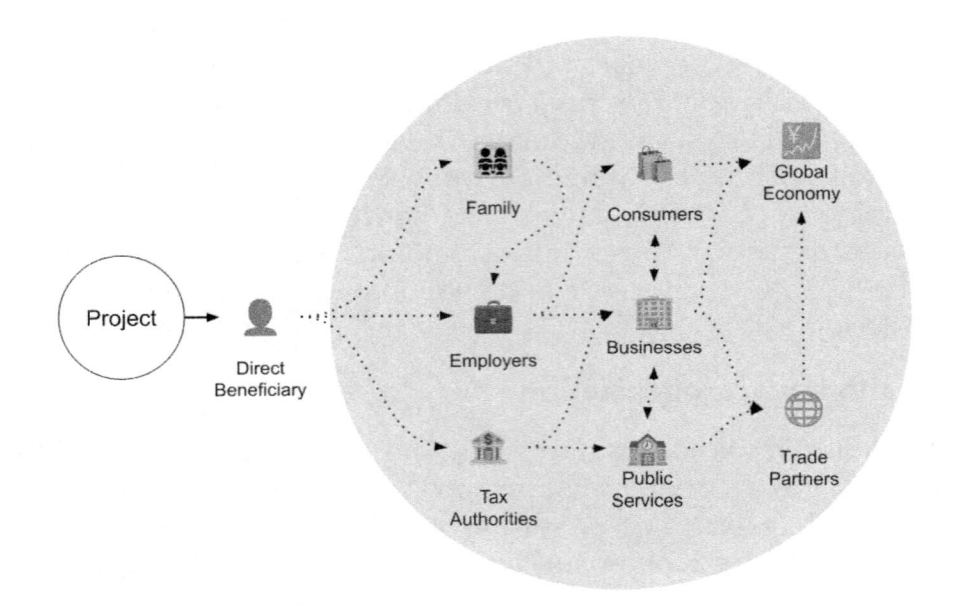

**Figure 6-2-B.** Different Pathways to Impact - Illustrating the knock-on effects that outcomes have in the world at large.

For example, the Global Fund claims to have saved 44 million lives over 20 years at a cumulative cost of $55.4 billion in disbursements plus approximately $6 billion in operating costs funded primarily by governments and philanthropists. Median estimates for the insurance value of a mortality risk reduction of this scale would come in at about $200 trillion dollars, attributing to the Global Fund an (undiscounted) outcomes-based return on investment (ROI) of over 3000:1. Accordingly, if the Global Fund could have captured a fraction of the insurance value of the outcomes it produced, it would be one of the most valuable entities in the world today, and everyone would want to buy its shares. In fact, everyone in the world already *does* own non-tradeable shares in the Global Fund, which pays out regular dividends in the form of reduced rates of disease contraction, increased economic growth and the benefits of loved ones living fuller lives among many other things. The question is how to raise revenue against these implicit, untraded shares to fund investment that can increase the benefits they pay out.[16]

1. We must be able to represent both the insurance and the broader social value of these investments. These can be tokenized based on digital certificates that use a combination of technocratic outcome evaluation, but also using "crowd-sourced" intelligence as highlighted, for example, in our 🗳 *Voting* chapter.
2. Build on this to coordinate fragmented funders and implementers through open impact pools that address the shortcomings noted with existing health financing. Develop an open coordination standard for subscription to pools that addresses the drawbacks of current health financing. Tokens can be used to participate in the governance of projects or of the funding pools. Projects can allocate tokens linked to contributions. Tokens can be used to participate in governance; to trade and invest; to exchange for selected services; or to fund further projects.
3. Harness generative foundation models (GFMs) and other applications to accelerate the process of forming such instruments and adapting them to investments. Through tokenization, bundling and trading, it can be

---

[16] In 2023, two of the contributors to this chapter created a Swiss-registered Association with the name *Unexia* that is pursuing the measures described here with a range of UN and other partner organizations.

made as simple to buy health impact as carbon credits. Tokens can be reinvested into projects or used to purchase health services according to a standardized impact model. Value can be linked to specific projects or aggregated into blocks, supporting the development of cascading ('fractal') health-impact markets.

## Incenting equitable benefit sharing

Health insurance consists of pooled mechanisms for the prepayment for health services that reduce mortality or morbidity risk, with a flexible element of benefit and risk redistribution. Benefit sharing in particular has bedeviled blended-finance agreements that promised to mobilize additional sources of funds from private, profit-seeking actors; instead of mobilizing new sources of funding, however, existing arrangements have tended to allow private investors to capture the benefits of public derisking while offering little or no financial incentive to ensure the active engagement of direct (or indirect) beneficiaries or to reward the commitment of, for example, biological, behavioral, or other services by stakeholders and participants. Open impact pools that allow for broad participation in governance including by beneficiaries themselves, and therefore also a broader entitlement to benefits through productizing benefit classes based on a standardized impact model, can more equitably distribute both risk and benefit and help incentivize the at-scale production of key goods.

## Deliberative tools for health cooperation

The world has experienced an increasing wave of pandemics, with 6 occurring already this century. In circumstances such as those in which COVID-19 emerged, one principle stands out: public health policy must be formulated in the presence of massive uncertainty about basic facts. For example, in early 2020, we knew we were confronted with two important unknowns: Q1. *How long would it take to develop an effective COVID vaccine?* and Q2. *Would populations tolerate the imposition of social distancing measures?* Policymakers got these questions badly wrong, estimating "at least 18 months" for the first and "no" for the second when "5 months" and "yes" were closer to correct. In fact, diverse publics worldwide largely led government response rather than following it during February and March of 2020.

If diffuse populations of individuals or loosely organized non-health associations, such as soccer clubs, can formulate *objectively better pandemic policy* than a government that is advised by the world's top epidemiological experts, then governments are turning a blind eye to a critical source of information and analysis. The use of online tools such as expert-elicitation databases maintained on a variety of collaborative, deliberative, voting or prediction-market (i.e. 'governance') technologies as we described in our chapter on *Augmented Deliberation* would have multiplied by orders of magnitude the power of 'the wisdom of the crowd'.[17] Indeed, in the long run, more important than 'getting policy right' is preserving social cohesion and public trust in policy-makers since without these 'policy' rapidly becomes meaningless anyway.

Taiwan followed a very different path, with rapid government support of citizen-led initiatives for, for example, tracking the supply of masks. By moving quickly to empower citizen-led online initiatives (g0v, Polis), Taiwan was able to harvest the power of localized and contextual knowledge as a 🔲 good without imposing centralized control while respecting privacy. Taiwan's "extitutional" approach was so successful that it has

---

[17] Kristin Shrader-Frechette, "Experts in Uncertainty: Opinion and Subjective Probability in Science.Roger M. Cooke," *Ethics* 103, no. 3 (April 1993): 599–601, https://doi.org/10.1086/293541.

now been institutionalized. With eloquent examples such as these, it follows that policymaking during the next novel pandemic will not be the sole prerogative of epidemiological experts in closed-room consultations, and that ⌬ technologies will be widely used for the large-scale formulation of and coordination around collective action.

In virtually every part of the world, healthcare is administered through a model originating in colonial powers, usually as a mirror of the forms of administration found in the respective imperial centers but with the additional mission of 'development' tacked on. Results have naturally been mixed. Nevertheless, in several former colonies, notably in Canada and Australia, concerted efforts are being made on the part of colonialist successor administrations to learn from Indigenous models of health and healthcare, to engage in the co-administration of healthcare and other health services in accordance with Indigenous community values, and to allow for the self-determination of solutions by Indigenous peoples. As these experiments remain few and far between, GFMs seem a promising tool to leverage the large and diffuse bodies of textual data produced in these initiatives for the purpose of interpreting, criticizing, reimagining, and eventually redesigning, systems of healthcare administration to be more responsive to cultural value systems. As discussed in our chapter on *Augmented Deliberation*, "points of view" that are held (albeit diffusely) by organizations and even entire cultures can be represented as an "individual" whose "synthetic wisdom" can be queried in real-time interactions, or who can be tasked with designing incentive-compatible healthcare and interventions along a post-colonial model.

## Post-symbolic communication for health

Brain computer interfaces (BCIs, see our chapter *Post-Symbolic Communication*) are not some futuristic fantasy of science fiction but familiar objects in common use. The usual operating system is that of the sensory and motor organs. Eyeglasses and hearing aids are low bitrate computing devices that interface (unidirectionally or write only) with our brains through the sensory organs; canes, crutches and wheelchairs are low bitrate mechanical computers that interface with the brain bidirectionally (i.e. read/write), through the intermediary of both the sensory and motor organs. Digital assistive devices, such as smart-phones or portable computers, are (slightly) higher bit-rate devices that interface with the brain (read/write) through the intermediary of the sensory-motor system (usually the visual, hearing and fine-motor systems) but also through higher-order domains of functioning such as speech (e.g. voice recognition), cognition (e.g. CAPTCHAs) and memory (e.g. passwords). These 'BCIs' interact through a range of input/output devices including keyboards, (touch)screens and a variety of other read/write interfaces. Such higher bit-rate digital computing tools have become for many people an indispensable part of what it means 'to be human': as anyone who has lost their smartphone knows, the experience is one of significant disability.

It would be futile to insist that such devices are not now an integral part of our (transhuman) personality.[18] Common applications of such technologies exist in the form of mobile health (e.g. text-message alerts, wearable devices, contact-tracing tools), telemedicine and telehealth (e.g. virtual fracture clinics)[19], and e-health (e.g. digital health records). It is natural

---

[18] Donna Haraway, "A Cyborg Manifesto: Science, Technology, and Socialist-Feminism in the Late Twentieth Century," in *Simians, Cyborgs and Women: The Reinvention of Nature* (New York; Routledge, 1991), pp. 149-181.

[19] Gillian Anderson, Paul Jenkins, David McDonald, Robert Van Der Meer, Alec Morton, Margaret Nugent, and Lech A Rymaszewski, "Cost Comparison of Orthopaedic Fracture Pathways Using Discrete Event

and obvious that the trend towards further modalities of interactivity, and higher bit-rate throughput, will have in time important implications for health, especially for visual, hearing, mobility, self-care, and speech disorders, notably through Extended Reality (XR) services. Biomedical engineering is already working to connect prosthetic devices at cellular level (i.e. bionics)[20], and BCIs hold out the corollary promise of allowing for such connectivity at cognitive, emotional and experiential level with, for example, powerful applications in speech and communication disorders, in the enhancement (or maintenance) of cognitive functions such as memory and, almost certainly, in novel applications for common mental disorders such as depression and anxiety, as well as for impulse control for addictive disorders.

Immersive shared reality (ISR) has thus far primarily been used in non-interpersonal medical settings, such as to de-risk medical training for health workers, much as flight simulators do for pilots. It is natural, however, to imagine the gamification of health-based ISR so as to incent the learning of complex cognitive, relational, and behavioral skills (such as self-care, self-insight, and self-management), as well as a suite of simulated interpersonal applications (see our *Immersive Shared Reality* chapter). Like the examples cited there, new horizons of simulated and non-simulated social interaction can

---

Simulation in a Glasgow Hospital," BMJ Open 7, no. 9 (September 2017): e014509, https://doi.org/10.1136/bmjopen-2016-014509.

[20] Laurent Frossard, Silvia Conforto, and Oskar Aszmann, "Editorial: Bionics Limb Prostheses: Advances in Clinical and Prosthetic Care Editorial on the Research Topic Bionic Limb Prostheses: Advances in Clinical and Prosthetic Care Context Importance of Residuum Health," *Frontiers in Rehabilitation Sciences* 3 (August 18, 2022). https://doi.org/10.3389/fresc.2022.950481.

be opened to those with disabilities that less immersive, lower-throughput, traditional assistive technologies cannot address.

## GFMs and data sharing to assist diagnosis and treatment

A human radiographer can at the upwards limit view and interpret perhaps as many one million diagnostic imaging scans during a lifetime of practice. While this is sufficient to achieve expert status in diagnosing common conditions, GFMs can fine-tune on datasets orders of magnitude larger and thus outperform human readers for the diagnosis of rarely seen conditions. Of course, human beings might specialize in such conditions and dedicate themselves to viewing a collection of many rare images, but the need for 🔲 technologies then becomes more acute: it seems impossible to imagine how large diagnostic databases of rare conditions can be compiled without established data-sharing practices across many image centers.

In this case too, we see diffuse pockets of diversity that show 'affinity' in terms of markers that cannot be organized into low-entropy pockets based merely on traditional variables such as place, profession, or parentage; in these cases, another organizing principle must be found, and online technologies are the obvious solution. Such technologies also need to respect privacy and confidentiality, both as a normative and legal principle. Various forms of privacy enhancing technologies (see our chapter *Association and 🔲 Publics*) such as zero- (or low-) knowledge proofs, allow for specific kinds of information to be reliably shared without over-sharing, helping enable simultaneous respect for medical privacy and large-scale data sharing.[21]

---

[21] Nicola Rieke et al. "The Future of Digital Health with Federated Learning" *npj Digital Medicine* 3 (2020): article 119.

In Web2 applications such as Facebook and Google, users "willingly" share their private information in exchange for the social benefits afforded by the platforms. That is, even knowing that their information is being harvested for profit by third-party entities, many individuals presumably still find that membership in online Web2 communities offers a net benefit. What if there was no trade-off between privacy and utility? What if accessing medical services did not incur an open-ended contingent liability for the privacy of the individual? Medical administrative data is 'safe' for everyone, until the system is hacked because of, for example, a phishing attack: in the long run, we all face data theft with Web2 systems. Rethinking medical practice (which requires patient data for the patient's own benefit) and medical research (which requires patient data for the benefit of others) to build in cryptographic principles from the foundation is an essential part of the Web3 project, with important health implications: no doubt some diseases today are still fatal only because of our failure to build such applications.

Extending the diagnostic example, medical notes of all kinds (e.g. admission, treatment, discharge) forming a part of a patient's record are a potentially vast source of information about care and outcomes that is not only highly diffuse and unstructured but also virtually unqueryable outside of a set of specific and restricted medicolegal contexts. If there is a way to extract weak, or highly confounded, signals as the basis for novel causal insights, GFMs are perhaps the only technology that might do so. Variations in medical practice and outcomes should in principle make it possible to identify and extract the relevant counterfactual, much as - at population level - regression discontinuity design does. Such practices could transform a variety of medical practices, such as making post-approval regulatory changes far more dynamic and adaptive.

## 6-2 Health

Given the enormous value currently 'left on the table' by the under-production of health, it is critical that ⌬ technologies increasingly be used to:

- Unlock successive layers of value for health funders, implementers, and beneficiaries.
- Attract a broader group of health funders, implementers, and beneficiaries who will want to work with novel mechanisms to coordinate around funding and production of health goods.
- Empower the construction of health-oriented communities of practice by funders, implementers, and beneficiaries.
- Ensure the reciprocal, symmetric, and equitable governance of pooled, co-created health assets by funders, implementers, and beneficiaries.
- Enable new forms of international, regional and local cooperation in the co-production of health.
- Unlock new avenues for healthy human (and transhuman) functioning.

The blockers noted above (lack of financing, missing markets, coordination failures, missing communities, misaligned incentives, and lack of enabling services) will be overcome, and the dark clouds blocking the path to another 20 years of healthy life expectancy will dissipate the world over.

## 6-3 Media

Immersive and telepathic media experiences promise to transform connection across difference, making the experiences of the marginalized as palpable to us as those of our neighbors. Collaborative journalism promises to increase by an order of magnitude the number of citizens who can meaningfully contribute to shaping our shared narration of history as it happens. Cryptographic securing of sources can increase freedom of the press, the equivalent of moving every country up a category (viz. from Satisfactory to Good in the Reporters without Borders World Press Freedom Index) by lessening the trade-offs between source confidentiality and state secrecy. Creating a more 數位 structure of attention allocation and business models to support it could at least undo the rise in affective polarization in many jurisdictions and possibly reduce them to the levels seen today in the least polarized jurisdictions like Taiwan and the Netherlands.

---

The direct experiences most of us have in our everyday lives exposes us to only a tiny sliver of global affairs. Almost everything we believe we know beyond this is mediated through relationships, schooling and, most of the time, "media", especially journalism (radio, television, newspapers) and social media, as well as directed small or large group communications such as email and group chats. An important promise of digital technology has been to transform media, a possibility we take up here with keen awareness of the dangers and harms to media that are widely attributed to digital technology and social media. We explore how 數位 could help correct many of these harms and help achieve something of the potential that internet pioneers like J. C. R. Licklider and Robert Taylor saw in digital media.[1]

In particular, we highlight how the coming tide of 🝔 may help increase empathy across social distance even more dramatically than photography and television did; how it could increase by an order of magnitude or more the number of people who can meaningfully and helpfully participate in the journalistic process; how it could help restore level of trust in media, as well as norms of respect for confidentiality, much of the way towards what they were at their mid-twentieth-century peak; how they could they could undo most of the rises in levels of "affective polarization" (viz. dislike across lines of political division) not just within national polities but across a range of other social organizations; and how it could help restore sustainable and aligned funding for media. In short, we show how 🝔 can help address and reverse many of the crises media face today.

## Walking in others' shoes

As noted above, a central role of journalism is to allow people to experience the events and sensations of parts of the world they may never visit. Every generation of technology has made this more vivid and thus created a "smaller world". Abolitionists like Frederick Douglass harnessed photography to bring the experience of slaves to Northerner whites.[2] Radio helped make the Great War a truly World War by allowing the sounds of conflict to echo around the world. Television

---

[1] Licklider and Taylor, op. cit.

[2] John Stauffer, Zoe Trodd, and Celeste-Marie Bernier, *Picturing Frederick Douglass: An Illustrated Biography of the Nineteenth Century's Most Photographed American* (New York: Liveright, 2015).

allowed millions to share Neil Armstrong's landing on the moon.

Immersive shared reality promise to create even deeper empathetic connections. Journalists may soon be able to bridge social divides with vivid empathy as never before. While they have reached a limited audience so far given the image quality and nausea-related challenges of existing virtual reality (VR) headsets, journalists and artists have already begun to pioneer a variety of empathetic VR experiences. Examples include Milica Zec and Winslow Porter's work to help people experience life as non-human life like a tree, Decontee Davis's portrait of one of the world's most horrific diseases from the eyes of an Ebola survivor and Yasmin Eyalat's animated immersion within the world of cyber-security.[3]

Yet these are only the first successful forays into an emerging medium. As shared reality technologies branch out into other senses (smell, touch, and taste), far more complete multisensory connections will be possible with even more surprising and enlightening results. Brain interfaces will be transformative in a way that is hard to even describe. The future of journalism empowering us to know things that are profoundly different is therefore bright.

**Citizen co-journalism**

One of the most important trends in the production of journalism in the internet era has been the rise of so-called "citizen journalism" and the allied "open-source intelligence" movement, both of which aim to empower a much broader diversity of people than those traditionally employed as formal journalists or intelligence analysts to document important

---

[3] Milica Zec and Winslow Porter, *Tree* (2017). Decontee Davis, *Surviving Ebola* (2015). Yasmin Elayat, *Zero Days VR* (2017).

events in the world around them. Such journalism has been central to documenting many of the most important events in recent years, from terrorist attacks to wars and police abuse. Yet it also faces significant criticism and social concern over bias, rigor of verification of facts and legibility and digestibility.

It is easy to see how many recent technological developments could dramatically exacerbate these problems. Generative foundation models (GFMs) will make the production of realistic fakes far easier and will spread distrust of any material without rigorous, multi-source validation. The echo chambers of anti-social media will allow fakes to spread even absent such vetting, proliferating misleading content and the conditions under which people believe it.

Yet there are equally clear precedents for how technology could offset these challenges. Wikipedia has shown the speed and scale at which distributed participation can produce roughly and broadly consensual accounts of many events, though not quite yet at the speed required of journalism. Many of the tools we have described above, and detail below, can help address challenges of rigorous verification at distance and scale and rapid achievement of rough and socially contextual consensus that is a more appropriate frame for thinking about "objectivity".

Perhaps one of the most interesting possibilities, though, is the way in which GFMs may allow for a new form of coherent, digestible, broadly traveling and yet authentic community voice. There is a long-standing tension in journalism between allowing a community to "speak for itself" (often through quotes or extended descriptions of community practices) and crafting a compelling narrative digestible to the target audience, and an even greater one that arises when articles are translated for other audiences. GFMs will increasingly allow communities to finesse these trade-offs, as they can learn from and synthesize the speech patterns of community members, incorporate verified facts and at the same time smoothly translate to a range of languages and subcultural standards and styles. This will empower groups of citizens who are not trained as journalists to convey the important stories they have to tell with precision and clarity to diverse publics.

## Cryptographically secure sources

One of the most frequently dramatized tensions in journalism surrounds the role of source confidentiality. Confidentiality obligations to the subject of the report are often broken by a confidential source to create the credibility of reports. Journalists must verify the authenticity of their sources and the information they provide, while ensuring their secrecy from (among others) the organizations they inform on and the credibility of their report to the public. In many cases, confidential informants are sharing information that the norms of their organization prohibit them from sharing. This creates strong tensions between many of the values we have highlighted above: protecting the associations, ensuring the integrity of the public sphere, etc. How might the tools of 數位 help navigate these challenging waters?

Many parts of the above process are naturally facilitated by the tools we highlight in the *"Identity and Personhood"* and *"Association and 數位 Publics"* chapters. Most of the tools for protecting 數位 publics could be applied by organizations to reduce the credibility of documents shared outside their intended social context. At the same time, zero-knowledge proofs (ZKPs) based on public credentials could allow sources to remain confidential even to journalists while proving (elements of) their position to journalists' audiences. Yet, absent some reconciliation, such strategies could quickly become an "arms race", escalating cryptography without arriving at a better social outcome.

A potential resolution of this impasse arises from the subtle distinctions these protocols make regarding verification. If someone publicly holds a position in an organization, they will typically be able to prove this to others using a ZKP without revealing other elements of their identity. They may then be able to harness the associated reputation, but no more, to make claims about things occurring in the organization. But for more sensitive information and expansive claims, especially if the person only holds a relatively low position in the organization, additional verification will usually be required to make this credible. One way is by revealing more (public) information about themselves, but this will narrow the pool of people they could be and thus expose them. Another is to provide direct verification ("receipts") of the claims. However, if these receipts are protected by technologies like designated verifier signatures, this is only possible by exposing their "private key" to another person (e.g. the journalist or legal authority), which puts them at risk of exploitation or exposure by that other person unless she is herself highly trustworthy.

Of course, the precise details vary greatly depending on which precise tools are used by each participant in this dance. But overall, it illustrates how cryptography can simultaneously allow for a quite intricate mix of trustworthy and private disclosures, protection of community norms of confidentiality and the ability to override these norms at personal cost in a broader social interest when critical.

## Stories that bring us together

While many Americans look back with nostalgia on the history of the press, the era of "press responsibility" against which they judge the harms of anti-social media, dates only to the 1940s. This was when the "Hutchins Commission on Freedom of the Press" developed a code of social responsibility under which the press would act as the "common carriers of public discussion", creating a baseline of shared understanding on which public debate could proceed.[4] That commission argued that a central role of a free press in a democratic society is to clarify to all citizens both the points of consensus (viz. the "Walter Cronkite effect" of commonly watched, consensual news) and fact and those of divergence (viz. the "fairness doctrine" and practice of balancing diverging perspectives) to allow self-government to thrive. While many appreciate what this era achieved at the national level for one country, the essence of 數位 is that we live (especially today) in a much richer and more diverse world, with many loci of democracy across, between, within and beyond nations. Whatever the many failings of social media, one thing it has achieved is to allow this diversity to shape the media ecosystem. How might it do this while still being pro-social media in the sense of the Hutchins report?

Our *Augmented Deliberation* chapter above suggests a natural strategy. Social media algorithms could create "communities" based both on patterns of behavior internal to the platform (e.g. views, likes, responses, propagation, choices to join) and on external data such as social science or group explicit self-identification (more on this below). For each such community, the algorithms could highlight "common content" (commonly agreed facts and values) of the group that span the divides internally, as well as important points of division within the community. Content could then be highlighted to members of the communities within this social context, making clear which content is rough consensus in communities that citizen is a member and which content is divisive, as well as offering opportunities for the citizen to explore content that is

---

[4] The Commission on Freedom of the Press, *A Free and Responsible Press: A General Report on Mass Communications* (Chicago: University of Chicago Press, 1947).

consensus on the other side of each divide from the one she is on within that community.

Such a design would continue to offer individuals and communities the agency social media affords them to respectively shape their own intersectional identities and self-govern. Yet at the same time it would avoid the rampant "false consensus" effect where netizens come to believe that extreme or idiosyncratic views are widely shared, fueling demonization of those who do not share them and a feeling of resentment when associated political outcomes are not achieved or "pluralistic ignorance" where netizens are unable to act collectively on "silent majority" views.[5] Furthermore, and perhaps most importantly, it would reshape the incentives of journalists and other creators away from divisive content and towards stories that bring us together. It is relevant beyond

---

[5] Gary Marks and Norman Miller, "Ten Years of Research on the False-Consensus Effect: An Empirical and Theoretical Review, *Psyhcological Bulletin* 102, no. 1: 72-90. Deborah A. Prentice and Dale T. Miller, "Pluralistic Ignorance and the Perpetuation of Social Norms by Unwitting Actors", *Advances in Social Psychology* 28 (1996): 161-209. An example of false consensus is that many observers believe SARS-Cov-2 escaped from a laboratory ('lab leak' hypothesis). The rationalist web site *Rootclaim* even assessed 'lab leak' at 89% probability (~8 to 1 in favour). Subsequently, educated laypersons were exposed to the evidence in over 18 hours of adversarial debate and found posterior probabilities on the order of ~800 to 1 *against* lab leak, implying a Bayes factor of ~100,000 to 1 against lab leak. Despite the strength of the evidence, the lab leak claim persists since not only does zoonosis lack emotional resonance but it also requires hard work to evaluate and offers no cathartic pay-off. Similarly, due to pluralistic ignorance, despite the fact that more than 81 million people in the United States voted for Joe Biden in 2020, a small crowd of several thousand highly motivated individuals almost succeeded in disrupting the Electoral College vote count on 6 January 2021. Jonathan E. Pekar et al., "The Molecular Epidemiology of Multiple Zoonotic Origins of SARS-CoV-2", *Science* 377, no. 6609 960-966. Michael Worobey et al., "The Huanan Seafood Wholesale Market in Wuhan was the Early Epicenter of the COVID-19 Pandemic", *Science* 377, no. 6609: 951-959.

"hard journalism" *per se* as many other cultural forms (e.g. music) benefit from audiences who want to share cultural objects and fandom with others.

## public media

The recommendations of the Hutchins Commission were largely adopted by leading media outlets as part of the then-prominent campaign for "social responsibility", which has recently made a comeback in the form of commitments to "environmental, social and governance" (ESG) goals among many companies. Yet a firmer foundation for encouraging such responsibility would be to align the funding sources of media more closely with the pro-social design goals above.

Neither individual subscriptions nor advertising offer a particularly promising path here, as both aim to appeal to *consumers* rather than *citizens* of diverse communities, and thus encourage serving consumers only the "dessert" they are tempted by rather than balancing this with the "vegetables" that bring them together with their communities. If we want social media to bring us together, we should aspire for it to be funded by organizations with a dedicated interest in achieving that goal: collective organizations including churches, civic associations, governments at many levels, charities, universities, corporations etc.

Replacing advertising with funding from a diversity of communities does not require much of a stretch of imagination from existing business models in adjacent industries. One of the largest and most profitable business models, pursued by corporations like Microsoft and Slack, is selling productivity software, which often includes social media-like components, to companies to boost productivity. These companies have no interest in "engaged" or polarized employees; the goal of the tools is to bring employees together to accomplish shared goals and adjust to change. A new, pro-social media model could thus naturally be incubated in such settings and then sold, in broader social contexts, to other organizations interested in solidarity and dynamism.

Furthermore, there are good reasons to believe such organizations could afford to displace advertising revenue. Most democratic governments (e.g. Germany, Finland, United States) spend more than a billion dollars a year supporting public media and far more than that subsidizing other culture.[6] Even religious media received more than $100 million in the United States alone in 2022.[7] This compares to roughly $5 billion in advertising revenue earned by X in 2022, at its peak.[8] It thus seems quite plausible that, together, a range of community representative organizations could replace advertising as a revenue stream, if community leaders focused on this space and social media channeled its attention to this new business model.

This might play out in a variety of ways, but a simple one would be for participants to opt into a set of communities they identify with. Each would "sponsor" their community members' use in exchange for the prioritization for their members' attention to the community-relevant content we discussed above. Users

---

[6] Kleis Nielsen, Rasmus, and Geert Linnebank, "Public Support for the Media: A Six-Country Overview of Direct and Indirect Subsidies," (Oxfordshire: Reuters Institute for the Study of Journalism: University of Oxford, 2011), https://reutersinstitute.politics.ox.ac.uk/sites/default/files/2017-11/Public%20support%20for%20Media.pdf.

[7] "Grants for Religious Media Organizations," Cause IQ, n.d., https://www.causeiq.com/directory/grants/grants-for-religious-media-organizations/.

[8] "Advertising Revenue of X (Formerly Twitter) Worldwide from 2017 to 2027," Statista, 2023, *https://www.statista.com/statistics/271337/twitters-advertising-revenue-worldwide/*.

數位 Plurality: Part 6: Impact

who did not sign up for communities paying sufficiently might have to accept some amount of advertising or pay a subscription fee, and the service could identify from its own patterns communities and approach their leaders to ask for payment. In short, social media might become a more ⌬ version of public media.

Overall, the examples above show how ⌬ can empower a new pro-social, ⌬ media environment: one where we can connect deeply with others from very different backgrounds as us, where people come together to tell their stories in authoritative and verifiable ways without compromising community or individual privacy and where we come to understand what unites and divides us in the interests of the dynamism and solidarity of all our communities.

# 6-4 Environment

🔲 may be even more core to addressing the most pressing environmental problems we face, from climate change to biodiversity loss, than even "green technologies" like clean energy are, because it provides a basis both for cooperation on developing those technologies and for establishing a positive communication with natural features that represents their interests in social decisions. As such, 🔲 may be central to the survival of the earth as a human-supporting habitat.

---

What does "Collaboration Across Difference" have to do with the environment? Local legends, stories, traditional religions, and many contemporary religions, spanning the length of human history, emphasize nature as a target of respect and a participant in cooperation with just as much as other humans are.

This chapter explores how 🔲 can transform our technological relationship with nature. In the past, technology has often been conceived of as a means to master nature, just as sometimes technology has previously been seen as a means to master fellow humans. Instead, we explore how 🔲 can facilitate communication, cooperation, and synergy with nature, empowered by data. Whether we see these ecosystems as alive and sentient, or as indispensable life-support systems for human societies, these approaches will enable us to co-exist with nature more sustainably.

Human activities – particularly our reliance on non-renewable energy sources – have profoundly altered the Earth since the 1950s. Deforestation, global warming, ocean acidification, and mass extinctions have all escalated as the climate changes. At the beginning of the 21st century, Nobel laureate Paul Jozef

Crutzen proposed the term "Anthropocene" to recognize this new epoch driven primarily by human influence.[1] Biodiversity has plummeted; between 2001 and 2014 alone, approximately 173 species vanished—25 times the historical extinction rate. During the 20th century, some 543 vertebrate species disappeared, an event that would typically unfold over 10,000 years.[2]

Of course, we humans are not immune to the effects. Air pollution alone kills nearly 6.7 million people every year, including half a million infants. In severely polluted countries, average life expectancy falls by up to six years.[3]

## Data coalitions for environmental action

Climate, air quality, and water data, which often rely on government agencies for input and maintenance, are resources that benefit each other internationally. Environmental awareness has become a distinctive feature of the implementation of the UN's Sustainable Development Goals, driven by open data organizations and environmental groups. The civic technology movement has opened a new space for digital social engagement; not simply providing tools, but also actively supporting civil society to work with the government to

---

[1] Will Steffan, Paul J. Crutzen and John R. McNeill, "The Anthropocene: Are Humans Now Overwhelming the Great Forces of Nature?" in Ross E. Dunn, Laura J. Mitchell and Kerry Ward, eds., *The New World History* (Berkeley, CA: University of California Press, 2016). Note that this proposal was recently rejected by the International Union of Geological Sciences.

[2] Gerardo Ceballos, Paul R. Ehrlich, and Peter H. Raven, "Vertebrates on the Brink as Indicators of Biological Annihilation and the Sixth Mass Extinction", *Proceedings of the National Academy of Sciences* 117, no. 24: 13596-13602.

[3] World Health Organization, "Air Pollution Resource Guide" at https://www.who.int/health-topics/air-pollution#tab=tab_1.

create more environmental knowledge, which can then be developed into a public movement that coordinates the interests of multiple parties.

In Taiwan, the Location Aware Sensor System (LASS), an open-source environment sensing network, empowers ordinary citizens to gather and share information freely, developing into a model of digital communication that incorporates local wisdom through citizen science. Instead of relying on authoritative organizations to shape public perceptions, LASS embraces direct action, extending community values into environmental care.

This type of citizen science community, which covers air, forest, and river sensing, is based on the spirit of open-source rainmaking, and contributes to the "Civil IoT" data coalition, which provides real-time sensing information updated every 3-5 minutes across the country, serving as a common ground for activists, and making it easier for ideas to solve problems to be examined and disseminated.

Data coalitions are interconnected with social movement-based civic technologies; a series of hackathon-themed fields have begun around the globe that will serve as mutually supportive gateways for mobility, acting as a technological conduit between natural environments and volunteers, and facilitating collective action on a global scale. It can be argued that the nature of collaborative networks is not just about information gathering and value re-engineering, but also about the foundation of community knowledge systems and the promotion of environmental justice.

Before conservationism was a widespread concept, conservative thinkers like Edmund Burke saw community groups as 'little platoons' – social hubs situated between individuals and the state.[4] Effective communication and cultivation are particularly important given that environmental problems often hit the most vulnerable first and hardest, such as low-income families or indigenous communities. The key is to ensure, through law and policy, that community members have an equal participation and voice in the development, resource allocation and implementation process, and that they are transformed from research subjects to data-driven actors.

**Conversations with nature**

Recent years have seen a growing movement to grant waterways 'natural legal personhood'. These waterways, with inherent rights and appointed guardians, include the Magpie River (Muteshekau Shipu) in Canada, the Whanganui in New Zealand, and the Ganga and Yamuna rivers in India.[5] This signifies a shared commitment to preserving these ecosystems for future generations.

Shared data can be transformed by data coalitions using generative foundation models (GFMs) into means of conversation with nature. These can serve as valuable tools for knowledge sharing and collective problem-solving regarding complex, cross-border problems. In promoting environmental sustainability, GFMs demonstrate a new model of co-existence between technology and humanity. As environmental data flows through verifiable relationships, it generates value (e.g., air and water quality monitoring), sending pulses of images,

---

[4] Edmund Burke, *Reflections on the Revolution in France and on the Proceedings in Certain Societies in London Relative to that Event* (London: James Dodley, 1790).

[5] Mihnea Tanasescu, "When a River is a Person: From Ecuador to New Zealand, Nature Gets its Day in Court", *Open Rivers* 8, Fall 2017 at https://openrivers.lib.umn.edu/article/when-a-river-is-a-person-from-ecuador-to-new-zealand-nature-gets-its-day-in-court.

sounds, and messages to engage people, offering real-time feedback to ideas, and encouraging more nature-conscious partners to join the effort.

It is important to emphasize that such advances can promote a mutually beneficial cocreation relationship, allowing all parties to work more closely together with the common goal of protecting the planet. Particularly in addressing trans-jurisdictional environmental issues, they offer unprecedented opportunities to analyze and address complex challenges such as global climate change, biodiversity loss and water management. By engaging in direct dialogues with nature, we can better understand environmental change and develop effective strategies and solutions based on it.

**Co-governance across borders**

Fluidity defines our natural world: oceans, rivers, and the atmosphere flow without regard for borders. Environmental solutions must transcend rigid hierarchical approaches that work within single towns, cities, or even countries. In response, we can draw from civic hacking culture, which celebrates cross-disciplinary teamwork among programmers, designers, and citizens across diverse communities.

Building GFMs models for natural environments involves challenges: open-source governance, capital and compute investments, and collaboration are key. Through GFMs, we can unlock deeper insights into our complex natural world. Scientific research and environmental management benefit from these insights, improving both and potentially reshaping society, as we have seen in the US National Aeronautics and Space Administration's ongoing collaboration with IBM on a Geospatial Foundation Model based on NASA's earth observation data, tackling crucial notions of environmental justice for natural spaces and human communities alike.[6]

Just as biometrics and sociometrics help establish identity, we need better ways to establish and protect the identity of natural ecosystems like rivers. A new conceptualization of identity is in order – one that factors in the connections between individual people and the ecosystems they rely on. ⌗publics, as explored earlier in this book, also establish and protect identity of collective entities, often devoted to cultural and care relationships. Some of these relate to natural ecosystems and can offer a foundation for conceptualizing the identity of such an ecosystem.

Notably, this perspective transcends the often-contentious debate around whether GFM systems can become legal agents; data coalitions can be viewed both as "little platoons" created by the people who benefit from the ecosystem, but also at the same time, through the legal positioning of natural personhood, the river's digital twin can be seen as a subject with rights and responsibilities. Similarly, a GFM created for whatever purpose of, by and for a community can exist both as a "person" and as a shared ⌗ good, depending on the perspective one adopts.

---

[6] Josh Blumenfeld, "NASA and IBM Openly Release Geospatial AI Foundation Model for NASA Earth Observation Data", *NASA Earth Data* August 3, 2023 at https://www.earthdata.nasa.gov/news/impact-ibm-hls-foundation-model.

# Part 7: Forward
## 7-0 Policy

If ⬚ succeeds, in a decade we imagine a transformed relationship among and across governments, private technology development and open source/civil society. In this future, public funding (both from governments and charitable initiatives) is the primary source of financial support for fundamental digital protocols, while the provision of such protocols in turn becomes a central item on the agenda of governments and charitable actors. This infrastructure is developed transnationally, by civil society collaborations and standard setting organizations supported by an international network of government leaders focused on these goals. The fabric created by these networks and the open protocols they develop, standardize, safeguard, and become the foundation for a new "international rules-based order", an operating system for a transnational ⬚ society.

Making these a bit more precise opens our eyes to how different such a future could be. Today, most research and development generally and software development occurs in for-profit private corporations. What little (half a percent of GDP in an average OECD country) funding is spent on research and development by governments is primarily non-digital and overwhelmingly funds "basic research." This contrasts with open-source code and protocols that can directly be used by most citizens, civil groups, and businesses. Spending on public software R&D pales by comparison to the several percent of GDP most countries spend on physical infrastructure.

In the future, we imagine that governments and charities will ensure we devote roughly 1% of GDP to digital public research, development, protocols, and infrastructure, amounting to nearly a trillion US dollars a year globally or roughly half of current global investment in information technology. This would increase public investment by at least two orders of magnitude and, given how much volunteer investment even limited financial investment in open-source software and other public investment has been able to stimulate, completely change the character of digital industries: the "digital economy" would become a 數位 society. Furthermore, public sector investment has primarily taken place on a national or regional (e.g. European Union) level and is largely obscured by broader publics. The investment we imagine would, like research collaborations, private investment, and open-source development, be undertaken by transnational networks aiming to create internationally inter-operable applications and standards like today's internet protocols. It would be at least as much a focus for the public as recently hyped technologies such as AI and crypto.

---

As we emphasized in the previous section, 數位 innovation does not take policy by a single government as a primary starting point: it proceeds from a variety of institutions of diverse and usually middling sizes outward. Yet governments are central institutions around the world, directing a large share of economic resources directly and shaping the allocation of much more. We cannot imagine a path to 數位 without the participation of governments as both users of 數位 technology and supporters of the development of 數位.

Of course, a full such embrace would be a process, just as 數位 is, and would eventually transform the very nature of governments. Because much of the book so far has gestured at what this would mean, in this chapter we instead focus on a vision of what might take place in the next decade to achieve the future we imagined above. While the policy directive we sketch is grounded in a variety of precedents (such as ARPA, Taiwan, and to a lesser extent India) that we have highlighted above, it does not directly follow any of the standard models employed by "great powers" today, instead drawing, combining, and extending elements from each to form a more ambitious agenda than any of these are today pursuing. To provide context, we therefore begin with a stylized description of these "models" before drawing lessons from historical models. We describe how these can be adapted to the global scope of today's transnational networks, how such investments can be financially supported and sustained, and finally the path to building the social and political support these policies will need, on which the next chapter focuses.

**Digital empires**

The most widely understood models of technology policy today are captured by legal scholar Anu Bradford in her *Digital Empires*.[1] In the US and the large fraction of the world that consumes its technology exports, technology development is dominated by a simplistic, private sector-driven, neoliberal free market model. In People's Republic of China (PRC) and consumers of its exports, technology development is steered heavily by the state towards national goals revolving around sovereignty, development, and national security. In Europe, the primary focus has been on regulation of technology imports from abroad to ensure they protect European standards of fundamental human rights, forcing others to comply with this "Brussels effect". While this trichotomy is a bit stereotyped and each jurisdiction incorporates elements of each of these

---

[1] Anu Bradford, *Digital Empires: The Global Battle to Regulate Technology* (Oxford, UK: Oxford University Press, 2023).

strategies, the outlines are a useful foil for considering the alternative model we want to describe.

The US model has been driven by a broad trend widely documented since the 1970s for government and the civil sector to disengage from the economy and technology development, focusing instead on "welfare" and national defense functions.[2] Despite pioneering the ARPANET, the US privatized almost all further development of personal computing, operating systems, physical and social networking and cloud infrastructure.[3] As the private monopolies predicted by J.C.R. Licklider (Lick) came to fill these spaces, US regulators primarily responded with antitrust actions that, while influencing market dynamics in a few cases (such as the Microsoft actions) were generally understood as too little too late.[4] In particular, they are seen as having allowed monopolistic dominance or tight oligopoly to emerge in the search, smartphone application, cloud services and several operating systems markets. More recently, American antitrust regulators under the leadership of the "New Brandeis" movement have doubled down on the primary use of antitrust instruments with limited success in court and have seen the challenges of emerging monopolies only expand in the market for chips and generative foundation models.[5]

---

[2] Daniel Yergin and Joseph Stanislaw, *The Commanding Heights: The Battle for the World Economy* (New York: Touchstone, 2002).

[3] Tarnoff, op. cit.

[4] Licklider, "Comptuers and Government", op. cit. Thomas Philippon, *The Great Reversal* (Cambridge, MA: Harvard University Press, 2019).

[5] Lina Khan, "The New Brandeis Movement: America's Antimonopoly Debate", *Journal of European Competition Law and Practice* 9, no. 3 (2018): 131-132. Akush Khandori, "Lina Khan's Rough Year," *New York Magazine Intelligencer* December 12, 2023 at

The primary rival model to the US has been the PRC, where the Central Committee of the Chinese Communist Party (CCP) has drafted a series of Five-Year plans that have increasingly in recent years directed a variety of levers of state power to invest in and shape the direction of technology development.[6] These coordinated regulatory actions, party-driven directives to domestic technology companies and primarily government-driven investments in research and development have dramatically steered the direction of Chinese technology development in recent years away from commercial and consumer applications towards hard and physical technology, national security, chip development and surveillance technologies. Investment that has paralleled the US, such as into large foundation models, has been tightly and directly steered by government, ensuring consistency with priorities on censorship and monitoring of dissent. A consistent crackdown on business activity not forming part of this vision has led to a dramatic fall in activity in much of the Chinese technology sector in recent years, especially around financial technology including Web3.

In contrast to the US and the PRC, the European Union (EU) and United Kingdom (UK) have (despite a few notable exceptions) primarily acted as importers of technical frameworks produced by these two geopolitical powers. The EU has tried to harness its bargaining power in that role, however, to act as a "regulatory powerhouse", intervening to protect the interests of human rights that it fears the other two powers often ignore in their race for technological supremacy. This has included setting the global standard for privacy regulation with their

---

https://nymag.com/intelligencer/2023/12/lina-khans-rough-year-running-the-federal-trade-commission.html.

[6] Central Committee of the Chinese Communist Party, *14th Five-Year Plan*, March 2021; translation available at https://cset.georgetown.edu/publication/china-14th-five-year-plan/.

General Data Protection Regulation, taking the lead on regulation of generative foundation models (GFMs) with their AI Act, and helping shape the standards for competitive marketplaces with a series of recent ex-ante competition regulations including the Digital Services Act, the Digital Markets Act and the Data Act. While these have not defined an alternative positive technological model, they have constrained and shaped the behavior of both US and Chinese firms who seek to sell into the European market. The EU also aspires to tight interoperability across the markets they serve, often leading to copycat legislation in other jurisdictions.

## A road less traveled

Just as Taiwan's Yushan (Jade) Mountain rises from the intersection of the Eurasian and Pacific tectonic plates, the policy approach we surveyed in our *Life of a Digital Democracy* chapter from its peak arises from the intersection of the philosophies behind these three digital empires as illustrated in Figure A. From the US model, Taiwan has drawn the emphasis on a dynamic, decentralized, free, entrepreneurial ecosystem open to the world that generates scalable and exportable technologies, especially within the open-source ecosystem. From the European model, it has drawn a focus on human rights and democracy as the fundamental aspirations both for the development of basic digital public infrastructure and on which the rest of the digital ecosystem depends. From the PRC model, it has drawn the importance of public investment to proactively advance technology, steering it toward societal interests.

7-0 Policy

**Figure 7-0-A.** An illustration of how the Taiwan policy model emerges from the intersection of PRC, US, and EU competing alternatives. Source: generated by authors, harnessing logos from the Noun Project by Gan Khoon Lay, Alexis Lilly, Adrien Coquet and Rusma Trari Handini under CC BY 3.0 at https://thenounproject.com/.

Together these add up to a model where the public sector's primary role is *active investment and support* to empower and protect *privately complemented but civil society-led, technology development* whose goal is *proactively* building a digital stack that *embodies in protocols principles of human rights and democracy*.

The Presidential Hackathon in Taiwan is a prime example of this unique model, blending public-sector support with civil society innovation. Since its inception in 2018, this annual event has drawn thousands of social innovators and public servants, as well as teams from numerous countries, all collaborating to enhance Taiwan's 🖥 infrastructure. Each year, five outstanding teams are honored with a presidential commitment to support their initiatives in the upcoming fiscal year – elevating successful local-scale experiments to the level of national infrastructure projects.

A key feature of the Presidential Hackathon is its use of quadratic voting for public participation in selecting the top 20 teams. This elevates the event beyond mere competition, transforming it into a powerful coalition-building platform for civil society leadership. For instance, environmental groups focused on monitoring water and air pollution saw their contributions gain national prominence through the Civil IoT project – backed by a significant investment of US $160 million – showcasing how the Taiwan model effectively amplifies the impact and reach of grassroots initiatives.

## Lessons from the past

Of course, the "Taiwan model" did not emerge *de novo* over the last decade. Instead, as we have highlighted above, it built on the synthesis of the Taiwanese tradition of public support for cooperative enterprise and civil society (see our *A View from Yushan* chapter) with the model that built the internet at the United States Department of Defense's Advanced Research Projects Agency (ARPA), which we highlighted in *The Lost Dao*. At a moment when the US and many other advanced economies are turning away from "neoliberalism" and towards "industrial policy", the ARPA story holds crucial lessons and cautions.

On the one hand, ARPA's Information Processing Techniques Office (IPTO) led by Lick is perhaps the most successful example of industrial policy in American and perhaps world history. IPTO provided seed funding for the development of a network of university-based computer interaction projects at the Massachusetts Institute of Technology (MIT), Stanford, University of California Berkeley, Carnegie Technical Schools (now Carnegie Mellon University or CMU) and University of California Los Angeles. Among the remarkable outcomes of these investments were:

1. The development of this research network into the seeds of what became the modern internet.
2. The development of the groups making up this network into many of the first and still the among the most prominent computer science and computer engineering departments in the world.
3. The development around these universities of the leading regional digital innovation hubs in the world, including Silicon Valley and the Boston Route 128 corridor.

Yet while these technology hubs have become the envy and aspiration of (typically unsuccessful) regional development and industrial policy around the world, it is critical to remember how fundamentally different the aspirations underpinning Lick's vision were from those of his imitators.

Where the standard goal of industrial policy is directly to achieve outcomes like the development of a Silicon Valley, this was not Lick's intention. He was instead focused on developing a vision of the future of computing grounded in human-computer symbiosis, attack-resilient networking, and the computer as a communication device. ⌗ builds closely on Lick's severely unfinished vision. Lick selected participating universities not based on an interest in regional economic development, but rather to maximize the chances of achieving vision of the future of computing.

Industrial policy often aims at creating large-scale, industrial "nation champions" and is often viewed in contrast to antitrust and competition policies, which typically aim to constrain excessively concentrated industrial power. As Lick described in his 1980 "Computers and Government" and in contrast to both traditions, the IPTO effort took the rough goals of antitrust (ensuring the possibility of an open and decentralized marketplace) but applied the tools of industrial policy (active public investment) to achieve them. Rather than constraining the winners of predigital market competition, IPTO aimed to create a network infrastructure on which the digital world would play out in such a way as to avoid undue concentrations of power. It was the failure to sustain this investment through the 1970s and beyond that Lick predicted would lead to the monopolization of the critical functions of digital life by what he at the time described as "IBM" but turned out to be the dominant technology platforms of today: Microsoft, Apple, Google, Meta, Amazon, etc. Complementing this approach, rather than directly fostering the development of private, for-profit industry as most industrial policy does, Lick supported the civil society-based (primarily university-driven) development of basic infrastructure that would support the defense, government, and private sectors.[7]

While Lick's approach mostly played out at universities, given they were the central locus of the development of advanced computing at the time, it contrasted sharply with the traditional support of fundamental, curiosity-driven research of funders like the US National Science Foundation. He did not offer support for general academic investigation and research, but rather to advance a clear mission and vision: building a network of easily accessible computing machines that enabled communication and association over physical and social distance, interconnecting and sharing resources with other networks to enable scalable cooperation.

Yet while dictating this mission, Lick did not prejudge the right components to achieve it, instead establishing a network of "coopetitive" research labs, each experimenting and racing to develop prototypes of different components of these systems that could then be standardized in interaction with each other and spread across the network. Private sector collaborators played important roles in contributing to this development,

---

[7] Licklider, "Computers and Government", op. cit.

including Bolt Beranek and Newman (where Lick served as Vice President just before his role at IPTO and which went on to build several prototype systems for the internet) and Xerox PARC (where many of the researchers Lick supported later assembled and continued their work, especially after federal funding diminished). Yet, as is standard in the development and procurement of infrastructure and public works in a city, these roles were components of an overall vision and plan developed by the networked, multi-sectoral alliance that constituted ARPANET. Contrast this with a model primarily developed and driven in the interest of private corporations, the basis for most personal computing and mobile operating systems, social networks, and cloud infrastructures.

As we have noted repeatedly above, we need not only look back to the "good old days" for ARPANET or Taiwan for inspiration. India's development of the "India Stack" has many similar characteristics.[8] More recently, the EU has been developing initiatives including European Digital Identity and Gaia-X. Jurisdictions as diverse as Brazil and Singapore have experimented successfully with similar approaches. While each of these initiatives has strengths and weaknesses, the idea that a public mission aimed at creating infrastructure that empowers decentralized innovation in collaboration with civil society and participation but not dominance from the private sector is increasingly a pattern, often labeled "digital public infrastructure" (DPI). We are largely advocating for this approach to be scaled up and become the central approach to the development of global ⌬ society. Yet for this to occur, the ARPA and Taiwan models need to be updated and

---

[8] Vivek Raghavan, Sanjay Jain and Pramod Varma, "India Stack—Digital Infrastructure as Public Good", *Communications of the ACM* 62, no. 11: 76-81.

adjusted for this potentially dramatically increased scale and ambition.

## A new 數位 order

The key reason for an updated model is that there are basic elements of the ARPA model that are a poor fit for the shape of contemporary digital life, as Lick began realizing as early as 1980. While it was a multisectoral effort, ARPA was centered around the American military-industrial complex and its collaborators in the American academy. This made sense in the context of the 1960s, when the US was one of two major world powers, scientific funding and mission was deeply tied to its stand-off with the Soviet Union and most digital technology was developed in the academy. As Lick observed, however, even by the late 1970s this was already becoming a poor fit. Today's world is (as discussed above) much more multi-polar even in its development of leading DPI. The primary civil technology developers are in the open-source community, private companies dominate much of the digital world and military applications are only one aspect of the public's vision for digital technology, which increasingly shapes every aspect of contemporary life. To adapt, a vision of 數位 infrastructure for today must engage the public in setting the mission of technology through institutions like digital ministries, network transnationally and harness open-source technology, as well as redirecting the private sector, more effectively.

Lick and the ARPANET collaborators shaped an extraordinary vision that laid the groundwork for the internet and 數位. Yet Lick saw that this could not ground the legitimacy of his project for long; as we highlighted central to his aspirations was that "decisions about the development and exploitation of computer technology must be made not only 'in the public interest' but in the interest of giving the public itself the means to enter into the decision-making processes that will shape their future." Military technocracy cannot be the primary locus for setting the agenda if ⌬ is to achieve the legitimacy and public support necessary to make the requisite investments to center ⌬ infrastructure. Instead, we will need to harness the full suite of ⌬ technologies we have discussed above to engage transnational publics in reaching an overlapping consensus on a mission that can motivate a similarly concerted effort to IPTO's. These tools include ⌬ competence education to make every citizen feel empowered to shape the ⌬ future, cultural institutions like Japan's Miraikan that actively invite citizens into long-term technology planning, ideathons where citizens collaborate on future envisioning and are supported by governments and charities to build these visions into media that can be more broadly consumed, alignment assemblies and other augmented deliberations on the direction of technology and more.

Digital (hopefully soon, ⌬) ministries, emerging worldwide, are proving to be a more natural forum for setting visionary goals in a participatory way, surpassing traditional military hosts. A well-known example is Ukraine's Mykhailo Fedorov, the Minister of Digital Transformation since 2019. Taiwan was a forerunner in this domain as well, appointing a digital minister in 2016 and establishing a formal Ministry of Digital Affairs in 2022. Japan, recognizing the urgency of digitalization during the pandemic, founded its Digital Agency at the cabinet level in 2021, inspired by discussions with Taiwan. The EU has increasingly formalized its digital portfolio under the leadership of Executive Vice President of the European Commission for a Europe Fit for the Digital Age Margrethe Vestager, who helped inspire both the popular television series *Borgen* and the middle name of the daughter of one of this book's authors.[9]

These ministries, inherently collaborative, work closely with other government sectors and international bodies. In 2023, the G20 digital ministers identified DPI as a key focus for worldwide cooperation, aligning with the UN global goals.[10] In contrast to institutions like ARPA, digital ministries offer a more fitting platform for initiating international missions that involve the public and civil society. As digital challenges become central to global security, more nations are likely to appoint digital ministers, fostering an open, connected digital community.

Yet national homes for 數位 infrastructure constitute only a few of the poles holding up its tent. There is no country today that can or should alone be the primary locus for such efforts. They must be built as at least international and probably transnational networks, just as the internet is. Digital ministers, as their positions are created, must form a network that can provide international support to this work and connect nation-based nodes just as ARPANET did for university-based nodes. Many of the open-source projects participating will not themselves have a single primary national presence, spanning many jurisdictions and participating as a transnational community, to be respected on terms that will in some cases be roughly equal to those of national digital ministries. Consider, for example,

---

[9] Danny Hakim, "The Danish Politician Who Accused Google of Antitrust Violations", *New York Times* April 15, 2015.

[10] Benjamin Bertelsen and Ritul Gaur, "What We Can Expect for Digital Public Infrastructure in 2024", *World Economic Forum Blog* February 13, 2024 at https://www.weforum.org/agenda/2024/02/dpi-digital-public-infrastructure. Especially in the developing world, many countries have ministries of planning that could naturally host or spin off such a function.

the relationship of rough equality between the Ethereum community and the Taiwanese Ministry of Digital Affairs.

Exclusively high-level government-to-government relationships are severely limited by the broader state of current international relations. Many of the countries where the internet has flourished have at-times had troubled relationships with other countries where it has flourished. Many civil actors have stronger transnational relationships than their governments would agree to supporting at an intergovernmental level, mirroring consistent historical patterns where civil connections through, for example, religion and advocacy of human rights have created a stronger foundation for cooperation than international relations alone. Technology, for better or worse, often crosses borders and boundaries of ideology more easily than treaties can be negotiated. For example, web3 communities and civic technology organizations like g0v and RadicalxChange have significant presences even in countries that are not widely understood as "democratic" in their national politics. Similar patterns at larger scales have been central to the transnational environmental, human rights, religious and other movements.[11]

While there is no necessary path from such interactions to broader democratization, it would also be an important mistake to miss the opportunity to expand the scope of interoperation in areas where it is possible while waiting for full government-to-government alignment. In her book *A New World Order*, leading international relations scholar Anne-Marie Slaughter sketched how such transnational policy and civil networks will

---

[11] Alexander Wendt, *Social Theory of International Politics* (Cambridge, UK: Cambridge University Press, 1999). For a recent case study of the role of religion in Middle East cooperation, see Johnnie Moore, "Evangelical Track II Diplomacy in Arab and Israeli Peacemaking", Liberty University dissertation (2024).

increasingly complement and collaborate with governments around the world and form a fabric of transnational collaboration.[12] This fabric or network could be effective than current international bodies like the United Nations. As such we should expect (implicit) support for these kinds of initiatives to be as important to the role of digital ministries as are their direct relationships with one another.

Some of the transnational networks that will form the key complements to digital ministries may be academic collaborations. Yet the element of the digital ecosystem most neglected by governments today is not academia, which still receives billions of dollars of research support. Instead, it is the largely ignored world of open source and other non-profit, mission-driven technology developers. As we have extensively discussed, these already provide the backbone of much of the global technology stack. Yet they receive virtually no measurable financial support from governments and very little from charities, despite their work belonging (mostly) fully to the public domain and their being developed mostly in the public interest.

Furthermore, this sector is in many ways better suited to the development of infrastructure than academic research, much as public infrastructure in the physical world is generally not built by academia. Academic research is heavily constrained by disciplinary foci and boundaries that civil infrastructure that is broadly usable is unlikely to respect. Academic careers depend on citation, credit and novelty in a way that is unlikely to align with the best aspirations for infrastructure, which often can and should be invisible, "boring" and as easily interoperable with

---

[12] Anne-Marie Slaughter, *A New World Order* (Princeton, NJ: Princeton University Press, 2005). This book has a special place in one of our hearts, as obtaining a prerelease signed copy was the first birthday present one author gave to the woman who became his wife.

(rather than "novel" in contrast to) other infrastructure as possible. Academic research often focuses on a degree and disciplinary style of rigor and persuasiveness that differs in kind from the ideal user experience. While public support for academic research is crucial and, in some areas, academic projects can contribute to 🔲 infrastructure, governments and charities should not primarily look to the academic research sector. And while academic research receives hundreds of billions of dollars in funding globally annually, open-source communities have likely received less than two billion dollars in their entire history, accounting for known sources as we illustrate in Figure B. Many of these concerns have been studied and highlighted by the "decentralized science" movement.[13]

Furthermore, open-source communities are just the tip of the iceberg in terms of what may be possible for public-interested, civil society-driven technology development. Organizations like the Mozilla and Wikimedia Foundations, while primarily interacting with and driving open source projects, have significant development activities beyond pure open source code development that have made their offerings much more accessible to the world. Furthermore, there is no necessary reason why public interest technology need inherit all the features of open-source code.

---

[13] Sarah Hamburg, "Call to Join the Decentralized Science Movement", *Nature* 600, no. 221 (2021): Correspondence at https://www.nature.com/articles/d41586-021-03642-9.

數位 Plurality: Part 7: Forward

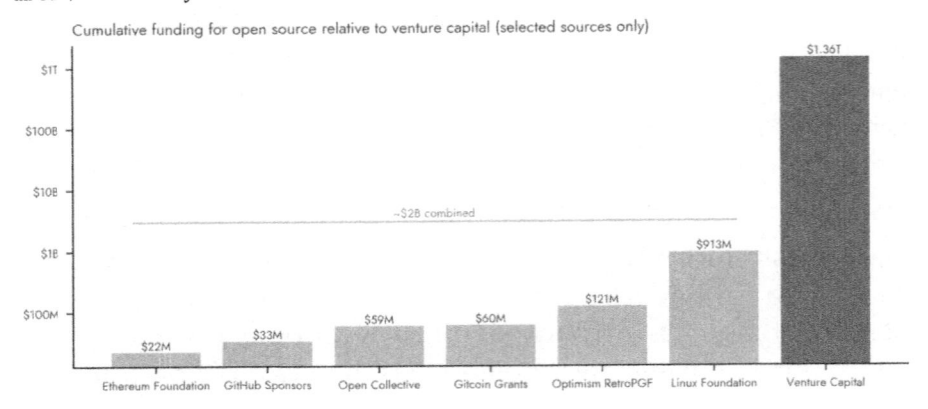

Cumulative funding for open source relative to venture capital (selected sources only)

**Figure 7-0-B.** Comparing known funding of open-source software and venture capital investment. Source: Chart by authors, sources various see footnote.[14]

Some organizations developing generative foundation models, such as OpenAI and Anthropic, have legitimate concerns about simply making these models freely available but are explicitly dedicated to developing and licensing them in the public interest and are structured to not exclusively maximize profit to ensure they stay true to these missions.[15] Whether they have,

---

[14] Jessica Lord, "What's New with GitHub Sponsors", *GitHub Blog*, April 4, 2023 at https://github.blog/2023-04-04-whats-new-with-github-sponsors/. GitCoin impact report at https://impact.gitcoin.co/. Kevin Owocki, "Ethereum 2023 Funding Flows: Visualizing Public Goods Funding from Source to Destination" at https://practicalpluralism.github.io/. Open Collective, "Fiscal Sponsors. We need you!" *Open Collective Blog* March 1, 2024 at https://blog.opencollective.com/fiscal-sponsors-we-need-you/. Optimism Collective, "RetroPGF Round 3", *Optimism Docs* January 2024 at https://community.optimism.io/docs/governance/retropgf-3/#. ProPublica, "The Linux Foundation" at https://projects.propublica.org/nonprofits/organizations/460503801.

[15] OpenAI, "OpenAI Charter", *OpenAI Blog* April 9, 2018 at https://openai.com/charter. Anthropic, "The Long-Term Benefit Trust", *Anthropic Blog* September 19, 2023 at https://www.anthropic.com/news/the-long-term-benefit-trust.

given the demands of funding and the limits of their own vision, managed to be ideally true to this aspiration or not, one can certainly imagine both shaping organizations like this to ensure they can achieve this goals using 🖬 technologies and structuring public policy to ensure more organizations like this are central to the development of core 🖬 infrastructure. Other organizations may develop non-profit 🖬 infrastructure but wish to charge for elements of it (just as some highways have tolls to address congestion and maintenance) while others may have no proprietary claim but wish to ensure sensitive and private data are not just made publicly available. Fostering a 🖬 ecosystem of organizations that serve 🖬 publics including but not limited to open-source models will be critical to moving beyond the limits of the academic ARPA model. Luckily a variety of 🖬 technologies are available to policymakers to foster such an ecosystem.

Furthermore, whatever the ideal structures, it is unlikely that such public interest institutions will simply substitute for the large, private digital ecosystem built up over the last decades. Many social networks, cloud infrastructures, single-sign-on architectures, and so forth would be wasteful to simply scrap. Instead it likely makes sense to harness these investments towards the public interest by pairing public investment with agreements to shift governance to respect public input in much the way we discussed in our chapters on 🖬 *Voting*, *Workplace* and *Media*. This closely resembles the way that a previous wave of economic democracy reform with which John Dewey was closely associated did not simply out-compete privately created power generation, but instead sought to bring them under a network of partially local democratic control through utility boards. Many leaders in the tech world refer to their platforms as "utilities", "infrastructure" or "public squares"; it stands to reason that part of a program of ⌘ digital infrastructure will be reforming them so they truly act as such.

Fostering a ⌘ ecosystem of organizations that serve ⌘ publics including but not limited to open-source models will be critical to moving beyond the limits of the academic ARPA model. Luckily a variety of ⌘ technologies are available to policymakers to foster such an ecosystem.

## ⌘ regulation

To allow the flourishing of such an ecosystem will depend on reorienting legal, regulatory, and financial systems to empower these types of organizations. Tax revenue will need to be raised, ideally in ways that are not only consistent with but promote ⌘ directly, to make them socially and financially sustainable.

The most important role for governments and intergovernmental networks will arguably be one of coordination and standardization. Governments, being the largest actor in most national economies, can shape the behavior of the entire digital ecosystem based on what standards they adopt, what entities they purchase from and the way they structure citizens' interactions with public services. This is the core, for example, of how the India Stack became so central to the private sector, which followed the lead of the public sector and thus the civil projects they supported.

Yet laws are also at the center of defining what types of structures can exist, what privileges they have and how rights are divided between different entities. Open-source organizations now struggle as they aim to maintain simultaneously their non-profit orientation and an international presence. Organizations like the Open Collective Foundation were created almost exclusively for the purpose of allowing them to do so and helped support this project, but despite taking a substantial cut of project revenues was unable to sustain itself and thus is in the process of dissolving as of this writing. The competitive disadvantage of Third-Sector technology providers could hardly be starker.[16] Many other forms of innovative, democratic, transnational organization, like Distributed Autonomous Organizations (DAOs) constantly run into legal barriers that only a few jurisdictions like the State of Wyoming have just begun to address. While some of the reasons for these are legitimate (to avoid financial scams, etc.), much more work is needed to establish legal frameworks that support and defend transnational democratic non-profit organizational forms.

Other organizational forms likely need even further support. Data coalitions that aim to collectively protect the data rights of creators or those with relevantly collective data interests, as we discussed in our *Property and Contract* chapter, will need protection similar to unions and other collective bargaining organizations that they not only do not have at present but which many jurisdictions (like the EU) may effectively prevent them from having, given their extreme emphasis on individual rights in data. Just as labor law evolved to empower collective bargaining for workers, law will have to evolve to allow data workers to collectively exercise their rights to avoid either being disadvantaged relative to concentrated model builders or so disparate as to offer insuperable barriers to ambitious data collaboration.

Beyond organizational forms, legal and regulatory changes will be critical to empowering a fair and productive use of data for

---

[16] Open Collective Team, "Open Collective Official Statement - OCF Dissolution" February 28, 2024 at *https://blog.opencollective.com/open-collective-official-statement-ocf-dissolution/*.

shared goals. Traditional intellectual property regimes are highly rigid, focused on the degree of "transformativeness" of a use that risk either subjecting all model development to severe and unworkable limitations or depriving creators of the moral and financial rights they need to sustain their work that is so critical to the function of these models. New standards need to be developed by judges, legislators and regulators in close collaboration with technologists and publics that account for the complex and partial way in which a variety of data informs the output of models and ensures that the associated value is "back-propagated" to the data creators just as it is to the intermediate data created within the models in the process of training them.[17] New rules like these will build on the reforms to property rights that empowered the re-purposing of radio spectrum and should be developed for a variety of other digital assets as we discussed in our *Property and Contract* chapter.

Furthermore, if properly concerted with such a vision, antitrust laws, competition rules, interoperability mandates and financial regulations have an important role to play in encouraging the emergence of new organizational forms and the adaptation of existing ones. Antitrust and competition law is intended to ensure concentrated commercial interests cannot abuse the power they accumulate over customers, suppliers, and workers. Giving direct control over a firm to these counterparties is a natural way to achieve this objective without the usual downsides in competition policy of inhibiting scaled collaboration. ⬚ technologies offer natural means to

---

[17] An interesting line of research suggesting possibility here is that of neural network and genetic algorithm pioneer John H. Holland, who tried to draw direct analogies between networks of firms in an economy linked by markets and neural networks. John H. Holland and John M. Miller, "Artificial Adaptive Agents in Economic Theory", *American Economic Review* 81, no. 2 (1991): 365-370.

instantiate meaningful voice for these stakeholders as we discussed in the *Workplace* chapter. It would be natural for antitrust authorities to increasingly consider mandating such governance reforms as alternative remedies to anticompetitive conduct or mergers and to consider governance representation as a mitigating factor in evaluating the necessity of punitive action.[18]

Mandating interoperability, in cooperation with standard setting processes that develop the meaning and shape of these standards, is a critical lever to make such standards workable and avoid dominance by an illegitimate private monopoly. Financial regulations help define what kinds of governance are acceptable in various jurisdictions and have unfortunately, especially in the US and UK, weighed heavily towards damaging and monopolistic one-share-one-vote rules. Financial regulatory reform should encourage experimentation with more inclusive governance systems such as Quadratic and other ⌾ voting forms that account for and address concentrations of power continuously, rather than offsetting the tendencies of one-share-one-vote to raiding with bespoke provisions like "poison pills".[19] They should also accommodate and support worker, supplier, environmental counterparty, and customer voice and steer concentrated asset holders who might otherwise have systemic monopolistic effects towards employing similar tools.

## ⌾ taxes

However, rules, laws and regulations can only offer support to positive frameworks that arise from investment, innovation, and

---

[18] Hitzig et al., op. cit.

[19] Eric A. Posner and E. Glen Weyl, "Quadratic Voting as Efficient Corporate Governance", *University of Chicago Law Review* 81, no. 1 (2014): 241-272.

development. Without those to complement, they will always be on the defense, playing catch up to a world defined by private innovation. Thus, public and multisectoral investment is the core they must complement and making such investments obviously requires revenue, thus naturally raising the question of how it can be raised to make ⌗ infrastructure self-sustaining. While directly charging for services largely reverts to the traps of the private sector, relying primarily on "general revenue" is unlikely to be sustainable or legitimate. Furthermore, there are many cases where taxes can themselves help encourage ⌗. It is to taxes of this sort that we now turn our attention.

The digital sector has proven one of the most challenging to tax, because many of the relevant sources of value are created in a geographically ambiguous way or are otherwise intangible. For example, data and networks of collaboration and know-how among employees at companies, often spanning national borders, can often be booked in countries with low corporate tax rates even if they mostly occur in jurisdictions with higher rates. Many free services come with an implicit bargain of surveillance, leading neither the service nor the implicit labor to be taxed as it would be if this price were explicit. While recent reforms to create a minimum corporate tax rate agreed by the G20 and Organization for Economic Cooperation and Development are likely to help, they are not tightly adaptive to the digital environment and thus will likely only partly address the challenge.

Yet while from one side these present a challenge, on the other hand they offer an opportunity for taxes to be raised in an explicitly transnational way that can accrue to supporting ⌗ infrastructure rather than, in an arbitrary way, to wherever the corporation may choose to domicile. Ideally such taxes should aim to satisfy as fully as possible several criteria:

1. Directly ▢ (D▢): Digital taxes should ideally not merely raise revenue, but directly encourage or enact ▢ aims themselves.[20] This ensures that the taxes are not a drag on the system, but part of the solution.
2. Jurisdictional alignment (JA): The jurisdictional network in which taxes are and can naturally be raised should correspond to the jurisdiction that disposes of these taxes. This ensures that the coalition required to enact the taxes is like that required to establish the cooperation that disposes of the revenue.
3. Revenue alignment (RA): The sources of revenue should correspond to the value generated by the shared value created using the revenue, ensuring that those disposing of the revenue have a natural interest in the success of their mission. It also ensures that those who pay for the tax generally benefit from the goods created with it, lessening political opposition to the tax.
4. Financial adequacy (FA): The tax should be sufficient to fund the required investment.

The principle of "circular investment" that we described in our *Social Markets* chapter suggests that eventually they can all be generally jointly satisfied. The value created by supermodular shared goods eventually must accrue somewhere with submodular returns, which can and should be recycled back to support those values sources. Extracting this value can

---

[20] Economists would refer to such taxes as "Pigouvian" taxes on "externalities". While a reasonable way to describe some of the below, as noted in our Markets chapter, externalities may be more the rule than the exception and thus we prefer this alternative formulation. For example, many of these taxes address issues of concentrated market power which do create externalities, but are not usually considered in the scope of Pigouvian taxation.

generally be done in a way that reduces market power and thus actually encourages assets to be more fully used.

Despite this theoretical ideal, in practice identifying practicable taxes to achieve it is likely to be as much a process of technological trial and error as any of the technological challenges we discuss in the Democracy part of the book. Yet there are several promising recent proposals that seem plausibly close to fulfilling many of these objectives as we iterate further:

1. Concentrated computational asset tax: Application of a progressive (either in rate or by giving a generous exemption) common ownership tax to digital assets such as computation, storage, and some kinds of data.[21]
2. Digital land tax: Taxing the commercialization or holding of scarce digital space, including taxes on online advertising, holding of spectrum licenses and web address space in a more competitive way and, eventually, taxing exclusive spaces in virtual worlds.[22]
3. Implicit data/attention exchange tax: Taxes on implicit data or attention exchanges involved in "free" services online, which would otherwise typically accrue labor and value added taxes.
4. Digital asset taxes: Common ownership taxes on pure-digital assets, such as digital currencies, utility tokens and non-fungible token.

---

[21] See the ongoing work developing this idea of Charlotte Siegmann, "AI Use-Case Specific Compute Subsidies and Quotas" (2024) at https://docs.google.com/document/d/11nNPbBctIUoURfZ5FCwyLYRtpBL6xevFi8YGFbr3BBA/edit#heading=h.mr8ansm7nxr8.

[22] Paul Romer, "A Tax That Could Fix Big Tech", *New York Times* May 6, 2019 advocated related ideas.

5. Commons-derived data tax: Profits earned from models trained on unlicensed, commons-derived data could be taxed.
6. Flexible/gig work taxes: Profits of companies that primarily employ "gig workers" and thus avoid many of the burdens of traditional labor law could be taxed.[23]

While a much more detailed policy analysis would be needed to comprehensively "score" these taxes according to our criteria above, a few illustrations will hopefully illustrate the design thinking pattern behind these suggestions. A concentrated computational asset tax aims simultaneously to encourage more complete use of digital assets (as any common ownership tax will), deter concentrated cloud ownership (thus increasing competition while decreasing potential security threats) and to drag on the incentives for accumulating the kind of computational resources that may allow training of potentially dangerous-scale models outside public oversight, all instantiating D⌬. Most forms of digital land tax would naturally accrue not to any nation state, but to the transnational entities that support internet infrastructure, access and content achieving JA. An implicit data exchange tax would provide a clearer signal of the true value being created in digital economies and encourage infrastructure facilitating this to maximize that value, achieving RA.

Of course, these are just the first suggestions and much more analysis and imagination will help expand the space of possibilities. However, given that these examples line up fairly closely with the primary business models in today's digital world (viz. cloud, advertising, digital asset sales, etc.) it seems plausible that, with a bit of elaboration, they could be used to raise a significant fraction of value flowing through that world and thus achieve the FA necessary to support a scale of

---

[23] Gray and Suri, op. cit.

⌑ 數位 Plurality: Part 7: Forward

investment that would fundamentally transform the digital economy.

While this may seem a political non-starter, an illuminating precedent is the gas tax in the US, which while initially opposed by the trucking industry was eventually embraced by that industry when policymakers agreed to set aside the funds to support the building of road infrastructure.[24] Though the tax obviously put a direct drain on the industry, its indirect support for the building of roads was seen to more than offset this by providing the substrate truckers needed for their work. Some would, rightly, object that there may have been even better targeted taxes for this purpose (such as road congestion charges), but gas taxes also carried ancillary benefits in discouraging pollution and were generally well-targeted at the primary users of roads at a time when charging for congestion might have been costly.

It is just possible to imagine assembling today an appropriate coalition of businesses and governments to support such an ambitious set of digital infrastructure supporting taxes. Doing so would require correct set asides of raised funds, more clever tax instruments harnessing the abundant data online, sophisticated, and low friction means of collecting taxes, careful harnessing of appropriate but not universal jurisdictions to impose and collect the taxes in a way that cajoles others to follow along and, of course, a good deal of public support and pressure as we discuss below. Effective policy leadership and public mobilization should, hopefully, be able to achieve these and create the conditions for supporting ⌑ infrastructure.

---

[24] John Chynoweth Burnham, "The Gasoline Tax and the Automobile Revolution" *Mississippi Valley Historical Review* 48, no. 3 (1961): 435-459.

## Sustaining our future

To embody 🔲, the network of organizations that are supported by such resources cannot be a *de novo* monolithic global government. Instead, it must be 🔲 itself both in its structure and in its connection to existing fora to realize the commitments of 🔲 to uplift diversity and collective cooperation. While we aspire to basically transform the character of digital society, we cannot achieve 🔲 if we seek to tear down or undermine existing institutions. Our aim should be, quite the reverse, to see the building of fundamental 🔲 infrastructure as a platform that can allow the digital pie to dramatically expand and diversify, lifting as many boats as possible while also expanding the space for experimentation and growth.

Different elements of our vision require very different degrees of government engagement. Many of the most intimate technologies, for example, such as immersive shared reality intend to operate at relatively intimate scales and thus should be naturally developed in a relatively "private" way (both in funding models and in data structures), with some degree of public support and regulation steering them away from potential pitfalls. The most ambitious reforms to the structure of markets, on the other hand, will require reshaping basic governmental and legal structures, in many cases cutting across national boundaries. Development of the fundamental protocols on which all this work rests will require perhaps the greatest degree of coordination but also a great deal of experimentation, fully harnessing the ARPA coopetitive structure as nodes in the network (such as India and Taiwan) compete to export their frameworks into global standards. An effective fabric of 🔲 law, regulation, investment, and control rights will, as much as possible, ensure the existence of a diversity of national and transnational entities capable of matching this variety of needs and deftly match taxes and legal authorities to empower these to serve their relevant roles while interoperating.

Luckily, while they are dramatically underfunded, often imperfectly coordinated, and lack the ambitious mission we have outlined here, many of the existing transnational structures for digital and internet governance have roughly these features. In short, while specific new capabilities need to be added, funding improved, networks and connections enhanced and public engagement augmented, the internet is already, as imagined by the ARPANET founders, 數位 in its structure and governance. More than anything, what needs to be done is build the public understanding of and engagement with this work necessary to uplift, defend and support it.

## Organizing change

Of course, achieving that is an enormous undertaking. The ideas discussed in this chapter, and throughout this book, are deeply technical and even the dry discussion here barely skims the surface. Very few will deeply engage even with the ideas in this book, much less the much farther ranging work that will need to be done both in the policy arena and far beyond it in the wide range of research, development, and deployment work that policy world will empower.

It is precisely for this reason that "policy" is just one small slice of the work required to build 數位. For every policy leader, there will have to be dozens, probably hundreds of people building the visions they help articulate. And for each one of those, there will need to be hundreds who, while not focused on the technical concerns, share a general aversion to the default Libertarian and Technocratic directions technology might otherwise go and are broadly supportive of the vision of 數位. They will have to understand it at more of an emotive, visceral and/or ideological level, rather than a technical or intellectual one, and build networks of moral support, lived perspectives and adoption for those at the core of the policy and technical landscape.

For them to do so, ⌗ will have to go far beyond a set of creative technologies and intellectual analyses. It will have to become a broadly understood cultural current and social movement, like environmentalism, AI and crypto, grounded in a deep, both intellectual and social, body of fundamental research, developed and practiced in a diverse and organized set of enterprises and supported by organized political interests. The path there includes, but moves far beyond, policymakers to the world of activism, culture, business, and research. Thus, we conclude by calling on each of you who touches any of these worlds to join us in the project of making this a reality.

數位 Plurality: Part 7: Forward

## 7-1 Conclusion

This book describes a vision for the future of technology and society that we hope is ambitious and serious enough to be a real competitor to, but will be more attractive to most readers than, that developed by Libertarians and Technocrats. If we are right and you share that vision, join us in the movement for 數.

Our concrete aspirations match our ambitious vision. By 2030, 數 will be as recognizable to people around the globe as a direction for technology as AI or blockchain are and as recognizable as a political movement as the Green movement. People will expect their democracy to progress as rapidly as their devices. They will see Taiwan as a guiding light and symbol for 數 and thus as important to the thriving of 數 as Israel is for the Jewish people or as Ukraine is for freedom in Europe. People around the world will find surprising allies and heroes through 數, like those concerned about authoritarian expansionism coming to admire a transgender Taiwanese leader on the front lines of that conflict and those seeking more 數 technology finding allies among devout conservatives in Africa.

---

Technology is the most powerful force transforming our world. Whether or not we understand its inner workings, deploy it tentatively or voraciously, or agree with the companies and policymakers that have shaped its development to date, it remains our single greatest lever to shape our collective future.

That collective is not simply a group of individuals but a fabric of relationships. Whether you look at it from a scientific,

## 7-1 Conclusion

historical, sociological, religious, or political point of view, it is increasingly clear that reality is defined not just by who we are, but how we connect.

Technology drives and defines those connections. From the railroad to the telegraph to the telephone to social media connecting us to old kindergarten friends and new like-minded allies to teleconferencing holding businesses and families together during Covid, we have benefited enormously from technology's capacity to forge and strengthen human connection while honoring our differences.

Yet, technology has also clearly driven us apart and suppressed our differences. Business models based on a fight for attention have prioritized outrage over curiosity, echo chambers over shared understanding, and proliferated mis- and disinformation. The rapid spread of information online, out of context and against our privacy expectations, has too often eroded our communities, driven out our cultural heritage and created a global monoculture. As a new generation of technologies including GFMs, Web3, and augmented reality spreads through our lives, it promises to radically increase technology's effects, good and bad.

Thus, we stand at a crossroads. Technology could drive us apart, sowing chaos and conflict that bring down social order. It could suppress the human diversity that is its lifeblood, homogenizing us in a singular technical vision. Or it could dramatically enrich our diversity while strengthening the ties across it, harnessing and sustaining the potential energy of ⌬.

Some would seek to avoid this choice by slamming on the breaks, decelerating technological progress. Yet, while of course some directions are unwise and there are limits to how rapidly we should proceed into the unknown, the dynamics of competition and geopolitics make simply slowing progress unlikely to be sustainable. Instead, we face a choice of directions more than velocity.

⿻ 數位 Plurality: Part 7: Forward

Should we, as Libertarians like Peter Thiel, Marc Andreesen and Balaji Srinavasan would have us do, liberate individuals to be atomistic agents, free of constraints or responsibilities? Should we, as Technocrats like Sam Altman and Reid Hoffman would have us do, allow technologists to solve our problems, plan our future and distribute to us the material comfort it creates?

We say, loudly and clearly, neither! Both chaos and top-down order are the antitheses not just of democracy and freedom, but of all life, complexity and beauty in human society and nature. Life and ⿻ thrive in the narrow corridor on the "edge of chaos". For life on this planet to survive and thrive, it must be the central mission of technology and politics to widen this corridor, to steer us constantly back towards that edge of chaos where growth and ⿻ are possible. That is the aspiration and the imperative of ⿻.

⿻ is thus the third way beyond Libertarianism and Technocracy, just as the life is the third way beyond rigid order and chaos. It is a movement we have perhaps three to five years to set in motion. Within that time frame, a critical mass of the technology that people and companies use every day will have become deeply dependent on "AI" and "the metaverse". At that point, we will not be able to reverse the *fait accompli* that Technocracy and Libertarianism have generated for us. But between now and then, we can mobilize to rechart the course: toward a relationship-centered, empowering digital democracy in which diverse groups of people, precisely because they do not agree, are able to cooperate and collaborate to constantly push our imaginations and aspirations forward.

Such a pivot will take a whole-of-society mobilization. Businesses, governments, universities, and civil society organizations must demand that our technology deepen and

## 7-1 Conclusion

broaden our connections across the many forms of diversity, show us that this is possible, build the tools we need to achieve it and make it a reality. That is the key, and the only path, to strengthening human stability, prosperity, and flourishing into the future. For all that it offers, the internet's potential for truly transformative progress has never materialized. If we want to realize that potential, we have a brief window of opportunity to act.

### Promise of

Over the last half century, most Western liberal democracies have learned to be helpless in the face of technology. They are intrigued by it and alternately delighted and frustrated by it, but tend to assume that it emerges inexorably, like modernity itself, instead of as the sum of the choices of small groups of engineers. Most citizens in these polities do not believe "we the people" have any ability, much less any right, to influence the direction of the platforms that are the operating system of our lives.

But we do have the right, and even the duty, to demand better. Some technology pulls us apart and flattens our differences; other technology brings us together and celebrates them. Some fuels our resentment and obedience, some helps us find interdependence. If we mobilize to demand the latter, *technologies* that are designed to help us collaborate across difference, we can re-engineer that operating system.

We see our opportunity to act across three horizons: the immediate, the intermediate, and the transformative.

*Immediate horizon*

Some of this change is ripe for action today. Anyone reading this book can explain, recommend, and tell its stories to friends and help spread various surrounding media content. Anyone can adopt a range of tools already widely available from meetings in immersive shared reality to open-source tools for making collective decisions with their communities.

Anyone can support political leaders and organize in political movements around the policy agenda we developed in the previous chapter, and especially political and policy leaders can work together to implement these ideas, as well as near-term political reforms in a ⿻ direction such as ranked-choice or approval voting. Anyone can choose to steer the diet of technology they use towards open-source tools and those of companies that adopt and incorporate ⿻ in their work. Business leaders, engineers, and product managers at these companies can both build ⿻ technologies into their products in modest ways, employ these tools in their productivity workflows, receive more effective feedback from customers and support public policies that embody them.

Academics can study ⿻ technologies and their impact on the ground today. They can devise rigorous measures to help us know what truly works. They can address key open questions in a range of fields that will allow the design of the next generation of ⿻ technologies and form relationships and collaborations across academic institutions through networks like the Plurality Institute. They can adopt ⿻ in the dissemination of research and peer review.

Cultural leaders, artists, journalists and other communicators can tell the stories of the ⿻ movement, like Oscar-winner Director Cynthia Wade and Emmy-winning Producer Teri Whitcraft are doing in a forthcoming documentary. They can incorporate ⿻ in their creative practice, as this book did and as we saw Mat Dryhurst and Holly Herndon doing. They can immerse citizens in constructive imagining of a more ⿻ future, like Miraikan in Tokyo does.

## Intermediate horizon

With more systemic imagination and ambition, there are opportunities to pursue ⌑ across a more intermediate horizon, reinventing institutions to include more diverse voices, build deeper connections and foster the regeneration of more diversity. Anyone can become part of local ⌑ communities around the world, telling in a wide variety of idioms, languages and forms the potential for a more ⌑ future and inviting friends to participate in co-creating it. Anyone can join what will be increasingly organized political movements explicitly dedicated to ⌑, contribute to a growing range of ⌑ civil and charitable causes, attend a growing number of hackathons and ideathons that help address the local concerns of diverse communities using ⌑.

Policy leaders can form political platforms and perhaps even political parties around comprehensive ⌑ agendas. Regulators and civil servants can deeply embed ⌑ into their practices, improving public engagement and speeding the loop of input. Employees of international and transnational organizations can begin to reform their structure and practices to harness ⌑ and to substantively embody ⌑, moving away from "international trade" to substantive, supermodular international cooperation and standards setting.

Business and more broadly organizational leaders can harness ⌑ to transform their internal operations, customer relations, hiring practice and corporate governance. They can promote more dynamic intrapreneurship by gradually shifting resources and power from siloed hierarchical divisions to emergent dynamic collaborations. They can harness augmented deliberation to facilitate better meetings and better customer research. They can apply generative foundation models (GFMs) to look for more diverse talent and to reorganize their corporate form to make it more directly accountable to a wider range of regulators, diffusing social and regulatory tension in the process.

Academics and researchers can form new fields of inquiry around 📱 and harnessing 📱 to empower these new collaborations bridging fields like sociology, economics, and computer science. They can invent disciplines that regularly train experts in 📱, teach a new generation of students to employ 📱 in their work and forge closer relationships with a variety of communities of practice to shorten the loop from research ideation to practical experimentation.

Cultural leaders can reimagine cultural practices harnessing 📱, creating powerfully empathetic emergent experiences that bridge cultural divides. They can sell this to media organizations that have adopted new business models serving public, civic, and business organizations rather than advertisers and end consumers. They can build participatory experiences that extend our ability to jointly design and imagine future, from the concrete design of physical spaces to the detailed interactive back-casting of potential science fiction scenarios.

*Transformative horizon*

For those of you with even more expansive vision, we have spent a good deal of this book articulating the kinds of truly transformative 📱 that could ultimately rewire the way humans communicate and collaborate. This ambition goes to the root of the 📱 movement's insight—that personhood, the core unit of democracy, is not merely atomistic or "monistic," but is also defined by social relationships – and it therefore gives rise to a broader conception of rights, going beyond individual rights to

## 7-1 Conclusion

recognize ▨ concepts of affiliation, commerce, property, and other building blocks of our society. All these will require fundamental rewriting of a range of technical infrastructures, social relationships and organizing institutions.

Such change cannot come directly, but instead must follow a gradual process of transformation, occurring in a range of social sectors that build on one another. To be truly ▨, these will need to engage and empower people across many lines of difference, which will in turn require that they understand and can articulate what they want from their future. Cultural creation, like those we have discussed above, will have to increasingly manifest ▨ in its form and substance to make this possible. This can create broad public understanding and expectation of public steering of the direction of technology and diverse social participation in its design.

This foundation of ▨ imagination across lines of difference can empower social and political organization around such goals. This in turn can allow political leaders to feature such visions as core to their agendas and to make the implementation in the functioning of governments, in their relationship to each other and private entities and in their policy agenda the creation of ▨.

Such policies and practices can in turn allow the development of novel technologies basically different, dramatically expanding the scope of the Third Sector and allowing the constant emergence of new social and democratic enterprise transnationally. These emergent enterprises can then take on an increasing range of responsibilities legitimately, given their democratic accountability, and blur the lines of responsibility usually assumed for nation states, building a new ▨ order.

Such enterprise can thus rely on new institutions of research and teaching that will cross disciplinary boundaries and the boundaries between knowledge creation and deployment, engaging deeply with such emerging social enterprises. That educational sector will continually produce new technologies that push the boundaries of ⌸, helping build the basis of new social enterprises and forming a base of ideas which will in turn support the progress of cultural imagination on which this all rests.

Thus, together culture, politics and activism, business and technology and research can form a mutually reinforcing virtuous circle: imagination drives action, which confirms the worth of imagination strengthening it further. This is why, whatever field you find yourself in, you have a chance to contribute to this truly transformative horizon, by being part of building that virtuous cycle, pushing momentum upwards by reinforcing others doing the same in other social sectors. There is no best or most important path to ⌸, because ⌸ is ⌸ and only succeeds by building on and proliferating the tremendous diversity of ways we all form part of networks of support and interdependence.

**Mobilization**

This is why, of course, there can be no top-down, one-size-fits all path to ⌸. What there can be, however – and soon, if this book has its intended effect – are intersecting circles of people, linked together in groups and individuals loosely federated across the globe, who are committed to ⌸ over its foils: Libertarianism and Technocracy. In charting a third course, pluralists are committed to technology strengthening and diversifying relationships, rather than tearing them down, and regenerating diversity, not fostering conformity. Relationships and the love, loss, adversity, and achievement that come with them are what makes life, not the violence of the jungle

## 7-1 Conclusion

manifested in books like *The Lord of the Flies* or the optimization of undifferentiated data points.[1]

If you believe that the central condition of a thriving, progressing, and righteous society is social diversity, and collaboration across such rich diversity – then come on board. If you believe that technology, the most powerful tool today, can yet be made to help us flourish, both as individuals and across our multiple, meaningful affiliations – then come on board. If you want to contribute to ⌗'s immediate horizon, intermediate horizon, or truly transformative horizon —or across all of them—you have multiple points of entry. If you work in tech, business, government, academia, civil society, cultural institutions, education, and/or on the home-front, you have limitless ways to make a difference.

This book is just one part of a great tapestry. One author of this book, for example, is also Executive Producer of a forthcoming documentary (mentioned above) about the life of another, which we suppose will reach a far broader audience than this book can; together we have founded another institution to *network academics* working on ⌗, obviously a much narrower audience. While these are just a couple of examples, they illustrate a crucial broader point: for 1000 people to be deeply involved (say in writing the book), they will need each 100 that will read it and they in turn will need each 100 who know about it and are supportive of the general idea. Thus, to succeed we need people at wide levels of engagement in mutually supportive relationships.

If 1000 people are deeply enough involved with this book to speak about it publicly, 10,000 are part of the community and actively contribute, 100,000 deeply digest the material, 1 million buy or download it, 10 million consume an hour of

---

[1] William Golding, *The Lord of the Flies* (London: Faber and Faber, 1954).

media content around it, 100 million see a film or other entertaining treatment of a related theme and 1 billion know about and are sympathetic to the aims, we will reach our 2030 goals.

Pluralists are in every country in the world, every sector of the economy. Connect, affiliate, rally, mobilize … and join us, in the deliberate and committed movement to build a more dynamic and harmonious world and let us free the future, together.

# Index

## ⿻ (Plurality / Plural) and 數位 (Digital / Plural)

數位　2
⿻　　88
⿻ approach　　96, 160, 197, 247
⿻ artist　344
⿻ book　391
⿻ competence education　　491
⿻ conversational and funding tools　　442
⿻ cryptography　　467
⿻ foundations　　110, 169
⿻ funding　　391, 402, 406
⿻ funding across boundaries 406
⿻ funding formula　391
⿻ future　183, 279, 410
⿻ governance　　153, 330, 407
⿻ group　402
⿻ hiring　437
⿻ identity　　203, 387, 407
⿻ identity Systems　203, 389, 407
⿻ infrastructure　　485, 490, 495, 502, 506
⿻ management　　286, 407
⿻ marketing　　420
⿻ mechanism　　449
⿻ media　472
⿻ memberships　　204
⿻ money 247, 409
⿻ perspective　　106, 110, 206
⿻ principles　　109, 408
⿻ property　　266, 272, 405

521

- public   449, 459, 478
- public media   470
- publics 208
- social science   106, 110
- society 180
- structure   125, 201, 462
- taxes   501
- technology   421, 480, 491, 497, 510, 513
- vision   171, 233
- voting   497, 501

# A

A Connected Society   88, 91, 113
*A New World Order*   173, 493
a priori   417
Aadhaar identity system   192
Abolitionist   11, 375, 463
Abuses Of Monopoly   398
Abusus   122, 264, 406
Academia Sinica   58
Academic peer review   349
Accelerationist   37
Access   277
Access with integrity   278
Acemoglu, Daron   5, 11, 27, 40
Active listening   351
Active public investment   487
ActivityPub   218, 227
Adaptive representation   386
Administration   351, 359
Administrative application   374
Administrative practice   372
Administrative state 364
Adobe Creative Cloud   335
Advanced Research Projects Agency (ARPA)   134, 481, 486, 489, 497, 507
Adverse selection   447
Advertising   188
Affective polarization   7, 83, 462
Affinity   346, 459

*Age of Surveillance Capitalism, The*   3, 10, 16, 188
Agglomeration   428, 432
AI Act   484
AI researcher   375
AI4Bharat   363
AIDS   445, 451, 457
Air pollution   474, 486
Algorithmic ranking system   352
Alien art   338
Alien intelligence   26, 338
Alignment assemblies   74, 491
All Our Ideas   354, 436
All-seeing   188
Allen, Danielle   88, 164, 371, 408
Alphabet   186, 441
AlphaGo   338
Altman, Sam   19, 33, 193, 512
Amazon   186, 488
*American democracy*   113, 127
American legislative Capitol   49
American Revolution   413
Analysis paralysis   349
Andersen, Hans Christian   213
Anderson, Laurie   338
Andreesen, Marc   512
Android   154, 167
Anonymity   181, 208, 331
Anthropic   176, 354, 403, 496
Anthropocene   474
Anthropologist   124, 133, 163, 203, 373
Anti-authoritarianism   62
Anti-social   5, 8, 465
Anti-social Media   71, 465
Antipathy   36
Antiretroviral Therapy   444
Antisocial   6, 26, 97
Antitrust   398, 403, 482, 487, 492, 500
Antitrust actions   482
Apple   186, 201, 488
Apple's torus spaceship   433
Approval Voting   301, 380, 514
Arab Spring   13
Arendt, Hannah   88, 198, 413
Arms Race   167, 418, 466

**523**

Armstrong, Neil   464
Arnott, Richard   405
ARPANET   138, 154, 257, 482, 489, 508
Arrow's Theorem   380
Arrow, Kenneth   380, 447
Articles 145 of the ROC   57
Artificial General Intelligence   34
Artificial Intelligence (AI)   4, 9, 23, 29, 105, 110, 367
Artificial Neural Network   105
Artistic cocreation   334
Artistic expression   333
Asana   251, 335
Asia Development Bank   78
Asimov, Isaac   26
Aspirations to equality   166
Asset sharing   253, 258, 266
Assimilation   52
Assisted real-time voting   387
Associated Identification Number   184
Association   208
Asynchronous communication   436
Athenian marketplace   347
Atomist   132
Atomistic agents   512
Attention exchange tax   504
Augmented Reality (AR)   167, 318, 511
Australia   44, 370, 456
Australian government   370
Authoritarian regimes   1, 12, 19
Authoritarian repressive state   60
Authoritarian rule   2
Authoritarianism   5, 62, 164, 170
Authority   413
Autodesk   335
Automated Clearing Houses (ACHs)   235
Autonomy   342

# B

Back-propagated   500
Background signals   384
Badges   371, 404
Bank accounts   188, 234
Banks   233, 239, 243
Banks, Ian   26

Baran, Paul 139, 203
Barlow, John Perry 37
Basic research 479
BBN 135, 138, 145
Bellamy, Edward 234
Benefits Data Trust 369
Benet, Juan 260
Berners-Lee, Tim 141, 145, 236
BERT 105
Bertelsmann Foundation 82
Bhagavad Gita 334
*Bible* 119, 334
Bidirectional equilibrium 106
Biodiversity 9, 104, 473, 477
Biodiversity Loss 9, 473, 477
Biomedical engineering 458
Biometrics 191, 194, 478
Bioweapons 9, 23
Birth certificates 115, 184
Bitcoin 13, 24, 35, 237, 248
Blended-Finance Agreement 454
Blindness of justice 365
Blitzscaling 414
Blockchain 4, 23, 196, 218, 227, 402
Blockchain-centric identity systems 197
Bluesky 158, 218
Bolt Beranek and Newman 489
Bottom-up 385
Bowling Alone 228
Boyd, danah 198, 218, 223
Bradford, Anu 481
Brain interface 301, 464
Brain-Computer Interfaces 310
Braver Angels 356
Bricolage 303
Bridging the crowd 345
Broadcast 66, 273, 348
Brussels Effect 481
Buddhism 81
Bureaucracies 365, 399
Bureaucratic rules 366
Burke, Edmund 475
By an invisible hand 395

525

# C

Cameron, Kim 195
Campus athletics 432
Canada 21, 408, 456, 476
Cancel culture 16
Capitalism 3, 8, 16, 20, 32, 35, 41, 392, 406
Carbon credit 454
Cash 232, 240
*Castle, The* 367
Cathy O'Neil 10, 16
Cellphone addiction 80
Center for Constructive Communication 355
Central Bank Digital Currencies 22, 232, 239
Central planning 34
Centralized surveillance 5, 197
Centralized top-down 4
Centralizing 6, 9, 97, 191
Centralizing structure 191
Certificates Of enrollment 184
Chains Of introductions 205
Chang, Simon 65
Chaos 97, 104
Chaos and top-down order 512
Chaotic effects 99
Chaotic states 97
Charity 230, 399
Charter cities 374
Checks and balances 241, 264
Chen Shui-bian 61
Cheques 234
Chiang Ching-Kuo 60
Chiang Kai-shek 55
Chinese Communist Party (CCP) 12, 55, 59, 483
Church-Turing Thesis 96
Church, Alonzo 98
*Circle, The* 223, 342
Circular investment 405, 503
Citizen co-journalism 464
Citizen journalism 464
Citizen volunteers 69
Citizen-led online initiative 455
Citizens of the Free Area 61
Civic hackers 64, 72

Civic hacking culture 477
Civic spaces 323
Civic Tech 158
Civic technology movement 474
Civil Clan 53
Civil IoT 475, 486
Civil Livelihood 54
Civil Rights Movement 58
Civil society 479, 485, 492, 495
*Civilization VI* 33, 377
Civilizing 393
Claude 303, 354
Clean energy 473
Climate change 179, 473, 477
Cloud Era 261
Cloud infrastructures 154, 489, 497
Co-construction of health agency 445
Cocreation relationship 477
Codetermination 398
Cofacts 73
Cogburn, Courtney 317
Cold War 19, 134, 164
Collaboration across difference 304, 473
Collaboration across diversity 409
Collaborative diversity 48, 92
Collaborative exchange 392
Collaborative filtering 345
Collaborative innovation 336
Collaborative journalism 462
Collaborative network 475
Collaborative platform 336, 341
Collaborative problem solving 55
Collaborative technologies 378
Collaborative technology 2, 285
Collaboratives 271
Collective action 212, 217
Collective alignment 355
Collective bargaining 172, 270, 499
Collective consciousness 315, 340
Collective creativity 328, 341
Collective decision 163, 248, 389, 514
Collective deliberation 375
Collective future 510
Collective intelligence 354, 437

Collective organization 35, 91, 470
Collective problem-solving 476
Collective response systems 354, 358
Collegia 142, 448
Colonial outsider 370
Colorado State Legislature 384
Commanding heights 12, 482
Common belief 214, 226
Common carriers 467
Common content 468
Common corporate infrastructure 427
Common European Asylum System 179
Common good 299, 395
Common interest 210
Common Knowledge 212, 223, 227
Common Ownership Tax 405, 504
Common will 362, 379
Commons-Based property 117
Commons-derived data tax 505
Communism 32
Community currency 247, 285
Community donation 390
Community Notes (CN) 345, 357
Community recovery 201
Community-based 117, 345, 415
Community-based identity 117
Compelling narrative 465
Competition policies 487
Competitive authoritarian regimes 164
Competitive effect 418
Complexity 202, 367
Complexity theory 104
Comprehensiveness 199
Compulsory Purchase 399
Computational complexity 98, 103
Computer as Communication Device 210
Computers And Government 132, 146, 487
Computer-simulated neuron 371
Concentrated computational asset tax 504
Confidential computers 268
Confidential computing 221
Conformity 375, 519
Confucian tradition 53, 58
Connected digital community 492

**528**

Connected Society 88, 91, 112
Consociational 117, 381, 386
Consociationalism 117, 386
Constitutional court 84
Context 211, 216, 226
Contextual confidence 226, 283
Contextual integrity 203, 206, 241, 281
Contribution 427, 439
Control 195, 204
Cooperative enterprise 54, 57, 128, 271, 398, 486
Coordination 498, 507
Copyright 23, 75
Corbyn, Jeremy 16
Corporate bureaucracy 364
Corporate campus 427, 432
Corporate control 146, 195, 330, 407
Corporate Libertarianism 33
Corporations 390, 394, 397, 403
Correlation discounting 386
Cortico 355
Countervail 398
Coursera 336
COVID-19 Pandemic 69, 72, 85, 428, 454, 469
Cowriting 334
Crackle 332
Creative collaborations 332
Creative Commons 285
Creative process 334, 340
Credit accounts 234
Credit card 234
Credit-scoring 188
Critical value 97
Cross-cultural collaboration 338
Cross-cultural Exchange 324
Cross-pollination 433, 442
Cross-Straits Services Trade Agreement 67
Crowdsourcing 334, 371
Crutzen, Paul Jozef 473
Crypto 5, 8, 13, 23, 29, 35, 480, 509
Cryptocurrency 8, 13, 23, 35, 194, 232, 237, 247
Cryptographic hypercapitalism 32
Cryptographic principle 460
Cryptographic standards 222
Cryptography 5, 31, 35, 193, 264, 462, 466

Cryptonomicon 35
Cultural diversity 281, 290, 343, 363
Cultural homogenization 344
Cultural norm 373
Cultural practice 260, 315, 373, 516
Currency 233, 239, 243, 247
Curriculum Vitae (CV) 365
Customers 96, 102, 111
Cybernetic society 129
Cybernetics 113, 129, 133

# D

Dao 50, 279
Daoism 50
dApps 423
Dark Web 190
DARPA 145, 148
Darwinism 96
Data Act 9, 255, 484
Data brokers 188
Data Coalitions 71, 424, 474, 499
Data collaboration 499
Data federation 263, 268
Data Governance Act 16, 263
Data sharing 257, 262
Data transparency 65, 75
Data-driven Actors 476
Davidson, James Dale 36
Davis, Decontee 464
De Tocqueville, Alexis 6, 210
Decentralization Of Cryptocurrencies 247
Decentralized Identifiers (DID) 196
Decentralized Identity 157, 177, 193
Decentralized Innovation 489
Decentralized Science 495
Decentralized Scientific Community 108
Decentralized Social Networking Protocol 218
Decentralized Social Technologies 19
Decentralized Web 158, 177
Decision Trees 368
Declaration for the Future of the Internet 279
Declaration of the Independence of Cyberspace 37
Decreasing Marginal Returns 395
Deepfakes 281

| | |
|---|---|
| DeepMind | 34, 338 |
| Deforestation | 325, 473 |
| Degressive Proportionality | 117, 384 |
| Deliberation | 286, 297, 300, 345, 468 |
| Deming, W. Edwards | 57, 133, 436 |
| Democracy | 1, 88, 278, 378, 484, 497, 504 |
| *Democracy in America* | 6, 209 |
| Democratic advocates | 59 |
| Democratic freedom | 62 |
| Democratic Inputs to AI | 70, 355 |
| Democratic participation | 4, 53, 160 |
| Democratic Progressive Party (DPP) | 49, 61 |
| Democratic Republican Government | 413 |
| Demonization | 469 |
| Descriptive | 90 |
| Designated Verifier Proofs (DVP) | 225 |
| Dewey, John | 54, 58, 91, 112, 126, 397, 497 |
| Deweyian pragmatism | 58 |
| Difference | 88 |
| Differential Privacy | 221, 269 |
| Differing degrees | 32, 122, 356, 380 |
| Diffusion of information | 352 |
| Digital access | 280 |
| Digital agency | 491 |
| Digital archaeology | 333 |
| Digital asset sharing | 253, 258, 266 |
| Digital asset taxes | 504 |
| Digital assets | 253, 263, 500, 504 |
| Digital assistant | 387 |
| Digital certificate | 453 |
| Digital civic engagement | 71 |
| Digital competence education | 75, 160 |
| Digital credentials | 179, 196 |
| Digital currencies | 19, 22, 35, 504 |
| Digital currency | 29, 239 |
| Digital democracy | 28, 33, 45, 280, 284, 370, 512 |
| Digital divide | 280, 330, 343 |
| Digital economy | 20, 253, 480, 506 |
| Digital ecosystem | 424, 484, 494, 497 |
| *Digital Empires* | 481, 484 |
| Digital freedom of association | 228 |
| Digital identity systems | 183, 191 |
| Digital infrastructure | 281 |
| digital innovation hubs | 487 |

Digital interaction     162, 166
Digital land tax     504
Digital legacies     328, 341
Digital life     166, 181, 278, 488
Digital mapping tool     370
Digital Markets Act  16, 484
Digital ministries     490
Digital nomads     429
Digital platform     188, 328, 343, 403
Digital protocols     176, 479
Digital Public Infrastructure (DPI)     177, 280, 484, 489
Digital public services     21, 283
Digital rights     212
Digital sector     502
Digital Services Act  16, 484
Digital social engagement     474
Digital stack     485
Digital stagnation     38
Digital technology     92, 365
Digital threats     283
Digital twins     339
Digital user experience     191
Digital workspace     335
Digital Yuan     24, 29
Digital-native Currency     177
Digital-native identity infrastructure     192
Digitally-related assets     272
Diia     283
Diplomatic Decisions     377
Diplomatic Favor     377
Diplomatic nuance  62
Direct collective representative     360
Direct election of the President     61
Direct neural interface     432
Directly ▢ (D▢)     503
Discrimination Law  10
Disinformation     352
Displacement     40
Disruption     9, 139, 440
Distributed Autonomous Organization (DAO)     190, 367, 385, 403, 499
Distributed Denial of Service (DDoS)     283
Distributed Ledger Technology (DLT)     196, 219, 237, 371
Distributed network 268, 372

Distributed participation 465
Distribution 203, 397, 400
Diverse legal system 372
Diverse perspective 336, 341
Diversification 374, 421
Diversity 412, 419
Diversity Of Cross-species Interactions, The 103
Diversity of groups 173, 414
Dividual identity 126, 129
Domain Names 274
*Domains of Identity* 189
Dominant narrative 343
DoNotPay 369
Dossiers 188
Double Coincidence Of Wants, The 244
Dream Machine, The 133, 256
Driverless Cars 22
Dryhurst, Mat 338, 514
Dunbar number 203, 243
Dunbar, Robin 203
Durkheim, Émile 124, 449
Duverger's Law 379
Dynamic 390, 393, 399, 403, 407
Dōka 52

# E

e-citizenship 429
E-Government 21, 160
e-health 457
e-sports 321, 432
Early adopter community 418
Early adopters 415, 419
Ease of Attacks Online 181
Ebola 464
Echo Chamber 345, 352, 465
Ecology 96, 104, 132
Economies of Esteem 404
Economist Intelligence Unit 82
Ecosystems 97, 102
Edge of chaos 97, 172, 512
Educational psychology 372, 415
edX 336
Egalitarianism 58, 447
EGDI 21

Eggers, Dave 223, 342
Eigenvalues 386
Eigenvoting 386
Einstein's Theories Of Relativity 101
Election 164, 170, 350, 355, 359, 379
Electromagnetic frequency 273
Electromagnetic spectrum 75, 254, 273
Electronic commerce 181, 244
Elite universities 369
Emergence 96, 103, 107, 110
Emergent publics 126, 129, 407
Eminent Domain 399
Emotional connectivity 318, 323
Empathy amplifiers 327
*Emperor's New Clothes, The* 213
Employment 181, 189, 195
Encounter with the East 339
Endowments 397
Engelbart, Douglas 136, 257
Enlightenment 117, 163
Entrepreneurship 58, 156, 393, 398
Environment sensing network 475
Environmental devastation 9
Environmental justice 475, 478
Environmental Movement 104
Environmental problem 411, 473, 476
Environmental Science 96
Environmental sustainability 476
Environmental, Social and Governance (ESG) 403, 470
Epigenetics 104
Establish and Protect Participant Identities 180
Estonia 28, 280, 283, 429
ETH Zurich 333
Ethereum 157, 237, 248, 493, 496
Ethereum community 493
Ethnic pluralism 53, 61
Ethnographer 373
EU 179, 194
Euclidean geometry 101, 118
European Digital Identity 489
European Union (EU) 483
Eusocial 103
Evacuation credentials 179
Excessive fragmentation 433

Excessive segregation 433
Existential risks 23
Experimentalism 55
Experimentation on 415
Experimentation with 416, 423
Expert 368
Export-orientation 62
Extended Evolutionary Synthesis 96, 102
Extended Reality (XR) 458
External surveillance 211, 216, 222, 242
Externalities 392, 397, 400, 404, 407
Extreme sports 432
Extremist parties 7

# F

Fabric of relationships 510
Faceted Identity 198
Facial recognition 24
Fact-checking 73, 345
Fairness 127, 364, 468
False consensus 469
Farritor, Luke 333
Fascism 32
Fast, Fun and Fair 74
Feature phone 363
Federal 381, 386
Federal Pension Insurance system 369
Federated learning 222, 268, 459
Fedorov, Mykhailo 491
Filecoin 177, 261
Financial adequacy (FA) 503
Financial capitalism 4
Financial innovation 7
Financial markets 5, 394
Financial technology 5, 13, 68, 483
Financial transactions 190, 241
Finnish government 369
Fintech 13, 250
Five star rating system 357
Five-Year Plans 483
Flexible/gig work taxes 505
Fluidity 477
Folk religion 81
For-profit private corporations 479

Fora        355
Formalism            98
Forms of diversity     290, 302, 513
Foundation Models  5, 19, 105
Foxconn   78
Fractals      99
Fractional reserve banking     234
Fragile democracies          13
Freddy Lim          67
free China          56
Free Markets Know Best     40
Free speech         161, 165, 171
Free trade          288, 394
Free trade agreements     394
Freedom House      82
Freedom of association    172, 207
Freedom of expression     279
Freedom of the press      462, 467
French Revolution   413
Frictions   393
Fridman, Lex        356
Fructus    122, 264, 406
Full multisensory shared experience    333
Full-time employment         398
Fundamental human rights    180, 481
Fundamental Welfare Theorems       395
Fundamentally Interactions    102
Funder    32, 390, 453, 461, 488
Funding pool        453
Fusion      303
Futarchy    387

# G

g0v        64, 71, 455, 493
Gaia-X      177, 263, 489
Galbraith, John Kenneth      215, 398
Galor, Oded         290
Gamification         458
Ganga River         476
Gates, Bill           61
Gathering Storm     33, 377
Gavi        444
General computation       96
General Data Protection Regulation    16, 222, 484

536

Generative AI 226, 279
Generative art 337
Generative artists 338
Generative Foundation Models (GFMs) 186, 253, 335, 365, 453, 465, 482, 496
Generative pre-trained transformer (GPT) 19, 49, 105, 416
Generative Pretrained Transformer 19
Geographical Information System (GIS) 370
Geopolitics 3, 76, 250, 511
George, Henry 54, 75, 91, 112, 119, 401, 405
Georgist land value tax 56
Germany 164, 369, 471
GFM-based Representative 360
GFM-driven Process 342
GFMs 511, 516
Ghost workers 254
Gig workers 505
Git 285
GitCoin 157, 390, 423, 496
GitCoin grants 390
GitHub 110, 186, 335
GitHub sponsors 390, 496
GitLab 156, 335
GitRules 286
Global anti-colonial movement 52
Global capitalism 392, 396
Global consciousness networks 328
Global Crossroad 47
Global Declaration on Information Integrity Online 279
Global Fund 451
Global GDP 1, 428
Global government 121, 410, 507
Global legitimacy 389
Global policies 377
Global positioning 14, 370
Global warming 473
Globalization 1, 41, 294
Gogolook 74
Gold Card 75, 429
Gold standard 200
Golden Age 8, 38, 45
Golgi, Camillo 104
Good Old-fashioned AI (GOFAI) 368
Google 392, 441, 488, 492, 504

537

Google DeepMind 338
Gordon-Levitt, Joseph 344
Government-issued Identities 186
Governments 479, 491, 498, 506
GovTech 158
Graeber, David 117, 243, 259, 413
Granovetter, Mark 105
Graphical user interface 137, 167
Graphics Processing Units (GPUs) 258
Grassroots Initiatives 486
*Great Firewall* 170
Great powers 3, 102, 481
Greatest Good For The Greatest Number, The 378
Green technologies 411, 473
Gross Domestic Product (GDP) 17, 77, 427
Group Works 351
Guard (hackathon) 208
Gödel's Theorem 96

# H

Hackathon 65, 71, 475
Hackathons 65, 71, 208, 515
HackMD 153
Hakka 50, 56, 62
Handmer, Casey 332
Hanson, Robin 387, 450
Haptic feedback 310, 322
Harberger, Arnold 401
Hard Journalism 470
Hawley, Josh 16
Health 411, 415, 425
Health financing 453
Health insurance 447, 454
Health Savings Account 448
Health Savings Plan 448
Healthy minds in healthy bodies 450
Hebbian Model Of Connections, The 105
Heisenberg's Uncertainty Principle 101
Henry George Theorem 120, 405
*Her* (film) 26
Herculaneum 332, 337
Herculean Task 201
Heritage Foundation 78
Herndon, Holly 338, 344, 514

Heterogeneity 110, 190, 390
High Modernism 95, 117
High-bandwidth communication 315
Higher-fidelity signals 379
HiredScore 370
Hiring Manager 366, 370, 438
Hirschman, Albert 393
Hit Rates 438
HIV 444, 450
Hock, Dee 235
Hodgkin, Alan 104
Hoffman, Reid 34, 416, 512
Holdout Issues 275
Hollowing-out 7
Holmes, Oliver Wendell 94
Holochain 177, 249
Homerian epics 334
Homogenization 306, 315, 373
Homogenization of Ideas 342
Homogenize 132, 302, 409
Homomorphic Encryption 220, 267
Horizontal Dialogue 437
Hsieh Tsung-min 58
Hu Shih 54
Hugging Face 335
*Human Condition, The* 88, 91, 95
Human cooperation 392
Human diversity 511
Human interactions 190, 319
Human resources platform 370
Human rights 180, 287, 481, 493
Human-Computer Symbiosis 487
*Humanocracy* 403
Humor over rumor 74
Hunter-gatherer model 411
Hutchins Commission on Freedom of the Press 467
Huxley, Andrew 104
Hybrid Reality environments 318, 322
Hybrid Work Style 429
Hypertext 137, 145, 153
Hypertext Transfer Protocol Secure (HTTPS) 267

# I

IBM 149, 256, 477, 488

Iceland   160, 385
ID2020   371
Ideathons   72, 491, 515
Identity and Access 424
Identity Foundation 177, 181
Identity information 188
Identity Provider, The   187
Identity systems   181, 186, 189, 197, 203, 206, 249
Ideologies of the Twenty-First Century   32
Ideology 42, 50, 56, 291, 493
Idiosyncratic project   441
Immersive learning 323
Immersive Shared Reality   317, 359, 421, 507
Immersive soundscapes   311
Impact   444
Impartial 365
Imperfections   393
Implementer   453, 461
Implicit data/attention exchange tax   504
In-person meeting 347
In-person team   431, 442
In-silico   339
Incompetent manager   439
India   28, 476, 481, 489, 498, 507
India stack   177, 192, 489, 498
India Stack Program 192
Indian Government 192
Indiastack   489
Indiegogo   336
Indigenous Land and Sea Corporation   370
Individual identity   113, 215
Industrial policy   486
Industrial Revolution   96
Inequality 343
Inequality in access 281
Influence function   269
Infodemic   44, 74
Information Age   36, 146, 278
Information commons   171, 279
Information integrity   229, 279
Information openness   283
Information Processing Techniques Office (IPTO)   136, 486
Information Technology   171
InformationCard   196

Infrastructure 399, 479, 502, 505
Infringement on privacy 206
Inji 193
Insurer 447, 451
Integrity of identity 229
Intelligence Augmentation 42
Inter-operation 142, 201, 222, 240
Inter-specific communication platform 328
Interactive agent 357
Intergalactic Computer Network 136, 150, 253
Intermediate horizon 515, 519
International Business Machines (IBM) 149, 256
International federation 184
International Monetary Fund 77
International rules-based order 479
International Telecommunication Union (ITU) 280
International trade 392, 406, 515
International trade treaties 406
Internet 1, 92, 352, 357
Internet access as a human right 282
Internet Corporation for Assigned Names and Numbers (ICANN) 274
Internet of Beings 64, 279
Internet of Things 5, 64
*Internet Tidal Wave* 61
Internet-compatible payments processor 239
Internet-mediated Writing 352
Interoperability 28
Interoperability Across Legal Regime 375
Interoperable Model 281
Interplanetary File System (IPFS) 260
Intersect 96, 106, 110
Intersectional Identity 91, 124, 359, 438
Intrapreneurship 428, 440, 515
Invasions of privacy 186
iOS 167
Irises 193
IVR junction 363

# J

J. D. Vance 36
Japanese occupation 52
Jefferson, Thomas 4
Jennifer Prah Ruger 445
Jetsons 26

Jobs, Steve 138, 143, 433
Johnson, Simon 27, 381
Joint Learning 431
Joseph Carl Robnett Licklider 132, 137, 210, 383, 482
Jothons 65
Journalism 462, 470
*Journey of Humanity, The* 290
Julian Schilliger 333
Jurisdictional Alignment (JA) 503
Jurisdictional boundaries 257, 394

# K

Kafka, Franz 367
Kaizen 57
Kao Chia-liang 64
Kaohsiung Incident 60
Karatani, Kojin 211, 247, 296, 385
Karya 363
Kazakhstan 21
Kela-Kelpo project 369
Khan Academy 336
Kickstarter 336
Kidd, David 371
Klein, Ezra 19, 35
Knappschaften 449
Know Your Customer (KYC) 188
knowledge is power 278
Kuomintang 50
Kurz, Sebastian 36
Kurzweil, Ray 26

# L

Labor augmentation 40
Labor automation 40
Labor Law 23, 499, 505
Labor markets 6, 394, 398, 408
Labor unions 60, 210, 398
Land to the Tiller 56
Lanier, Jaron 202
Large Language Model (LLM) 70, 339, 360, 438
Latour, Bruno 360
Laws of Identity 195
Le Guin, Ursula 26

Lean manufacturing 57
Lean startup 58
Lee Teng-hui 60
Legal agent 478
Legal grounding 189
Legal jurisdiction 374
Legal Robot 369
Legal tender 233
Legislative Yuan 66
Legitimacy 215, 413
Legitimation 23
Lego 403
Levels of assurance 182
Levitsky, Steven 7, 164, 412
Liberal democracy 87
Liberal democratic polities 206
Liberalization of Taiwan 60
Liberating structures 351
Libertarian ideology 42
Libertarian vision 110
Libertarianism 33, 40, 89
Libertarians 174, 240, 367, 510
Life expectancy 444, 461
Limited Cultural Groups 409
Linkage 182
LinkedIn 186, 205, 416
Linton, Michael 247
Linux 154, 166, 496
Liquid Democracy 359, 385
Little Platoons 475, 478
Liu Cixin 101
Livestream-based communication 66
Local Exchange Trading Systems (LETS) 247
Local language 363
Local communities 515
Location Aware Sensor System (LASS) 475
Long-distance cooperation 48
Long-term work permits 408
Lorax 360
Lord Kelvin 100
*Lord of the Flies, The* 519
Los Alamos 334
Lost Dao, The 176, 335

**543**

Low-skilled workers 40

# M

Ma, Jack 34
Machine learning 5, 368
Machine translation tool 357
Macro badges 372
Macrobiology 102
Magpie River 476
Malaria 450
Man-Computer Symbiosis 135, 487
Management challenges 270
Mandarin 2, 50, 65, 92
Mandelbrot set 99
Manipulation 314
Mao Zedong 55
Marginal Revolution 395
Market 390
Market design 273, 404
Market power 11, 39, 396, 403
Marxism 51, 55
Mask App 72
Mass extinction 473
Mass surveillance 12
Massachusetts Institute of Technology (MIT) 355
Massive Multi-user Online Laboratories (MMOLs) 323
Masters of Scale 416
Masters, Blake 36
Mastodon 21, 158, 218
Matching fund 390, 402, 406, 442
Material redistribution 34
Maternal mortality 444
Mathematics 96, 135, 375
Maximize utility 95
Maximum Flow (maxflow) 205, 248
Mechanism design 275, 401
Media 411, 417, 420, 423, 462
Media ecosystem 468
Mediated reality 306, 319
Mediators of Individual Data (MIDs) 202, 271
Meetings Deemed Unproductive 427
Mental health 312, 325, 330, 444
Meta 186, 356, 392, 488
Metascience 107

Metaverse 25, 35, 512
Metaverses 174
Mezzo Badges 372
Microsoft (MSFT) 186, 195, 363, 440, 470, 482, 488
Military scenario 432
Mimetic Models 281
Minister of Digital Affairs 49
Minister without Portfolio 67, 76
*Ministry for the Future* 360, 406
Ministry of Digital Affairs 76, 260, 491
*Minitel* 18, 143
Minority 81, 106, 194, 343
Minquán 54
Minzú 53
Miraikan 305, 491, 515
Misinformation 347, 352
Misleading 345
Mix Of Diversity And Interconnectedness, The 100
Mixed Reality (MR) 157, 318, 430
Mobile Operating System 489
Mobile Telephones 188
Modernity 113, 117, 370, 513
Modular Open-Source Identity Platform (MOSIP) 193
Molecular biology 104
Monarchy 55
Monist 132
Monist Atomism 89, 95
Monopolization 146, 330, 488
Monopoly 119
Moore's Law 33, 256
Moore's Law for Everything 33
Moral Bio-enhancement 312
Mount Vesuvius 332
Move fast and break things 417
Mozilla 495
mRiik 283
MSFT 196
Multi-factor authentication 182, 189
Multi-sectoral alliance 489
Multidisciplinary renaissance 340
Multiemployer 6
Multiple accounts 183, 196
Multiple perspective 337
Multipolarity 298

545

Multiscale organization 103
Musk, Elon 19, 34, 218, 239
Mutualism 103
Mycorrhizal fungi 282
MyGoPen 74
Mínshēng 54

# N

Nadella, Satya 363, 440
Nader, Youssef 332
Name spaces on the Internet 273
Narrow Corridor 5, 97, 512
Narrow Educational and Career Path 370
Narrow Signals Of Identity 186
NASA 134, 137, 477
Nation-state 37, 113, 120, 125, 129, 146, 172, 177, 211, 291, 392, 398, 408, 448, 505, 518
National Coalition for Dialogue and Deliberation 351
National insurance model 449
National language 363
National politics 60, 437, 493
National Security Agencies 188
National Socialist German Workers (Nazi) party 164
Nationalism 36, 53, 398
Nationalist 36, 52
Nationalist backlash 37
Natural ecosystem 478
Natural language processing 355
Natural leadership 440
Natural legal personhood 476
Natural sciences 97, 112, 131
Natural selection 102
Negative freedom of speech 165
Nelson, Ted 140, 145, 150, 334
Neoliberal 41
Neoliberal reaction 400
Neoliberalism 148, 393, 486
Neom 22
Netflix Prize 337
Netherlands 462
Netizen 469
Network architectures 197
Network Of Processes 94
Network sociology 105

*Network State, The* 36
Network States 374
Networked and probabilistic structure 371
Networked value 119
Networks of human minds 371
Neural interfaces 306, 313, 432
Neural network 96, 105, 337, 368, 372
Neurofeedback 312
Neuromodulation 312
Neurons 104, 122, 371
Neuroscience 96, 103, 312, 326
New Associationist Movement (NAM) 211, 247, 385
New Brandeis 482
New England town hall 347
New money 234, 239
New public 112, 127
New Republic, The 55
New Yorker 181
New Zealand 160, 476
New ▢ Order 490, 518
News feed algorithm 339, 345
Newtonian mechanics 96, 118, 129
Nicholas Bostrom 26, 34
Nissenbaum, Helen 206, 211
Nixon's visit to PRC 59
Nixon, Richard 59
Nobody Movement 65
Nodes 105, 368
Non-aligned incentives 446
non-believers 81
Non-communicable disease 445
Non-Euclidean Geometries 96
Non-fungible Token (NFT) 402, 504
Non-human Perspective 340
Non-market 6, 409, 451
Non-profit ▢ Infrastructure 497
Non-renewable energy sources 473
Non-verbal communication 307, 347
Normative 90, 275, 459
North star 420
Notion 335

# O

OAuth 183, 187
Objective quality 346
Objectivity 465
Occupy 48, 440
Ocean acidification 9, 473
Octavia Butler 26
OECD 17, 78, 479
Office of Chief Technology Officer 440
Office politics 437
Olfactory technology 322
On Revolution 413
On the ground 441, 514
On the Internet, Nobody Knows You're A Dog 181
One China 59
One Country, Two Systems 62
One-dimensional Spectrum 225, 346
One-Person-One-Vote 117
One-Share-One-Vote 114, 381, 394, 407, 501
Online collaboration platform 334
Online deliberation 150, 158
Online democracy 181
Online gaming 318
Online platform 300, 320, 334
Opacity of bureaucracy 374
Open and decentralized marketplace 487
Open Collective Foundation 496
Open conversation 436
Open Government Data 283
Open Government Movement 67
Open Impact Pool 453
Open protocols 479
Open source 18, 22, 285, 399, 479, 494
Open source code 18, 285, 495
Open source community 399, 490
Open source ecosystem 390, 484, 494, 497
Open source intelligence (OSINT) 464
Open source models 335
Open source projects 495
Open Source Software (OSS) 22, 68
Open source technology 490
Open space technology 348
Open standard 139

Open standards-based collaborations    263
Open-source project    335, 492
Open-source rainmaking    475
Open-source software (OSS)    245
OpenAI    19, 33, 70, 193, 354, 403, 417, 441, 496
OpenID Connect    187
OpenMined    268
Operating System    161, 287
Optimism Collective    496
Orderly states    97
Outcome    451, 460
Output    451, 457
Ovadya, Aviv    353
Over-shared information    207
Ownership    196, 200

# P

Packet switching    139, 145, 197, 201, 205, 371
PageRank    274, 386
Paradigm shift    314, 352
Paradox.ai    370
PARC    137, 143, 489
Park of Aging    305, 310
Parker, Seth    332
Parliament of Things    360
Partial Common Ownership    401
Participation    4, 14, 23
Participative production    57
Participatory design    403
Participedia    351
Passports    115, 184
Password    182, 225, 457
Path of least action    95
Paucity of attention    217
Payment In digital spaces    232
PayPal    150, 239
PDCA (Plan-Do-Check-Act) cycle    57
Peer Production    152
Peng Ming-min    58
Penrose, Lionel    383
People's Republic of China (PRC)    17, 28, 34, 50, 59, 62, 481
Peripheral    27, 35
Personal computing    256, 482, 489
Personal identities    91

549

Phishing attack 223, 460
Phone 179, 187, 192, 196, 205
Physical Government-issued IDs 186
Physical work 429
Physics 94, 100
Pigouvian taxes 400, 503
Piketty, Thomas 79
Pixar's headquarters 433
Place of Convergence 48
Plural Funding 386, 390
Plural management protocol 407
Plural spirit 48
Pluralism 53, 61
Pluralistic ignorance 469
Pluralists 518
Plurality 2
Plutocracy 181
Polarization 4, 43
Policy 479
Polis 68, 353, 357, 436, 455
Political polarization 7, 43, 83, 345
Polycentrism 203, 206
Polypolitan migration policy 408
Pompeii 332
Populist movement 398
Portals Policing Project 324, 356
Porter, Winslow 464
Positive freedom of speech 165
Post-capitalist world 26
Post-colonial futurism 26
Post-gender 26
Post-state 26
Post-symbolic communication 305, 340, 375, 421
Power concentration 387
Pragmatic 54, 133, 300
PRC surveillance regime 28
Pre-digital associations 211
Precious metals 233
Prediction market 285, 387, 403
Predictive futurism 26
Predictive voting 387
Premature optimization 288, 298
Prepayment 447, 454
Prescriptive 90, 383

Presidential Hackathon 71, 485
Press freedom 411, 462
Press responsibility 467
Principles of ⬚ 162, 344
Privacy 182, 185, 191, 194, 203, 206, 231, 237, 240, 342
Privacy budget 269
Privacy regulations 222, 264
Privacy-enhancing technologies (PETs) 220
Private club 216
Private community-based sponsorship 408
Private corporations 150, 177, 479, 489
Private health insurance 447
Private information 182, 460
Private key 220, 467
Private monopolies 482
Private organizations 409
Private property 112, 122, 273, 392, 399
Private providers 189
Private sector 18, 29, 185, 192, 481, 488, 498, 502
Private technology development 479
Private, for-profit corporations 187
Pro-social media 468, 471
Production Possibilities Frontier (PPF) 296
Productivity Software 470
Programmer 368, 477
*Progress and Poverty* 119
Progress prizes 332
Progressive authentication 200
Project Liberty 176, 218
Projection mapping 311
Proof of Work 238
Propagational investment currency system (PICSY) 385
Property 251
Property rights 272, 392, 397
Proportional representation 116, 382, 385
Protocol Labs (PL) 260
Pseudonymity 181
Pseudonyms 184, 196
*Public and its Problems, The* 112, 126, 397
Public consent 23
Public data repositories 196
Public Digital Innovation Space (PDIS) 70
Public expenditure 17, 369

Public funding  154, 479
Public goods  374, 392, 395, 399, 402, 405, 409
Public health policy 454
Public investment  480, 484, 487, 497
Public key cryptography  220
Public mission  489
Public participation 14, 283, 351, 486
Public perception  475
Public sector  14, 17, 23, 32
Public service  363, 369
Public signals  186
Public square  21, 172, 217, 497
Public welfare schemes  400
Public will 376, 379
Public/supermodular goods  402
Purchasing Power Parity (PPP) 77
Putnam, Robert  228

# Q

Qing  51
Quadratic Funding (QF)  391, 402
Quadratic Liquid Democracy 387
Quadratic Voting (QV)  71, 378, 486, 501
Quantitative markers  404
Quantum computer 222
Quantum mechanics  101, 132
Quantum physics  101, 130
Quick fixes  264

# R

RadicalxChange  247, 382, 387, 493
Rainbow flags  50
Rainforest Foundation US  370
Raj  28, 32, 301
Ramón y Cajal, Santiago  104
Rand, Ayn  35
Randomized controlled trials 414
Ranked Choice  380
Rationality  95, 117, 298, 370
*Ready Player One*  329
Real-time auction  274
Realistic avatar  431
Receipts  233, 467

552

Reckless monopolies 393
Recovery 183, 189, 196, 200
Reddit 190, 271
Redistribution 397, 400, 447, 454
Reductionism 98
Redundancy 139, 199, 260
Rees-Mogg, Jacob 36
Rees-Mogg, Lord William 36
Regenerating diversity 288, 294, 302, 519
Region 211
Regression discontinuity design 460
Regulatory powerhouse 483
Reinstatement 40
Relationality 100, 103
Relevant public 128, 400
Remesh 354, 436
Remix and replace 10
Remote collaboration tool 429
Remote employee 431
Remote fitness classes 321
Remote Shared Reality 432, 438
Remote teams 427, 431, 442
Renaissance 117, 340
Reporters without Borders 462
Representation 349, 359
Representative statement 353
Representing consensus position 358
Republic of China (ROC) 50
Research and development 17, 29
Research policy 399
Resolution 2758 59
Restrepo, Pascual 11, 40
Revenue alignment (RA) 503
Reverse mentors 49
Revive China Society 53
Revolutionary Democratic Direction 53
rhizomatic association 211
Rich get richer 369
Rights Of association 183
Rights of free speech 165
Risk pooling 447
River Of democracy 2
Robinson, James 5
Robinson, Kim Stanley 360

Roblox 403
Ropes course 431
Rorty, Richard 216
Rosenblatt, Frank 105
Rough consensus 354, 358, 362, 468
Rovelli, Carlo 95, 102
Rule Of law 392
Run-off 380
Rural Land Reform 56
Russian Revolution 55

## S

Saez, Emmanuel 39, 79
Same-sex Marriage 84
San Francisco 120, 236
Sardinia 429
Saudi Arabia 20
Scaling collaboration 396
Scandinavian countries 20, 87, 165, 448
Science and Technology Studies 27
Science Fiction 25, 34, 89, 516
Science of Science 107
Scientific Management 95
Scott, Kevin 440
Seales, Brent 332
Search Engines 10, 21, 274, 375
Seasteads 35, 374
Secret Information 183
Secure Multi-Party Computation (SMPC) 220, 267
Securities Laws 23
Security 182, 193, 200, 204
Security protocols 167
Seeds 419
Self-determination 53, 456
Self-organizing Criticality 98
Sen, Amartya 382
Sensitivity 99, 221
Sensory integration 318, 326
SERVIR Amazonia 370
Seuss, Dr. 360
Shared goods 392, 396, 503
Shared knowledge base 332
Shield Of Trust and Safety 180
Sidewalk Labs 23

Signal 220
Signatures 221, 269, 467
Silent majority 469
Silicon Valley 487
Simard, Suzanne 282
Simmel, Georg 112, 123
Simon, Herbert 217, 350
Simulated military exercise 431
Single Point of Failure 195, 200
Single Tax 119
Single-sign-on Architectures (SSO) 187, 497
Sino-Japanese war 52
Siraya 50
Slack 335, 436, 470
Slaughter, Anne-Marie 172, 494
Smaller world 463
Smallpox 444
Smart city 22
Smart contract 157, 237, 265, 367
Smith, Noah 35
SnapChat 224
Snow Crash 25, 35, 329
Snowden, Edward 222
Social and behavioral psychology 106
Social collapse 5
Social connectedness 88
Social control 12, 24
Social Credit Score 24
Social currencies 249
Social difference 288, 292, 297
*Social Dilemma, The* 16
Social distance 391, 410
Social distancing measure 455
Social diversity 110, 392, 519
Social divide 386, 418, 464
Social division 345, 388, 420
Social dynamism 127
Social equity 399
Social esteem 245, 404
Social fabric 5, 174, 210
Social graph 183, 439
Social identity system 438
Social inclusivity 284
Social insurance 400

Social interaction 393
Social interactions 173, 198, 228, 251, 282
Social leakage 270
Social media 5, 13, 21, 43, 345, 352, 359, 462, 465
Social media accounts 181
Social media platform 13, 170, 339, 345, 425
Social network 337, 482, 489, 497
Social order 374, 511
Social organization 113, 129
Social recovery 200
Social responsibility 467, 470
Social science experts 128
Social sciences 27, 96, 131, 415
Social Sector 417, 425
Social Security Number (SSN) 115, 184, 317, 351
Social system 95
social welfare function 298, 381, 447
Social worker 369
Socialism 54, 349, 393
Socialism Takes Too Many Evenings 349
Socially isolated 6
Society for Worldwide Interbank Financial Telecommunication (SWIFT) 236
Society Library 356
Sociometrics 198, 478
Solidarity and Dynamism 440, 471
Sortition 297, 350, 359
Soulbound Tokens (SBTs) 197
Source confidentiality 462, 466
South China Sea 51
Sovereign Individual, The 36
Soviet Union 134, 392, 490
SpaceX 333
Spatial computing 311
Speciation 374
Spectrum sharing 275
Square Root 384, 402, 421
Square-root Voting 384
Srinavasan, Balaji 36, 512
Stagnant democratic stories 92
Stakeholder Corporation 402
Stakeholder remedies 403
Stakeholders 403, 407
Stakeholding 407
Standard career paths 437

Standardization   417, 498
*Star Trek*   26, 89, 302
Start-ups   145, 394, 407
State of Wyoming   499
Statistical Process Control (SPC)   57
Steam   190
Stephenson, Neal   25, 35, 299, 329
Stiglitz, Joseph   405
StoryCorps   356
String Theory   101
Su Tseng-chang   74
Subcultural translation   286
Submodular   245, 503
Submodular returns   503
Subscriptions   181, 470
Sun Yat-Sen   53, 401
Sunflower Movement   50, 61, 66, 83
Superintelligence   26, 32
Supermodular collaboration   399
Supermodular international cooperation   515
Supermodular investments   405
Supermodular production   406
Supermodular shared goods   503
Supermodularity   287, 294, 392, 396
Superposition   101
Superpower   10, 73
Surveillance   3, 10, 16, 24, 28, 318, 330
Sustainable Development Goals (SDGs) 444
Suzuki, Ken   385
Swartz, Lana   239
Symbiotic relationship   2, 106
Symphony of minds 340
Synchronous meeting   436
Synthetic instrument   337
Synthetic Technocracy   33
Systems of rights   169

# T
Taigi   50, 56, 62
Taishō Democratic   53
Taivoan   48
Taiwan   28, 38, 88, 280, 283, 390, 402, 408, 429, 462, 475, 481, 484, 489, 507, 510
Taiwan Self-Salvation Manifesto   58

Taiwan's Digital Civic Infrastructure 64
Talk to the City 357, 360
Tang Jingsong 52
Tang, Audrey 64, 88, 354
Tangible Potential 411
Taoism 55, 81
Taste retargeting 322
Taxes 501
Taylor, Robert 138, 210, 463
Taylorism 95
Teams 427, 435, 442
Tech Left 34
Techlash 14, 147
Technocracy 89
Technocratic vision 110
Technocrats 174, 510
Technological agenda 92
Technology addiction 80
Technology investment 29, 37
Technology policy 481
Telecommuting 6
Telehealth 457
Telemedicine 457
Telepathic creative exchange 340
Telepathic exchange 340
Telepathy 313
Temporal collaboration 341
Terminator 26
Territorial And Intellectual Property Treaties 394
Theocracy 32
Theory of change 412
Thiel, Peter 36, 239, 512
Thin shell 409
Thin signals 186, 297
Third sector 58, 399, 517
Thorburn, Luke 353
time sharing 136
Time Travel 341
Time-sharing 256, 262, 415
Top employer 369
Top-down 190, 368
Tornado Cash 241
Total Factor Productivity (TFP) 38
Towards a Connected Society 88

Toyota Production System (TPS) 57
Tradable Carbon Permits 404
Trading Cycles 244
Traditional practice 372
Transformativeness 500
Transhuman 457, 461
Transitive trust 202, 206
Translation 373
Transnational corporations 394
Transparent database 371
Trello 436
Trichotomy 481
Tridemism 51, 56, 62
True democracy 128
Trump, Donald 36
Trust falls 431
Trust Over IP Foundation 201, 249
Trusted Network 283
Tsai, Jaclyn 49, 67
Tuberculosis 451
Turing 370
Twitter 14, 21, 44, 217, 239, 345, 471
Tyranny of structurelessness 351
Tyranny of the majority 380

# U
Ukraine 283, 491
UN global goals 492
Uncertainty Principle, The 96, 99
Undecidable 98
Unforgeable and undeniable signatures 221
Uniform Resource Locator (URL) 254
Union of Japanese Scientists and Engineers (JUSE) 57
Unique Identification Authority of India (UIDAI) 192
United Arab Emirates (UAE) 20
United Kingdom (UK) 483
United Nations (UN) 268, 381, 474
United States (US) 480, 501, 506
Universal Basic Income (UBI) 34, 194
Universal birth registration 115
Universal Coded Character (unicode) 91
Universal Declaration of Human Rights 163, 166, 279
Unorthodox Thinking 437
Untapped 370

User engagement   13, 345
User experience   64, 191, 353, 495
User perspective   353
Ushahidi   159, 370
Usus   122, 263, 406
Utilities   218, 497
Utility regulation   398
Utility tokens   504

# V

V-Dem   2, 49, 82
Vaccine Alliance   444
Venture capital   29, 36, 394, 416
Venture capitalist   36, 416
Ventures   394, 406
Verifiable Credentials (VCs)   176, 193, 197, 372
Vesuvius Challenge   332, 337
Vickrey, William   401, 405
Violent revolution   412
Virtual gatherings   319
Virtual meeting   352, 434
Virtual music festivals   318, 321
Virtual Reality (VR)   147, 156, 317, 324
Virtual replica   339
Virtual tourism   321
Virtuous circle   518
Visa   235
Voice-based internet   363
Volume cartographer   332
Vote   378
Voting   23, 246
Voting based on measures of power   381
Voting based on population size   381
Vouch   199, 247
VR therapy   325
vTaiwan   67, 353
Vulcans   89

# W

Wade, Cynthia   514
Wage system   394
Waldrop, M. Mitchell   97, 133
War of Independence   413

Water Management 477
Watermarking 269
Way, Lucan 412
Wealth Taxes 399
*Weapons of Math Destruction* 10, 16, 375
Weather Systems 99
Web 2.0 19, 371
Web of group-affiliation 123
Web2 application 460
Web3 19, 28, 35, 177, 181, 190, 200, 390, 407, 423, 511
Web3 communities 181, 200
Weber, Max 117, 124, 365
Wei Ting-chao 58
Weighted voting 381, 384
Weimar Republic 164
WEIRD societies 114
Welfare 482
Welfare capitalism 287
Western capitalist countries 28
Western liberal democracies 28, 513
Whanganui 476
What's App 364
Whitcraft, Teri 514
White collar 432, 435
White Terror 56, 59
Wiener, Norbert 113, 129
Wikimedia Foundation 495
Wikipedia 22, 140, 151, 335, 465
Wikisurvey 68, 354
Wilde, Oscar 349
Will Of The Group 380
will.i.am 344
Windows 143, 166, 196
Wisdom of the crowd 455
Withdrew 59
Women Talking 347
Work-life Balance 429
Workplace 411, 425
Workspace 335
World Cafe, The 348
World Congress 377
World Economic Forum 363, 492
World Health Organization (WHO) 80
World Press Freedom Index 462

World Trade Organization, 394
World War 19, 57, 133, 164, 463
World Wide Web Consortium (W3C) 176, 190, 196, 218
Worldcoin 193
Wu, Michelle 355

# X
X (formerly Twitter) 345, 471
Xerox PARC 138, 143, 489

# Y
Yamuna River 476
Yarvin, Curtis (aka Mencius Moldbug) 36
Yasmin Eyalat 464
Year of AI 49, 363
Year of Elections 49
Yglesias, Matthew 35
Young, Kaliya 189, 249
Yu Yong-Ding 34
Yuans 54
Yushan 47, 484

# Z
Zero Trust 75
Zero-Knowledge Proofs (ZKPs) 466
Zetlin, Ariana 371
Zheng Chenggong 51
Zoning Restrictions 400
Zuboff, Shoshanna 3, 16
Zuckerberg, Mark 356
Zucman, Gabriel 39, 79

# Number
12-Year basic education curriculum 75
20% time model 442
2050 net zero 86
3D Audio 311
4chan 35, 190
51% Attack 381
5G 20, 45, 273

Printed in Great Britain
by Amazon